PROFESSIONAL
ANDROID™ PROGRAMMING WITH MONO®
FOR ANDROID AND .NET/C#

D1552174

PROFESSIONAL

Android™ Programming with Mono® for Android and .NET/C#

Wallace B. McClure
Nathan Blevins
John J. Croft IV
Jonathan Dick
Chris Hardy

John Wiley & Sons, Inc.

Professional Android™ Programming with Mono® for Android and .NET/C#

Published by
John Wiley & Sons, Inc.
10475 Crosspoint Boulevard
Indianapolis, IN 46256
www.wiley.com

Published by John Wiley & Sons, Inc., Indianapolis, Indiana

Published simultaneously in Canada

ISBN: 978-1-118-02643-4
ISBN: 978-1-118-22215-7 (ebk)
ISBN: 978-1-118-23581-2 (ebk)
ISBN: 978-1-118-26075-3 (ebk)

Manufactured in the United States of America

10 9 8 7 6 5 4 3 2 1

For general information on our other products and services please contact our Customer Care Department within the United States at (877) 762-2974, outside the United States at (317) 572-3993 or fax (317) 572-4002.

Wiley also publishes its books in a variety of electronic formats and by print-on-demand. Not all content that is available in standard print versions of this book may appear or be packaged in all book formats. If you have purchased a version of this book that did not include media that is referenced by or accompanies a standard print version, you may request this media by visiting http://booksupport.wiley.com. For more information about Wiley products, visit us at www.wiley.com.

Library of Congress Control Number: 2011930295

CREDITS

EXECUTIVE EDITOR
Bob Elliott

SENIOR PROJECT EDITOR
Kevin Kent

PROJECT EDITOR
Victoria Swider

TECHNICAL EDITORS
Stephen Long
Jordan Cobb

PRODUCTION EDITOR
Daniel Scribner

COPY EDITOR
Gayle Johnson

EDITORIAL MANAGER
Mary Beth Wakefield

FREELANCER EDITORIAL MANAGER
Rosemarie Graham

ASSOCIATE DIRECTOR OF MARKETING
David Mayhew

MARKETING MANAGER
Ashley Zurcher

BUSINESS MANAGER
Amy Knies

PRODUCTION MANAGER
Tim Tate

VICE PRESIDENT AND EXECUTIVE GROUP PUBLISHER
Richard Swadley

VICE PRESIDENT AND EXECUTIVE PUBLISHER
Neil Edde

ASSOCIATE PUBLISHER
Jim Minatel

PROJECT COORDINATOR, COVER
Katie Crocker

PROOFREADER
Louise Watson, Word One New York

INDEXER
Ron Strauss

COVER DESIGNER
Ryan Sneed

COVER IMAGE
© Antonis Papantoniou / iStockPhoto

ABOUT THE AUTHORS

 WALLACE B. (WALLY) MCCLURE graduated from the Georgia Institute of Technology (Georgia Tech) in 1990 with a Bachelor of Science degree in electrical engineering. He continued his education there, receiving a Master's degree in the same field in 1991. Since that time, he has done consulting and development for such companies as the United States Department of Education, Coca-Cola, Bechtel National, Magnatron, and Lucent Technologies, among others. McClure has authored books on architecture, ADO.NET, SQL Server, AJAX, and Mobile Devices with Mono. He has authored two books on iPhone programming with MonoTouch and one book on Mono for Android. He specializes in mobile applications, application scalability, and application user interfaces. He is a Microsoft MVP, an ASPInsider, and a partner in Scalable Development, Inc. You can read Wally's blog at www.morewally.com. Wally is married and has two children. When not writing software, he explores entrepreneurial efforts, plays golf, exercises, and hangs out with his family.

 NATHAN BLEVINS is a husband and father who has been working in application development for the past 10 years. Always intrigued by logical puzzles, mechanics, and problem solving, Nathan found his calling in software development and has been playing at work ever since. Living by the philosophy of "work to become, not to acquire," Nathan has devoted himself to being a lifetime student, also working within the community as a speaker, educator, and overall technology enthusiast. In the past, Nathan has worked with various national and local businesses via his personal consulting company, Blevins Consulting. At present, Nathan is serving as a developer and business analyst for Bush Brothers & Company.

Though his career began on the open source development stack in languages such as PHP and Python, Nathan's main focus has been on ASP.NET and C# development since 2004. During the past few years, Nathan's work has included mobile development platforms such as Android, Blackberry, and Windows Phone 7. Currently, Nathan is involved in the community as a member of the ASP.NET Insiders and as a public speaker. If you would like to get into contact with Nathan Blevins, please feel free to contact him through his personal blog at http://nathanblevins.com or via his Twitter account, @nathanblevins.

 JOHN J. CROFT IV graduated from the Georgia Institute of Technology in 1991, receiving a Bachelor's degree in mechanical engineering. He then spent 5 years consulting for large companies, including Coca-Cola, BellSouth, and MCI. Work at these companies primarily involved C and C++ programming and object-oriented systems analysis. In 1995, Croft embarked on his entrepreneurial career by starting Computing Solutions. Computing Solutions is a technology firm that has provided quality service to over 200 clients nationwide. Computing Solutions clients have varied in both size and need, from Fortune 100s to small startup companies. Their problems have varied drastically as well, from large databases and executive information systems to lithotripter control and satellite telemetry. In 2003,

Computing Solutions merged with McClure Development to become Scalable Development, Inc. SDI's technology performances have included projects with Java, C#, and .NET applications. Recently, John has returned to the corporate world as a senior technical manager for Turner Broadcasting Systems. John has coauthored two other books on programming with .NET. He currently lives in Atlanta with his wife, Valerie, and his two sons.

 JONATHAN DICK is a database administrator and software developer and has been working with .NET since its beta days. He now focuses on mobile application development, and has written several MonoTouch applications. He currently maintains open source .NET libraries for Apple iOS Push Notifications and Google Android Cloud to Device Messaging (APNS-Sharp and C2DM-Sharp), while contributing to other mobile-focused projects such as MonoTouch.Dialog and MonoDroid.Dialog.

 CHRIS HARDY, a Microsoft ASPInsider, is a .NET consultant focusing on MonoTouch and Mono for Android development working with Xamarin. Ever since MonoTouch was in beta, Chris has been developing and evangelizing MonoTouch and was one of the first users to get a MonoTouch application onto the App Store. Speaking at conferences around the world on the subject, Chris has been a key part of the community and extended this by contributing to the Wrox book *Professional iPhone Programming with MonoTouch and .NET/C#.* You can follow him on Twitter @chrisntr.

ABOUT THE TECHNICAL EDITORS

STEPHEN LONG is a senior developer currently focusing on .NET and specializing in web and mobile development. He enjoys working with MVC frameworks, such as those provided with ASP.NET and the Android SDK, leveraging new and emerging technologies, and being a mentor to those around him. He is a self-described Google/Android fanboy, husband, and father of two wonderful daughters currently residing in Knoxville, Tennessee. Stephen graduated from the University of Memphis with a BSEE degree with a concentration in computer engineering. He can be found on twitter @long2know.

JORDAN COBB has been fascinated by technology ever since receiving his first computer, a 486 DX2, at the age of 12. His first passion was network systems and hardware, but after becoming frustrated in relying on third-party applications, or the lack thereof, to get the job done he delved into the world of software development. After dabbling in the PHP language for some time he moved to the .NET Framework and has been developing professionally for the past 9 years. Jordan enjoys interfacing software with physical devices, like Arduino, as well as other hobby electronics projects. When he is not at the keyboard, Jordan enjoys playing the occasional round of paintball, attending conferences, and spending time with his new wife, Christine. The couple is expecting their first child, Zoey, in April 2012.

ACKNOWLEDGMENTS

I'VE ALWAYS LOVED MOBILE DEVELOPMENT. After years of working with Wrox, we were able to create content based on MonoTouch, which is the elder sibling of Mono for Android. After more twists and turns, Mono for Android is now out and available. I'd like to thank the Mono for Android team for staying the course and creating a great product; Bob Elliott, who allowed us to create the Mono for Android book; Jim Minatel, who originally asked if such a product might exist; Kevin Kent, who worked with us on a daily basis and kept us on track; and a great set of coauthors, who all helped get a great book out the door.

I also want to thank my family. They did a great job allowing me to work on the book and to work for customers as well. I owe Ronda, Kirsten, and Brad a huge "Thank you!"

Finally, I want to thank you for purchasing this book. We hope you enjoy reading this book as much as we enjoyed writing it.

—WALLACE B. MCCLURE

We are all the products of our experiences. With this in mind, I would like to thank my friends, family, coworkers, and tweeps for all the support and advice they have provided me throughout this process. It would be difficult not to succeed with so many wonderful people in my life. Specifically, I'd like to thank Mom, who tirelessly worked to instill within me some sense of linguistics, and Dad, who taught me the value of hard work and perseverance. Also, I'd like to take a moment to thank my brother, Dave, for his patience and to formally apologize for all those missed Halo nights. In addition, I'd like to thank Andrew May for his sanity checks and Android advice, Rodney Stephens and the CIT for new beginnings, and the wonderful folks at Bush Brothers & Company for their encouragement and for simply being the outstanding people that they are.

Finally, I'd like to thank my fellow authors for being such a pleasure to work with. I am grateful to Bob, Kevin, and the other folks at Wiley whose vision and amazing attention to detail made even me sound intelligent. Finally, I owe the biggest thanks to my loving wife, Crystal, for her understanding and her willingness to allow me to play at working for long hours into the night.

—NATHAN BLEVINS

I would like to thank all those who helped me in writing this book, particularly my editors, Kevin Kent, Stephen Long, and Jordan Cobb, whose feedback was of immense help. Also I would like to thank my coauthors and our lead author Wally McClure, who pulled the project together.

— JOHN J. CROFT IV

Thanks to the entire Mono team. You are all fantastic, make extraordinary products, and it has been a pleasure getting to work with you! Thanks to Wally for bringing me on board, and to my coauthors for sticking with it to the end to make this book happen! I'd especially like to thank my family for their enthusiastic support, and my wonderful wife, Jennifer, for her understanding and encouragement of all my crazy endeavors and the countless hours she's allowed me to obsess over technology!

—JONATHAN DICK

A huge thanks to all the Wrox team for letting me contribute to the book, the Mono team for creating an awesome product with Mono for Android, and to the whole MonoTouch and Mono for Android community for being amazing!

—CHRIS HARDY

CONTENTS

FOREWORD

Mono for Android is a blend of two fascinating and incredibly enjoyable worlds: the C# language and the Android operating system. We designed Mono for Android to bring those two universes together, and we did this by tapping into years of experience designing and implementing languages, APIs, and bindings.

Our passion for the Android OS is very simple to explain: Like everyone else we were smitten by the growth rate of the platform, the well-thought-out design, and the powerful development platform. This combination was hard to resist.

Our love for C# goes back to the year 2000, when Microsoft unveiled their new language to the world. And just like C# rocked the Windows world, it rocked our world. By the year 2000 we had been working on the GNOME Desktop and the Evolution mail client for Linux for a few years, and we had learned our share of lessons in developing desktop applications.

We were developing software in a competitive space, and we needed to produce software faster, with fewer developers. One option was to work harder and work more hours. Instead we chose to raise the programming level: We kept performance-sensitive code written in C and produced bindings for high-level languages that developers could exploit.

When Microsoft announced C# and the .NET framework, the language was an immediate improvement that raised the programming level. The .NET framework ensured that our hands would not be bound to a single language, but also ensured that we could continue to re-use any existing code that we had written in C or C++. C# made the world, ourselves included, vastly more productive.

Over the years, Mono grew in every possible direction. It quickly permeated beyond the desktop comfort zone where it originated and was implemented on everything from embedded controllers to MP3 players, servers, video games, and industrial controls.

MonoTouch was created purely out of user demand. Our main-line e-mail address was bombarded during 2008 and 2009 with requests to bring Mono to the iPhone, and by the summer of 2009 we had a full stack offering that was released later that fall. By early 2010, we were receiving a volume of requests from developers to expand our toolkit to support the Android platform in addition to our existing support for iOS. Just one short year later, we released Mono for Android with a full complement of cutting-edge APIs and the ability to write Android applications using Visual Studio 2010. It is simply amazing just how far we've come in such a short amount of time.

The authors of this book are among the early beta testers of Mono for Android: They were there on the first days of the Mono for Android release, they were there to explore the original API design, they were there to help us shape the final product, and they continue to help us prioritize what matters most to developers when targeting the Android OS.

You might know some of the authors already:

Wally McClure has been a recent convert to Mono through his interest in MonoTouch and now Mono for Android. He released the first e-book for MonoTouch in record time, and was the lead author on the first MonoTouch book published. Both of these books have helped thousands of developers to get applications up and running on the iPhone within months of the initial MonoTouch release.

Chris Hardy is well known in the Windows/ASP.NET world and is also a very active member of the MonoTouch and Mono for Android communities. In 2011 he joined Xamarin and has to date engaged with tons of developers to help improve their applications and has answered countless questions on the Xamarin mailing lists, forums, Stack Overflow, and IRC. Chris jumped into MonoTouch and Mono for Android with the passion that only a rocker from Manchester can exhibit. He also created the open source MonoTouch iPhone application for Scott Hanselman's podcast "Hanselminutes," to much acclaim.

Jon Dick is a database administrator and software developer and has been working with .NET since its beta days. He now focuses on mobile application development, and has written several MonoTouch applications. He currently maintains open source .NET libraries for Apple iOS Push Notifications and Google Android Cloud to Device Messaging (APNS-Sharp and C2DM-Sharp), while contributing to other mobile-focused projects such as MonoTouch.Dialog and MonoDroid.Dialog.

Nathan Blevins has been on ASP.NET and C# development since 2004. During the past few years, Nathan's work has included mobile development platforms such as Android, Blackberry, and Windows Phone 7.

John Croft spent years consulting for large companies, including Coca-Cola, BellSouth, and MCI, primarily doing work involving C and C++ programming and object-oriented systems analysis. Then John's work with his own Computing Solutions technology firm had him working with everything from large databases and executive information systems to lithotripter control and satellite telemetry. Then Computing Solutions merged with McClure Development to become Scalable Development, Inc., and John's work included projects with Java, C#, and .NET applications. Additionally, John has coauthored two other books on programming with .NET. Currently, John is a senior technical manager for Turner Broadcasting Systems.

Building applications with C# and the Android OS is really the best of both worlds. You get a strongly typed, type safe, garbage collected language with the hottest APIs for mobile applications, and the best libraries created natively for Android as well as for C# in .NET.

I leave you in the good hands of Wally, Chris, Jon, Nathan, and John.

—MIGUEL DE ICAZA
Chief Technology Officer
Xamarin, Inc.

INTRODUCTION

SINCE ITS INTRODUCTION IN THE FALL of 2008, Android has grown and matured to the point where it is currently the number one smartphone platform in terms of shipments worldwide. Along with that growth is an interest in writing applications that run natively on the device and that take advantage of the device's features, such as the camera and voice recognition.

Since the release of the .NET Framework in January 2002, its growth has been impressive. It is the most popular development framework in use today. While the .NET Framework was in initial development, Miguel de Icaza, who worked for Ximian, created his own C# compiler, and from that the Mono framework was born. In 2003, Novell purchased Ximian. In 2011, Attachmate purchased Novell. Later in 2011, Xamarin was formed and all of the products associated with Mono, MonoTouch, Mono for Android, and MonoDevelop were transferred to Xamarin. The payoff for us as developers is that Xamarin is laser-focused on Mono for Android and MonoTouch, and on making those the best products available for development on mobile with Android and iPhone. Throughout all of this, the Mono framework has grown to run across various platforms. Initially, Mono was designed to run on Linux. Since that time, Mono has branched out and is available across several non-Windows platforms. In the summer of 2009, the MonoTouch framework was shipped. This allowed developers to write applications with the .NET Framework and using the C# language to run applications written for the iPhone. In February 2010, de Icaza confirmed on his blog that the Mono team were working on an implementation of Mono for Android similar in concept to MonoTouch. This implementation initially was called MonoDroid and finally was named Mono for Android.

To .NET developers, the ability to write applications in C# using many of the existing APIs that they are already familiar with is very attractive. .NET developers are not required to learn the ins and outs of the Java language, nor are they required to learn the Eclipse IDE. .NET developers can stay within the Visual Studio IDE that they are already accustomed to, use the C# language that they already know, make calls in the .NET Framework that they are already familiar with, and create an application for the Android platform. I'm excited about the possibilities that this offers.

The ability to run natively on the device should not be understated. HTML5 is a great emerging standard for providing applications. Frameworks that are being built will take advantage of what the web browser allows. Unfortunately, it has several problems. For example, a web application cannot access all of the device, so currently you can't access the camera or voice recognition or run applications in the background. Also, HTML5 won't be a full and accepted standard for several years.

But wait; there's more.

One of the frustrations with writing applications for mobile devices is that developers are required to write an ObjectiveC application for the iPhone, a Java application for Android, and a Silverlight/ .NET application for Windows Phone 7. The time and expense to develop for these platforms is non-trivial. If a team decides to develop an ObjectiveC application, a Java application, and a Silverlight/ .NET application for each platform, it would be impossible to share code among those platforms. Thankfully, the Mono platform allows developers to share business logic across those platforms. Imagine having a class library for interacting with your Amazon web services that you can use across all your platforms. When you add some new functionality in one platform, all platforms get this functionality. When a bug is fixed in one platform, the fix is available to all platforms.

The Mono platform lets you target multiple platforms using the languages you already know. This is a great thing for both developers and development managers. The idea of building a native application for a device and reusing some of the same code across various platforms is very appealing. This will definitely cut the cost of building mobile applications and bringing them to market across multiple platforms. And what developer, manager, or business doesn't like that?

WHO THIS BOOK IS FOR

This book is for .NET developers who want to use their existing knowledge to create native Android applications written in .NET/C#. .NET developers are always interested in learning, but they know that learning Java, Eclipse, and the specifics of Android can be overwhelming. Developers interested in Mono for Android will recognize that its cost is easily made up by the ability to quickly target Android using a language they already know.

This book is intended for .NET developers who want to target Android. It is designed to get you up to speed with Android, not to teach you about the .NET Framework or C# language, which we assume you already know.

Chapters 1 through 4 contain introductory material; you should read them sequentially. These chapters introduce the Mono for Android product, the basics of developing with Mono for Android, the Visual Studio plugin and MonoDevelop, and the basics of presenting data to a user with screen and data controls and how to develop a user interface for Android. When you are comfortable with these concepts, you probably can move from one chapter to another without necessarily reading them sequentially.

WHAT THIS BOOK COVERS

This book covers .NET/C# development with Mono for Android. Mono for Android allows a developer to target Android devices running version 1.6 and later. This includes tablets based on Android. Unless otherwise noted, all the development is geared toward Android 2.3, a.k.a. Gingerbread. At the time of the writing of this book, Android 2.3 is the most widely deployed version of the platform. However, the technology world changes fast. More recently, Google shipped Honeycomb (a.k.a. Android 3.x), which is the version of Android geared toward tablets. Android 3.x shipped in various tablet devices from various vendors during 2011.

Toward the end of 2011, Google shipped Android 4.0, a.k.a. Ice Cream Sandwich (ICS). This version of Android unifies the phone-optimized 2.x line with the tablet-optimized 3.x line. Unfortunately, at the time of the writing of this book, we haven't had Android 4.0 ICS devices to test our code with. In addition, the Android marketplace tends to not upgrade their devices as fast as the iPhone community. As a result, it's highly likely that the Android 2.x series will continue to have a majority of phone installations for the foreseeable future.

With all of these versions of Android out in the marketplace, we've tried to target Android 2.3 as our base platform. However, having said that, we've also covered Android tablet support in its own chapter. In addition, while we've targeted 2.3, we have made sure our code runs in Android 4.0 as well.

HOW THIS BOOK IS STRUCTURED

This book is essentially divided into two parts. Chapters 1 through 4 make up the first part, which covers the essentials of developing for Android, the essentials of Mono for Android, and the development experience for users targeting the Android platform. Again, it makes sense to read that part of the book from beginning to end. When you feel comfortable with these concepts, you can move on to the second part of the book, which contains discrete chapters from which you can pick and choose.

WHAT YOU NEED TO USE THIS BOOK

You need several things to successfully use this book:

➤ **An Android device:** This could be a phone or tablet running Android.

➤ **The Android SDK:** You need to download and install the latest version of the Android SDK on your computer.

➤ **The Java SDK:** Android development requires the Java SDK. In spite of the fact that Mono for Android is an implementation of .NET/C# for Android, many pieces of development on Android require Java. Therefore, Java is required for Mono for Android.

➤ **A Development IDE:** .NET developers are familiar with the Visual Studio .NET. Visual Studio is featured throughout the book. MonoDevelop for the Mac and Windows is supported. MonoDevelop has additional requirements. Check out the Mono for Android website at `http://mono-android.net/` for additional information.

➤ **Mono for Android:** The Mono for Android product is necessary. Additional features may be added over time. Therefore, it's a good idea to check the Mono for Android website at `http://mono-android.net/`.

CONVENTIONS

To help you get the most from the text and keep track of what's happening, we use a number of conventions throughout the book.

 Boxes with a warning icon like this one hold important, not-to-be forgotten information that is directly relevant to the surrounding text.

 The pencil icon indicates notes, tips, hints, tricks, or asides to the current discussion.

As for styles in the text:

➤ We *italicize* new terms and important words when we introduce them.

➤ We show keyboard strokes like this: Ctrl+A.

➤ We show filenames, URLs, and code within the text like so: `persistence.properties`.

➤ We present code in two different ways:

```
We use a monofont type with no highlighting for most code examples.
We use bold to emphasize code that's particularly important in the present context.
```

SOURCE CODE

As you work through the examples in this book, you may either type in all the code manually or use the source code files that accompany the book. All the source code used in this book is available for download at `www.wrox.com`. When at the site, simply locate the book's title (use the Search box or one of the title lists) and click the Download Code link on the book's detail page to obtain all the source code for the book. Code that is included on the Web site is highlighted by the following icon:

Available for download on Wrox.com

Listings include the filename in the title. If it is just a code snippet, you'll find the filename in a code note such as this:

Code snippet filename

 Because many books have similar titles, you may find it easiest to search by ISBN; this book's ISBN is 978-1-118-02643-4.

After you download the code, decompress it with your favorite compression tool. Alternatively, you can go to the main Wrox code download page at `www.wrox.com/dynamic/books/download.aspx` to see the code available for this book and all other Wrox books.

 Again, please note we've tried to target Android 2.3 as our base platform for the code you will download, but we've made sure the code runs in Android 4.0 as well.

Also, if you have problems with the code that you can't explain, doing a Clean and Full Rebuild of your solution can often solve your problems. When in doubt, we recommended you try this.

ERRATA

We make every effort to ensure that there are no errors in the text or code. However, no one is perfect, and mistakes do occur. If you find an error in one of our books, such as a spelling mistake or a faulty piece of code, we would be grateful for your feedback. By sending in errata, you may save another reader hours of frustration. At the same time, you will help us provide even higher quality information.

To find the errata page for this book, go to www.wrox.com and locate the title using the Search box or one of the title lists. Then, on the book details page, click the Book Errata link. On this page you can view all errata that have been submitted for this book and posted by Wrox editors. A complete list that has links to each book's errata is also available at www.wrox.com/misc-pages/booklist.shtml.

If you don't spot "your" error on the Book Errata page, go to www.wrox.com/contact/techsupport.shtml and complete the form there to send us the error you have found. We'll check the information and, if appropriate, post a message to the book's errata page and fix the problem in subsequent editions.

P2P.WROX.COM

For author and peer discussion, join the P2P forums at http://p2p.wrox.com. The forums are a web-based system for you to post messages related to Wrox books and related technologies and to interact with other readers and technology users. The forums offer a subscription feature through which you can receive e-mail on topics of interest when new posts are made to the forums. Wrox authors, editors, other industry experts, and your fellow readers are present on these forums. The forums will help you not only as you read this book, but also as you develop your own applications. To join the forums, follow these steps:

1. Go to http://p2p.wrox.com and click the Register link.

2. Read the terms of use, and click Agree.

3. Complete the required information to join, as well as any optional information you want to provide, and click Submit.

4. You will receive an e-mail with information describing how to verify your account and complete the joining process.

 You can read messages in the forums without joining P2P, but to post your own messages, you must join.

After you join, you can post new messages and respond to messages other users post. You can read messages at any time on the Web. If you would like to have new messages from a particular forum e-mailed to you, click the Subscribe to this Forum icon by the forum name in the forum listing.

For more information about how to use the Wrox P2P, be sure to read the P2P FAQs for answers to questions about how the forum software works, as well as many common questions specific to P2P and Wrox books. To read the FAQs, click the FAQ link on any P2P page.

1

Introduction to Android, Mobile Devices, and the Marketplace

WHAT'S IN THIS CHAPTER?

➤ A short history of Mono and its relationship to the .NET Framework

➤ How Mono for Android opens the Android platform to .NET developers

➤ Why Mono for Android is so attractive to developers

➤ The history of Android and its mind share

➤ Exploring cross-platform alternatives

The past several years have seen an amazing growth in the use of smartphones. *USA Today* recently reported on how smartphones have become an indispensable part of people's lives. With growth and popularity comes competition, and, unlike desktop computers, no single vendor or platform dominates the mobile device marketplace; devices based on Symbian, Research in Motion (Blackberry), Windows Mobile, Android, and other platforms are available. In addition, devices may run the same operating system and be presented to the user in separate form factors. This fracture in the marketplace is problematic for developers: How can they take a development framework or tool that they already know and use that knowledge in a device that has a large and growing market share?

This chapter looks at how the largest segment of developers (.NET/C# developers) can target the smartphone that has the highest mind share (Android). It also looks at how the smartphone is growing faster in market share than any other device.

PRODUCT COMPARISON

This section takes a quick look at the .NET Framework, Mono, and Mono for Android. These products have allowed the largest segment of developers to target the Android family of mobile devices — the fastest-growing mobile platform currently on the market.

The .NET Framework

Over the past decade, the popularity of the .NET Framework has grown. In the late 1990s, Microsoft began working on the .NET Framework. The first version shipped in 2002. Microsoft recently introduced .NET Framework 4. The .NET Framework comes in various versions, including 32-bit, 64-bit, a version for the Xbox gaming platform, and a version for Microsoft's mobile devices called the Compact Framework (CF). Here are a few key facts about the .NET Framework to keep in mind as you begin to look at the Mono framework:

➤ Microsoft released a development tool, *Visual Studio .NET*, with this framework. This tool is the integrated development environment for .NET.

➤ This framework is based on a virtual machine that executes software written for the framework. This virtual-machine environment is called the *Common Language Runtime* (CLR), and it is responsible for security, memory management, program execution, and exception handling.

➤ Applications written in the .NET Framework are initially compiled from source code, such as Visual Basic or C#, to an intermediate language, called MSIL. The initial compilation is performed by calling the language-specific command-line compiler, Visual Studio, or some other build tool. A second compilation is typically performed when an application is executed. This second compilation takes the intermediate language and compiles it into executable code that can be run on the operating system. This second compilation is called *just-in-time* (JIT) *compilation*.

➤ This framework is language-independent, and numerous languages are available for it. In Visual Studio, Microsoft has shipped various languages, including Visual Basic, F#, C++, and C#.

➤ This framework has a series of libraries that provide consistent functionality across the various languages. These libraries are called the *base class libraries*.

➤ Microsoft has submitted various parts of the .NET Framework to various standards organizations, including those for the C# language, the Common Language Infrastructure, Common Type System (CTS), Common Language Specification (CLS), and Virtual Execution System (VES).

➤ This framework has the largest number of developers of any development framework. As a result, more developers are familiar with the .NET Framework than any other development framework.

➤ A disadvantage of the .NET Framework is that it is unavailable for non-Microsoft platforms.

The significance of all this is that Microsoft has created a standards-based environment for the .NET Framework. Though most developers working on the Microsoft platform are not worried about the standards compliance of the .NET Framework, the significance of this aspect of the .NET Framework cannot be understated. By defining these standards and submitting these standards to compliance committees, Microsoft has created a group of developers that can integrate at fairly low levels into the .NET Framework. In this environment, Miguel de Icaza had a vision and stepped up to create the Mono framework discussed next.

Mono

Mono is an open source project that provides a C# compiler and CLR on non-Windows operating systems. Mono is currently licensed under GPL version 2, LGPL version 2, the MIT, and dual licenses. Mono runs on Mac, Linux, BSD, and other operating systems. Along with the C# compiler, additional languages run on Mono, including F#, Java, Scala, Basic, and others.

Mono, the brainchild of Miguel de Icaza, was officially announced in 2001. Version 1.0 shipped in 2004, and currently Mono is at version 2.10, though it is continually being upgraded and will most likely be at a later version by the time you read this. Currently, Mono has parity with many of the features in .NET 4. Mono continues to be directly led by de Icaza. Recently, the steward-ship of Mono has passed to Xamarin. Xamarin leads the direction of Mono. Mono started as an open source implementation of a C# compiler. It grew from this initial design into the current open source implementation of .NET. It is now Xamarin's responsibility to nurture Mono. Xamarin is responsible for the development of Mono for Android, MonoTouch, and the software that makes these products work for the developer. Given that Xamarin is laser-focused on Mono in the mobile area, I think these products are in good hands.

As much as there is a desire to match the .NET Framework's features, this is not possible because Microsoft has more resources and a head start on the development of those features. At the same time, the Mono project has parity with a large number of .NET Framework features. The best that Xamarin will most likely accomplish is to be shortly behind the .NET Framework for most of the APIs that are possible.

Along with Mono is the open source IDE called *MonoDevelop*, which started as a port of the *SharpDevelop* IDE. MonoDevelop began as a project to allow for Mono development on Linux, but with the release of MonoDevelop 2.2, the ability to develop with Mono expanded to the Mac, Windows, and several other non-Linux UNIX platforms.

Although the .NET Framework is very popular, two issues make it unsuitable for running on Android:

➤ At some level Google and Microsoft are competitors and are probably not too excited to work together. Microsoft has had Windows Mobile devices for years, which compete directly with Google's Android operating system.

➤ The .NET Framework fundamentally is a major competitor for the Java Virtual Machine that is at the heart of an Android device. This Java VM is called Dalvik. The .NET Framework and Java have been competitors since the initial announcements of the .NET Framework.

A disadvantage of .NET/Mono and Android is that .NET/Mono developers cannot take their .NET/Mono/C# knowledge and apply it to the Android platform. Figure 1-1 shows this concept. .NET/Mono developers can't target Android because they're two separate entities.

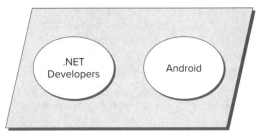

FIGURE 1-1

In 2009, the Mono team announced and shipped MonoTouch, the forerunner to Mono for Android. MonoTouch allows developers familiar with C# to target the Apple iPhone. Based on the experience of building MonoTouch, the Mono team learned how to effectively and efficiently build a C#/Mono layer that sits on top of the device's native application programming interface (API).

Mono for Android

In April 2010, Apple introduced fear, uncertainty, and doubt into the mobile development marketplace by making changes to its software development kit (SDK) licensing. This change caused many developers to question developing for the iPhone and iOS. At that point in time, the Mono team had been experimenting with creating a Mono product for Android similar to its MonoTouch product. Due to Apple's SDK changes, the Mono team announced the Mono for Android product and put significant resources behind it. Mono for Android shipped in the spring of 2011. While Apple eventually rescinded their SDK issues, the 5 months during which MonoTouch sat in limbo allowed the Mono team to put significant resources into developing Mono for Android. The result of this is that Mono for Android is further along than it would have been if Apple had not put MonoTouch into limbo for all those months in 2010.

Mono for Android allows .NET developers to create native applications that run on Android. These applications look and feel like native Java applications running on Dalvik. With Mono for Android, applications are compiled into executable code that runs on Android devices. The significance of this should not be understated: .NET/Mono developers can target Android through Mono for Android, as illustrated in Figure 1-2

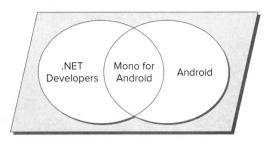

FIGURE 1-2

How does Mono for Android accomplish this? Does it somehow allow Windows Forms applications to be translated or recompiled and deployed on Android? Mono for Android provides a .NET layer over the native programming layer present on the Android OS. Developers targeting Dalvik would write applications in Java. Mono for Android does not provide a mechanism to cross-compile Windows Forms applications, but it allows developers to build applications that run natively on Android.

Overall, the API exposed by Mono for Android is a combination of the .NET 4 Framework's core features, Silverlight APIs, and the native Dalvik Java VM. Mono for Android provides a bridge (interop) layer between Android's native APIs and the APIs that .NET and C# developers are accustomed to.

Mono for Android Components

Mono for Android is made up of a set of assemblies, namespaces, and classes that are optimized for mobile platforms. This code is a combination of the .NET 4, Silverlight, and Windows Phone profiles, as well as code that allows a developer to take advantage of the Android platform.

Namespaces and Classes

Mono for Android provides a rich set of namespaces and classes to support building applications for the iPhone. Here are some of the most popular assemblies and the functionality that they provide:

➤ `Mono.Android.dll`: This assembly provides the C# bindings to the Android APIs. This includes namespaces that support the `Android.*` namespaces.

➤ `System.dll`: This assembly provides much of the .NET Framework functionality for Mono for Android.

➤ `Mono.data.Sqlite.dll`: This assembly is an ADO.NET provider for the native SQLite database.

➤ `Mono.Data.Tds.dll`: This assembly provides the support for the TDS protocol, which is used to connect to SQL Server.

➤ `OpenTK.dll`: This assembly has support for OpenGL.

➤ `System.Json.dll`: This assembly provides support for using JSON.

➤ `System.ServiceModel.dll`: This assembly provides support for WCF.

➤ `System.Xml.dll`: This assembly provides support for XML.

➤ `System.Xml.Linq.dll`: This assembly provides support for LINQ to XML.

Within these assemblies, Mono for Android also provides namespaces that may be important to you. These are:

➤ `Android`: The `Android.*` namespace provides resources, classes, and application permission support.

➤ `Android.Bluetooth`: This namespace provides support for Bluetooth.

➤ `Android.Database`: This namespace provides support for the SQLite database on the device.

➤ `Android.Graphics`: This namespace provides support for graphic display.

➤ `Android.Hardware`: This namespace provides support for hardware on an Android device such as the camera.

➤ `Android.Locations`: This namespace provides the necessary support for location.

➤ `Android.Net`: This namespace provides support for networking, including support for Voice over IP (VoIP) and WiFi.

These namespaces are a small subset of what is available inside of Mono for Android and are fairly self-explanatory in their functionality. Also, these namespaces are specific to Android. Code that is written using these namespaces will only run on Android-based devices.

Development Tools

No matter what type of project you are building, development tools are an integral part of creating an application. Long gone are the days of a bunch of files, a character-based editor, command-line output for debugging, and a make file as the only way to build an application.

Developers who work in the .NET Framework are familiar with Visual Studio. Visual Studio is Microsoft's development tool. It includes support for solutions, projects, a visual design surface, databases, and numerous other features.

Similarly, Mono has its own development tool; MonoDevelop is a free IDE used for developing with Mono and is an early branch of the SharpDevelop IDE. Originally, MonoDevelop ran only on Linux, but with version 2.2, MonoDevelop began running on the Mac and Windows. MonoDevelop lets you create and manage numerous projects as well as debug and deploy to the simulator and devices for testing.

Thankfully, the Mono team has produced Mono for Android, which will work across Visual Studio and MonoDevelop, as well as a plug-in for operating systems other than Windows. This facilitates writing code with Mono for Android across Visual Studio, MonoDevelop on the Mac, and MonoDevelop on Windows. Developers are free to use whichever of these development IDEs they prefer. At this point in time, I have personally found that Windows and the Mac each have their own advantages, including:

➤ Debugging on Windows is where most developers starting with Mono for Android will probably start.

➤ Debugging on the Mac seems to work very well in the Android emulator.

MOBILE DEVELOPMENT

Developers need to keep a few key ideas in mind when building applications on Android with Mono for Android:

➤ The Android simulator is good for initial testing; however, it is not necessarily accurate for all testing. Just because something works in the simulator doesn't mean it will run on all Android devices in the same way. Final testing should be completed on different versions of Android devices.

 As of the Android SDK available for the writing of this book, testing on a device is typically more accurate for advanced features. For basic development, the emulator is easier to work with. Thanks to snapshots, it's typically quicker to work with as well.

➤ .NET executables are fairly small because they can use a shared copy of the framework. Mono for Android can have applications deployed two different ways. The most common way is to have the application and Mono for Android bound together. A second way is for the applications to share the Mono framework. This makes application executables small, but it also means that a copy of the Mono framework for Mono for Android must be installed on the device.

At the time of this writing, it is suggested that the application be bound with the Mono for Android runtime. This is currently what is done when a "Release" build of the application is done.

➤ It is important to be a good citizen on a device. Developers will need to continually think about how to implement features that are good citizens.

Getting Around Support Issues

Although Mono for Android is a commercially licensed product, it is still under continual development, so it might not support a specific namespace or assembly. You have two options in this situation:

1. Wait on the implementation of that assembly from the Mono for Android product.

2. Pull the necessary code or reference the necessary assembly in your project. This is fairly common if the application needs to use code within the `System.Web.*` namespaces. For example, imagine an application that needs to call a REST-based web service and needs to encode data before it is sent. `System.Web.HttpUtility.HtmlEncode()` should be called. Unfortunately, the `System.Web` namespace is not part of Mono for Android by default. You must add this namespace by referencing the `System.Web` assembly in your application.

Design Issues

In addition to the technical issues of building an application for Android, here are some design issues developers should be aware of:

➤ **Don't design an application for a desktop environment and think that it can be scaled down to Android or any mobile device.** Android does not have the display, hardware, or storage of a desktop computer. Android and mobile device applications are good for simple, limited-purpose functions, but they should not be expected to do everything that a desktop application does.

➤ **The Android simulator is a fine tool, but don't limit your testing to it.** A simulator is just that. A keyboard and mouse are associated with the Android simulator since it is primarily running on the desktop. Also, understand that the simulator is ultimately using the CPUs of the development system. While the CPU of a device is fine for the device, it really isn't comparable in terms of performance with a desktop. The desktop has a high click speed, more memory, and typically has higher speed and higher quality Internet bandwidth. To really test a complicated design, you must test the application from Android on a mobile device while running on a mobile network.

➤ **When testing on a device, though WiFi is a mobile network, the WiFi in your office or home is typically of a higher quality than a mobile provider's network.** Typically, WiFi will have lower latency and higher bandwidth than a 3G (or worse) connection. Applications must be tested in a mobile scenario. Get a coworker to drive you around to test an application.

ANDROID

There's no doubt that Android devices took off in the first half of 2010. Although the Android phone was not the first graphical phone, it was the first product that provided its software free to phone device manufacturers, made it easy to use, and provided an easy-to-use marketplace to purchase applications.

History of Android

In July 2005 Google purchased a small company called Android, Inc., which was involved in mobile software. With this purchase, Google began heading in the direction of mobile devices. Rumors regarding Google's entry into mobile devices began to ramp up in December 2006. In the fall of 2007, the Open Handset Alliance (OHA) was formed, with the goal of creating a set of standards for mobile devices. The alliance has at its core a mobile device architecture based on the Linux Kernel version 2.6 (and later), along with an SDK that can be used to build native Android applications. In the fall of 2008, the first Android phone shipped.

The initial shipment of Android was not well received in the marketplace. It was criticized significantly by the media and by the first users of the platform. However, Android had several big advantages over competing platforms that were not evident at the time. Android is an open platform. As such, manufacturers are competing against other mobile device manufacturers as well as against other members of the Open Handset Alliance. This means the pace of innovation at the hardware level is significant, and the Android platform shows it compared to other platforms. Android devices are not limited to one manufacturer or one telecommunications carrier either. As such, telecommunications carriers must compete with each other. These two factors and others have led to a significant amount of innovation and advancement in the Android and mobile device marketplaces.

After some initial teething pains, the Android SDK has grown up. (You can find a discussion of the tools available in the Android SDK — and pertinent to Mono for Android developers — later in this chapter.) After numerous beta releases in 2007 and 2008, the 1.0 release of the SDK occurred in September 2008. Since that time, many additional SDK versions have shipped.

In the fall of 2009, OHA introduced the Android 2.0 (Eclair) operating system. This was a watershed event for Android. Along with the shipment of Android 2.0, Motorola released the Droid phone, and Verizon began significantly marketing the product. From that point Android has quickly grown in the marketplace.

In 2010, OHA shipped Android 2.1. In addition, HTC, Motorola, and others produced a family of high-end devices. The shipment of these items further accelerated Android's growth and mind share. At the same time, a number of manufacturers introduced tablet devices based on Android.

In early 2011, devices based on Android 3.0 (a.k.a. Honeycomb) shipped. This version of Android is optimized for the tablet environment. Unfortunately, this version of Android has not been well received in the marketplace.

In late 2011, Google announced and shipped Android 4.0 (a.k.a. Ice Cream Sandwich). Ice Cream Sandwich is the version of Android that unifies the programming APIs for Android phones and tablets.

Growth has been a hallmark of the Android platform. Since its first availability in 2008, Android shipments have grown significantly. Gartner Group is predicting that Android will see tremendous growth at least through 2015. Considering that Android had so few devices in the marketplace in 2008, this growth is mind-boggling.

Writing Web-Based Applications for Android

Writing a web-based application for Android is fairly simple. The WebKit web browser is a great tool; it does an excellent job of scaling web-based applications to run on an Android-sized screen. It also does well at running applications that are highly dependent on JavaScript. Upgrading an Android web-based application is also a simple matter of deploying a new version of the application to a web server. Many applications have taken this approach. And although HTML5 has a number of great features, a web-based environment has some inherent limitations.

 Unfortunately, web applications are not suitable for all applications. Applications that require some background processing and access to local resources must work when a network connection is unavailable, and some other application types don't work well in this model.

So, the question becomes how you write a native application that fits into Android.

Writing Native Applications for Android

These native applications are a great improvement over web-based applications, which are limited in what they can do on a device. Fundamentally, web-based applications have to be loaded over the web and cannot access all device features. Native applications tend to have more support for device features such as the accelerometer, file system, camera, cross-domain web services, and other features that are not available in HTML and JavaScript. In addition, native applications do not depend on the wireless network to be loaded, whereas a web application is dependent on the wireless network for nearly everything.

Android Development Issues

Developers must consider several issues when running applications on the device:

> There are a tremendous number of form factors, screen sizes, and devices. An application may look great on an HTC device but not on a slightly older Droid device. Developers must take device differences into account. For example, while Twitter for Android runs on an HTC Android device as shown in Figure 1-3, it definitely has a different look than when it runs in a Motorola Xoom Android device, as shown in Figure 1-4 (note that user pictures have been removed from these figures to protect privacy).

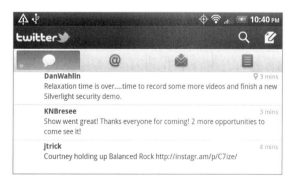

FIGURE 1-3

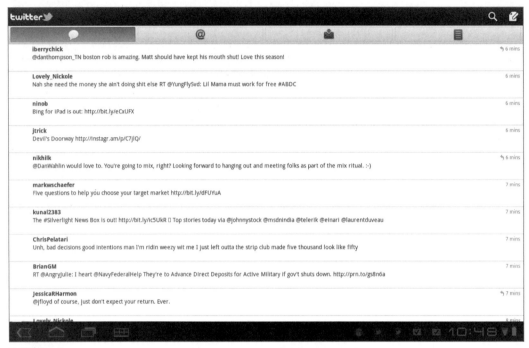

FIGURE 1-4

➤ Developers must take into account the various versions of the Android operating system. Some users may be running Android 2.0, and others may be running 3.0.

➤ Developers must be realistic about the sales numbers of applications delivered through the Android Market. Even though Android has experienced a phenomenal growth rate, this excitement must be tempered, because the Android Market has a higher percentage of free applications compared to the Apple App Store. Your sales numbers may be more for an Android version of an application, but average sales prices for applications on Android are less than average sales prices for iPhone devices.

Developers need to be aware of these issues. They may require you to spend more time in development when building applications for Android.

Android SDK Tools

The Android SDK contains a number of tools, including a set of libraries for the Android platform, a debugger, a simulator, and various pieces of documentation. The following tools are the most important to the Mono for Android developer:

➤ **Libraries:** Mono for Android is a layer over the top of the existing Dalvik-based APIs. So, learning the API calls of the Dalvik libraries will help you learn Mono for Android.

➤ **Simulator:** The simulator is the first tool that developers use to test their applications. It allows them to create various simulated versions of Android, screen resolutions, memory, and other hardware factors.

One thing that developers will find missing, at least in the initial versions of Mono for Android, is a design surface. When the Mono team shipped MonoTouch, it used the Interface Builder SDK tool. Unfortunately, the Android SDK has no design surface. Further, due to time constraints, the initial shipments of Mono for Android also don't include a design surface.

Fortunately, all is not lost for developers. There are currently two ways to create a user interface for Mono for Android:

1. Edit the user interface XML by hand. Obviously, this method is error-prone.

2. Design the user interface through third-party tools such as DroidDraw. DroidDraw is a standalone design surface for building an Android user interface. DroidDraw can be seen in Figure 1-5.

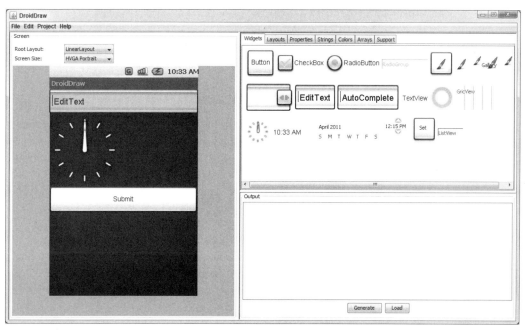

FIGURE 1-5

Android Development Costs

The SDK is a free download. However, to release software for Android, a developer must join the Android Market Development Program. The current cost to join in the United States is $25 a year. The cost of joining varies from country to country. The ability to distribute applications to devices depends on having the necessary development certificates. These are available through the Android Developer site after you join the Android Development Program. Certificates are discussed more in Chapter 16.

CROSS-PLATFORM ALTERNATIVES

The choice of using a cross-platform development tool, such as Mono for Android or MonoTouch, is not one to be made lightly. Even though Mono for Android offers a superior combination of native development and integration with the .NET stack and leverages the power of Visual Studio, it is important to not only be aware of the differences between native and non-native development tools, but also understand the differences between the various cross-platform options.

Other Cross-Platform Tools

In addition to Mono for Android, there are several other options out there that can be used to develop mobile applications that can target Android as well as other platforms. Here are a few examples of other cross-platform mobile development tools:

➤ **PhoneGap** is a cross-platform mobile development tool that focuses on using standards-based web technologies, including HTML5, jQuery Mobile, and so on. Like Mono for Android, PhoneGap uses a common technology to allow developers to not only write applications for their target mobile devices but also to directly access some of the native features of the device, such as the compass, the camera, or the file system.

➤ **Appcelerator Titanium** is another cross-platform tool that allows a developer to write applications using HTML, JavaScript, and their own library of APIs that grant access to several of the mobile device's features. Much like Mono for Android, Titanium can be compiled into the native language, meaning that you can present the same kind of experience that other native applications may offer.

➤ **RhoMobile Rhodes** is a Ruby-based framework that allows you to build cross-platform applications. This tool allows you to compile into native applications that can access many of the device's features.

These tools are among the most popular of the many other cross-platform tools in the market today. Because needing to target multiple mobile platforms with as little effort as possible is a common problem, you have many different solutions to consider.

Considerations for Selecting a Cross-Platform Tool

When selecting a cross-platform tool, you have to consider many different things. In some cases, some options may provide too simple a solution and maintenance/features could quickly become unwieldy or even impossible. Other tools could offer many, many native features, but in the process, introduce additional complexity beyond what a native approach might have offered. Because of this, making the right tool selection is critical. The following sections discuss a few things developers should ask themselves about the tool before making their selection.

How Does the Tool Allow You to Author Your Application?

As far as cross-platform tools go, they tend to take one of two approaches to allow developers to write their applications. The first approach is to utilize a mobile device's natural support for web browsing, whereas the second approach is to develop the means to translate or compile a common language, such as C# or JavaScript, into the native language, such as Java for Android/Dalvik or Objective-C for iOS.

Utilizing a mobile device's natural affinity with web browsing allows developers to work primarily with HTML and JavaScript, which makes development approachable for a very large subset of potential mobile developers. In addition, there are a plethora of development tools and environments that make the development process fluid and painless. A great example of this approach would be PhoneGap.

Unfortunately, this approach tends to have a couple of flaws. For starters, this approach results in a web application with native features rather than a full, native application. Although web applications have come a very long way in the past few years, they are quite different than native applications and have their own special foibles. In addition, users tend to appreciate the experience of a native application over that of a web application. The second flaw with this approach is that support of native features can be limited and, in some cases, impossible. Generally, access to native features is achieved through a custom JavaScript API.

The second approach, translating or compiling from a common language to the native language, allows the users to harness the native speed and features of the application while also writing in another, more accessible language. The large benefit to this approach is that you end up with the look and feel of a native application as well as native performance speeds. Mono for Android is a great example of this approach.

The flaws of this approach are that these solutions tend to require a slightly more advanced skill set. Whereas the web browser–based approach usually requires a basic understanding of HTML and browser page request life cycles, the compiled approach requires an understanding of the underlying architecture and design paradigms of the mobile platform. For instance, a Mono for Android developer needs to have at least a basic understanding of Android before they can begin writing an application. Finally, some of the cross-platform tools may require some platform-specific code to fully compliment the solution — particularly when it comes to handling UI logic.

What Device Features Does the Tool Support?

When considering the tool to select, you need to have a good idea of what features are most important for you as an application developer. If you are writing a simple application that will display some kind of data to the user, you probably have little concern over whether or not your solution supports the accelerometer. However, if you are developing a simple game, this could be a make-or-break feature. For the most part, every tool provider expressly lists the limitations of their product.

When working with a cross-platform tool such as Mono for Android, a developer is often trading features or flexibility for simplicity and familiarity. Before you choose a cross-platform tool, be sure to have a general concept of what you are trying to create and ensure that the tool supports the features that you desire. Thankfully, Mono for Android has very few limitations and has them clearly defined at `http://docs.xamarin.com/android/about/limitations`.

What Platforms Does the Tool Support?

There are a wide variety of cross-platform tools out there, and each of them supports a different number of platforms that range from most mobile device OSs to even the various desktop OSs. When selecting your tool, consider where you plan to deploy your application as well as whether the deployed application's design and usage patterns would fit with the target platform.

For instance, Appcelerator Titanium boasts the ability to deploy not only to some of the major mobile platforms but also to Windows, Linux, and Mac. On the other hand, Rhodes focuses on supporting the major mobile platforms — including Windows Phone 7, RIM, and Windows Mobile.

Although we have discussed the feature support consideration, make sure that your needed feature is supported across all the platforms that you want to deploy to. For instance, if you have an application that is dependent upon the compass feature of the device and you want to target Android and WebOS, PhoneGap would not be the platform for you.

What Skill Sets Does the Tool Require?

Each approach offers some kind of common language to begin application development. Whether that language is HTML or C#, it is important to ensure that you have the skills in house to cover the development needs of the tool. In addition to this, some solutions require you to have intimate knowledge of the mobile platform's framework or, at times, intimate knowledge of the tool's custom APIs.

With the HTML approach, a strong understanding of HTML and JavaScript can take a developer a long way. On the other hand, the translation/compilation approach often requires a basic understanding of the target platform framework — especially in regards to developing the user interface.

What Tools Exist to Support Development?

One of the most important considerations of your cross-platform tool is what kind of development tools exist to support the coding process. Development time for a solution can be vastly different when using a specialty, proprietary tool versus a full-featured development environment, such as Visual Studio.

How Active Are the Development Community and Support Channels?

When considering the cross-platform tool of your choice, take some time to familiarize yourself with the development community. Are there active mailing lists or forums? How frequently do developers respond to users' requests? How often are other developers answering each other's issues? Solutions with poor developer support or a stagnant community are unhealthy signs.

What Are the Successful Application Deployments for This Tool?

Most cross-platform tool vendors will quickly list any application success stories as a way to brag about their solution. Take some time to download these applications and see how they interact and perform on your target mobile devices. Given the chance, take a moment to communicate with the application developer to ask them about their development experience using this toolset.

If you are reading this book, you are clearly interested in Mono for Android as a solution. With that in mind, it may seem somewhat strange to discuss alternative approaches to cross-platform development. The reason for this approach is to help you make an informed decision about a development tool rather than an incidental one. By taking the time to understand the strengths and weaknesses of other solutions, you will, hopefully, be able to make the best choice for your application. Mono for Android (and Mono Touch) has many strong features that enable it to accommodate just about any development scenario.

To answer our own previous question, there are very clear reasons why Mono for Android stands out as an excellent cross-platform development tool:

➤ Mono for Android gives a developer access to the tooling and developer stack as provided by Microsoft. Considering the kind of investment that Microsoft puts into Visual Studio, this is a huge benefit to the developer. You can continue to work in Visual Studio and use your existing tools, like ReSharper.

➤ Mono for Android runs natively, providing almost all of the native capabilities. In addition, by supporting mobile platform–specific UI elements, it allows developers to reuse large portions of their code without sacrificing the performance and agility to match user expectations.

➤ Mono for Android has a large, active development community. Mono for Android developers actively work to address any developer concerns or issues.

SUMMARY

This chapter looked at the following items:

➤ A product comparison of the .NET Framework and Mono

➤ Mono for Android, which allows .NET developers to target Android

➤ The Android platform, its licensing, and its operating system

➤ Cross-platform alternatives for developing Android applications

You should now understand which tools are needed to build a native application with .NET/C# for Android. The next chapter explores the specifics of building a Mono for Android application with Visual Studio and MonoDevelop. Chapters 4 and 5 describe how to work with the user controls for user input and how to present data to the user in a standard form factor. Other chapters in the book discuss specific parts of Android, such as maps and acceleration.

2

Introduction to Mono for Android

WHAT'S IN THIS CHAPTER?

➤ Introduction to Mono and Mono for Android

➤ Configuring the development environment

➤ Mono for Android tools for Visual Studio

➤ Debugging and deploying

What is Mono for Android? This chapter provides the basis for Mono for Android development. It starts with an overview of Mono and then moves to a discussion of Mono for Android, configuring the development stack, and developing and deploying a "Hello Mono for Android" application — first to an emulator and then to your Android-based phone.

BEFORE YOU BEGIN DEVELOPING

Before getting started with development, you need to learn about a number of items that will help you understand the development environment and the tools that are involved. This section covers what Mono is and how it is implemented. Then it discusses what Mono for Android is, along with its benefits and implementation. Finally, this section discusses the development stack before moving on to development.

What Is Mono?

Mono is an open source project sponsored by Xamarin to create an Ecma standard implementation of the .NET common language infrastructure (CLI), a C# compiler, and an open development stack. The Mono project was started by Ximian in 2001, and version 1.0 was released in 2004.

Mono Implementation Goals

The Mono implementation is currently targeting three goals:

➤ An open source CLI

➤ A C# compiler

➤ An open development stack

The CLI provides the runtime environment for languages that have been compiled to the Common Intermediate Language (CIL). The C# compiler is responsible for compiling C# code to CIL for execution on the runtime. The open development stack facilitates development and includes an IDE in MonoDevelop and several libraries beyond the core libraries to provide open cross-platform development. These libraries include GTK# for graphical user interface development, POSIX libraries for UNIX/Linux compatibility, Gecko libraries, database connectivity libraries, and XML schema language support via RELAX NG.

Mono Standards

Mono adheres to the Ecma Standard. Ecma International was formed in 1961 to support the standardization of information and communication technology. In 2005, Ecma approved version 3 of C# and CLI as updates to Ecma 334 and 335. Currently, a working draft of the Ecma 335 CLI is in progress.

The Mono C# compiler is currently feature-complete per the Ecma standards for C# versions 1, 2, and 3 in version 2.6. Version 2.6 also includes a preview of C# 4, with a feature-complete version of C# 4 available in the trunk of version 2.8.

What Is Mono for Android?

Mono for Android is a runtime and development stack that allows .NET developers to leverage their knowledge of Visual Studio and C# to develop applications for Android-based devices.

➤ **Runtime:** The Mono for Android runtime is an application that runs on the Linux kernel in the Android stack. It interprets the Mono byte code and handles communication with the Dalvik runtime for calls to native Android APIs.

➤ **Development stack:** Mono for Android is also a development stack, providing the tools necessary to create and package applications for Android devices.

Why Do I Need Mono for Android?

Given that the Android platform has an open development stack based on Java with Eclipse as a visual development environment, it would be reasonable to ask why you need Mono for Android. A .NET developer who uses Visual Studio has three main reasons: a familiar development environment, familiar APIs, and, as a result, rapid start-up.

Familiar Development Environment

As every developer knows, learning a new development stack is time-consuming and can be painful. Mono for Android allows the .NET developer to stick with the two core tools of .NET development: Visual Studio and C#.

➤ **Visual Studio:** Visual Studio is an excellent and robust IDE geared toward .NET. By using the Mono for Android tools for Visual Studio, you won't have to change your IDE or the settings you like.

➤ **C#:** Some .NET developers work only with Visual Basic .NET, but most .NET developers are familiar with C#. Although C# and Java are similar in structure, many differences in the idioms of each language make for fluent writing. And although proficient C# developers would not have to spend extensive amounts of time learning the Java idioms, they would not have to spend any time if they could stick with a language they already knew.

Familiar API and Library Structure

Staying within the .NET world allows you to work with a familiar API and library structure. Table 2-1 shows the assemblies that are a part of Mono for Android 4.0.1.

TABLE 2-1: Mono for Android Assemblies

ASSEMBLY	DESCRIPTION
Mono.Android.dll	This assembly contains the C# binding to the Android API.
Mono.CompilerServices.SymbolWriter.dll	For compiler writers
Mono.Data.Sqlite.dll	ADO.NET provider for SQLite
Mono.Data.Tds.dll	TDS protocol support; used for System.Data.SqlClient support within System.Data
Mono.Security.dll	Cryptographic APIs
mscorlib.dll	Silverlight
OpenTK.dll	The OpenGL/OpenAL object-oriented APIs, extended to provide Android device support
System.dll	Silverlight, plus types from the following namespaces: System.Collections.Specialized System.ComponentModel System.ComponentModel.Design System.Diagnostics System.IO.Compression

continues

TABLE 2-1 *(continued)*

ASSEMBLY	DESCRIPTION

	`System.Net`
	`System.Net.Cache`
	`System.Net.Mail`
	`System.Net.Mime`
	`System.Net.NetworkInformation`
	`System.Net.Security`
	`System.Net.Sockets`
	`System.Security.Authentication`
	`System.Security.Cryptography`
	`System.Timers`

`System.Core.dll`	Silverlight
`System.Data.dll`	.NET 3.5 with some functionality removed
`System.Json.dll`	Silverlight
`System.Runtime.Serialization.dll`	Silverlight
`System.ServiceModel.dll`	WCF stack as present in Silverlight Alpha quality

`System.ServiceModel.Web.dll`	Silverlight, plus types from the following namespaces:
	`System`
	`System.ServiceModel.Channels`
	`System.ServiceModel.Description`
	`System.ServiceModel.Web`
	Alpha quality

`System.Transactions.dll`	.NET 3.5; part of `System.Data` support
`System.Web.Services`	Basic web services from the .NET 3.5 profile, with the server features removed
`System.Xml.dll`	.NET 3.5
`System.Xml.Linq.dll`	.NET 3.5

http://mono-android.net/Documentation/Assemblies

So, with your favorite development environment to leverage as well as familiar APIs, you will have a rapid start-up for Android development.

What Are the Trade-Offs of Working with Mono for Android?

When you decide not to work with a native API and development stack, trade-offs will be necessary. They need to be weighed against the advantages of working with a more comfortable, but abstract, layer.

Waiting for Improvements

Although moving away from the native Java and Eclipse in favor of Visual Studio has the benefits just mentioned, it also has some downsides. The first is that you generally have to wait for the latest improvements. That is, usually as soon as a new feature or performance enhancement is available in the Android SDK, you have to wait for the next release of Mono for Android for it to be available.

Taking a Potential Performance Hit

The second trade-off is performance. The Mono for Android runtime has to communicate with the Dalvik runtime to get a number of things done. This overhead, however, generally is minor and is more than offset by the benefits mentioned previously.

After you install the Mono for Android tools for Visual Studio, starting a new Mono for Android project is as easy as selecting File ➪ New ➪ Project ➪ C# ➪ Mono for Android. We will cover this in more detail next.

Memory Management

Many of the objects that are allocated by Mono for Android are wrappers for the Java objects they represent. So what happens is this: Every time you allocate a type which is wrapping a corresponding Java type, two objects are created:

1. The Java object, in the Java heap
2. The Mono "proxy" object, in the Mono heap

Mono for Android does some work to ensure that both objects stay alive as long as one is referencing the other. That is, as long as the Mono garbage collector (GC) refers to an object, the Java-side object will be kept alive and vice versa. This is accomplished by the proxy objects that are created by the mandroid.exe tool at build time.

However, the GCs are by nature lazy, only performing a collection on demand and not simply when objects go out of scope. So that means that cross-VM garbage will stick around longer than average, and this is unavoidable.

So, when allocating a large number of objects for temporary use, it is worthwhile to explicitly dispose of those objects. A convenient approach to this is to use a `using` block with a new object, as this will implicitly dispose of the new object that is the target of the `using` clause, and thereby dispose of the Mono-side wrapper, which will allow the Java-VM to collect the object, preventing too many temporary objects from sticking around for too long.

 For more details on garbage collection, you should refer to the docu- mentation at the following link: http://mono-android.net/index. php?title=Documentation/GC&highlight=garbage+collection.

What Do I Need for the Mono for Android Development Environment?

Although the development environment for Mono for Android is geared toward working in Visual Studio with C#, many pieces beyond that are required.

Java SDK

First, you need to install the Java SDK, which can be found at http://java.sun.com. You might wonder why you need Java if Mono for Android is supposed to allow you to develop with C# on Visual Studio. The Android SDK is developed in Java, so it is required to run all the tools that come with the SDK. The most significant tool is the Android emulator, which is required for rapid debug- ging and testing before deploying to an actual device. However, other tools you will become familiar with are also Java-dependent.

Android SDK

Following the installation of the Java SDK, the Android SDK can be installed. The Android SDK can be downloaded from http://developer.android.com/sdk/index.html, where you will find a link to download a Windows installer. After you have downloaded the SDK, the installation has four steps.

1. The first step is to run the SDK installation. This is as straightforward as it sounds. Run the Windows installer, and you're done.

2. The second step is to download the APIs that you want to use. Run the program AVD Manager.exe, and select the "Available packages" item on the left. This allows you to install the different Google APIs and SDK platforms that you will use in the next step. You may install all the platforms you want, but for our purposes, ensure that you install at least the Level 8 platform, which corresponds to Android 2.2. If you install all the available packages, you should have a view that looks like Figure 2-1.

3. Now that the SDK is fully set up, the third step is to configure an Android emulator. In the Android SDK and AVD Manager, select "Virtual devices," and then click the Create but- ton. You see the window shown in Figure 2-2. In the Name field, type **Android_22**. In the Target drop-down, select Android 2.2 - API Level 8. In the SD Card radio group, select Size and enter **512**. Now click Create AVD. You should get a dialog that confirms that the Android_22 AVD was successfully created.

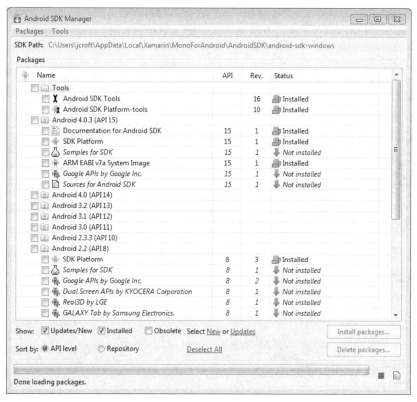

FIGURE 2-1

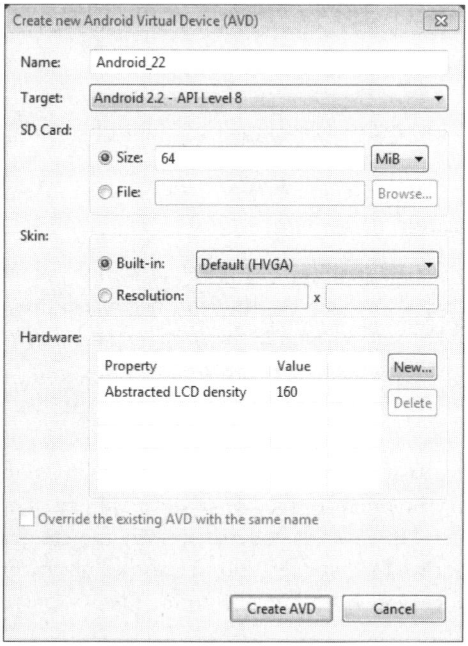

FIGURE 2-2

4. The fourth step is to start the emulator you have configured. Select the Android_22 AVD from the list, and click the Start button. The dialog box that appears lets you change some launch settings. For now, the defaults are fine, so click the Launch button. After a short time you should see an image like the one shown in Figure 2-3. After a minute or two you should see the familiar Android logo, but it may take several minutes before the emulator is fully booted, as shown in Figure 2-4.

FIGURE 2-3

Once the emulator is running, you can leave it running to save some start-up time during the "Hello Android" development process.

Visual Studio

For Mono for Android development you must have Visual Studio 2010 Professional or better to run the Mono for Android plug-in. Visual Studio 2010 Express is insufficient, because it does not support plug-ins. The installation process for Visual Studio is outside the scope of this discussion, but you need to ensure that Visual Studio 2010 is installed before proceeding.

Mono Tools for Visual Studio

Mono Tools for Visual Studio are tools added to Visual Studio as a plug-in that helps with cross-platform compatibility of .NET development for the open source Mono development stack. These tools are not required for what we are doing here. However, if you are broadly interested in Mono development or deploying code written on Windows in Visual Studio to another platform that Mono supports, these tools are worthwhile and easy to install at this point. The tools can be found at http://mono-tools.com/download/.

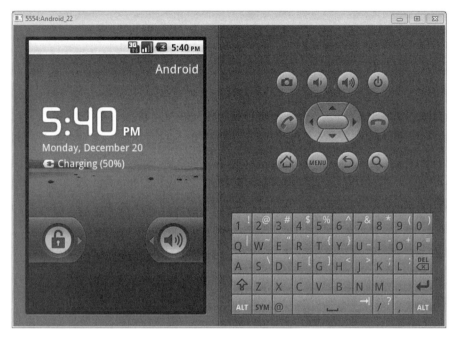

FIGURE 2-4

Installing the Mono for Android Plug-in

As soon as all the prerequisites are in place, you can install the Mono for Android plug-in for Visual Studio. The plug-in can be downloaded from `http://mono-android.net/Store`. Close Visual Studio if it is open, and run the installation program. It takes a few minutes to install, but after it is complete, you are ready to proceed to Mono for Android development.

VISUAL STUDIO DEVELOPMENT WITH MONO FOR ANDROID

This section covers developing a basic "Hello Android" application for your Android device working with the Android plug-in for Visual Studio 2010. You start by setting up a new Mono for Android project in Visual Studio and then follow through with building and debugging the application. After that you add some logging and unit tests to the project before deploying the application to a physical device.

Although some of the specifics are focused on Visual Studio, everyone is encouraged to read this section, as it explains some aspects of Android and Mono for Android that are not covered in the section specifically geared toward development with MonoDevelop.

General Setup

The first thing you do is create the new application in Visual Studio. Start Visual Studio 2010 and select File ➪ New ➪ Project. When the New Project dialog appears, select Mono for Android Application from the available C# templates, as shown in Figure 2-5. In the Name field, type **HelloAndroid**. That will also appear as the solution name. Then click OK. Your project opens to `Activity1.cs`.

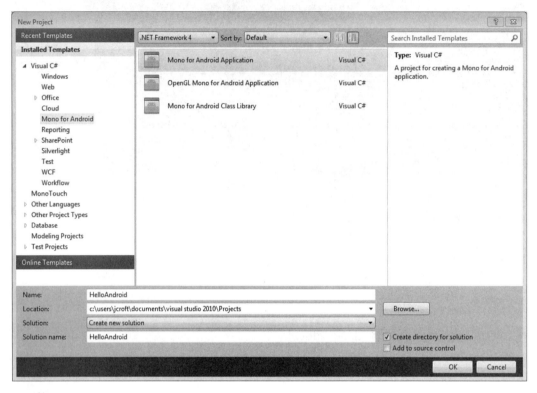

FIGURE 2-5

Building Hello Android

Before you build the application, you need to consider the template code and make some quick changes. The template code is as follows:

```csharp
using System;

using Android.App;
using Android.Content;
using Android.Runtime;
using Android.Views;
using Android.Widget;
using Android.OS;

namespace HelloAndroid
{
    [Activity(Label = "My Activity", MainLauncher = true)]
    public class Activity1 : Activity
    {
        int count = 1;

        protected override void OnCreate(Bundle bundle)
```

```
        {
            base.OnCreate(bundle);

            // Set our view from the "main" layout resource
            SetContentView(Resource.layout.main);

            // Get our button from the layout resource,
            // and attach an event to it
            Button button = FindViewById<Button>(Resource.id.myButton);
            button.Click += delegate { button.Text = string.Format("{0} clicks!",
count++); };
        }
    }
}
```

This block of code shows a few things.

➤ First are the using clauses needed for this code.

➤ Then you have the namespace declaration that is set to your application name,
   HelloAndroid.

➤ Then you have the class declaration for Activity1, which is of type Activity.

   An Activity is central to the design of Android-based programs, and they are discussed
   more in upcoming chapters, particularly Chapter 3. However, the annotations on this class
   are also of note. First is the label My Activity, which will be the label seen in the Android
   application window. Second is the MainLauncher annotation, which indicates that this
   Activity is the main one to be launched in this application.

➤ Finally, you have the OnCreate function. Activity creation is just one of several life cycle
   steps that an Activity may be subjected to. The whole life cycle will be discussed further in
   Chapter 3. In this function you initialize a resource bundle, set your view, get a button from
   the view, and attach an event to it.

Now you are ready to build the new application. Click the Debug button on the toolbar. You are
prompted to select a running device to deploy the code to, as shown in Figure 2-6. You should see
listed the emulator that you started running earlier. If there is no running device, you can select a
device to start.

FIGURE 2-6

Select that emulator, and click OK. The Mono for Android toolkit then checks for an installed version of the Mono for Android runtime. If the runtime is not found, the toolkit installs it. This process can take quite some time. Once the runtime is installed, the toolkit signs and installs the application into the running emulator.

After that process has finished you can run your application. Go to the emulator, unlock it, and click the Applications button. You should see an image similar to Figure 2-7. Click the My Activity application. You should see the application running, as shown in Figure 2-8.

FIGURE 2-7

Logging

To follow the flow of the program execution, it is often helpful to log program activity. This section briefly examines how you can implement logging messages in Mono for Android. The Log class can be found in the android.util namespace. You can add a few lines to the code you had before to get the following source:

```
using System;

using Android.App;
using Android.Content;
using Android.Runtime;
using Android.Views;
using Android.Widget;
using Android.OS;
using Android.Util;
```

```
namespace HelloAndroid
{
    [Activity(Label = "Hello Android", MainLauncher = true)]
    public class Activity1 : Activity
    {
        int count = 1;

        protected override void OnCreate(Bundle bundle)
        {
            Log.I("HA", "Start OnCreate");
            base.OnCreate(bundle);

            // Set our view from the "main" layout resource
            SetContentView(Resource.layout.main);

            // Get our button from the layout resource,
            // and attach an event to it
            Button button = FindViewById<Button>(Resource.id.myButton);
            button.Click += delegate { button.Text = string.Format("{0} clicks!",
count++); }

            Log.I("HA", "End OnCreate");
        }
    }
}
```

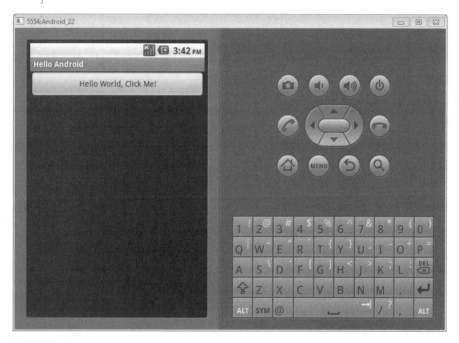

FIGURE 2-8

Here you can see the added `using Android.Util` that provides access to the `Log` class, which contains the following convenience functions (among others):

➤ `Log.I(string tag, `*`string message`*`)` logs information.

➤ `Log.W(string tag, `*`string message`*`)` logs warnings.

➤ `Log.E(string tag, `*`string message`*`)` logs errors.

The `tag` parameter provides context for the log message. In this case you can use a tag of "HA" for HelloAndroid. To view the messages in Visual Studio, select View ➪ Other Windows ➪ Android Device Logging, and all the messages will be available.

Debugging

Having successfully executed the application in your emulator, you can look at how to debug a problem that we will introduce. If you are using a physical phone, you need to go to the applications page on your phone and select Settings. Then select Applications, Development, and check USB Debugging. After that, return to your code.

Change the following line:

```
Button button = FindViewById<Button>(Resource.id.myButton);
```

To the following:

```
TextView button = FindViewById<TextView>(Resource.id.myButton);
```

Rerun the application. This time the application will throw an error on start-up because you are trying to treat a `Button` as a `TextView`. While this example may be contrived, take a look at how you can debug the application.

Set a break point on the following line:

```
base.OnCreate(bundle);
```

Now, click the run/debug button on the toolbar. This time, as the application starts up the software will stop at the break point. You can now step through the application until you arrive at the offending line. Trying to step over that instruction will result in the previously seen error, and, in this case, fixing it is trivial.

Testing

The days of merely testing software through usage are long gone. All reliably built software relies on unit tests as a best practice and to make the testing cycle shorter and more reliable. So, how do you build unit tests with Mono for Android?

The short answer is NUnit, just as it is for any other Mono application. The longer answer involves structuring your program to make it amenable to testing. That is, the NUnit testing framework is not geared toward UI testing, so it is best to isolate your non-UI code into a separate library and set up any tests to run against that library.

It is also worth noting that if you intend to leverage code for other platforms, for example, the iPhone with MonoTouch or Windows Phone 7 with Mono or .NET, then you also want to isolate platform-specific code from generically reusable code. This code would also be good code to build test cases against.

So for non-UI and platform-independent code, instead of building program logic into the Android activities you want to extract that code to an Android library. You can create an Android library by creating a new solution, but instead of selecting Android application, select Android library. Then use NUnit to provide automated tests for that code.

Deploying

Having run the gamut from "Hello Android" through debugging, logging, and testing, it's now time to look at deploying an application to an actual Android device. This process has three steps: connect the phone via USB, set the phone into development mode, and deploy the application.

1. The first step is obvious.

2. The second step requires you to go into the phone's settings and select Application Settings. Under Application Settings, check the option for Unknown Sources. This lets you install non-Android market apps, which you want. Second, on the same page, select the Development option. This takes you to a screen with three options. Select USB Debugging and Stay Awake. You aren't using mock locations, so don't worry about that now.

3. Now for the final step: click the Debug button on the toolbar. This time, when the Running Devices list comes up, your device is on it! Select your device. This time the installation process runs over USB to your device.

When it is finished, give the Hello Android app a try.

MONO FOR ANDROID DEVELOPMENT WITH MONODEVELOP

This section covers developing a basic "Hello Android" application for your Android device working with the Android plug-in for MonoDevelop. If you skipped the Visual Studio section because you are on a Mac or use MonoDevelop anyway, I would encourage you to read the Visual Studio section because it covers some generally applicable concepts, but if you want to jump right in and catch up along the way you should be fine.

General Setup

Installing the development environment on the Mac is straightforward. There are six steps to the process:

➤ **Install the Android SDK:** This can be found at `http://developer.android.com/sdk/index.html`. This is Java-based and leverages the Java SDK installed by default on OSX.

➤ **Install Mono for Mac:** This can be found at `http://www.go-mono.com/mono-downloads/download.html`. This provides the Mono platform, which is the basis for the Mono development tools that will also be installed.

➤ **Install MonoDevelop for Mac:** This can be found at `http://monodevelop.com/download`. This provides an IDE for developing Mono applications on the Mac. Also, it is required because Mono for Android for the Mac installs as a plug-in for this IDE.

➤ **Install Mono for Android for Mac:** This can be found at `http://mono-android.net/Store`. At the store page you can also download a trial version of the software.

➤ **Configure the Mono for Android MonoDevelop add-in:** Once the plug-in is installed you need to go to MonoDevelop ➪ Preferences, which will display the preferences dialog. After this, select the Other category and select Mono for Android SDKs. This will allow you to configure the Java and Android SDKs that you are using.

➤ **Configure your Android Emulator:** Finally, run the Android SDK installer and select Virtual Devices. Create a new virtual device. It's important to note that you may find developing on an actual device to be somewhat faster than it is on an emulated device.

If you want to read about this process in more detail please refer to the following link: `http://mono-android.net/Installation/Installation_for_Mac`.

 Also, if you are running in a Mono for Windows environment you may want to refer to the installation instructions at `http://mono-android.net/Installation/Windows`, *as there are some minor differences in setup.*

Building Hello Android

To get a program up and running with MonoDevelop and Android is very simple. If you read the Visual Studio section, you can probably skip this section and find the details on your own, but for those who skipped the Visual Studio section you can run through the process now.

Go to File ➪ New ➪ Solution and select the Mono for Android template as shown in Figure 2-9.

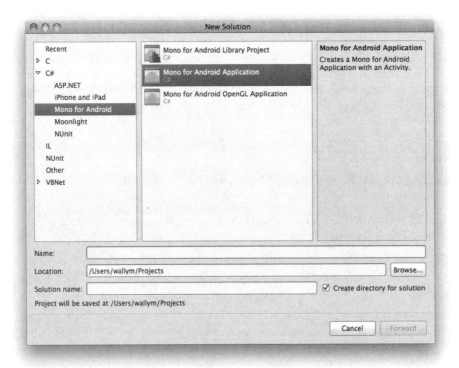

FIGURE 2-9

For the solution name, key in HelloAndroid. Then click OK. The new application will appear in the window. Go to the Run menu and select Run. After a moment a window will appear prompting you to choose the device to run the application on. If you have a running emulator or an Android device plugged in, it will be listed. If not, select "Start an Emulator Image" and you will receive a list of images that are configured on your machine, one of which will be the emulator you configured during the general setup.

Select the device or emulator that you want your application to run on, then select OK. If an emulator has to start up, it could take awhile. Otherwise, messages will appear notifying you that it is checking for installed applications, installing Mono for Android, if necessary, and, finally, running the application, as shown in Figure 2-10.

FIGURE 2-10

Logging

Logging in MonoDevelop is identical to logging in Visual Studio, as it is a function of the API and not of the IDE. To recap, in case you skipped the Visual Studio section, here are the logging functions:

➤ `Log.I(string tag, string message)` logs information.

➤ `Log.W(string tag, string message)` logs warnings.

➤ `Log.E(string tag, string message)` logs errors.

The `tag` parameter provides context for the log message. For instance, if you add some logging to your HelloAndroid application, you might use a tag of "HA" in the logging functions.

Debugging

Having successfully executed the application in the emulator, it's time to look at how to debug a problem that we will introduce. If you are using a physical phone, you need to go to the Applications page on your phone and select Settings. Then select Applications, Development, and check USB Debugging. After that, return to your code.

Change the following line:

```
Button button = FindViewById<Button>(Resource.id.myButton);
```

To the following:

```
TextView button = FindViewById<TextView>(Resource.id.myButton);
```

Rerun the application. This time the application will throw an error on start-up because you are trying to treat a `Button` as a `TextView`. While this example may be contrived, take look at how you can debug the application.

Set a break point on the following line:

```
base.OnCreate(bundle);
```

Now, click the Run/Debug button on the toolbar. This time, as the application starts up the software will stop at the break point. You can now step through the application until you arrive at the offending line. Trying to step over that instruction will result in the previously seen error, and, in this case, fixing it is trivial.

Testing

The days of merely testing software through usage are long gone. All reliably built software relies on unit tests as a best practice and to make the testing cycle shorter and more reliable. So, how do you build unit tests with Mono for Android?

The short answer is NUnit, just as it is for any other Mono application. The longer answer involves structuring your program to make it amenable to testing. That is, the NUnit testing framework is not geared toward UI testing, so it is best to isolate your non-UI code into a separate library and set up any tests to run against that library.

Deploying

Deployment of your HelloAndroid application to a device is very simple.

This process has three steps: connect the phone via USB, set the phone into development mode, and deploy the application.

1. The first step is obvious.

2. The second step requires you to go into the phone's settings and select Application Settings. Under Application Settings, check the option for Unknown Sources. This lets you install non-Android market apps, which you want. Second, on the same page, select the Development option. This takes you to a screen with three options. Select USB Debugging and Stay Awake. You aren't using mock locations, so don't worry about that now.

3. Now for the final step: click the Debug button on the toolbar. This time, when the running devices list comes up, your device is on it! Select your device. This time the installation process runs over USB to your device.

When it is finished, give the HelloAndroid app a try.

SUMMARY

In this chapter you covered installing the development environment for Android on Windows using the Visual Studio 2010 plug-in, and you covered installing the development environment on the Mac using MonoDevelop. In each case, the process is similar: install the software stack including the Java SDK, the Android SDK, and the Mono SDK. Have your IDE installed, either Visual Studio or MonoDevelop. Then install the Mono for Android add-in. If you are using MonoDevelop, configure the add-in. Then, using the installed platform, create a default HelloAndroid application.

In addition, this chapter covered logging, testing, and deploying applications. You saw that logging was a simple matter of adding one of the three log calls to your application, and that these logs can be seen in the console of either Visual Studio or MonoDevelop. Testing is always considered a best practice to assist in validating the behavior of your software before it is deployed. Deployment is what software development is about. These skills will be used over and over in all the chapters to come.

3

Understanding Android/Mono for Android Applications

WHAT'S IN THIS CHAPTER?

➤ What comprises Android and Mono for Android applications

➤ Explaining the Android core components

➤ Describing purpose of intents and how they interact within the Android platform

➤ Exploring the Android manifest file and its key features

To develop Mono for Android applications, you need a good working knowledge of the key components of an Android application. Not only will this understanding enable you to build a feature-rich application, but it also will help you communicate between other applications and processes on the Android device.

One of the selling points of Mono for Android is that it enables you to write Android applications in a .NET-specific language. However, this does not imply that you do not need a basic understanding of the Android runtime as well as the underlying Java-based architecture. To write a full-featured application, you must be able to interface with Android's Java APIs and, potentially, other applications that are not necessarily written using Mono for Android. Furthermore, it is imperative that you understand the "Android way" of writing an application, because the Mono for Android runtime is built on that understanding and, in many ways, reflects those "Androidisms" in its architecture. The overall goal of this chapter is to provide the foundation for that understanding.

To accomplish its goals, this chapter gives you a broad understanding of the Android platform but does so *in a Mono for Android context* where applicable. All key differences between Mono for Android and Android are called out specifically. This chapter introduces the different components of the Android stack and how they interact with one another to form an application. In addition, it spends some time reviewing how the Android OS manages those application components in terms of priority, memory usage, resources, and other life cycle–related topics. If you are already familiar with Android, you may consider this chapter a review or even skip it. If you're new to the Android platform, this is a great place to get a broad understanding of the system. Either way, this chapter should serve as a great introduction to the bridge between Android and the Mono for Android runtime.

 Although most of this chapter's content focuses on features that are specific to the Android core classes, all code samples and naming conventions are presented as if you are working in a Mono for Android environment. For the most part, Mono for Android namespaces mirror those of Android. However, the casing, nonalphanumeric character usage, and names are sometimes modified to favor the suggested practices of the C# language.

WHAT IS AN ANDROID APPLICATION?

Most applications have one entry point at which the developer can define start-up procedures, resource initialization, and other steps. In the case of Windows programming, this is characterized by the `Main()` function. Although Android applications have settings that identify an application's default entry point, Android apps are not what you would consider typical. When you look at an Android application, no single function unilaterally instantiates the entire application. This is because Android applications behave and interact much like a group of related subapplications rather than a single rigid entity.

Android applications are an association of core components that can be called and instantiated upon demand. In fact, these components can work independently of each other but still maintain a cohesive story via loose coupling and preestablished means of communicating with one another. Furthermore, the interactions between the application's components are not limited to the application but may be accessed from other Android applications as well.

The reason for this structure is to allow for as much fluidity between different applications, components, and features within an Android device as possible. Although this may increase the complexity of speaking from component to component, it gives the developer a lot of freedom to share data, share behaviors, or even create something of a distributed application.

For example, suppose you needed to create an application to store grocery data while a person was shopping. For this application to succeed, you would need to leverage the bar code on the back of the grocery item by reading it with the device. In most situations, you would likely have to download a bar code–scanning library and include it as part of your application build.

In addition to the application architecture, you should keep in mind a few other key points when developing any Mono for Android or Android application:

> **Every Android application runs in its own process.** When an Android application is started, the Android OS starts a single Linux process. This makes it much simpler for the Android OS to create and destroy application processes upon request or when the system needs additional resources.

➤ **Android starts only one thread per process.** If you remember nothing else from this chapter, remember this! When you are dealing with different application components within an Android application, it is easy to forget that, with a few exceptions, everything in an application runs in a single thread. Although it is a small matter to create additional threads to complete work, it is up to you as a developer to do so.

➤ **Every application runs in its own instance of the Dalvik virtual machine.** This sandboxing method protects your application from being corrupted by other running applications. One badly planned application does not affect the stability of other applications on the device.

➤ **Every application is protected so that only the device user and the application can access the application's data or resources.** By default, all applications live in a silo in which other applications cannot see stored or sensitive data or user actions. As a developer you can expose as many features or as much data as you want, but it has to be explicitly named. In addition, upon application installation or update, the user can accept or refuse any permission requests that the installing application may make of other applications.

Although these are default rule settings for applications, you can bend them by specifically writing the appropriate code or requesting the appropriate permission level from the device user. These rules are intended to help ensure the stability of your application and the Android device by allowing each application to live in its own world. In addition, they play a large role in protecting your application data from malicious attacks.

The Building Blocks of an Android Application

Android applications are composed of four building blocks that are often called the Android *components*. These components encapsulate different usage patterns and behaviors on the Android platform. Specifically, they can be defined as follows:

➤ Activities

➤ Services

➤ Content providers

➤ Broadcast receivers

An Android application may have one or many of each of these components. The following sections walk through what each of these items is, discuss their usage scenarios, and define what native versions of these items exist in the Android platform.

Activities

An *activity* is a user interface component that can be used to accomplish a single task. If you are working with Mono for Android or Android applications for the first time, odds are that the first application component you develop will be an activity. When you are running an Android application, every screen that the application displays or that you interact with is launched by one or more activities. Broadly speaking, activities comprise the application's presentation layer. They handle the logic to display information to the user, present controls and collect their data, and direct the user to other activities as needed.

An application may consist of one or many activities. The number that an application may have is based on an application's complexity and the developer's design decisions. Since each component of an Android application is expected to be able to function independently of the others, activities can be launched by being marked as the application's startup activity in the Android manifest or by the current activity launching a new activity directly.

> *In Android, you can identify the start-up activity by adding the appropriate action to the activity's intent filter. This occurs within the Android manifest. This differs quite a bit from Mono for Android in that Mono for Android allows you to specify the start-up activity by using the following attribute in your activity's class declaration:*
>
> ```
> [Activity(Label = "My Activity", MainLauncher = true)]
> public class Activity1 : Activity
> {
>         //Activity class implementation...
> }
> ```
>
> *The Android manifest, intent filters, and actions are covered later in this chapter and in Chapter 11.*

An activity is probably the simplest of the application components to work with. For the most part, you can think of an activity as having two basic operating parts:

➤ **A collection of one or more views:** These items comprise the different interfaces that can be presented to the user. This can vary from simple Toast() messages to full, complex data tables to animations. Views are discussed at more length in the following sections.

➤ **The activity class:** This acts as the controller for the activity. Based on user interaction, it handles the launching of additional layouts and views, the fetching and binding of appropriate data, and the collection and delegating of collected data.

If you're familiar with the MVC pattern, you will quickly recognize how activities are structured, because Android activities and views were developed with this in mind. The Activity class acts as the controller. The class receives input and acts on that input, calling the appropriate model objects and presenting various views. On the other hand, Android views are responsible for knowing how to present the model objects they are passed. One Android activity (controller) may present many different views, based on the user input.

The Activity Life Cycle

The life cycle of an Android component runs from the time when the component is created to the time when it is destroyed. In the larger scheme of things, component life cycles are a part of the overall Android resource management process. By gauging where different components are within their life cycle pattern, the Android OS can decide how to allocate resources and manage memory requirements. Specifically, an activity's life cycle is a series of states that starts with the activity's being created in `OnCreate()` and ends with its being removed in `OnDestroy()`. Activities have basically three states: active, paused, and stopped:

➤ The activity is *active* when it is running on the device and is in the foreground of the screen. When using an application on your Android device, the activity you are working with and viewing is in an active state.

➤ The activity is *paused* when it is still visible but does not have screen focus. Typically, this occurs when another activity overlies the current one. Although it does not have focus, it is still running with resources as if it were active.

➤ An activity is *stopped* when it is obscured by another activity. It can still carry information, such as state and member information, but its window is hidden. When an activity is in a stopped state, it is an excellent target to be killed by the Android OS to free up resources.

Typically, an activity's state changes due to the user's interactions or the Android OS managing resources. Figure 3-1 shows the theoretical states of the Gmail application while a user interacts with it. In this example, imagine that you are checking your Gmail application on your Android device.

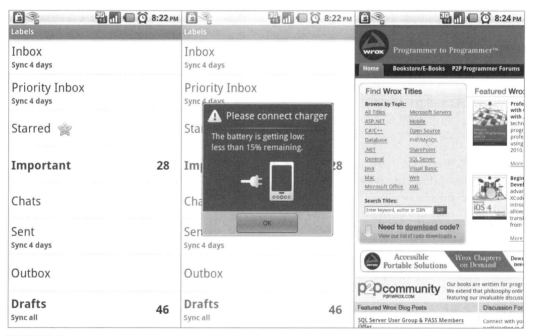

FIGURE 3-1

When you first launch the application, an activity displays a list of all your e-mails. The Gmail application is in an active state, as shown on the left side of Figure 3-1.

Suppose that, as you begin working through your e-mails, the battery on your device begins running low, and you receive a notification. The notification screen overlies the currently active screen to warn you, as shown in the middle of Figure 3-1. You can see your Gmail application in the background, but it is in a paused state.

You clear the warning message and find the e-mail you are looking for. You open it and follow a link within it. This launches the browser app, which completely covers the Gmail activity (the right side of Figure 3-1). At this point, the Gmail activity is in a stopped state. Even though it may still be running and may contain some instance values, the Android OS will possibly kill it as more resources are requested by your browsing or by using other applications.

As an activity is moved from one state to another, the application developer needs to be able to respond to the changes in state. Therefore, the `Activity` class exposes several events that trigger when the activity state changes. These events allow you to respond to the state change appropriately to preserve your application's data and free unnecessary resources. The available events are `OnCreate()`, `OnStart()`, `OnRestart()`, `OnResume()`, `OnPause()`, `OnStop()`, and `OnDestroy()`.

Although you may have occasion to use any of these events, `OnCreate()` and `OnPause()` typically are the ones that are used most frequently:

➤ The `OnCreate()` method is reserved for defining whatever initialization activities your application may require. In this method, you define the first view that you will present to the user by using the `SetContentView()` method of the `Activity` base class. Also, you may choose to request access to various system resources. Finally, you use this class to assign delegates to the appropriate event handlers for controls such as a button press.

➤ The `OnPause()` method is a key tool for handling situations in which your activity is going into the background. During an activity's life cycle, this method is called when the user navigates away from your activity. This method lets you clean up your application's resource usage by closing access to system resources, such as the device's camera, or halt expensive tasks such as animations.

By understanding the activity life cycle, you can ensure the stability of your application, protect the integrity of your data, and improve system performance by proactively freeing resources when they are no longer necessary.

Activities and Views

To fully utilize activities, you need a pretty solid understanding of what views are, as well as how they are used throughout Mono for Android and Android. When an activity runs, the Android OS assigns that activity a window in which it can draw whatever content it needs to present. The content to display within this window space is communicated via *views*. In short, views are the basic building blocks used to define the controls and layout that the activity presents to the user to interact with.

Each activity can present a single view or a hierarchy of views within its window space. This is accomplished by calling the activity's `SetContentView()` method and by providing the appropriate view item to display. In addition to setting the initial view within the `OnCreate()` event of the `Activity` class, activities can change the view that is displayed based on triggered events or by launching into a different activity.

The Android platform has several different implementations of views. Every view type extends the `View` class, which defines the basic interface behaviors such as creation, layout, event processing, and drawing. Some of the more common views that you will work with in your applications are items such as a `Button`, `ImageView`, and `TextView`. Inheriting from the `View` class, all of these are a type of view, although they are more commonly called *controls* or *widgets*.

A special kind of view known as a *view group* contains its own collection or hierarchy of views. Not only does a view group perform all the same functionality of a typical view, but it also handles the flow and layout of its children. View groups are a great tool because they allow a developer to make a collection of reusable, complex controls. In addition, they serve as the foundation for layouts.

A *layout* is a view group that is used to manage the flow or presentation of a group of views. The layout is typically defined using an XML-based syntax similar to HTML. This allows a developer to quickly place several views in a single layout and also individually set property values for each view within that layout.

Often, the terms *view*, *control*, *widget*, and *layout* are used interchangeably. This can lead to some confusion, because these terms move from generic to specific. In addition, these terms can be confused with other Android features such as application widgets. To help resolve this confusion, consider this code snippet:

```xml
<?xml version="1.0" encoding="utf-8"?>
    <LinearLayout xmlns:android="http://schemas.android.com/apk/res/android"
        android:orientation="vertical"
        android:layout_width="fill_parent"
        android:layout_height="fill_parent">

    <ImageView android:layout_height="wrap_content"
        android:layout_width="wrap_content"
        android:layout_margin="5dip"
        android:src="@drawable/icon" />

    <TextView android:id="@+id/text"
        android:layout_width="wrap_content"
        android:layout_height="wrap_content"
        android:text="@string/welcomeText" />

    <Button android:id="@+id/helloButton"
        android:layout_width="fill_parent"
        android:layout_height="wrap_content"
        android:text="@string/hello"/>
</LinearLayout>
```

In this example, the XML syntax defines a group of different user interface components to present to the user. This is a typical snippet of what is loaded when an activity's `SetContentView()` method is called. At the root node of this snippet is the `LinearLayout` node. `LinearLayout` inherits from `View` and `Viewgroup`. Thus, this is a view. Since it contains child views, this is also a *viewgroup* or *layout*. In this case, `LinearLayout` places each child view in a single column.

Within `LinearLayout` are several *controls* (or *widgets*) that are predefined in the Android framework. Each of these controls—`Button`, `Image`, and `TextView`—derives from the `View` base class.

Chapter 4 delves deeper into types of views and how to utilize them in conjunction with your activities.

Services

A *service* is a unit of work defined by the developer that can run for an indefinite period of time. Unlike activities, services do not have a visual component. In addition, they do not rely on the application user to function. They can be used for a plethora of tasks, such as fetching data from the network, playing music while you are browsing through other applications, or working on a longer-running task. When you think of any kind of automated or timed task on an Android device, you are most likely thinking of something that runs as a service.

Services often confuse those who have not worked in the Android environment before. When developers hear the term *service*, they often think of a "background service." Although services are used for just this purpose, developers often make the mistake of assuming that services run on a different thread than other components of an application. This is not the case. As a developer, you are responsible for creating additional threads as necessary. *All items in an Android application run within the same thread unless specifically handled by the developer.*

In a nutshell, services are the workforce of an Android application. They can be used to queue a set of tasks to be processed or to systematically check the status of a network resource. Also, a service is a way to expose a task to other applications, allowing them to interact with that particular work. Services are a great way to handle repetitive or ongoing tasks, even when your application's activities are inactive or closed. Typical Android services include mail applications, RSS readers that periodically check for updates, podcast playback applications, and Twitter clients.

Services are both a broad and deep topic that goes beyond the scope of this chapter. Chapter 11 digs deeper into the inner workings of a service, the different aspects of the service life cycle, and how to implement services in your Mono for Android applications.

 When an application is initially asked to run, Android starts a process for it with a single thread. All components within that application run in that single thread. *To prevent the application from locking while the service is being executed, it is vital to spawn different threads or define different processes to handle the service task while allowing the user to enjoy a responsive interface.*

Content Providers

Content providers are the preferred means of sharing information across multiple applications. They can be thought of as a type of community data storage that allows developers to expose specific sets of data to be queried or even manipulated by other applications and processes. Because the Android platform has no universal data storage mechanism, content providers are a great way to create common data pools for Android applications.

Content providers have the flexibility to allow you to define one or many data sets that target different subsets of your data. With this flexibility, you can protect data that you want to exist in only your application, such as personal user data, while sharing other data with applications that meet the security criteria you specify. In addition, a content provider can implement different actions for each data set. This means that interaction with each of your data sets can range from read-only to mass inserts.

The advantage of these data types being exposed is that the users have options for what applications they want to manage their data; they are not forced to use a native player. And, as a developer, you have exposure to write your own applications to improve upon native performance.

> *As a developer, you may be tempted to forgo using content providers and use data storage that only your application can access. However, by using the content provider as a community data pool, you do yourself and your potential customers a favor. You get a prepopulated data pool directly on installation, and the users do not have to manually migrate data. It is a way to be a good citizen on an Android device.*

Native Content Providers

The best way to get a clear understanding of content providers is to look at those that are already established in the Android platform. These native providers can give you a real sense of why you should use content providers and also how they are best implemented.

There are several native content providers. The content they provide ranges from access to basic data types such as contacts and phone call history to more complex types such as images and video. Table 3-1 describes a few of the most commonly used native content providers.

TABLE 3-1: Common Content Providers

PROVIDER NAME	DESCRIPTION
AlarmClock	Gives access to the system's alarm clock application, allowing different applications to set alarm modes and times.
Browser	Exposes data sets such as web searches, history, and bookmarks for viewing or editing.
CallLog	Provides information about outgoing, incoming, and missed calls, including phone numbers, timestamps, and duration.
ContactsContract	Used to view or modify contact data. For those who were early Android developers, this replaces the deprecated `Contact` provider.
MediaStore	Provides universal access to media on the Android device, including images, videos, and audio. In addition, this provider exposes metadata for the media on your device, such as genre and artist.
Settings	Accesses the global system settings and preferences for the Android device. Some common settings queried are Bluetooth, locale, and network settings.
UserDictionary	Allows insertion or viewing of user-defined words to use for predictive text. In addition, this provider stores usage frequency and locale information for those words.

A list of available default content providers can be found in the Android developer documentation for the `android.provider` namespace.

How Content Providers Work

Whether you are using the default content providers or creating your own, Android gives you a universal way to access them. This is not achieved by allowing direct access to the content providers, however; this is a very important facet of content providers. Rather than giving hundreds of different content providers access to methods or schemes, the Android platform unifies all current and future access by utilizing a mediator object. Specifically, the `ContentResolver` object handles all interactions with a content provider. `ContentResolver` ensures that any new content providers can be universally accessed by other applications while not limiting the methods by which the developer might want to store his or her application data.

 `ContentResolver` *acts as a mediator to a data store. This approach not only simplifies the consumption of data from content providers but also ensures that all content providers are equal. This type of interaction is a great example of the mediator design pattern.*

The content resolver follows two basic rules. First, all content stores have a unique URI. This URI is very similar to a web address. It provides a unique way to locate the content provider you want to access. In addition, the URI can be used to target specific data sets within the content provider or to specify key arguments and values.

The second rule of content providers is that the `ContentProvider` base class defines all possible actions that can be performed on an implemented provider. While writing a custom provider, it is up to you to implement the logic of whatever methods you choose to support. The advantage of this approach is that, if you know how to connect to one provider, you can connect to any provider. Of course, the downside is that you do not have the privilege of writing your own access methods. Thankfully, `ContentResolver` has just the right amount of simplicity and flexibility to support most data needs.

Table 3-2 lists `ContentResolver` functions that most providers implement in some form or fashion.

TABLE 3-2: Common Content Resolver Functions

FUNCTION NAME	DESCRIPTION
query()	Accepts arguments for the provider URI, the selection string, the selection arguments, and the result set sort order. Used to return a cursor with the target result set.
update()	Accepts arguments for the provider URI, the new field values, and the filter to target specific rows to be updated. This returns the number of rows affected by the update statement.
insert()	Accepts arguments for the provider URI and the name-value pairs to be added to the data store. This returns the URI for the newly inserted item.

FUNCTION NAME	DESCRIPTION
delete()	Accepts arguments for the provider URI, the selection string, and the selection arguments. Used to delete one or more entities from the data store. Returns the number of rows affected.
getType()	Accepts arguments for the provider URI. This returns the text MIME type of the data stored within the content provider.

Inserting, deleting, or updating items within a content provider is a fairly straightforward process. Since they return simple data types, you can work directly with the ContentResolver instance associated with your current activity. One of the advantages of the Activity class is that it automatically initiates a ContentResolver object. By calling the methods directly, you can perform your work and not have to worry too much about memory management. This is not quite the case with the query() method.

When performing a query through the ContentResolver, you receive a cursor object. This object can be used to iterate through the result set and leverage the data as you see fit. When you are using the query() action on the ContentResolver object, it is up to you to manage the life cycle of that query as a sensitive resource. In other words, you must be sure to call close() on the cursor object appropriately to avoid memory leaks.

Thankfully, there is a better way to query a content provider if you do not need to directly manage your query cursor. Each activity has an abstraction of the ContentResolver.query() method via the ManagedQuery() function. This too is a basic function of the Activity class. This function associates a query cursor with the activity's life cycle, handling the finer details of closing the query on application destroy() or pause() events and requerying the data when the application is restarted. Unless you need finer control over the query, using the ManagedQuery() method is a better practice.

> *If you find yourself directly using the* ContentResolver.query() *method, you can still allow your application to manage the cursor without using the* ManagedQuery() *method. This is achieved by calling the* StartManagingCursor() *method of the current activity and passing it the appropriate cursor instance.*

Finally, we would be remiss not to consider the security implications of accessing and sharing application data. Although you might want to expose user data, ultimately it is the device user's decision whether he or she wants his or her data used in this manner. When accessing content providers, you may have to request certain application permissions. Likewise, you can state what permissions are needed before someone can access your custom provider. All this configuration is managed in the Android manifest file, which is covered later in this chapter.

Broadcast Receivers

A *broadcast receiver* is an application component that listens for and reacts to events. Broadcast receivers let you listen for specific events and, if need be, initiate activities and services in response. Broadcast receivers comprise the core event-handling system in the Android OS. Broadcast receivers share many similarities with services. They do not have any user interface components, and they are used to accomplish a kind of work. However, receivers differ from services in that they only exist to listen for a type of message and *initiate* the appropriate response to that message.

 Initiate *is an operative word when describing what broadcast receivers do. Broadcast receivers are intended solely to respond to an event that has occurred, not to handle the processing of any response to that event. Major processing should not be handled in the receiver itself but should be passed to an activity or service. To enforce this distinction, Android has a 5-second execution limit for broadcast receiver responses.*

Broadcast Messages

As we describe the details of a broadcast receiver, it is important to understand where the messages that receivers act on originate. First, many different system-level events broadcast messages. These events can be anything from incoming phone calls to low battery warnings to network availability. In addition, individual applications can broadcast messages. These messages may pertain to new data being available or a status change on an application.

Whenever a message is broadcast, it is called a *broadcasting intent*. Intents serve as a messaging facility for different components within the Android platform. This section covers a specific part of what intents do as a whole. Intents are covered in greater depth in the next section and in subsequent chapters.

As with content providers, some intents require special permissions before they can be received by broadcast receivers. These permissions must be requested from the user of the device during the installation of the application onto the device.

Table 3-3 lists some of the more common broadcast messages. As you read through this list, imagine how an Android application could respond to each event. As you might suppose, these events give the developer a significant amount of control to make sure his or her app runs smoothly in a variety of situations.

TABLE 3-3: Common Broadcast Events

ACTION_TIME_TICK	ACTION_TIME_CHANGED
ACTION_TIMEZONE_CHANGED	ACTION_BOOT_COMPLETED
ACTION_PACKAGE_ADDED	ACTION_PACKAGE_CHANGED
ACTION_BATTERY_CHANGED	ACTION_POWER_CONNECTED
ACTION_POWER_DISCONNECTED	ACTION_POWER_DISCONNECTED
ACTION_SHUTDOWN	ACTION_UID_REMOVED

Broadcast Receiver Life Cycle

A broadcast receiver has the simplest life cycle of all the components. Basically, it has only one call-back method, `OnReceive()`. When a message is received, the intent message's data is passed to the receiver. At this point, the receiver is considered to be active while it handles the message and performs the proper actions. Once the `OnReceive()` method returns, a receiver is considered to be in an inactive status again.

Any process that has an active receiver is protected from being killed by the OS. This is an important point to bear in mind, because it can interfere with the system's ability to free needed resources. Therefore, as previously noted, receivers have a 5-second execution limit. Any long-running work should be pushed to a different component, such as a service.

> *For more information regarding the basic building blocks of a Mono for Android or an Android application, please refer to the application fundamentals sections of the official Android documentation at* `http://developer.android.com/guide/topics/fundamentals.html`.

Communicating between Components: Android Intents

Now that you have had a look at the core components of an Android application, you need to work on understanding how those application pieces interact. To allow different pieces of the Android platform to communicate with one another, Android needed a universal messaging system. This messaging system had to support a variety of different usage scenarios while respecting the autonomy of the application components. In addition, this messaging system would have to be a generic, passive system that could be consumed by any application component *whether or not the originating process knew who was receiving the message.* These notions led to the creation of *intents.*

Intents form the messaging system for the Android platform. Because Android components operate in proverbial silos, intents provide a critical function by allowing them to communicate with one another seamlessly. In particular, intents can be used to do the following:

➤ Interact with an activity either by requesting that the activity start a new task or by starting a new activity

➤ Interact with a service by either initializing a new service or delivering a new instruction set to an ongoing service

➤ Interact with broadcast receivers by serving as the medium by which messages are broadcast

In some ways, you can think of the intent system as a way to transform your application into part of a much larger, distributed application. This allows you to make significant time savings by leveraging another application's functionality for your own. Some common usage scenarios for intents include playing a piece of downloaded music, notifying interested applications that the cell phone signal has been lost, or passing changes in an application state to other listening applications.

Android uses intents as a core design principle. Using this messaging system, the Android platform can allow its components to be very loosely coupled, even within the same application. This adherence to the publish/subscribe pattern allows components to be easily switched in and out without causing massive overhaul of other systems.

So, what makes up an intent? At the most basic level, an intent is an abstraction of the details needed to accomplish a task. Several pieces of information are stored in an intent object—either the instruction for the receiving component to execute or simply some data that a component may choose to react to. Upon receiving an intent, it is up to that receiver to know how to respond to and leverage the data stored in the intent message. Table 3-4 describes the core pieces of an intent.

TABLE 3-4: Core Information within an Intent

NAME	DESCRIPTION
Action	Specifies the action that needs to be performed. Examples include `ACTION_GET_CONTENT`, `ACTION_RUN`, and `ACTION_SYNC`.
Data	Represents the data that needs to be acted upon. An example is a URI for a particular record in a content provider.
Category	Used to give more information about the action to execute. It can be used to specify the context of how to operate the action, such as `CATEGORY_HOME`, or even as a filter for the given action results.
Type	Allows you to override automatic resolution of type and specify your own MIME type of the intent data.

Throughout the rest of this book, you will encounter many different scenarios in which intents are being utilized. As the messaging system for the Android platform, intents are necessary to accomplish any kind of interaction between applications and device features.

BINDING THE COMPONENTS: THE ANDROID MANIFEST

So far this chapter has discussed all the key components of an Android application, in particular, discussing how each component is, in many ways, its own autonomous entity that can run independently of other components of the application. Although this is advantageous in terms of reusability and design, some kind of binding mechanism is needed to keep the application cohesive and to store universally accessed values and settings. In Android, this is achieved via the *Android manifest*.

The Android manifest is an XML configuration file that resides in the root directory of an Android application. This file contains the information necessary for the Android OS to create a process in which this application will run. In addition, the Android manifest file is used for several other functions:

➤ It contains metadata information for the application, such as the unique package name, minimum SDK level, the icon or application theme, and application version.

➤ It binds the application components. This includes the core components of activities, services, broadcast receivers, and content providers.

➤ It describes the capabilities of each of its components by stating which intent's messages are bound to which application component.

➤ It states what permissions the application must have to operate, as well as what permissions other applications must have to utilize its functionality.

➤ It defines the other code libraries that the application must have to operate.

 If you're familiar with ASP.NET web development, the Android manifest and web.config *share much of the same functionality. Just as an ASP.NET web application must have a* web.config*, all Android applications must have an Android manifest to operate.*

Android Manifest Basics

The Android manifest is a structured document that supports many different configuration scenarios. At first glance, it can seem somewhat overwhelming and possibly even a nightmare to maintain. Even though it can sometimes be a bit of a pain in terms of maintenance, having a basic understanding of the manifest's underlying rules and structure will go a long way toward demystifying and simplifying it.

First, the Android manifest has a limited number of nodes that can be used. As a developer, you cannot define new nodes within the Android manifest. With that in mind, The following XML snippet displays the main nodes that are possible within the Android manifest as well as the general hierarchy.

```xml
<?xml version="1.0" encoding="utf-8" ?>
<manifest>
    <permission />
    <uses-permission />
    <permission-tree />
    <permission-group />
    <instrumentation />
    <uses-sdk />
    <uses-configuration />
    <uses-feature />
    <supports-screens />
    <application>
        <activity />
        <activity-alias />
        <service />
```

```
            <receiver />
            <provider />
        </application>
    </manifest>
```

Although this defines the overall structure of the Android manifest, it does not imply that nodes of the same level need to appear in a particular order. In fact, the only node that has a required sequence is the activity-alias node. This node must always follow the activity that it is aliasing.

Now that you have an idea of the general structure of the Android manifest, it's time to review the capabilities of each of the available nodes. Table 3-5 lists most of the available nodes and describes their general purposes. By cross-referencing the hierarchy shown in the preceding snippet, you can get a good idea of how the manifest works and what configuration options you have at your disposal. This table is not exhaustive, but it gives you a working knowledge of what each node does so that you can recognize the developer's intent when you see them within any Android application.

TABLE 3-5: Android Manifest Elements

ELEMENT	DESCRIPTION
manifest	The root node of any Android manifest. This is a required node. In addition to serving as the root node for the Android manifest, it can contain the attributes to define the package name, version number and name, Linux user ID, and preferred installation location.
uses-permission	Used to define what permissions that application must have to operate correctly. Whatever permissions you request are presented for the user's approval before the application is installed on his or her device.
permission	Allows developers to define permissions required to access shared application components. When another application tries to use your application's features, it must use the `uses-permission` attribute to request the specified permission from your application. You can define different protection levels to imply the potential risk in allowing this access by using predetermined string values such as "normal" and "dangerous."
permission-tree	Acts as a "placeholder" for permissions that the application can add dynamically. By using the `PackageManager` class, an application can determine what `permission` elements to add upon request.
permission-group	Creates a logical grouping of permissions. This allows the Android OS to group these permissions visually when presenting them to the application user for verification.
instrumentation	Gives the developer access to testing and monitoring hooks to check to see how the application interacts with the system and its resources. To accomplish this, instrumentation objects are instantiated before any other application components.

ELEMENT	DESCRIPTION
uses-sdk	Allows you to set the compatibility level for your application. You have the flexibility to set the min, max, and target SDK level. Do not confuse the SDK level with the Android OS version number.
uses-configuration	Allows you to specify the hardware and software input features that your application can use or needs to use to run. Items bound in this section can include a hardware keyboard, trackball, scroll wheel, and touch screen. This is also used to warn the user if he or she is installing an application that depends on a feature that his or her device does not support. You may also define multiple items per feature.
uses-feature	Allows you to determine an individual software or hardware feature that will be used in your application. In addition, you can state whether that feature is required, meaning that your application must have it to run, or whether it is simply preferred. Examples of hardware features requested include Bluetooth, camera, location, and microphone.
supports-screens	Defines the screen sizes that your application will support. In a world with Google TV and Android tablets, this node becomes increasingly important, because you can define what screens you want your application to run on. By default, Android applications are set to support all screen sizes unless otherwise stated.
application	Used to define the application's metadata. Values set this way are considered to be the default values for all application components. There can be only one application node per manifest. In addition to the metadata, this node also contains the subnodes that describe the application components (services, broadcast receivers, content providers) as well as their means of communication and configuration.
activity	Serves as the declaration for the activity component. All activities must be declared in the manifest before the Android OS can run them. Also, you can set activity metadata and settings such as the name, label, and screen orientation.
activity-alias	Used to present a target activity as a separate entity to the Android OS. By doing so, you can alter the original attributes of the activity target, such as intent filters and attributes.
service	Declares a service component. All services must be declared in the manifest before the Android OS can run them.
receiver	Declares a broadcast receiver component. This is one of the two ways to create a broadcast receiver to listen for events. The second way to declare a receiver is by calling the Context.registerReceiver() method.

continues

TABLE 3-5 *(continued)*

ELEMENT	DESCRIPTION
`provider`	Specifies each of your application's content providers. If your application is creating a custom provider, the system is unable to use that content provider unless it is declared within the Android manifest.
`intent-filter`	Specifies the kind of intents that a given application component can respond to. This can be a subnode of the `activity`, `service`, and `receiver` nodes. This node allows you to define a type of intent you would like to receive, while filtering out all other kinds of intents.
`meta-data`	Contains additional developer-defined key-value pair data that can be utilized by the application component in which it is located. This serves as a subnode of `activity`, `service`, `provider`, and `receiver`.
`uses-library`	Allows you to specify any shared libraries on which your application may depend.

Do not let the number of available nodes and attributes overwhelm you. Despite the number of options within the manifest, the Android OS requires only the `manifest` *and* `application` *nodes. Other nodes are used to define details and permissions to perform actions you will add as you develop your application.*

The Android manifest is a powerful tool that serves as the "glue" for your application. Not only does it give your application an identity and purpose, but it also brings together all the individual components of your application. Finally, you can use the Android manifest to fine-tune the permissions and general configuration properties for all your application components in a single location.

For more information regarding the Android manifest or any of its components, please check out the Mono for Android documentation or the official Android documentation:

➤ **Mono for Android:** `http://mono-android.net/Documentation/Guides/Working_with_AndroidManifest.xml`

➤ **Official Android:** `http://developer.android.com/guide/topics/manifest/manifest-intro.html`

Editing the Manifest for Mono for Android via Visual Studio

Although many "Androidisms" carry over quite nicely into the Mono for Android world, some areas pertain to Mono for Android alone. In this case, the location and the toolset used to edit the Android manifest differ greatly from those of a typical Android application.

When a new application is created, the Android manifest is not part of the project. As you learned in the previous chapter, Mono for Android is possible because it generates the appropriate Java and configuration code when built. Therefore, the Android manifest is not a required part of a Mono for Android application, because it automatically generates a manifest for you when you publish your application.

Even though the Mono for Android toolset autogenerates your manifest file, this does not mean that you do not have to edit or understand the inner workings of the manifest.

Within Visual Studio, you have three main ways to edit the Android manifest. Of those three, two do not require utilizing the physical manifest file.

➤ The first way that Mono for Android enables you to edit the Android manifest is by creating a plethora of class attributes for many of the different Android components. These attributes allow you to define configuration options in code. When the application is compiled, the runtime reads those attributes and adds the appropriate information to the generated manifest file. One such example is the activity, which we discussed earlier in this chapter.

When you decorate a class with the `Activity` attribute, the framework automatically appends the proper activity nodes to your Android manifest. In addition, setting the values of properties results in the correct subnodes for the activity to be generated. Consider the following code snippet:

```
[Activity(Label = "Demo_Application", MainLauncher = true,
Permission = "READ_CONTACTS",MultiProcess = false,
ScreenOrientation = Android.Content.PM.ScreenOrientation.Landscape)]
```

Once your application is compiled, the runtime generates the following XML within the Android manifest:

```
<activity android:label="Demo_Application" android:multiprocess="false"
    android:permission="READ_CONTACTS" android:screenOrientation="landscape"
    android:name="testing_01.Activity1">
    <intent-filter>
        <action android:name="android.intent.action.MAIN" />
        <category android:name="android.intent.category.LAUNCHER" />
    </intent-filter>
</activity>
```

As you can see, the resulting XML fits the hierarchy and rules of the Android manifest that we discussed earlier.

➤ The second way to edit the Android manifest file within Visual Studio is by changing select settings within the Visual Studio application properties window. For your convenience, Mono for Android has included global configuration tooling within this window to allow you to quickly add and edit different items in the Android manifest. Figure 3-2 shows the configuration window for adjusting the global application permissions in Visual Studio.

➤ Finally, the third way to edit the Android manifest is by physically editing the manifest XML within Visual Studio. Although it is not generated by default, the `AndroidManifest.xml` file is located in the `Properties` folder of your application. If you do not see the file there, you can force the system to generate a manifest for you by going to your application settings and selecting the link "No AndroidManifest.xml found. Click to add one." under the Application tab, as shown in Figure 3-3.

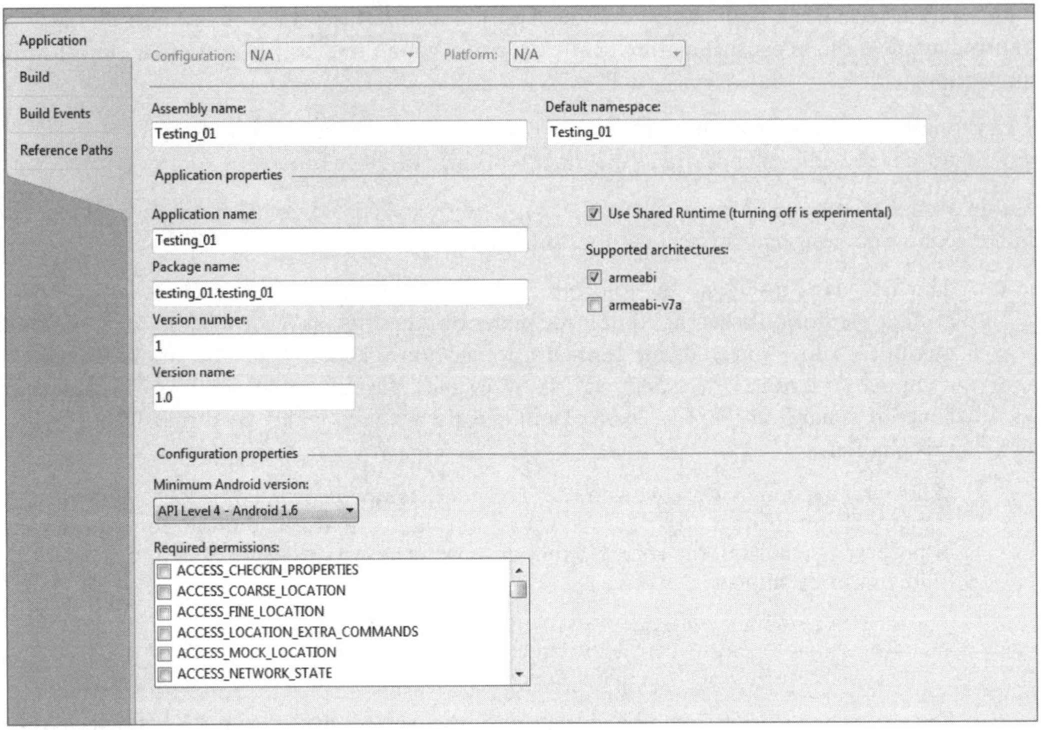

Application

Build

Build Events

Reference Paths

Configuration: N/A   Platform: N/A

Assembly name:
Testing_01

Default namespace:
Testing_01

Application properties

Application name:
Testing_01

☑ Use Shared Runtime (turning off is experimental)

Supported architectures:

Package name:
testing_01.testing_01

☑ armeabi

☐ armeabi-v7a

Version number:
1

Version name:
1.0

Configuration properties

Minimum Android version:
API Level 4 - Android 1.6

Required permissions:
☐ ACCESS_CHECKIN_PROPERTIES
☐ ACCESS_COARSE_LOCATION
☐ ACCESS_FINE_LOCATION
☐ ACCESS_LOCATION_EXTRA_COMMANDS
☐ ACCESS_MOCK_LOCATION
☐ ACCESS_NETWORK_STATE

FIGURE 3-2

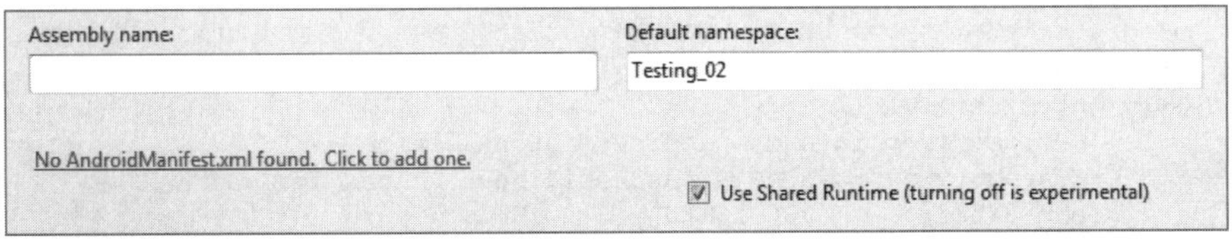

Assembly name:

Default namespace:
Testing_02

No AndroidManifest.xml found. Click to add one.

☑ Use Shared Runtime (turning off is experimental)

FIGURE 3-3

Although it should go without saying, take care when editing your Android manifest by hand. Although you can edit manually, it is generally a good idea to allow the system to generate the appropriate nodes for you by using the proper attribute values. Since parts of the Android manifest in Visual Studio are the result of code generation, some manual edits within the manifest could be lost between compilations.

SUMMARY

Mono for Android goes a long way toward easing the way to developing Android applications for C# and .NET developers. With its adherence to the general intent and naming structure of the Java APIs, it makes the development experience feel as if you are working against the native APIs.

However, this does not mean that you do not need a good understanding of the Android platform and how its basic components function and interact. By having a great understanding of the underlying ideas behind intents, content providers, services, broadcast receivers, and activities, you can develop applications that not only fully utilize the features of the Android device but also interact with other Java-based applications.

Finally, you create a cohesive application of independent but cooperating components by using the Android manifest.

Planning and Building Your Application's User Interface

WHAT'S IN THIS CHAPTER?

➤ Mobile UI guidelines

➤ Building a UI for Android

➤ Examining the layout of controls

➤ Exploring the UI controls

➤ Designing screen-independent UI

In this chapter you'll learn about creating your application's user interface (UI). You'll get a look at a base set of guidelines for building a successful user interface on Android, examine the options for building a user interface, and see how controls are laid out in Android. Finally, you'll get to explore the controls available to Android developers.

GUIDELINES FOR A SUCCESSFUL MOBILE UI

Before you dig into building a user interface, it's important to understand some guidelines for doing so successfully. These guidelines affect how users will use applications when they are mobile, as well as how your applications can be good citizens when running:

➤ The device's screen size is much smaller than that on a desktop system. As such, applications should limit the number of screen controls presented to the user at one time.

➤ Applications should require the users to enter the smallest amount of data possible. A spinner control (similar to a drop-down list box), where the user is required to select a pre-entered value, is preferable to requiring the user to type in some amount of text. Typing on a mobile device is problematic. Tapping several times is preferable to entering 30 letters into a text form.

➤ Be a good citizen on the device. Caching data locally is preferred to pulling data over a wireless connection. For example, a spinner control is populated once with data from a web service. The next time that data is needed, there is no reason to pull that data from the web service. The data should be cached locally on the device and reused from the cache as much as possible.

➤ Users typically are moving when they are using their devices. Think about the number of users who are walking through an airport, walking the halls of an office, or exercising when accessing an application. An application's user interface needs to take movement and jarring into account. For example, presenting data in a listview is common. The user expects to select a cell and get more detailed information. The size of the cell should be such that there is some margin for error when selecting a cell. This will improve the user's ability to select the correct item.

➤ Because mobile devices have small screens, the text that is presented to the user needs to be large enough for the user to easily view the data presented.

➤ There is no control over where a mobile device is located when it is running an application. It may be directly in the sunlight, or it could be in a parking lot at midnight. The application needs to be easily readable when it runs. This may involve a combination of screen colors or the application's theme.

 Of course, this is a very short list of some of the most common guidelines to keep in mind. For more guidelines, we recommend that you check out the Android User Interface Guidelines. The various documents can be found at `http://developer.android.com/guide/practices/ui_guidelines/index.html.`

BUILDING AN ANDROID UI

Developers who are building a user interface in Android will find concepts that are similar to those of their existing .NET applications. Android uses the concept of controls that programmers are familiar with. Here are some characteristics of controls that will seem familiar:

➤ Properties can be set to get a control's value or change a control's default functionality.

➤ A program can process events, such as a button click or value change.

➤ Controls can be grouped in a hierarchy known as a `View` or `ViewGroup`.

➤ Controls can be themed so that the look of a set of controls can be changed in a group.

Views

An Android user interface is based on `View` and `ViewGroup` objects. A `View` class is the basis for widgets, which are UI objects such as text fields, spinners, buttons, clocks, and date pickers. A `ViewGroup` is the basis for layout subclasses. An `Activity`'s user interface consists of a tree of `View` and `ViewGroup` nodes. The top of the tree is a `ViewGroup`. To display a view hierarchy, an `Activity` calls `SetContentView(Resource)` to load the `Resource` view and begin drawing the tree.

Design Surface

.NET developers building a user interface with WebForms, WinForms, or other applications are familiar with the concept of a design surface. With a design surface, you can use a set of controls to display data to the user. The Android Developer Tools contain an Eclipse plug-in that lets you create a user interface. However, this has not been integrated into Mono for Android and does not work with Visual Studio. Mono for Android does not have its own design surface at the time of this writing. It does offer IntelliSense for manually creating the user interface. However, given that manually creating the user interface is prone to errors, we recommend that you look for a high-level tool for creating your user interface, such as DroidDraw. DroidDraw has a website that you can use to build your app's UI, as well as a downloadable Java application. For more information on DroidDraw, go to `http://droiddraw.org`.

Figure 4-1 shows DroidDraw. The left side displays the user interface that has been defined. The top-right section shows the options you can set, allowing you to set the properties of the UI elements. The bottom-right section shows the XML generated for the UI. The XML is not updated automatically; you must create it by clicking the Generate button.

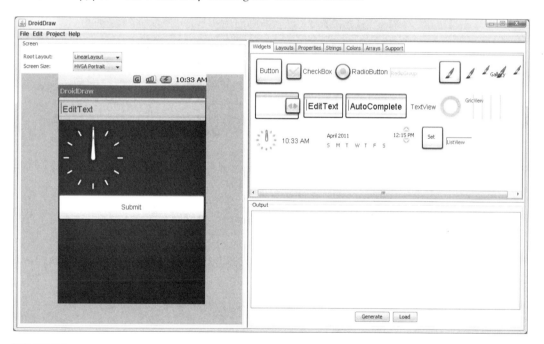

FIGURE 4-1

CHOOSING A CONTROL LAYOUT

Android UIs have different layouts that can be used. A layout defines how its child controls are arranged onscreen. Android has five standard layouts:

➤ `AbsoluteLayout` places all controls at a defined location. This layout has been deprecated. `FrameLayout` or `RelativeLayout` is suggested instead.

➤ `FrameLayout` displays a single item, such as an image.

➤ LinearLayout displays child controls along a single line, either horizontal or vertical.

➤ RelativeLayout places controls at a location relative to other controls.

➤ TableLayout displays controls in a row/column-style layout.

AbsoluteLayout

The AbsoluteLayout is the layout that allows a developer to place views at a defined location. The AbsoluteLayout has been deprecated. The FrameLayout or RelativeLayout is suggested instead. Having said that, if you need to use the AbsoluteLayout, Listing 4-1 shows the necessary XML.

LISTING 4-1: AbsoluteLayout XML

```xml
<?xml version="1.0" encoding="utf-8"?>
<AbsoluteLayout
android:id="@+id/widget31"
android:layout_width="fill_parent"
android:layout_height="fill_parent"
xmlns:android="http://schemas.android.com/apk/res/android"
>
  <Spinner
  android:id="@+id/widget27"
  android:layout_width="wrap_content"
  android:layout_height="wrap_content"
  android:layout_x="170px"
  android:layout_y="12px"
>
  </Spinner>
  <EditText
  android:id="@+id/widget29"
  android:layout_width="wrap_content"
  android:layout_height="wrap_content"
  android:text="EditText"
  android:textSize="18sp"
  android:layout_x="225px"
  android:layout_y="102px"
>
  </EditText>
  <AnalogClock
  android:id="@+id/widget30"
  android:layout_width="wrap_content"
  android:layout_height="wrap_content"
  android:layout_x="20px"
  android:layout_y="62px"
>
  </AnalogClock>
</AbsoluteLayout>
```

This code is contained in Layouts\Layouts\Resources\Layout\absolute.axml

Figure 4-2 shows the output of the `AbsoluteLayout` previously defined.

FIGURE 4-2

FrameLayout

`FrameLayout` is the simplest layout option. It is designed to display a single object on the screen. All elements within the `FrameLayout` are pinned to the top-left corner of the layout. If multiple elements are within a `FrameLayout`, they are drawn in the same location, and their displays interfere with each other.

LinearLayout

`LinearLayout` aligns all objects either vertically or horizontally. The direction displayed depends on the `orientation` attribute. All the elements are displayed one after the other. If the `orientation` attribute of `LinearLayout` is set to `vertical` (as shown in Listing 4-2), the UI displays vertically. If the `orientation` attribute of `LinearLayout` is set to `horizontal`, the UI displays horizontally.

LISTING 4-2: LinearLayout XML

```
<?xml version="1.0" encoding="utf-8"?>
<LinearLayout
android:id="@+id/widget28"
android:layout_width="fill_parent"
android:layout_height="fill_parent"
xmlns:android="http://schemas.android.com/apk/res/android"
android:orientation="vertical"
>
```

continues

LISTING 4-2 *(continued)*

```xml
      <Spinner
      android:id="@+id/widget27"
      android:layout_width="wrap_content"
      android:layout_height="wrap_content"
  >
      </Spinner>
      <EditText
      android:id="@+id/widget29"
      android:layout_width="wrap_content"
      android:layout_height="wrap_content"
      android:text="EditText"
      android:textSize="18sp"
  >
      </EditText>
      <AnalogClock
      android:id="@+id/widget30"
      android:layout_width="wrap_content"
      android:layout_height="wrap_content"
  >
      </AnalogClock>
</LinearLayout>
```

This code is contained in Layouts\Layouts\Resources\Layout\linear.axml

Figure 4-3 shows a sample `LinearLayout` displaying items vertically.

FIGURE 4-3

Creating a horizontal `LinearLayout` is simple. The value of `android:orientation` is changed to `horizontal`, as shown in Listing 4-3.

LISTING 4-3: LinearLayout XML oriented horizontally

```xml
<?xml version="1.0" encoding="utf-8"?>
<LinearLayout
android:id="@+id/widget289"
android:layout_width="fill_parent"
android:layout_height="fill_parent"
xmlns:android="http://schemas.android.com/apk/res/android"
android:orientation="horizontal"
>
  <Spinner
  android:id="@+id/widget279"
  android:layout_width="wrap_content"
  android:layout_height="wrap_content"
>
  </Spinner>
  <EditText
  android:id="@+id/widget299"
  android:layout_width="wrap_content"
  android:layout_height="wrap_content"
  android:text="EditText"
  android:textSize="18sp"
>
  </EditText>
  <AnalogClock
  android:id="@+id/widget309"
  android:layout_width="wrap_content"
  android:layout_height="wrap_content"
>
  </AnalogClock>
</LinearLayout>
```

FIGURE 4-4

Figure 4-4 shows a sample horizontal LinearLayout.

RelativeLayout

With RelativeLayout, the child elements are positioned relative to the parent element or to each other, depending on the ID that is specified (see Listing 4-4):

LISTING 4-4: RelativeLayout XML

```xml
<?xml version="1.0" encoding="utf-8"?>
<RelativeLayout
android:id="@+id/widget32"
android:layout_width="fill_parent"
android:layout_height="fill_parent"
xmlns:android="http://schemas.android.com/apk/res/android"
>
  <Spinner
  android:id="@+id/widget27"
  android:layout_width="wrap_content"
  android:layout_height="wrap_content"
  android:layout_alignParentTop="true"
  android:layout_alignParentRight="true"
>
```

continues

LISTING 4-4 *(continued)*

```
    </Spinner>
    <EditText
    android:id="@+id/widget29"
    android:layout_width="wrap_content"
    android:layout_height="wrap_content"
    android:text="EditText"
    android:textSize="18sp"
    android:layout_below="@+id/widget27"
    android:layout_toLeftOf="@+id/widget27"
>
    </EditText>
    <AnalogClock
    android:id="@+id/widget30"
    android:layout_width="wrap_content"
    android:layout_height="wrap_content"
    android:layout_centerVertical="true"
    android:layout_toLeftOf="@+id/widget27"
>
    </AnalogClock>
</RelativeLayout>
```

This code is contained in Layouts\Layouts\Resources\Layout\relative.axml

Figure 4-5 shows the output from a RelativeLayout.

FIGURE 4-5

TableLayout

TableLayout arranges its elements into rows and columns. Conceptually, this is similar to an HTML table. With TableLayout, a number of TableRows are used to define the TableLayout. Listing 4-5 shows an example of TableLayout:

LISTING 4-5: TableLayout XML

```xml
<?xml version="1.0" encoding="utf-8"?>
<TableLayout
android:id="@+id/widget33"
android:layout_width="fill_parent"
android:layout_height="fill_parent"
xmlns:android="http://schemas.android.com/apk/res/android"
android:orientation="vertical"
>
  <Spinner
  android:id="@+id/widget27"
  android:layout_width="wrap_content"
  android:layout_height="wrap_content"
>
  </Spinner>
  <EditText
  android:id="@+id/widget29"
  android:layout_width="wrap_content"
  android:layout_height="wrap_content"
  android:text="EditText"
  android:textSize="18sp"
>
  </EditText>
  <TableRow>
    <AnalogClock
    android:id="@+id/widget30"
    android:layout_width="wrap_content"
    android:layout_height="wrap_content"
>
    </AnalogClock>
    <Button
    android:id="@+id/widget34"
    android:layout_width="fill_parent"
    android:layout_height="wrap_content"
    android:text="Button"
>
    </Button>
  </TableRow>
</TableLayout>
```

This code is contained in Layouts\Layouts\Resources\Layout\table.axml

Figure 4-6 shows a sample `TableLayout`.

FIGURE 4-6

Optimizing Layouts

Opening layouts in an `Activity`, called "inflating," is an expensive operation. Each layout that is nested and each view that is displayed requires additional CPU processing and memory consumption on the device. The general idea is to keep layouts as simple as possible. Here are some general rules for layouts:

➤ Avoid nesting layouts to the extreme. Sometimes applications have a business need for nested layouts. However, the nesting of layouts should be kept to a minimum.

➤ Watch out for unnecessary nesting. Two layouts set to `FILL_PARENT` will add unnecessary time to the inflation of the layouts.

➤ Watch for an extreme number of `Views`. A layout with too many `Views` will confuse the user and will take a long time to display due to the need to inflate the `Views`.

Obviously, this is not an exhaustive list of rules. The key is to create simple user interfaces that meet the users' needs and that do not overload the processor's and device's memory.

 All the sample code for the user interface controls can be found in the UIControls project.

DESIGNING YOUR USER INTERFACE CONTROLS

For the user, the most important part of any application is the user interface; in essence, for the user the user interface is the application. Desktop applications can have rather complicated user interfaces, but creating a user interface for a mobile device is the single most important feature of an application.

Here are some guidelines for creating a successful mobile user interface:

➤ **Number of form elements:** Because of the display size of a mobile device, the user should not be subjected to a large number of form elements.

➤ **Size of form elements:** Mobile devices are, by definition, mobile. Users may be in an industrial plant, on the elliptical at the gym, or taking their children for a walk in the park. Form elements must be large enough to be readable and to allow users to make selections when they are not standing still. At the same time, form elements must be small enough to fit on the screen rather easily.

➤ **Testing:** Android devices have different screen sizes and resolutions. As a result, thinking about and testing your application on various screen sizes and capabilities is important.

Android provides a set of controls that developers can use to create a user interface. These controls can be used individually or as part of a composite control. In addition, these controls allow you to create an application with a consistent look and feel as well as simplify and speed development. Here are some of the more valuable controls:

➤ `TextView` is similar to a label. It allows data to be displayed to the user.

➤ `EditText` is similar to a .NET textbox. It allows for multiline entry and word wrapping.

➤ `AutoCompleteTextView` is a textbox that will display a set of items that a user can pick from. As the user enters more data, the set of items displayed narrows. At any point, the user may select on the displayed items.

➤ `ListView` is a view group that creates a vertical list of views. This is similar to a gridview in .NET. The `ListView` is covered in Chapter 6.

➤ `Spinner` is a composite control. It contains a textview and an associated listview for selecting items that will be displayed in the textview. This control is similar to a drop-down list box in .NET.

➤ `Button` is a standard push button, which should be familiar to .NET developers.

➤ `Checkbox` is a button that contains two states — checked and unchecked. The check box should be familiar to all .NET developers.

➤ `RadioButton` is a two-state button in a group. The group of radio buttons allows only one item to be selected at a time. The radio button should be familiar to all .NET developers as a radio button list.

➤ `Clock` has digital and analog clock controls. They are time picker controls and allow the developer to get or set the time.

➤ `TimePicker` is associated with the clock controls. The time picker is an up/down control along with a button.

➤ `Image`(s) are a series of controls that are used to deal with images. These controls include a single image, an image button, and an image gallery.

➤ While not available in all devices, **virtual keyboards** are a feature available for touch devices like the HTC and Motorola lines of Android devices.

These are just some of the controls that are available to a developer. Many more are available with Android. They are contained within the `Android.Widget` namespace.

The next sections examine the definition of these controls, the values they support, and the controls themselves.

SOMETHING FAMILIAR — XML, ATTRIBUTES, AND VALUES

ASP.NET developers will be familiar with the concept of the XML layout for Android files. ASP.NET WebForms keeps its display information in its front-end `.aspx` files, and the back-end logic is contained within the `.cs` and `.vb` files. Android applications use a similar concept. The display information is contained within the `Views`. An `Activity`'s user interface can be loaded by calling `SetContentView` and passing in a layout resource ID or a single `View` instance. As a result, a developer can actually create his or her own user interface programmatically.

TextView

`TextView` is a control that displays text to the user. By default, the `TextView` class does not allow editing. For the .NET developer, this control is similar in concept to a label in WinForms or WebForms. Take a look at a couple members that the class exposes from a programmability standpoint:

➤ The `Text` property of the `TextView` allows a program to get/set the value that is displayed in the `TextView`.

➤ The `Width` property sets the width of the `TextView`. This can be set with the value `fill_parent` or in pixels as an integer.

EditText

`EditText` is a subclass that allows the user to input and edit text. Figure 4-7 shows sample output for `EditText`.

FIGURE 4-7

AutoCompleteTextView

`AutoCompleteTextView` is an editable `TextView` that shows suggestions while the user is typing. The list of suggestions is displayed in a drop-down menu. As the user types, he or she can choose an item. If an item is chosen, the text is then displayed in the text view. The list of suggestions that is displayed to the user is formed from a data adapter.

Spinner

The spinner control is used to present the user with a defined set of data from which he or she can choose. The data in the spinner control is loaded from an `Adapter` that is associated with the spinner control. Listing 4-6 shows the XML UI for a spinner activity:

Available for download on Wrox.com

LISTING 4-6: Spinner XML

```xml
<?xml version="1.0" encoding="utf-8"?>
<LinearLayout
android:id="@+id/widget28"
android:layout_width="fill_parent"
android:layout_height="fill_parent"
android:orientation="vertical"
xmlns:android="http://schemas.android.com/apk/res/android"
>
  <Spinner
  android:id="@+id/Sp"
  android:layout_width="fill_parent"
  android:layout_height="wrap_content"
>
```

continues

LISTING 4-6 *(continued)*

```
    </Spinner>
    <TextView
    android:id="@+id/tvSp"
    android:layout_width="193px"
    android:layout_height="35px"
    android:text="TextView"
>
    </TextView>
</LinearLayout>
```

This code is contained in UIControls\Resources\Layout\spinner.axml

Listing 4-7 provides the code for a spinner control:

LISTING 4-7: Spinner code

```
Spinner state;
TextView tvSp;
ArrayAdapter<String> aas;

protected override void OnCreate(Bundle bundle)
{
    base.OnCreate(bundle);
    SetContentView(Resource.Layout.spinner);

    state = FindViewById<Spinner>(Resource.Id.Sp);
    tvSp = FindViewById<TextView>(Resource.Id.tvSp);
    aas = new ArrayAdapter<String>(this,
        Android.Resource.Layout.SimpleSpinnerDropDownItem);
    state.Adapter = aas;
    aas.Add(String.Empty);
    aas.Add("Alabama");
    aas.Add("Arizona");
    aas.Add("California");
    aas.Add("Tennessee");
    aas.Add("Texas");
    aas.Add("Washington");
    state.ItemSelected += new EventHandler<ItemEventArgs>(sp_ItemSelected);
}

void sp_ItemSelected(object sender, ItemEventArgs e)
{
    tvSp.Text = Convert.ToString(aas.GetItem(e.Position));
}
```

This code is contained in UIControls\UIControls\spinneract.cs

In this example, an `ArrayAdapter` that contains type `String` is created and associated with the spinner control. The `ArrayAdapter` has strings added to it, and then the strings are added to the spinner control and ultimately are presented to the user.

Notice the second parameter in the `ArrayAdapter` *initializer. It is the layout type that is displayed when the spinner control is opened.*

Figure 4-8 shows opening a spinner.

FIGURE 4-8

Button

The user can press the button control to perform some type of action. This button is the Android equivalent of a button in WinForms and WebForms. It supports an `OnClick` event that developers can use to process code when the button is clicked.

Check Box

A check box is a button control that supports two states — checked and unchecked. This is similar to a check box in WinForms/WebForms for .NET developers. This control supports an `OnClick` event that developers can use to process code when an item is clicked.

Radio Buttons and Groups

A radio button is a button control that supports two states — checked and unchecked. However, this control is slightly different from a check box. Once a radio button is checked, it cannot be unchecked.

A radio group is a class that creates a set of radio buttons. When one radio button within a radio group is checked, any other checked radio button is unchecked. The initial state of a radio group has all items unchecked. The radio group is a container control for a group of radio buttons that work together. Programmatically, the radio group is created by creating individual radio buttons and adding them to the radio group.

Listing 4-8 provides a short example of XML with the check box, radio button, and radio group.

LISTING 4-8: Radio buttons and check boxes XML

```xml
<?xml version="1.0" encoding="utf-8"?>
<LinearLayout
xmlns:android="http://schemas.android.com/apk/res/android"
    android:orientation="vertical"
    android:layout_width="fill_parent"
    android:layout_height="fill_parent">
  <CheckBox
  android:id="@+id/cb1"
  android:layout_width="wrap_content"
  android:layout_height="wrap_content"
  android:text="CheckBox"
></CheckBox>
  <TextView
  android:id="@+id/tvcb"
  android:layout_width="wrap_content"
  android:layout_height="wrap_content"
  android:text=""
></TextView>
  <RadioButton
  android:id="@+id/rb"
  android:layout_width="wrap_content"
  android:layout_height="wrap_content"
  android:text="RadioButton"
></RadioButton>
  <TextView
  android:id="@+id/rbtv"
  android:layout_width="wrap_content"
  android:layout_height="wrap_content"
  android:text=""
></TextView>
  <RadioGroup
  android:id="@+id/rg"
  android:layout_width="wrap_content"
  android:layout_height="wrap_content"
  android:orientation="vertical"
/>
    <TextView
  android:id="@+id/rgtv"
  android:layout_width="wrap_content"
  android:layout_height="wrap_content"
  android:text=""
></TextView>
  <Button
  android:id="@+id/btnCloseRadioCheckBoxes"
   android:layout_width="fill_parent"
```

```
        android:layout_height="wrap_content"
        android:text="Close" />
</LinearLayout>
```

This code is contained in UIControls\Resources\Layout\radiocheckboxes.axml

Listing 4-9 gives the code listing for buttons, check boxes, radio buttons, and radio groups:

LISTING 4-9: Radio buttons, radio groups, and check boxes

```csharp
[Activity(Label = "Radio & Checkboxes", Name="uicontrols.radiocheckboxes")]
public class radiocheckboxes : Activity
{
Button btn;
RadioButton rb;
CheckBox cb;
RadioGroup rg;
TextView rbtv, cbtv, rgtv;
protected override void OnCreate(Bundle bundle)
{
    base.OnCreate(bundle);
    SetContentView(Resource.Layout.radiocheckboxes);
    // Create your application here
    rg = FindViewById<RadioGroup>(Resource.Id.rg);
    rg.Click += new EventHandler(rg_Click);
    cb = FindViewById<CheckBox>(Resource.Id.cb1);
    rb = FindViewById<RadioButton>(Resource.Id.rb);
    btn = FindViewById<Button>(Resource.Id.btnCloseRadioCheckBoxes);
    rbtv = FindViewById<TextView>(Resource.Id.rbtv);
    cbtv = FindViewById<TextView>(Resource.Id.tvcb);
    rgtv = FindViewById<TextView>(Resource.Id.rgtv);
    btn.Click += new EventHandler(btn_Click);
    cb.Click += new EventHandler(cb_Click);

    rb.Click += new EventHandler(rb_Click);

    RadioButton rb1;
    for (int i = 0; i < 3; i++)
    {
        rb1 = new RadioButton(this);
        rb1.Text = "Item " + i.ToString();
        rb1.Click += new EventHandler(rb1_Click);
        rg.AddView(rb1, i);
    }
}

void rg_Click(object sender, EventArgs e)
{
    rgtv.Text = ((RadioButton)sender).Text;
}void rb1_Click(object sender, EventArgs e)
{
```

continues

LISTING 4-9 *(continued)*

```
        RadioButton rb1 = (RadioButton)sender;
        rgtv.Text = rb1.Text + " was clicked.";
    }

    void rb_Click(object sender, EventArgs e)
    {
        rbtv.Text = "Radio Button Click";
    }

    void cb_Click(object sender, EventArgs e)
    {
        cbtv.Text = "Checkbox Clicked";
    }

    void btn_Click(object sender, EventArgs e)
    {
        this.Finish();
    }
```

This code is contained in UIControls\radiocheckboxes.cs

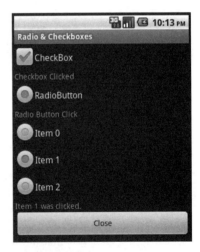

Figure 4-9 shows the display and output associated with a check box, radio button, and radio group.

This example contains a check box, a single radio button, and a radio group. Here are a few things to note:

➤ A loop is used to add radio buttons to the radio group.

➤ Click events are set up for each screen control.

➤ The Click event of the radio group is set up on the Click event of the individual radio buttons.

Clocks

Clocks and time are important in many mobile applications. Many mobile phone users don't wear a watch, so they depend on their phone and its applications for the current time. Applications depend on the time to know when to fire scheduled events through background services.

FIGURE 4-9

For user interaction, Android can display two types of clocks. These types are:

➤ **Analog Clock:** The analog clock displays hands for hours and minutes.

➤ **Digital Clock:** The digital clock is similar to the analog clock, except that the display is digital. The hours, minutes, and seconds are contained in separate views.

Pickers

Android provides a time picker and a date picker. These controls allow the user to select the date and time.

➤ **Time Picker:** The time picker allows the user to select the hours and minutes. The time picker can be configured for 12- or 24-hour days, with a.m./p.m. as necessary.

 `TimePicker` *only seems to expose a change event that can be used to obtain the time that is currently selected.*

➤ **Date Picker:** The date picker allows the user to select the month, day, and year. Thankfully, the date picker exposes the selected day, month, and year in the control as properties.

 The `Month` *integer that the* `DatePicker` *returns runs from 0 to 11.*

Listing 4-10 shows a sample XML layout involving date and time pickers.

LISTING 4-10: Date and time pickers XML

```
<?xml version="1.0" encoding="utf-8"?>
<LinearLayout
xmlns:android="http://schemas.android.com/apk/res/android"
    android:orientation="vertical"
    android:layout_width="fill_parent"
    android:layout_height="fill_parent">
  <DigitalClock
  android:id="@+id/dc"
  android:layout_width="wrap_content"
  android:layout_height="wrap_content"
  android:text="11:00 PM"
></DigitalClock>
  <TextView
  android:id="@+id/dctv"
  android:layout_width="wrap_content"
  android:layout_height="wrap_content"
  android:text="TextView"
></TextView>
  <DatePicker
  android:id="@+id/dp"
  android:layout_width="wrap_content"
  android:layout_height="wrap_content"
></DatePicker>
  <TextView
```

continues

LISTING 4-10 *(continued)*

```
      android:id="@+id/dptv"
      android:layout_width="wrap_content"
      android:layout_height="wrap_content"
      android:text="TextView"
  ></TextView>
    <TimePicker
      android:id="@+id/tp"
      android:layout_width="wrap_content"
      android:layout_height="wrap_content"
  ></TimePicker>
    <TextView
      android:id="@+id/tptv"
      android:layout_width="wrap_content"
      android:layout_height="wrap_content"
      android:text="TextView"
  ></TextView>
    <Button
      android:id="@+id/btnTimeValues"
      android:layout_width="wrap_content"
      android:layout_height="wrap_content"
      android:text="Get Values"
  ></Button>
    <Button
      android:id="@+id/btnTimeClose"
      android:layout_width="wrap_content"
      android:layout_height="wrap_content"
      android:text="Close"
  ></Button>
  </LinearLayout>
```

This code is contained in UIControls\Resources\Layout\time.axml

Listing 4-11 shows an example of the class for the date controls:

LISTING 4-11: Date and time pickers

```
[Activity(Label = "Time Activity")]
public class timeact : Activity
{
    Button btnClose, btnTimeValues;
    int nowHour, nowMinute;
    TimePicker tp;
    protected override void OnCreate(Bundle bundle)
    {
        base.OnCreate(bundle);
        SetContentView(Resource.Layout.time);
        btnClose = FindViewById<Button>(Resource.Id.btnTimeClose);
        btnClose.Click += new EventHandler(btnClose_Click);
        btnTimeValues = FindViewById<Button>(Resource.Id.btnTimeValues);
```

```
        btnTimeValues.Click += new EventHandler(btnTimeValues_Click);
        nowHour = DateTime.Now.Hour;
        nowMinute = DateTime.Now.Minute;
        tp = FindViewById<TimePicker>(Resource.Id.tp);
    }
    void btnTimeValues_Click(object sender, EventArgs e)
    {
        TextView tv = FindViewById<TextView>(Resource.Id.dctv);
        DigitalClock dc = FindViewById<DigitalClock>(Resource.Id.dc);
        tv.Text = dc.Text;
        TextView tptv = FindViewById<TextView>(Resource.Id.tptv);
        DatePicker dp = FindViewById<DatePicker>(Resource.Id.dp);
        TextView dptv = FindViewById<TextView>(Resource.Id.dptv);
        DateTime dt = new DateTime(dp.Year, dp.Month + 1,
            dp.DayOfMonth, nowHour, nowMinute, 0);
        dptv.Text = dt.ToString();
    }
    void tp_TimeChanged(TimePicker view, int hourOfDay, int minute)
    {
        nowHour = hourOfDay;
        nowMinute = minute;
    }
    void btnClose_Click(object sender, EventArgs e)
    {
        this.Finish();
    }
}
```

This code is contained in UIControls\timeact.cs

The time and date examples show how to get the time and date properties of the various controls. One thing to note in the code is that the time picker's `TimeChanged` event is used to get the values. Those values are saved as private variables in the `Activity`'s class and can be used as needed. Figure 4-10 shows the `Activity` with its output from the date and time picker controls.

Images

Applications tend to be about the information users digest. Typically, this information is presented in the form of text. However, as the saying goes, a picture is worth a thousand words. As such, the appropriate use of images can provide tremendous value to users. With this fact in mind, Android provides several image controls. Here are a few points to keep in mind when working with images:

➤ Images can be of types png, jpg, gif, and bmp.

FIGURE 4-10

➤ Images should be placed in the /Resources/drawable directory.

➤ Images should be marked as AndroidResource, as shown in Figure 4-11. This should happen automatically.

➤ IntelliSense is provided for images. The association between the images and their values is stored in the file ResourcesDesigner.cs, as long as the build action of the image is set to AndroidResource.

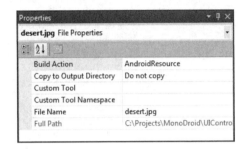

FIGURE 4-11

➤ The IntelliSense provided for images does not contain file extensions.

➤ Loading an image over WiFi or a wireless network requires more power than loading an image locally. Don't load an image from a remote resource unless absolutely necessary.

ImageView

The ImageView class is used to display an image. Images can be loaded from various resources and content providers. ImageView computes the images' measurements. In addition, it supports various options such as scaling.

ImageButton

The ImageButton class displays an image in place of text in a button. An ImageButton looks like a regular Button. The ImageButton supports several states. An image can be associated with the states of a Button, such as the default state, focused, and pressed.

Gallery

The Gallery is a View that is used to show items in a center-locked horizontal scrolling list. Listing 4-12 shows the XML user interface for images:

LISTING 4-12: Images XML

```xml
<?xml version="1.0" encoding="utf-8"?>
<LinearLayout
xmlns:android="http://schemas.android.com/apk/res/android"
    android:orientation="vertical"
    android:layout_width="fill_parent"
    android:layout_height="fill_parent">
  <ImageButton
  android:id="@+id/ib"
  android:layout_width="wrap_content"
  android:layout_height="wrap_content"
></ImageButton>
  <TextView
  android:id="@+id/ibtv"
  android:layout_width="fill_parent"
  android:layout_height="wrap_content"
```

```
></TextView>
  <Gallery
  android:id="@+id/gal"
  android:layout_width="wrap_content"
  android:layout_height="wrap_content"
></Gallery>
  <TextView
  android:id="@+id/galtv"
  android:layout_width="wrap_content"
  android:layout_height="wrap_content"
></TextView>
  <ImageView
  android:id="@+id/iv"
  android:layout_width="fill_parent"
  android:layout_height="wrap_content"
></ImageView>
  <Button
  android:id="@+id/btnImageClose"
  android:layout_width="wrap_content"
  android:layout_height="wrap_content"
  android:text="Close"
></Button>
</LinearLayout>
```

This code is contained in UIControls\Resources\Layout\images.axml

Listing 4-13 exemplifies the `Activity` for displaying images:

Available for download on Wrox.com

LISTING 4-13: Working with images

```
[Activity(Label = "Image Activity")]
public class imagesact : Activity
{
    Button btnImageClose;
    ImageButton ib;
    ImageView iv;
    Gallery g;

    protected override void OnCreate(Bundle bundle)
    {
        base.OnCreate(bundle);
        SetContentView(Resource.layout.images);
        btnImageClose = FindViewById<Button>(Resource.Id.btnImageClose);
        btnImageClose.Click += new EventHandler(btnClose_Click);
        g = FindViewById<Gallery>(Resource.Id.gal);
        TextView gtv = FindViewById<TextView>(Resource.Id.galtv);
        ib = FindViewById<ImageButton>(Resource.Id.ib);
        ib.SetImageResource(Resource.Drawable.blue);
        ib.Click += new EventHandler(ib_Click);
        ib.FocusChange += new EventHandler<View.FocusChangeEventArgs>
            (ib_FocusChange);
        iv = FindViewById<ImageView>(Resource.id.iv);
```

continues

LISTING 4-13 *(continued)*

```
            iv.SetImageResource(Resource.drawable.desert);
            g.Adapter = new ImageAdapter(this);
        }

    void ib_FocusChange(object sender, View.FocusChangeEventArgs e)
    {
        if (e.HasFocus)
        {
            ib.SetImageResource(Resource.drawable.red);
        }
        else
        {
            ib.SetImageResource(Resource.drawable.purple);
        }
    }
    void ib_Click(object sender, EventArgs e)
    {
        ib.SetImageResource(Resource.drawable.purple);
    }
    void btnClose_Click(object sender, EventArgs e)
    {
        this.Finish();
    }
//menu items are included in this .cs file; however
// they are not used in this section.
}
```

This code is contained in UIControls\imagesact.cs

Listing 4-14 gives a custom image array class for filling an image gallery.

Available for download on Wrox.com

LISTING 4-14: ImageAdapter for the gallery

```
public class ImageAdapter : BaseAdapter
{
    Context context;
    Dictionary<int, ImageView> dict;
    public ImageAdapter(Context c)
    {
      context = c;
      dict = new Dictionary<int, ImageView>();
    }

    public override int Count { get { return thumbIds.Length; } }

    public override Java.Lang.Object GetItem(int position){ return null; }

    public override long GetItemId(int position){ return 0; }

    // create a new ImageView for each item referenced by the Adapter
    public override View GetView(int position, View convertView, ViewGroup parent)
    {
```

```
        bool bOut;
        ImageView i;// = new ImageView(context);
        bOut = dict.TryGetValue(position, out i);

        if (bOut == false)
        {
            i = new ImageView(context);
            i.SetImageResource(thumbIds[position]);
            i.LayoutParameters = new Gallery.LayoutParams(150, 100);
            i.SetScaleType(ImageView.ScaleType.CenterInside);
            dict.Add(position, i);
        }

        return i;
    }

    // references to our images
    int[] thumbIds = {
        Resource.Drawable.chrysanthemum,
        Resource.Drawable.desert,
        Resource.Drawable.hydrangeas,
        Resource.Drawable.jellyfish,
        Resource.Drawable.koala,
        Resource.Drawable.lighthouse
    };
}
```

This code is contained in UIControls\ImagesArray.cs

Here are a few points to note about the custom image array class:

➤   The class inherits from the `BaseAdapter`.

➤   The class overrides the `Count` property. The count returns the total number of items that will be provided by the image array class.

➤   The `GetItem` method returns an item. In this case, the value is not needed, so a null is returned.

➤   The `GetItemId` method returns the item's unique identifier at a position. It is not needed in this example, so a value of 0 is returned.

➤   The `GetView` method returns the `View` necessary for an image view. This code stores the various image views in a dictionary. As the user scrolls through the images, the image view is pulled from the dictionary if it exists in the dictionary. If the image view does not exist within the dictionary, the image view is created and stored in the dictionary.

FIGURE 4-12

Figure 4-12 shows an `ImageButton`, `ImageView`, and a `Gallery`.

Virtual Keyboards

As we've already said many times in this book, mobile devices have limits. These include limits regarding their displays and keyboards. As a result, developers need to provide the users with some type of help inputting data into an application. Android provides this functionality through an attribute on the controls named inputType, as shown in Listing 4-15.

LISTING 4-15: Setup for virtual keyboards

```xml
<?xml version="1.0" encoding="utf-8"?>
<LinearLayout
android:id="@+id/lll"
android:layout_width="fill_parent"
android:layout_height="fill_parent"
android:orientation="vertical"
xmlns:android="http://schemas.android.com/apk/res/android"
>
  <EditText
    android:id="@+id/UriAddress"
    android:layout_width="fill_parent"
    android:layout_height="wrap_content"
    android:hint="Url"
    android:textSize="18sp"
    android:inputType="text|textUri" />
  <EditText
  android:id="@+id/To"
  android:layout_width="fill_parent"
  android:layout_height="wrap_content"
  android:hint="To"
  android:textSize="18sp"
  android:inputType="text|textEmailAddress"
/>
  <EditText
  android:id="@+id/subject"
  android:layout_width="fill_parent"
  android:layout_height="wrap_content"
  android:hint="Subject"
  android:textSize="18sp"
/>
  <EditText
    android:id="@+id/Message"
    android:layout_width="fill_parent"
    android:layout_height="240px"
    android:hint="Message"
    android:textSize="18sp"
    android:gravity="top"
/>
  <Button
  android:id="@+id/btn"
  android:layout_width="fill_parent"
  android:layout_height="wrap_content"
```

```
        android:text="Send"
        android:textSize="18sp"/>
    </LinearLayout>
```

This code is contained in softkeyboards\Resources\Layout\Main.axml

Figure 4-13 shows the three different virtual keyboards that are presented to the user in Android 2.x. Figure 4-14 shows the three different virtual keyboards that are presented to the user in the Android 4.0 emulator. These keyboards are set up based on the `inputType` attribute in the XML layout file. These virtual keyboards have only a few subtle differences among them.

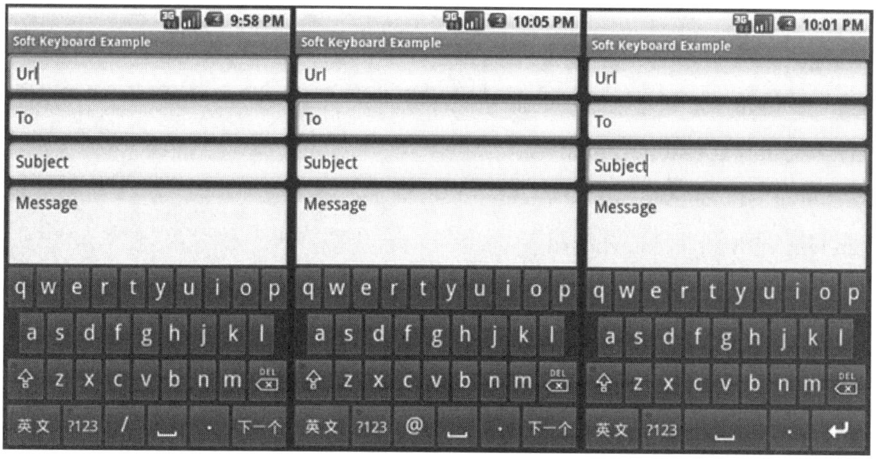

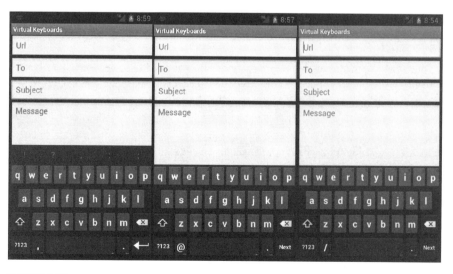

FIGURE 4-13

FIGURE 4-14

You may want to set the keyboard support in the emulator to true to get a more realistic visual when using an emulator session. To do this, the parameter to set is Keyboard Support to yes in an Android 2.3 Emulator Session. In an Android 4.0 Emulator Session, set the Keyboard Support to no to get the virtual keyboard support.

Selecting Your Virtual Keyboard

Many types of keyboards can be used to help users input data. These keyboards fall into the areas of text, number, phone, and date/time. Here are some of the possible virtual keyboards:

➤ `none`: The text is not editable.

➤ `datetime`: The input will be used for a date/time.

➤ `number`: The input text will be a number.

➤ `phone`: The input will be used as a phone number.

➤ `text`: Plain text with a basic keyboard.

➤ `textAutoCorrect`: Autocorrection support is provided.

➤ `textCapCharacters`: Text with all the characters in uppercase.

➤ `textEmailAddress`: The text will be used as an e-mail address.

➤ `textPassword`: The text will be displayed as a password input.

➤ `textUri`: The text will be used as a URI.

Many more input types can be specified, of course.

Removing the Keyboard

When the user is done with input, he or she wants the virtual keyboard to slide away. There is a user interface control within a virtual keyboard that allows the user to specify when the keyboard should slide away. If this needs to be performed programmatically, the following code will make the virtual keyboard slide away:

```
Android.Views.InputMethods.InputMethodManager imm =
        (Android.Views.InputMethods.InputMethodManager)
GetSystemService(Context.InputMethodService);
imm.HideSoftInputFromWindow(btn.WindowToken,
        Android.Views.InputMethods.HideSoftInputFlags.None);
```

This code can be placed in a number of locations that are particular to a specific application.

Programmatically hiding a virtual keyboard is not commonly done in Android applications, so this is not a requirement for you to implement.

CONTROLLING YOUR MENUS

Because screen real estate is at a premium with a mobile application, Android exposes a mechanism to provide application functionality without sacrificing too much screen real estate. Android allows each `Activity` to display its own menu when the device's menu button is selected. In addition, Android supports a context menu system that can be assigned to any `View`. Context menus are triggered when the user holds the touch screen for 3 seconds or longer within a `View`, presses the trackball, or presses the middle D-pad button; this depends on the device's input mechanism. Activity and context menus support additional submenus and context menus on the UI controls.

Introducing the Menu System

Given the small screen and the need to navigate applications that may have a large number of onscreen options, Android provides a multistage menu system. This menu system is optimized for small screens and the input they allow. These menu stages are as follows:

➤ **The icon menu:** The icon menu appears along the bottom of an `Activity` when the Menu button is pressed and an `Activity` has the menu setup. The icon menu does not display check boxes, radio buttons, or shortcut keys for menu items. When an `Activity`'s menu has more items than the maximum, an option to display more is shown.

➤ **The expanded menu:** The expanded menu appears when the user clicks the More option on a menu. The expanded menu displays items not shown in the icon menu's first set of options.

➤ **The submenu:** Faced with the icon menu and the possible expanded menu, the user can be overwhelmed with menus. Thankfully, Android implements a submenu system. This allows an application to present the user with a simple hierarchical set of menus that the user may drill into. At this time, submenus cannot be nested. Note that controls may be displayed, but icons are not displayed within the submenu items.

➤ **The context menu:** Context menus are associated with a `View`. A context menu offers options associated with that view.

Menus

The first issue in creating a menu is to understand where and when it is created. Menus are associated with an `Activity`. The menu is created by overriding the `OnCreateOptionsMenu` method of an `Activity`. The method is called when the device's Menu button is pressed while the `Activity` is being displayed. When the Menu button is pressed, the method is called, and a menu is displayed. Take a look at some sample code in Listing 4-16:

LISTING 4-16: Adding menu items

```
public override bool OnCreateOptionsMenu(Android.Views.IMenu menu)
{
    base.OnCreateOptionsMenu(menu);
    int groupId = 0;
    // Unique menu item Identifier. Used for event handling.
    int menuItemId = Android.Views.Menu.First;
    // The order position of the item
    int menuItemOrder = Android.Views.Menu.None;
    // Text to be displayed for this menu item.
    int menuItemText = Resource.String.menuitem1;
    // Create the menu item and keep a reference to it.
    IMenuItem menuItem1 = menu.Add(groupId, menuItemId, menuItemOrder,
        menuItemText);
    menuItem1.SetShortcut('1', 'a');
    Int32 MenuGroup = 10;
    IMenuItem menuItem2 =
        menu.Add(MenuGroup, menuItemId + 10, menuItemOrder + 1,
        new Java.Lang.String("Menu Item 2"));
    IMenuItem menuItem3 =
        menu.Add(MenuGroup, menuItemId + 20, menuItemOrder + 2,
        new Java.Lang.String("Menu Item 3"));
    ISubMenu sub = menu.AddSubMenu(0, menuItemOrder + 30,
        menuItemOrder + 3, new Java.Lang.String("Submenu 1"));
    sub.SetHeaderIcon(Resource.Drawable.plussign);
    sub.SetIcon(Resource.Drawable.plussign);
    IMenuItem submenuItem = sub.Add(0, menuItemId + 40, menuItemOrder + 4,
        new Java.Lang.String("Submenu Item"));
    IMenuItem submenuItem2 =
        sub.Add(MenuGroup, menuItemId + 50, menuItemOrder + 5,
        new Java.Lang.String("sub-1")).SetCheckable(true);
    IMenuItem submenuItem3 =
        sub.Add(MenuGroup, menuItemId + 60, menuItemOrder + 6,
        new Java.Lang.String("sub-2")).SetCheckable(true);
    return true;
}
```

This code is contained in UIControls\menus.cs

There are a few things to notice when a menu item is created:

➤ Calling the `.Add()` method creates a menu item and returns a reference to that item.

➤ The first parameter is the group value. It separates the menu's items for ordering and processing.

➤ The second parameter is an identifier that makes a menu item unique. The `OnOptionsItemSelected()` method uses this value to determine which menu item was clicked.

➤ The third parameter is an order parameter in which the order will be displayed.

➤ The final parameter is the text that the menu item displays — either a string resource or a string.

➤ After the menu items are created and populated, `true` should be returned.

➤ Check boxes and radio buttons are available on expanded menus and submenus. These are set in the `SetCheckable` method.

➤ A radio button group is created by `SetGroupCheckable`, by passing the group identifier, and by passing `true` to the exclusive parameter.

➤ Shortcut keys are set by calling the `SetShortcut` method.

➤ An icon can be set by calling the `SetIcon` method and passing a drawable resource.

➤ A condensed title can be set by calling an `IMenuItem`'s `.SetTitleCondensed()` method and passing a string. Because the state of a check box/radio button is not shown, the condensed title can be used to communicate the state to the user.

When a menu item is selected — including a submenu item, the menu item that represents the submenu, and an expanded menu item — the event `OnMenuItemSelected()` handles a selection. The application can tell which item was selected by looking at the `item.ItemID` property. The code in Listing 4-17 shows the `OnMenuItemSelected()` method:

LISTING 4-17: Processing a menu item selection

```
public override bool OnMenuItemSelected(int featureId, IMenuItem item)
{
    switch (item.ItemId)
    {
        case(0):
        //menu id 0 was selected.
            return (true);
        case(1):
        //menu id 1 was selected
            return (true);
        // additional items can go here.
    }
    return (false);
}
```

This code is contained in UIControls\menus.cs

Figure 4-15 shows the menu items running in the emulator.

As mentioned previously, when two menu items need to appear on one screen, items are displayed in an expanded menu. Figure 4-16 shows the menu items that are displayed as part of the expanded menu.

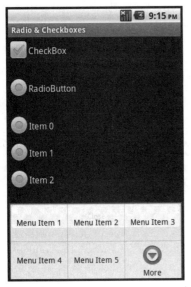

FIGURE 4-15

FIGURE 4-16

Submenus

Submenus are menu items that logically and hierarchically appear under menu items. Submenus are displayed when a menu item is selected and programmed to display the items. Here are some important points about submenus:

➤ Submenus are created by calling the AddSubMenu() method of an IMenuItem.

➤ The AddSubMenu() method uses the same parameters as when adding a menu item.

➤ Adding icons and the rest of the submenu items is the same as with a menu item.

Selecting the Menu button on the device brings up the menu items shown in Figure 4-17.

The submenu item is displayed along with a graphic signifying that additional information is displayed when the item is selected. Figure 4-18 shows Submenu 1 selected.

Context Menus

Context menus are displayed for a given view, such as a control. They are within the view's "context." In this source code, the context menu is created when the user selects the ImageView control. This is done within the OnCreate() method of a view that is displayed.

```
iv.SetImageResource(Resource.drawable.desert);
RegisterForContextMenu(iv);
```

After the view has been passed to the RegisterForContextMenu() method, when the user selects the view through some action, such as by pressing the trackball, selecting the middle D-pad button, or selecting the view for at least 3 seconds, the context menu is shown. Figure 4-19 shows an example of the context menu that is displayed when selecting an image view.

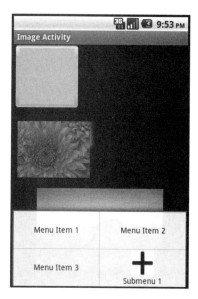

FIGURE 4-17

FIGURE 4-18

FIGURE 4-19

The code in Listing 4-18 creates the context menu. Note that the methods to add items accept the same parameters and allow for the same options as the menus and submenus.

LISTING 4-18: Creating a context menu

```
public override void OnCreateContextMenu(Android.Views.IContextMenu menu, View v,
        Android.Views.IContextMenuContextMenuInfo menuInfo)
{
    base.OnCreateContextMenu(menu, v, menuInfo);
    Java.Lang.ICharSequence str0 = new Java.Lang.String("Context Menu");
    Java.Lang.ICharSequence str1 = new Java.Lang.String("Item 1");
    Java.Lang.ICharSequence str2 = new Java.Lang.String("Item 2");
    Java.Lang.ICharSequence str3 = new Java.Lang.String("Item 3");
    Java.Lang.ICharSequence strSubMenu = new Java.Lang.String("Submenu");
    Java.Lang.ICharSequence strSubMenuItem = new Java.Lang.String("Submenu Item");
    menu.SetHeaderTitle(str0);
    menu.Add(0, Android.Views.Menu.First,
        Android.Views.Menu.None, str1).SetIcon(Resource.Drawable.koala);
    menu.Add(0, Android.Views.Menu.First + 1, Android.Views.Menu.None, str2)
        .SetCheckable(true);
    menu.Add(0, Android.Views.Menu.First + 2, Android.Views.Menu.None, str3)
        .SetShortcut('3', '3');
    ISubMenu sub = menu.AddSubMenu(strSubMenu);
    sub.Add(strSubMenuItem);
}
```

This code is contained in UIControls\menus.cs

When the user selects a context menu item, the following code determines which menu item was
selected:

```
public override bool OnContextItemSelected(IMenuItem item)
{
    base.OnContextItemSelected(item);
    switch (item.ItemId)
    {
        case (0):
            return (true);
        case (1):
            return (true);
    }
    return (false);
}
```

This code is contained in UIControls\menus.cs

Defining Menus as a Resource

In addition to manually creating menus programmatically, you can create menus from an XML
resource. The menus that are created can be either standard menus created when the user clicks the
menu item or context menus.

Menus

Menu resources are stored as XML files in the layout directory and have their `build` attribute set to `AndroidResource`. The menu starts with the `<menu>` tag as the root, along with the `<item>` tag for menu items and the `<menu>` and `<item>` tags shown on `item04` for submenu items. Listing 4-19 shows the XML used for an embedded resource.

LISTING 4-19: Menu defined in XML

```
<menu xmlns:android="http://schemas.android.com/apk/res/android"
android:name="Embedded Resource - Context Menu">
   <item
   android:id="@+id/item01"
   android:icon="@drawable/jellyfishsmall"
   android:title="Menu item 1">
   </item>
   <item
   android:id="@+id/item02"
   android:checkable="true"
   android:title="Menu item 2">
   </item>
   <item
   android:id="@+id/item03"
   android:numericShortcut="3"
   android:alphabeticShortcut="3"
   android:title="Menu item 3">
   </item>
   <item
   android:id="@+id/item04"
   android:title="Submenu items">
      <menu>
        <item
        android:id="@+id/item05"
        android:title="Submenu item 1">
        </item>
      </menu>
   </item>
</menu>
```

This code is contained in UIControls\Resources\Layout\menu.xml

The following code shows the menu being loaded and inflated into the display when the user clicks the Menu button when an `Activity` is loaded:

```
public override bool OnCreateOptionsMenu(Android.Views.IMenu menu)
{
    base.OnCreateOptionsMenu(menu);
    MenuInflater inflater = new Android.Views.MenuInflater(this);
    inflater.Inflate(Resource.layout.menu, menu);
    return (true);
}
```

This code is contained in UIControls\menu.cs

Figure 4-20 shows the output of loading the embedded menu into the display.

FIGURE 4-20

Context Menus

An embedded resource can be used as a context menu and then be created from a `View`, just like when a context menu is created programmatically. Listing 4-20 shows the creation of the context menu from an embedded resource.

LISTING 4-20: OnCreateContextMenu method with an XML resource

```
public override void OnCreateContextMenu(Android.Views.IContextMenu menu, View v,
    Android.Views.IContextMenuContextMenuInfo menuInfo)
{
    base.OnCreateContextMenu(menu, v, menuInfo);
    MenuInflater inflater = new Android.Views.MenuInflater(this);
    inflater.Inflate(Resource.layout.menu, menu);
    menu.SetHeaderTitle("My Context Menu");
}
```

This code is contained in UIControls\menu.cs

Figure 4-21 shows the context menu that is created when an embedded resource is used.

From the embedded resource, Figure 4-22 shows the context menu's submenu item.

FIGURE 4-21

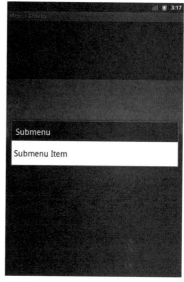

FIGURE 4-22

RESOLUTION-INDEPENDENT UI

Initially, designing a UI for Android was simple. All the initial devices had the same screen size and pixel density. Basically, if you designed a UI for a single device layout, it worked across the rest of the devices.

Unfortunately, the marketplace is a fickle beast. As the saying goes, "One size fits all" never fits you. Starting with Android 2.0 in late 2009, the marketplace has seen a tremendous increase in the number of devices. Each of these devices seems to have a slightly different screen size and pixel density. Creating a UI that looks good across all the devices you want to support is not difficult, but it can take some thought. This section looks at some of the features in Mono for Android (and Android) that help developers write a resolution-independent UI. These include supporting various resources, supporting varying screen sizes, and working from a set of best practices.

Supporting Various Screen Resources

In general, resources dealing with the screen can be divided into two areas — screen sizes and pixel density.

Supporting Screen Sizes

There are three generalized screen sizes. Based on the device's screen size, an application can provide various layouts. The currently supported screen sizes are as follows:

➤ **Extra Large:** An extra large screen in Android is a screen that is larger than a large screen.

➤ **Large:** A large screen typically is much larger than the screen on a standard-sized smart-phone. Usually this is a tablet–or netbook-size screen or larger.

➤ **Medium:** A medium screen equates to the typical screen size of a smartphone.

➤ **Small:** A small screen is smaller than a standard 3.2-inch smartphone screen.

Screen size support for an application can be placed within the `AndroidManifest.xml` file that is stored within the `Properties` folder of an Android application. The support is set by the following XML:

```
<supports-screens android:smallScreens="false" android:normalScreens="true"
   android:largeScreens="true" android:xlargeScreens="true"
   android:anyDensity="true" />
```

The attributes have the following meanings:

➤ `android:smallScreens` indicates whether the application supports screen form factors with a smaller aspect ratio than the traditional HVGA screen (smaller than "normal"). If an application does not support small screen sizes, it will be unavailable to a device with a small screen. By default, this value is `true` for API level 4 and later, so it is `true` for Mono for Android.

➤ `android:normalScreens` indicates whether a normal size screen is supported. By default, this attribute is `true`.

➤ `android:largeScreens` indicates whether a larger-than-normal (tablet or netbook) screen size is supported. By default, this setting is `true` for API level 4 and later, so it is `true` for Mono for Android.

➤ `android:xlargeScreens` indicates whether or not an extra large screen is supported. By default, this setting is false for API level below 9. This attribute will require the API level to be 9 or higher.

➤ `android:anyDensity` indicates whether an application can support any screen density. This is `true` by default for API level 4 and later, so it is `true` for Mono for Android.

 The values for `true` and `false` are slightly different from what developers assume. A value of `false` does not mean that an application will not run on the device. It means that Android will attempt to apply some sizing features and fit the application into the device. A value of `true` means that the application has been checked by the application developer, should support that resolution, and does not need the device to apply any screen-sizing magic.

Supporting Pixel Densities

Pixel density is another issue that must be figured into an application. Resources are stored in the `drawable` directory and may be stored in several subdirectories, depending on their screen resolution. Android has these standard pixel densities:

➤ **ldpi:** Low-density resources are designed for devices with a screen pixel density of 100 to 140 dpi. These resources are stored in the `Resources/drawable-ldpi` folder.

➤ **mdpi:** Medium-density resources are designed for devices with a screen pixel density of 140 to 190 dpi. These resources are stored in the `Resources/drawable-mdpi` folder.

➤ **hdpi:** High-density resources are designed for devices with a screen pixel density of 190 dpi and higher. These resources are stored in the `Resources/drawable-hdpi` folder.

➤ **xhdpi:** Extra high-density resources are designed for devices with a screen pixel density of 320 dpi. These resources are stored in the `Resources/drawable-xhdpi` folder.

Mono for Android running in Visual Studio provides a `drawable` folder. The other directories may be created manually based on the need. Mono for Android running in MonoDevelop on the Mac provides the `drawable-hdpi`, `drawable-mdpi`, `drawable-ldpi` folders. These are optional directories and are provided as a convention to provide alternative resources depending on the device's capabilities. The decision as to which resources to use is determined at runtime. The order for determining the resources is `ldpi`, `mdpi`, `hdpi`, `xhdpi`, and `nodpi`.

> *For the most up-to-date information on the support for resources in Android, check the Android Developer site on Providing Resources. The url is* `http://developer.android.com/guide/topics/resources/providing-resources.html`.

> *It is worth noting that Google did a survey and found that, as of August 2, 2010, 97 percent of devices have a pixel density of mdpi or hdpi. Developers are probably safe to assume that devices are mdpi or better.*

Using Android Market Support

In addition to application support for various screen sizes and pixel densities, the Android Market uses the `<support-screens />` attributes. Applications that specify these values are filtered within the marketplace so that the user is presented with only applications that fit the device that is currently being used to connect to the Market. If an application does not support a small screen, the application will not be listed when a small screen device searches the Android Market.

Multiple Screen Resolution Best Practices

The following are best practices for building an application that supports multiple screen resolutions:

➤ `AbsoluteLayout` should not be used. `AbsoluteLayout` uses the concept of specific positions for controls. Although this will work for the initial screen design, it will most likely cause problems when an application is run on a different device with a different screen resolution. It is suggested that developers use `RelativeLayout` and `FrameLayout` and set `layout_margin` attributes within the child controls.

➤ Use `fill_parent`, `wrap_content`, and dip (density-independent pixel) units instead of pixel sizes in UI attributes.

➤ Avoid placing pixel values directly in code. Although the Android framework uses pixel values in code for performance reasons, it is suggested that dips be used for calculations and conversions as necessary. The class `Android.Util.DisplayMetrics` can be used to get the necessary screen dimensions for the currently running device.

➤ Use the density and image-specific resources.

➤ Test your application in the simulator in various configurations as well as on multiple devices.

CONSTRUCTING A USER INTERFACE: A PHONE AND TABLET EXAMPLE

Putting together an application's user interface using these standard controls and having that application run across multiple form factors is the goal of any Android application. In this example, the user is presented with a user registration screen. The user is provided with assistance during the registration process. The assistance provided in this app is as follows:

➤ Scrolling is turned on via the `ScrollView` control. This allows for the user interface of an application to scroll as needed. (For a tablet, or larger screen device, this is not an issue.) The `ScrollView` enables the controls to be scrolled.

➤ Virtual keyboards are used in the various input fields. For example, the e-mail field provides the keyboard layout optimized for e-mail, while the phone number field provides the keyboard optimized for numeric input.

➤ A spinner is used to provide a list of states. Instead of typing the state in, the user selects the spinner, navigates to the appropriate state, and then selects the state.

➤ An autocomplete is used to enter the country of the user.

➤ Location services are used to calculate the user's current location. From this location, the user's city and zip code are then prefilled. Once the location is determined, the location services are no longer used and are turned off.

Figures 4-23 and 4-24 show the same application running in a tablet device (the Motorola Xoom) and on a phone (an HTC EVO 4G device).

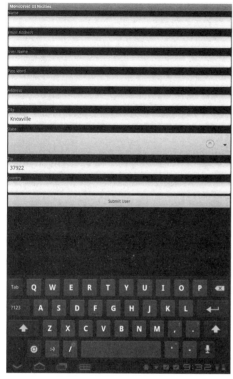

FIGURE 4-23

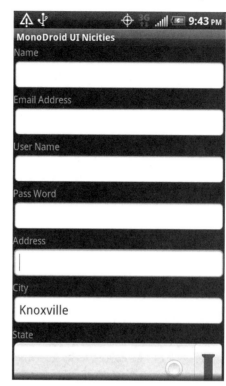

FIGURE 4-24

Listing 4-21 shows the XML layout for this user interface, which runs across the Motorola Xoom and the HTC EVO 4G.

LISTING 4-21: XML layout with inputType attributes

```xml
<?xml version="1.0" encoding="utf-8"?>
<ScrollView  xmlns:android="http://schemas.android.com/apk/res/android"
  android:id="@+id/sv"
  android:layout_width="fill_parent"
  android:layout_height="wrap_content"
  >
  <LinearLayout
    android:orientation="vertical"
    android:layout_width="fill_parent"
    android:layout_height="fill_parent"
```

continues

LISTING 4-21 *(continued)*

```xml
          android:isScrollContainer="true"
          >
    <TextView android:id="@+id/tvName"
        android:layout_width="fill_parent"
        android:layout_height="wrap_content"
        android:text="@string/Name"
/>
    <EditText android:id="@+id/Name"
      android:layout_width="fill_parent"
      android:layout_height="wrap_content"
      android:inputType="text|textCapWords" />

      <TextView android:id="@+id/tvEmail"
          android:layout_width="fill_parent"
          android:layout_height="wrap_content"
          android:text="@string/Email"
/>
    <EditText android:id="@+id/Email"
      android:layout_width="fill_parent"
      android:layout_height="wrap_content"
      android:inputType="text|textEmailAddress"
/>

      <TextView android:id="@+id/tvUserName"
          android:layout_width="fill_parent"
          android:layout_height="wrap_content"
          android:text="@string/UserName"
/>
    <EditText android:id="@+id/UserName"
      android:layout_width="fill_parent"
      android:layout_height="wrap_content"
/>
    <TextView android:id="@+id/tvPassWord"
        android:layout_width="fill_parent"
        android:layout_height="wrap_content"
        android:text="@string/PassWord"
/>
    <EditText android:id="@+id/PassWord"
      android:layout_width="fill_parent"
      android:layout_height="wrap_content"
      android:inputType="text|textPassword"
/>
    <TextView android:id="@+id/tvAddress"
        android:layout_width="fill_parent"
        android:layout_height="wrap_content"
        android:text="@string/Address"
/>
    <EditText android:id="@+id/Address"
      android:layout_width="fill_parent"
      android:layout_height="wrap_content"
/>
```

```
   <TextView android:id="@+id/tvCity"
     android:layout_width="fill_parent"
     android:layout_height="wrap_content"
     android:text="@string/City"
     android:inputType="text|textAutoCorrect"
           />
   <EditText android:id="@+id/City"
     android:layout_width="fill_parent"
     android:layout_height="wrap_content"
  />
   <TextView android:id="@+id/tvState"
       android:layout_width="fill_parent"
       android:layout_height="wrap_content"
       android:text="@string/State"
  />
   <Spinner android:id="@+id/State"
         android:layout_width="fill_parent"
         android:layout_height="wrap_content"
  />
   <TextView android:id="@+id/tvZip"
       android:layout_width="fill_parent"
       android:layout_height="wrap_content"
       android:text="@string/Zip"
  />
   <EditText android:id="@+id/Zip"
     android:layout_width="fill_parent"
     android:layout_height="wrap_content"
     android:inputType="number"
  />
   <Button
     android:id="@+id/Submit"
     android:layout_width="fill_parent"
     android:layout_height="wrap_content"
     android:text="@string/Submit"
     />
</LinearLayout>
</ScrollView>
```

This code is contained in MonoDroidUiNicities\Resources\Layout\ui.axml

Now that you have created a user interface, you can create the activity code (Listing 4-22). The key items of note in the code are:

➤   The spinner control is populated from a resource.

➤   The autocomplete textbox control is populated from a resource.

➤   A location manager object is created to get the location updates.

➤   Once a location is detected, the location manager no longer sends updates to the application. This keeps the UI from being updated by the application and the user wondering why the update occurred.

LISTING 4-22: Code listing for setting up the user interface

```
[[Activity(Label = "Mono for Android UI Nicities", MainLauncher = true)]
public class Activity1 : Activity, ILocationListener
{
    private Spinner States;
    private Button button;
    private EditText etAddress;
    private EditText etCity;
    private EditText etZipCode;
    private AutoCompleteTextView actvCountry;
    private LocationManager lm;
    protected override void OnCreate(Bundle bundle)
    {
        base.OnCreate(bundle);
        SetContentView(Resource.Layout.ui);
        try
        {
            button = FindViewById<Button>(Resource.Id.Submit);
            button.Click += new EventHandler(button_Click);
            States = FindViewById<Spinner>(Resource.Id.State);
            var fAdapter = ArrayAdapter.CreateFromResource(this,
                    Resource.Array.states,
            Android.Resource.Layout.SimpleSpinnerDropDownItem);
            int spinner_dd_item = Android.Resource.
                    Layout.SimpleSpinnerDropDownItem;
            fAdapter.SetDropDownViewResource(spinner_dd_item);
            States.Adapter = fAdapter;
            Criteria cr = new Criteria();
            cr.Accuracy = Accuracy.Fine;
            cr.AltitudeRequired = false;
            cr.BearingRequired = false;
            cr.SpeedRequired = false;
            cr.CostAllowed = true;
            String serviceString = Context.LocationService;
            lm = (LocationManager)GetSystemService(serviceString);
            string bestProvider = lm.GetBestProvider(cr, false);
            actvCountry = FindViewById<AutoCompleteTextView>(Resource.Id.Country);
            etAddress = FindViewById<EditText>(Resource.Id.Address);
            etCity = FindViewById<EditText>(Resource.Id.City);
            etZipCode = FindViewById<EditText>(Resource.Id.Zip);
            string[] countries = Resources.GetStringArray(
                    Resource.Array.Countries);
            var adapter = new ArrayAdapter<String>(this,
                    Resource.Layout.ListItem, countries);
            actvCountry.Adapter = adapter;
            lm.RequestLocationUpdates(bestProvider, 5000, 1f, this);
        }
        catch (System.Exception sysExc)
        {
            Toast.MakeText(this, sysExc.Message, ToastLength.Short).Show();
        }
    }
```

```csharp
void GetAddress(double Lat, double Lon)
{
    try
    {
        IList<Address> al;
        Geocoder geoc = new Geocoder(this, Java.Util.Locale.Default);
        al = geoc.GetFromLocation(Lat, Lon, 10);

        if ((al != null) && (al.Count > 0))
        {
            var firstAddress = al[0];
            var addressLine0 = firstAddress.GetAddressLine(0);
            var City = firstAddress.Locality;
            var zip = firstAddress.PostalCode;

            if (!String.IsNullOrEmpty(City))
            {
                RunOnUiThread(() => etCity.Text = City);
            }
            else
            {
                RunOnUiThread(() => etCity.Text = String.Empty);
            }
            if (!String.IsNullOrEmpty(zip))
            {
                RunOnUiThread(() => etZipCode.Text = zip);
            }
            else
            {
                RunOnUiThread(() => etZipCode.Text = String.Empty);
            }
            lm.RemoveUpdates(this);
        }
    }
    finally { }
}
void button_Click(object sender, EventArgs e)
{
    EditText ev = FindViewById<EditText>(Resource.Id.Name);
    string message = "Your values will now be processed.";
    Toast.MakeText(this, message, ToastLength.Short).Show();
}
public void OnLocationChanged(Location location)
{
    GetAddress(location.Latitude, location.Longitude);
}
public void OnProviderDisabled(string provider)
{    }
public void OnProviderEnabled(string provider)
{    }
public void OnStatusChanged(string provider, Availability status,
    Bundle extras)
{    }
}
```

This code is contained in MonoDroidUiNicities\Activity1.cs

SUMMARY

This chapter has introduced some of the ideas, concepts, and controls you can use in building your Android user interface. Some of the key concepts presented include the following:

➤   Views and ViewGroups

➤   Layouts for placing controls on an Activity

➤   Some of the key controls used to build a user interface

➤   Some of the key ideas behind building a successful user interface

This chapter completes the first part of the book on building the basics of an application with Mono for Android.

5

Working with Data

WHAT'S IN THIS CHAPTER?

➤ Working with the SQLite database

➤ Working with remote data using SOAP-based web services

➤ Working with REST-style web services using XML and JSON

➤ Storing data efficiently

➤ Connecting and talking to a database off the device directly

Data is the lifeblood of companies and the applications they build for public and private consumption. The application might be an app to interact with Twitter, an instant-message application, or your own personal address book. This chapter looks at interacting with device databases, the SQLite database engine, and some of the strategies to store data off the device on a central server through SOAP and REST without tying up the user interface.

WORKING WITH SQLITE

SQLite is a data engine running in Android and is the native database on Android. It is different from client/server-style databases, such as SQL Server, Oracle, and DB/2. With a client/server-style database, a query or operation is sent to the database engine, the operation is performed, and the result is sent back to the client. With this type of database engine, the database runs in a separate process and typically on a separate machine. SQLite does not run on a separate machine; it runs on the same machine, Android, and runs in the same process as the application. SQLite is embedded in the application and linked to the app during the compilation process. Calls made to SQLite are not made over a network, but stay on the physical device. SQLite, a free application, uses SQL (Structured Query Language) to interact with it.

This chapter is not meant to be an introduction to the SQL language, databases, tables, columns, data types, foreign keys, rows, or any other type of database feature. You are expected to understand these concepts. For more information on the SQLite database, check the website http://sqlite.org/. *For more information on the SQL language, check out any number of books from Wrox and Wiley on the subject.*

The data provider for SQLite is contained within the Mono.Data.Sqlite assembly, which supports SQLite version 3. The assembly is intended for ADO.NET 2.0, which isn't a problem for writing an application in Mono for Android.

The Mono.Data.Sqlite.dll assembly and the Mono for Android files are located in the directory for the Android assemblies. Another option for adding these assemblies in is to just use the list capability in Visual Studio for adding a reference.

Setting Up a Database

The first step in getting an app to work with SQLite is to set up the database. With server-based databases, this is done once by a DBA. With SQLite, the database must be created on the initial run of an application on a device, and it must be done on each device that the application runs on. Because the application must run on the end user's device, the database setup process must work without user intervention, and it must run within the device's time constraints. Listing 5-1 is the code that creates a database.

Dealing with data can be a time-consuming process. Locking the main thread in an application for too long can result in the Android operating system attempting to stop the application. Database operations are a good candidate for background threads.

Sometimes there are operations that work on a device and not in the Android emulator. SQLite's CreateFile method has been one of these. Please be aware of this issue if you have problems in this area.

LISTING 5-1: Creating a database on a device

```
string DatabaseName = "UserData.db3";
string documents =
    System.Environment.GetFolderPath(System.Environment.SpecialFolder.Personal);
```

```
string db = Path.Combine(documents, DatabaseName);
bool exists = File.Exists(db);
if (!exists)
{
        SqliteConnection.CreateFile(db);
}
```

This code is contained in InternalNetworkData\InternalNetworkData\Activity1.cs

The following are notable occurrences in this code:

➤ A database name is selected. This is where the tables and other data objects will be stored.

➤ The personal directory is determined.

➤ The full path to the database file is created.

➤ A test is performed to determine if the file exists. If it does not, the file is created.

Setting Up Tables

Now that your database has been created, the next step is to set up tables, indexes, triggers, and any other particular database objects that are needed. Listing 5-2 shows code that creates tables, triggers, and indexes.

LISTING 5-2: Creating tables in a database

```
var conn = new SqliteConnection("Data Source=" + db);
var commands = new[] {
    "CREATE TABLE IF NOT EXISTS STATE (STATEID INT PRIMARY KEY, " +
    "STATENAME VARCHAR(50))",
    "CREATE TABLE IF NOT EXISTS CUSTOMER(CUSTOMERID BIGINT PRIMARY KEY, " +
    "NAME VARCHAR(100), CONTACTNAME VARCHAR(100), DATEJOINED DATETIME, " +
    "PHONE VARCHAR(25), ADDRESS VARCHAR(100), CITY VARCHAR(50), " +
    "STATEID INT, ZIPCODE VARCHAR(25), DATEENTERED DATETIME, " +
    "DATEUPDATED DATETIME, FOREIGN KEY(STATEID) REFERENCES STATE(STATEID))",
    "CREATE TRIGGER IF NOT EXISTS CUSTOMER_INSERT INSERT ON CUSTOMER " +
    "BEGIN UPDATE CUSTOMER SET DATEENTERED=DATE('now') " +
        "WHERE CUSTOMERID=NEW.CUSTOMERID; END;",
    "CREATE INDEX IF NOT EXISTS IDX_CUSTOMERNAME ON CUSTOMER (NAME)",
    "CREATE INDEX IF NOT EXISTS IDX_STATEID ON CUSTOMER (STATEID)",
    "CREATE INDEX IF NOT EXISTS IDX_DATEENTERED ON CUSTOMER (DATEENTERED)",
    "INSERT INTO STATE (STATENAME) VALUES ('TENNESSEE');",
    "INSERT INTO STATE (STATENAME) VALUES ('GEORGIA');"};
foreach (var cmd in commands)
    using (var sqlitecmd = conn.CreateCommand())
    {
        sqlitecmd.CommandText = cmd;
        sqlitecmd.CommandType = CommandType.Text;
        conn.Open();
        sqlitecmd.ExecuteNonQuery();
        conn.Close();
    }
```

continues

LISTING 5-2 *(continued)*

```
SqliteCommand sqlc = new SqliteCommand();
sqlc.Connection = conn;
conn.Open();
string strSql = "INSERT INTO CUSTOMER (NAME, CONTACTNAME, STATEID) " +
        "VALUES (@NAME, @CONTACTNAME, @STATEID)";
sqlc.CommandText = strSql;
sqlc.CommandType = CommandType.Text;
sqlc.Parameters.Add(new SqliteParameter("@NAME", "The Coca-Cola Company"));
sqlc.Parameters.Add(new SqliteParameter("@CONTACTNAME", "John Johns"));
sqlc.Parameters.Add(new SqliteParameter("@STATEID", 1));
sqlc.ExecuteNonQuery();
if (conn.State != ConnectionState.Closed)
{
    conn.Close();
}
conn.Dispose();
tv.Text = "Commands completed.";
```

This code is contained in InternalNetworkData\InternalNetworkData\Activity1.cs

Look at the sequence of events that are happening in this code:

➤ A `Connection` object is created for the SQLite database.

➤ A series of commands is loaded into an array of strings.

➤ A loop is performed. It will execute each individual command in the `foreach` loop.

➤ A command is performed to insert a customer name. Note that this command uses database parameters.

➤ Finally, the connection is closed and disposed of, and the user is informed that the commands have been completed.

Using SQL Statements

Creating, altering, and dropping database objects is interesting. However, CRUD (create, read, update, delete) is the lifeblood of database applications. The ability to select, insert, update, and delete data through SQL is at the core of an application. The following sections cover some useful SQL statements.

Using Read/Select to Read Data

Reading data is a very important operation for an application. Reading data from a database table is the operation that is done most often in an application. The .NET Framework provides data readers, connections, and a series of objects that allows us to access database tables. Mono for Android provides an implementation of these .NET methods for Android. Listing 5-3 shows some code that reads data from a table.

LISTING 5-3: Reading data

```csharp
string DatabaseName = "UserData.db3";
string documents =
    System.Environment.GetFolderPath(System.Environment.SpecialFolder.Personal);
string db = Path.Combine(documents, DatabaseName);
var conn = new SqliteConnection("Data Source=" + db);
var strSql = "select Name from Customer where STATEID=@STATEID";
var cmd = new SqliteCommand(strSql, conn);
cmd.CommandType = CommandType.Text;
cmd.Parameters.Add(new SqliteParameter("@STATEID", 2));

try
{
    conn.Open();
    SqliteDataReader sdr = cmd.ExecuteReader();
    while (sdr.Read())
    {
        tv.Text = Convert.ToString(sdr["Name"]);
    }
}
catch (System.Exception sysExc)
{
    tv.Text = sysExc.Message;
}
finally
{
    if (conn.State != ConnectionState.Closed)
    {
        conn.Close();
    }
    conn.Dispose();
}
```

This code is contained in the InternalNetworkData\InternalNetworkData\Activity1.cs

This code does the following:

➤ Creates a database connection.

➤ Creates a parameterized database query.

➤ Adds values to the parameter.

➤ Opens the database connection.

➤ Performs the query by returning a data reader.

➤ Outputs values to the TextView. The table has only one value, so the final value is obtained and displayed to the user.

As you can see, it's possible to use objects that you know and understand. You can create a connection object and then create a data reader. With the data reader, you can iterate through the records returned and use the records just like in a .NET application.

> *Another option is to use the* using *statement. The* using *statement will call the* .Dispose() *method for you when the* using *statement is executed. I prefer the* try-catch-finally *syntax written out. Either case is syntactically correct and can be used at the developer's discretion.*

Using SQL Statements to Insert Data

Now that you know how to read data from a database table, the next obvious question is how to put data into a table. Your first step is to acquire some data. In this case, put some data in a table using a SQLite command object, as shown in Listing 5-4.

LISTING 5-4: Writing data

```
var conn = new SqliteConnection("Data Source=" + db);
SqliteCommand sqlc = new SqliteCommand();
sqlc.Connection = conn;
conn.Open();
string strSql = "INSERT INTO CUSTOMER (NAME, CONTACTNAME, STATEID) " +
"VALUES (@NAME, @CONTACTNAME, @STATEID)";
sqlc.CommandText = strSql;
sqlc.CommandType = CommandType.Text;
sqlc.Parameters.Add(new SqliteParameter("@NAME", "The Coca-Cola Company"));
sqlc.Parameters.Add(new SqliteParameter("@CONTACTNAME", "John Johns"));
sqlc.Parameters.Add(new SqliteParameter("@STATEID", 1));
sqlc.ExecuteNonQuery();
if (conn.State != ConnectionState.Closed)
{
    conn.Close();
}
conn.Dispose();
```

This code is contained in the InternalNetworkData\InternalNetworkData\Activity1.cs

In this method, a record is inserted using a SQLite command object, parameters, and a connection. Now that you can insert data into the table, handling other operations is similar. Update and Delete operations can easily be handled through SQLite's command object. The command can be a direct SQL statement or a prepared statement. Either will work. One word of warning: If you choose to use a simple SQL statement, don't open up code to a SQL injection attack.

UPGRADING STRATEGIES

A web application typically has only one database instance to manage. With an application installed on Android and using SQLite, there are as many database instances as installations of the application. A new version of your application most likely has a new version of the database schema to support the new features in that upgraded application. This section discusses strategies that can be inserted into an application to handle upgrading a database that is out in the wild.

Upgrading in Place

With an existing application's database, one strategy is to track the application's version within a table. By tracking the database schema version, the application can check the version on startup. If the version is not the current one, the schema can be upgraded by executing a series of SQLite-commands against the database. This strategy requires a check on each startup of the application and works well for a complicated database schema.

Copying Data

The upgrade-in-place solution requests a check each time the application starts. Another option is to check on startup. If the schema is not the correct version, you can create a new instance of the database and copy the necessary data. Then you can assume that the schema is correct. This strategy requires a significant number of commands to be executed and potentially a lot of data to be moved. The more commands that must be executed and the more data that is moved, the more opportunity there is for a mistake to be made. This option would be a good idea for an application that must make many changes.

Either of these options is most likely preferable to deleting the existing database along with its data.

ANDROID-SPECIFIC DATABASE OPTIONS

If you review all of the previous code from this chapter, you will notice that it runs the same on MonoTouch on the iPhone. That is a good thing. One of the goals of Mono for Android, and MonoTouch, is that as much code as possible runs on the other Mono platform. However, there are a couple Android-specific options for interfacing with the SQLite database on Android. These two options are creating a database and its tables and performing the CRUD operations. It is definitely possible to perform both of these options in a cross-platform way as shown previously in this chapter. Therefore, caution should be used in using these Android-specific options. If an application uses these Android-specific mechanisms, there are several issues:

➤ .NET developers familiar with ADO.NET are not familiar with these Android-specific features.

➤ The parts of an application written with Android-specific methods will not be usable under MonoTouch on the iPhone or any other mobile platforms supported by Mono.

SQLiteOpenHelper

`SQLiteOpenHelper` is a helper class. It is designed to assist with the process of creating databases as well as version management of those databases. The process to use this class is as follows:

➤ Inherit from the `SQLiteOpenHelper` class.

➤ Implement three methods: `OnCreate`, `OnUpgrade`, and `OnOpen`. These methods can be modified to suit the needs of a specific application.

Listing 5-5 shows an example of using the SQLiteOpenHelper to open a database:

LISTING 5-5: SQLiteOpenHelper usage

```
class DBHelper : Android.Database.Sqlite.SQLiteOpenHelper
{
    private const string DbName = "GolfScore";
    private const int DbVersion = 1;

    public DBHelper(Context context) : base(context, DbName, null, DbVersion)
    {   }
    public override void OnCreate(Android.Database.Sqlite.SQLiteDatabase db)
    {
        db.ExecSQL(@"CREATE TABLE IF NOT EXISTS GolfScore " +
"(GolfID INTEGER PRIMARY KEY AUTOINCREMENT," +
            "ScoreDate varchar(30) NOT NULL, ScoreNumber NOT NULL, " +
"Rating double NOT NULL, Slope int not null)");
    }
    public override void OnUpgrade(Android.Database.Sqlite.SQLiteDatabase db,
        int oldVersion, int newVersion)
    {
        db.ExecSQL("DROP TABLE IF EXISTS GolfScore");
        OnCreate(db);
    }
}
```

This code is contained in SQLiteAndroidSpecific\SQLiteAndroidSpecific\DBHelper.cs

Listing 5-6 shows an example using the native Android data access APIs to perform common database operations.

LISTING 5-6: Using the SQLiteOpenHelper

```
class dbCommands
{
    private DBHelper dbHelp;
    public dbCommands(Context context)
    {
        dbHelp = new DBHelper(context);
        dbHelp.OnCreate(dbHelp.WritableDatabase);
    }

    public IList<Score> GetAllScores()
    {
        Android.Database.ICursor golfCursor = dbHelp.ReadableDatabase.
Query("GolfScore", null, null, null, null, null, null, null);
        var scores = new List<Score>();
        while (golfCursor.MoveToNext())
        {
            Score scr = MapScores(golfCursor);
            scores.Add(scr);
        }
```

```
        return scores;
    }

    public long AddScore(int ScoreNumber, DateTime ScoreDate,
        double rating, double slope)
    {
        var values = new ContentValues();
        values.Put("ScoreNumber", ScoreNumber);
        values.Put("ScoreDate", ScoreDate.ToString());
        values.Put("Rating", rating);
        values.Put("Slope", slope);
        return dbHelp.WritableDatabase.Insert("GolfScore", null, values);
    }

    public void DeleteScore(int ScoreID)
    {
        string[] vals = new string[1];
        vals[0] = ScoreID.ToString();

        dbHelp.WritableDatabase.Delete("GolfScore", "ScoreId=?", vals);
    }
    private Score MapScores(Android.Database.ICursor cursor)
    {
        Score scr = new Score();
        scr.ScoreID = cursor.GetInt(0);
        scr.ScoreDate = cursor.GetString(1);
        scr.ScoreNumber = cursor.GetInt(2);
        scr.Rating = cursor.GetDouble(3);
        scr.Slope = cursor.GetInt(4);
        return (scr);
    }
}
```

This code is contained in SQLiteAndroidSpecific\SQLiteAndroidSpecific\dbCommands.cs

The code items in Listing 5-6 show how to call into the SQLiteOpenHelper that was featured in Listing 5-5.

Storing Data Remotely

The options just described — and there are most likely others — both result in data being stored in the application. Neither takes into account what happens if the device is lost or damaged. From a business perspective, there may be a desire to keep potentially sensitive data from being stored on a device. To solve this problem, it is possible to store data remotely to the device. The next section focuses on the web services support necessary to store data remotely.

WORKING WITH REMOTE DATA

Applications no longer live as little islands of data. Everything is interconnected, or will be. The ability to connect with remote data is not only nice to have, but a requirement with today's applications. When I got my first cell phone, I often lost the signal or never got a signal. Those days are over. Signal connections are available all over the place now, making connecting to data services online a simple task.

Typically, the remote-data issue is seen as a problem that has been solved. This section looks at two primary ways to connect to data services over the Internet: SOAP and REST. Each operates over HTTP and port 80. Other mechanisms exist to interchange data, but this section looks at just these two.

Accessing Enterprise Services

Working with data is the lifeblood of any business. This data can be in a database, ERP application, accounting system, or any other potential data source. The question that developers must ask is, "How do we best get at our data?" Unfortunately, the answer to this question is "It depends." Some of the options that developers will have to consider are:

➤ Does my database have direct support within Mono for Android? SQL Server has direct support in Mono for Android. If the application is running over a private network, this is an option. Unfortunately, exposing a SQL Server database to the Internet is a security concern. As a result, making a direct connection to SQL Server is really only an option within a private network.

➤ With the release of .NET 1.0, Microsoft released support for SOAP Services through ASMX. Over the past few years WCF has become popular amongst .NET developers. Visual Studio has had great support for SOAP Services. Mono for Android uses this support for these SOAP Services. Unfortunately, SOAP has met resistance in the marketplace.

➤ Developers can set up a REST web service and make data available in the XML or JSON format. Mono for Android can call REST Services in this scenario. REST has the most support amongst devices. Unfortunately, REST requires the most work for developers.

As you can see, there are several issues that developers must navigate through when integrating Enterprise Services with Mono for Android. No one size fits all. As you build an application (and read the rest of this chapter), you must be aware of the options for building an application and must make choices as to what you will use.

One of the problems that I ran into when working on this section was creating examples of code with which I was familiar. My first thought was to create a series of examples using the `Twitter.com` *API. Unfortunately, it is based on REST, and there is no SOAP-based API. Therefore, Twitter has no ASMX or WCF native solution. I decided to use some simple web services to illustrate the issues. I found the ASMX web service example through* `w3schools.com`. *Unfortunately, getting WCF, REST, and JSON examples was much more problematic. For those, I will demonstrate the calls against a service that I use for my test Windows Azure application as well as an example from* `parasoft.com`. *Parasoft provides web service testing facilities. These calls are for example purposes only and the APIs may have changed after this content was written. Please use this as a general guide for web services options.*

A second problem when writing demos is to know what developers are using. After speaking with many other developers, I found a lot of new development being done with WCF. However, a large number of ASMX-based web services currently are used in production, so I decided that it was important to add a short section on ASMX-based web services.

Using SOAP

Simple Object Access Protocol (SOAP) is a mechanism to exchange information in the form of web services over computer networks. SOAP is highly reliant on XML and web standards. Due to this reliance, SOAP is a natural tool to easily allow different systems to communicate. For example, a Windows-based system can communicate with a UNIX or mainframe system over HTTP without requiring the heavy layer of access software that is normally associated with such communication. One of SOAP's big advantages is that developers are familiar with creating and using SOAP-based web services in Visual Studio. With .NET, ASMX-based and WCF-based web services support SOAP.

Working with ASMX Web Services

ASMX web services were the first mechanism in ASP.NET for building web services. ASMX shipped with .NET 1.0 in January 2002. They are still in wide usage today. Many applications have been developed with them and continue to work properly today. ASMX web services operate with the Web Services Description Language (WSDL) and SOAP. Consuming an ASMX web service with Mono for Android is similar in concept to consuming a WCF web service in Mono for Android.

 I do not have an ASMX web service handy to work with. Instead of creating one and potentially causing my own DDOS attack on one of my services with a sample application, I decided to use a simple web service that converts from Celsius to Fahrenheit and back; it is hosted by `w3schools.com`.

The next example looks at how to call an ASMX-based web service using Mono for Android. The steps are as follows:

1. Add a reference to the web service's WSDL within a project. You do this by right-clicking the project and adding the location of the URL, which is
`http://www.w3schools.com/WebServices/TempConvert.asmx`.

2. Now that the reference has been created for the code, it is possible to program against the web service's API. The code shows programming against the API exposed by the web service.

Now that this is set up, take a look at Listing 5-7.

Available for download on Wrox.com

LISTING 5-7: Calling ASMX web services

```
void btnCallASMX_Click(object sender, EventArgs e)
{
    com.w3schools.www.TempConvert tc = new com.w3schools.www.TempConvert();
    tc.CelsiusToFahrenheitCompleted += new
        com.w3schools.www.CelsiusToFahrenheitCompletedEventHandler(
          tc_CelsiusToFahrenheitCompleted);
    tc.CelsiusToFahrenheitAsync("27");
}
```

continues

LISTING 5-7 *(continued)*

```
void tc_CelsiusToFahrenheitCompleted(object sender,
    com.w3schools.www.CelsiusToFahrenheitCompletedEventArgs e)
{
    this.RunOnUiThread(() => tv.Text = gResult + e.Result);
}
```

This code is contained in WebServices\WebServices\Activity1.cs

Notice the following points in Listing 5-7:

➤ In the `OnCreate` method, a button is created to handle user interface operations along with the assignment of a `.Click` event handler.

➤ Within the event handler, a class representing the web service is created, and an asynchronous call is made. The calling sequence for an asynchronous web service call is to assign a `.MethodCompletedEventHandler` and then call the method's asynchronous proxy method.

➤ A final parameter that can be passed is a user state object that might be useful in the callback.

➤ The callback method, `tc_CelsiusToFahrenheitCompleted`, accepts the `CelsiusToFahrenheitCompletedEventArgs` parameter. This parameter is used to get the asynchronous state that was passed in as well as to get the output result.

➤ The final issue is how to return the value to the user interface so that the data can be available to the user. This is done through the `RunOnUIThread` method. `RunOnUIThread` must be used because the response from the web service is handled in a different thread from the main thread. To write to the user interface, the command must be written on the main thread.

Because the operation is performed asynchronously, the work is completed in a different thread. To write back to the UI, this must be performed on the main thread by calling the `RunOnUIThread` method.

The proxy is created by Visual Studio when using ASMX. The proxy is created for a project similar to that shown in Figure 5-1, which appears later in the chapter.

Working with Windows Communication Foundation (WCF)

This section explores WCF-based web services. WCF was released with .NET 3.5 and has evolved into .NET 4.0. It is an API designed to build service-oriented applications.

Manually Create Your Own Proxy

Visual Studio hides a number of the complexities of SOAP-based web services from developers. One of the complexities is the creation and generation of web service proxies. These proxies allow developers to generate and use these web services as if they were local libraries on a computer. Here are the steps to manually create an application proxy and then get things running:

1. Manually generate the runtime proxy. Silverlight version 3 ships with a utility to generate a proxy. This utility is available on a Windows system with Silverlight version 3 installed and is called by `C:\Program Files\Microsoft SDKs\Silverlight\v3.0\Tools\SlSvcUtil .exe/noConfig http://example.com/service.svc?wsdl`. The result is a proxy that can be used in a Mono for Android application. The resulting file can be imported into a Visual Studio or MonoDevelop project.

2. Add the generated proxy to your project.

3. Add references to `System.Runtime.Serialization`, `System.ServiceModel`, and `System.ServiceModel.Web` to your project.

4. Make requests against the service. The constructor for the method should use the `BasicHttpBinding` type and the endpoint address.

Listing 5-8 shows the Mono for Android code for calling a remote method hosted in WCF.

LISTING 5-8: Calling WCF asynchronously via manual proxy

```
void btnCallWSDLClient_Click(object sender, EventArgs e)
{
    try
    {
        WebServiceWSDLClient wsClient = new WebServiceWSDLClient(
            new BasicHttpBinding(),
                new EndpointAddress(
                "http://www.twtmstr.com/webservices/webservicewsdl.svc"));
        wsClient.LoginCompleted += new EventHandler<LoginCompletedEventArgs>(
            wsClient_LoginCompleted);
        wsClient.LoginAsync("MonoDroidBook", "MonoDroidIsGreat", "blah");
    }
    catch (System.Exception sysExc)
    {
        tv.Text = "Exception: " + sysExc.Message;
    }
}

void wsClient_LoginCompleted(object sender, LoginCompletedEventArgs e)
{
    this.RunOnUiThread(() => tv.Text = gResult + e.Result.ToString());
}
```

This code is contained in WebServices\WebServices\Activity1.cs

Note the following in Listing 5-8:

➤ On a simple button click event, code is called.

➤ The `AddNumberServiceClient` class is created. When the class is instantiated, `BasicHttpBinding` is passed as the binding, and `EndPointAddress` is created and passed with the URI to the WCF service.

➤ Because the WCF service is asynchronous, the completed event is set up. In this case, it calls a defined method; however, it could just as easily call a delegate.

➤ In the callback, the result is received through the event arguments that are passed in.

➤ The final step is to do something with the result. In this case, the code just displays data to the user. The result is that `InvokeOnMainThread` is called to put data back in the UI.

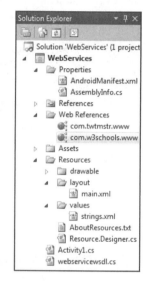

Although it would work to manually create a proxy and use it to call WSDL web services, just like in MonoTouch, Visual Studio provides the necessary infrastructure to create proxies and such. Adding a proxy and calling a WCF-based web service works as .NET developers would expect. As shown in Figure 5-1, the web references can be referenced and created. After the reference is created, Visual Studio creates the necessary proxies in the project and allows the Mono for Android project to call the web service. Let's look at calling an ASMX service. In Listing 5-9, the code calls a login method I have used for a service that is used for a personal project.

FIGURE 5-1

LISTING 5-9: Calling WCF synchronously via runtime proxy

```
void btnCallWSDL_Click(object sender, EventArgs e)
{
    com.twtmstr.www.WebServiceWSDL ws = new com.twtmstr.www.WebServiceWSDL();
    bool result, loginResult;
    ws.Login("MonoDroidBook", "MonoDroidIsGreat", "blah", out result,
        out loginResult);
    tv.Text = gResult + result.ToString();
}
```

This code is contained in WebServices\WebServices\Activity1.cs

This call is synchronous. An app running on a carrier's network has a number of unknowns, including the availability of the network in a particular location, signal strength within a building, and other factors that affect the signal's reliability at any moment in time.

Listing 5-10 is an asynchronous code sample running with the Parasoft web service.

LISTING 5-10: Calling WCF asynchronously via runtime proxy

```
void btnCallAsyncWSDL_Click(object sender, EventArgs e)
{
    com.parasoft.soatest.Calculator calc =
        new com.parasoft.soatest.Calculator();
    calc.addCompleted += new com.parasoft.soatest.addCompletedEventHandler(calc_
addCompleted);
    calc.addAsync(2.0f, 3.0f);
}

void calc_addCompleted(object sender, com.parasoft.soatest.addCompletedEventArgs e)
{
    RunOnUiThread(delegate
    {
        tv.Text = String.Format("result:{0}", e.Result);
    });
}
```

This code is contained in WebServices\WebServices\Activity1.cs

In this code, an asynchronous request is made to the WSDL service. The `LoginCompleted` event handler is created, and the `Login` method is called asynchronously.

Using REST-Based Web Services

REST (Representational State Transfer) is a general architecture for distributed systems, such as the World Wide Web. REST architectures are made up of clients and servers. Servers process requests that come from clients. Clients make requests against the servers. Conceptually, these requests are how web browsers (clients) work against web servers.

REST-based web services run over HTTP and implement a more readable (and simpler) interface than SOAP. With REST, there is no need for proxies or some of the other things that make SOAP somewhat complicated.

REST-based web services typically have these three features:

➤ Addressability of the resources. Some portion of the data is available over a URL.

➤ Data is sent over various HTTP verbs, such as GET, POST, PUT, and DELETE. The verbs typically are used as follows:

  ➤ In a GET operation, input data is sent over the URL. This is thought of as a request for data.

  ➤ In a POST operation, input data is sent in the body of the request. A POST is used to add/insert data.

➤ In a PUT operation, input data is sent in the body of the request. A PUT is used to update data.

➤ In a DELETE operation, all data is sent in the body of the request. A DELETE is used to delete data.

Some purists will argue the point, but there may be valid reasons to perform REST-style operations by using different HTTP verbs. In addition, some operating systems and devices do not support all the HTTP verbs. The examples here use the GET and POST verbs for operations.

➤ Data may be sent encoded in various formats, such as text, XML, JSON, and any other valid data type. Officially, this is referred to as the MIME type.

Using JavaScript Object Notation (JSON)

Most developers are familiar with eXtensible Markup Language (XML), which is used for data interchange. JSON is a similar technology; it is a data-interchange format based on the JavaScript scripting language. The JSON format uses a series of conventions that are familiar to most programmers who use the C family of languages. JSON is built on two concepts:

➤ Data is transmitted as a series of name-value pairs. The values may be a single value or a series of values, such as an array.

➤ Data is stored in a structure that can be thought of as a sequence.

Because these concepts are commonly accepted, they are available across nearly all modern programming languages. As a result, nearly all programming languages have some support for JSON. In .NET, Microsoft introduced support for JSON with the ASP.NET 2 AJAX library that shipped in 2007. Now programmers have various options for JSON in .NET thanks to System.Json, WCF, the popular JSON.NET library, and various other libraries.

Here is an example of a JSON data packet:

```
"ld":{
        "UserName":"tiger",
        "PassWord":"scott",
        "AppKey":"blah"
},
"TwitterId":"wbm",
"PageIndex":"1"
```

This example contains three parameters:

➤ ld: This object contains three properties:

➤ UserName has a value of tiger.

➤ PassWord has a value of scott.

➤ AppKey has a value of blah.

➤ TwitterId: This property has a value of wbm.

➤ PageIndex: The PageIndex property has a value of 1.

Now, take a look at a short example to call a REST-based web service (see Listing 5-11). This service is set up to accept JSON and a JSON response. This code sends a complex request to return the timeline of the user's Twitter friend. This request is set up for asynchronous request. Because the password is sent across the wire, a secure connection should be made, and the data should be sent over a post.

LISTING 5-11: Calling a REST service asynchronously with POST

```
void btnRESTJSON_Click(object sender, EventArgs e)
{
    string Url =
      "http://www.twtmstr.com/webservices/remoteapi.svc/GetUserTimeLine";
        string Url =
  "http://www.twtmstr.com/webservices/remoteapi.svc/GetUserTimeLine";
    System.Json.JsonObject ld = new System.Json.JsonObject()
    { { "UserName", "MonoDroidBookEx" },
        { "PassWord", "MonoDroidIsGreat" },
        { "AppKey", "blah" } };
    System.Json.JsonObject bd = new System.Json.JsonObject()
    { { "ld", ld },
        { "TwitterId", "monodroidbookex"},
        { "PageIndex", 1 }};
    string Body = bd.ToString();
byte[] byteData = System.Text.UTF8Encoding.UTF8.GetBytes(Body);
    try
    {
        // Create the web request
        HttpWebRequest request = WebRequest.Create(Url) as HttpWebRequest;
        request.ContentLength = Body.Length;

        // Set type to POST
        request.Method = "POST";
        request.ContentType = "application/json";

        // Write the parameters
        StreamWriter stOut = new StreamWriter(request.GetRequestStream(),
            System.Text.Encoding.ASCII);
        stOut.Write(Body);
        stOut.Close();

        request.BeginGetResponse(new
            AsyncCallback(ProcessRestJSONHttpResponse), request);
    }
    catch (WebException we)
    {
        tv.Text = we.Message;
        Android.Util.Log.E("http request", "Exception: " + we.Message);
        //System.Diagnostics.Debug.WriteLine("Exception: " + we.Message);
    }
```

continues

LISTING 5-11 *(continued)*

```
        catch (System.Exception sysExc)
        {
            tv.Text = sysExc.Message;
            Android.Util.Log.E("http request", "Exception: " + sysExc.Message);
        }
    }


//Note: A secure connection is not made in this example. A secure connection
//(https) should be made. However, due to time and complexity it is not set up on
//the server.

void ProcessRestJSONHttpResponse(IAsyncResult iar)
{
    try
    {
        HttpWebRequest request = (HttpWebRequest)iar.AsyncState;
        HttpWebResponse response;
        response = (HttpWebResponse)request.EndGetResponse(iar);
        System.IO.StreamReader strm = new System.IO.StreamReader(
            response.GetResponseStream());
        System.Json.JsonArray jsonArray = (System.Json.JsonArray)
            System.Json.JsonArray.Load(strm);
        List<Tweet> twt = new List<Tweet>();
        foreach (System.Json.JsonObject jsonTweet in jsonArray)
        {
            Tweet t = new Tweet();
            t.ProfileImage = jsonTweet["ProfileImage"].ToString();
            t.Status = jsonTweet["Status"].ToString();
            t.StatusDate = jsonTweet["StatusDate"];
            t.StatusId = Convert.ToInt64(jsonTweet["StatusId"].ToString());
            t.UserName = jsonTweet["UserName"].ToString();
            twt.Add(t);
        }
        this.RunOnUiThread(() => tv.Text = "Records returned: " +
            twt.Count.ToString());
        Android.Util.Log.D("http response", "finished");
    }
    catch (System.Exception sysExc)
    {
        Android.Util.Log.E("http response", "Exception: " + sysExc.Message);
        this.RunOnUiThread(() => tv.Text = "Exception: " + sysExc.Message);
    }
}
```

This code is contained in WebServices\WebServices\Activity1.cs

When the data is returned, the `System.Json` namespace is used. This namespace allows for the easy processing of JSON results. In this case, a `foreach` loop is used to process the results. In the `foreach` loop, a `Tweet` object is created and added to a list.

Listing 5-12 is slightly different. In this example, the asynchronous request is made through a POST to a JSON-based web service using REST.

LISTING 5-12: Calling a REST service via POST and returning JSON and using LINQ

```
void btnRESTJSONLINQ_Click(object sender, EventArgs e)
{
    string Url =
      "http://www.twtmstr.com/webservices/remoteapi.svc/GetUserTimeLine";
    string Url =
      "http://www.twtmstr.com/webservices/remoteapi.svc/GetUserTimeLine";
    System.Json.JsonObject ld = new System.Json.JsonObject()
    { { "UserName", "MonoDroidBookEx" },
        { "PassWord", "MonoDroidIsGreat" },
        { "AppKey", "blah" } };
    System.Json.JsonObject bd = new System.Json.JsonObject()
    { { "ld", ld },
        { "TwitterId", "monodroidbookex"},
        { "PageIndex", 1 }};
    string Body = bd.ToString();
    byte[] byteData = System.Text.UTF8Encoding.UTF8.GetBytes(Body);
    try
    {
        HttpWebRequest request = WebRequest.Create(Url) as HttpWebRequest;
        request.ContentLength = Body.Length;
        request.Method = "POST";
        request.ContentType = "application/json";
        // Write the parameters
        StreamWriter stOut = new StreamWriter(request.GetRequestStream(),
        System.Text.Encoding.ASCII);
        stOut.Write(Body);
        stOut.Close();
        request.BeginGetResponse(new
                AsyncCallback(ProcessRestJSONLINQHttpResponse), request);
    }
    catch (WebException we)
    {
        tv.Text = we.Message;
        Android.Util.Log.E("http request", "Exception: " + we.Message);
    }
    catch (System.Exception sysExc)
    {
        tv.Text = sysExc.Message;
        Android.Util.Log.E("http request", "Exception: " + sysExc.Message);
    }
}
```

This code is contained in WebServices\WebServices\Activity1.cs

In the callback shown in Listing 5-13, the JSON response is placed in a JsonArray object. The JsonArray object is then queried using Language Integrated Query (LINQ), and a list of type Tweet is created. This is conceptually the same as the `foreach` loop seen earlier, but the use of LINQ makes this potentially much more powerful.

LISTING 5-13: Handling HTTP response of JSON with LINQ

```
void ProcessRestJSONLINQHttpResponse(IAsyncResult iar)
{
    try
    {
        HttpWebRequest request = (HttpWebRequest)iar.AsyncState;
        HttpWebResponse response;
        response = (HttpWebResponse)request.EndGetResponse(iar);
        System.IO.StreamReader strm = new System.IO.StreamReader(
            response.GetResponseStream());
        System.Json.JsonArray jsonArray =
            (System.Json.JsonArray)System.Json.JsonArray.Load(strm);
        var twt = (from jsonTweet in jsonArray
                    select new Tweet
                    {
                        ProfileImage = jsonTweet["ProfileImage"].ToString(),
                        Status = jsonTweet["Status"].ToString(),
                        StatusDate = jsonTweet["StatusDate"],
                        StatusId = Convert.ToInt64(jsonTweet["StatusId"].
                                ToString()),
                        UserName = jsonTweet["UserName"].ToString()
                    }).ToList<Tweet>();
        this.RunOnUiThread(() => tv.Text = "Records returned: " +
            twt.Count.ToString());
        Android.Util.Log.D("http response", "finished");
    }
    catch (System.Exception sysExc)
    {
        Android.Util.Log.E("http response", "Exception: " + sysExc.Message);
        this.RunOnUiThread(() => tv.Text = "Exception: " + sysExc.Message);
    }
}
```

This code is contained in WebServices\WebServices\Activity1.cs

Posting Data with POST

Now that you have learned how to get data from a service, you need to take a closer look at how to post data to a service. In this example, you look at posting data to a service with JSON.

First, some background on the service: TwtMstr is a service that provides a number of enhancements to businesses that are using Twitter as part of their social media efforts. TwtMstr exposes a set of REST-based JSON web services that allow third-party applications to integrate with it. One of the features that TwtMstr provides is the ability to associate multiple Twitter ideas with a single TwtMstr ID.

Listing 5-12 shows some sample code that logs into the TwtMstr service and returns data from a user's timeline over JSON. Note the following in the code:

➤ You create the URL for calling this method. This is stored in the `Url` variable.

➤ The body of the method is created. Ideally, this would be done with a custom object that is serialized. The reason for showing it here is merely to display the content. The body is put into a byte array.

➤ An `HttpWebRequest` is created with several properties set. The key is the `Method` and the `ContentType`. The `Method` is set to `POST`, and the `ContentType` is set as a JSON data packet.

➤ Finally, `BeginGetResponse()` is called. This causes the web request to be made asynchronously.

➤ When the response returns, the method `ProcessRestJSONLINQHttpResponse()` is called. This method handles the callback event.

➤ The `ProcessRestJSONLINQHttpResponse()` method, shown in the code block, does nothing more than close the web request when it is finished.

RETRIEVING DATA USING LINQ AND XML

This section is an introduction to getting data in XML and using LINQ. In this example, we'll return data from Twitter using APIs. LINQ is a set of methods, operations, rules, and types that allow data to be queried within a .NET language such as Visual Basic or C#. LINQ initially shipped within the .NET 3.5 Framework, and LINQ support for several data providers exists within the Mono project.

LINQ to XML is a technology that allows XML documents to be converted into XElement objects, queried based on some criteria, and converted into a collection of objects. The queries are performed within the local execution engine. In Listing 5-14, an asynchronous request is performed against the Twitter API to return a specific user's timeline — my own in this case.

LISTING 5-14: GET Operation using XML and LINQ

Available for
download on
Wrox.com

```
void btnRESTXML_Click(object sender, EventArgs e)
{
    string Url =
"http://api.twitter.com/1/statuses/user_timeline.xml?screen_name=wbm";
    try
    {
        // Create the web request
        HttpWebRequest request = WebRequest.Create(Url) as HttpWebRequest;
        request.Method = "GET";
        request.ContentType = "application/xml";
        request.BeginGetResponse(new
            AsyncCallback(ProcessRestXmlLINQHttpResponse),
```

continues

LISTING 5-14 *(continued)*

```
                request);
        }
        catch (WebException we)
        {
            tv.Text = we.Message;
            Android.Util.Log.E("http request", "Exception: " + we.Message);
        }
        catch (System.Exception sysExc)
        {
            tv.Text = sysExc.Message;
            Android.Util.Log.E("http request", "Exception: " + sysExc.Message);
        }
    }

    void ProcessRestXmlLINQHttpResponse(IAsyncResult iar)
    {
        try
        {
            HttpWebRequest request = (HttpWebRequest)iar.AsyncState;
            HttpWebResponse response;
            response = (HttpWebResponse)request.EndGetResponse(iar);
            System.IO.StreamReader strm = new System.IO.StreamReader(
                response.GetResponseStream());
            //string responseString = strm.ReadToEnd();
            System.Xml.Linq.XDocument xd = XDocument.Load(strm);
            var twt = (from x in xd.Root.Descendants("status") where x != null
                        select new Tweet
                        {
                            StatusId = Convert.ToInt64(x.Element("id").Value),
                            UserName = x.Element("user").
                                Element("screen_name").Value,
                            ProfileImage = x.Element("user").
                                Element("profile_image_url").Value,
                            Status = x.Element("text").Value,
                            StatusDate = x.Element("created_at").Value
                        }).ToList<Tweet>();
            Response.Close();
            this.RunOnUiThread(() => tv.Text = "records: " + twt.Count.ToString());
            Android.Util.Log.D("http response", "finished");
        }
        catch (System.Exception sysExc)
        {
            Android.Util.Log.E("http response", "Exception: " + sysExc.Message);
            this.RunOnUiThread(() => tv.Text = "Exception: " + sysExc.Message);
        }
    }
```

This code is contained in WebServices\WebServices\Activity1.cs

In this example, a query is made against the Twitter API to get a user's timeline. The programmatic steps are as follows:

1. An asynchronous request is made against the Twitter API to obtain a user's timeline.

2. When the data is returned, it is loaded into an XDocument from the response stream.

3. A query is formed against the XDocument. When the query is executed, the data is converted from an XML format into a collection of objects.

4. LINQ queries are executed when the results are enumerated. The `.ToList()` method is called to cause the data to be retrieved. `.ToList()` is unnecessary and is used to return the data to the application.

You may have noticed that the code makes a request asynchronously. There is one negative to performing synchronous operations. Performing a synchronous operation over a wireless network may not be a reliable mechanism. If the connection is unreliable, the application may freeze for more than Android's self-imposed time limit. The result would be that Android would detect the timeout and close the application. The easiest way around this issue is to perform the operation asynchronously. Therefore, this and most of the examples are performed using asynchronous operations.

Using Asynchronous Data Retrieval

Performing an asynchronous call to a REST-based web service is possible. Although Android is limited in its ability to multitask third-party applications, it is possible to make asynchronous calls through Mono for Android. Calling a REST-based web service asynchronously is an easy way to get around Android's time limit spent in an application executing code. Another positive is that this is done through the exact same API as in .NET. Most developers probably are familiar with the .NET asynchronous programming methodologies of calling Begin*XXX*/End*XXX*.

In Listing 5-14, the code makes asynchronous requests against the API hosted on the `twitter.com` domain.

Here are the specifics of this code:

1. A URL to call is set up. This URL is to a REST-based XML service. This method returns a set of user statuses and has ID information, images, and similar information that can be extracted from the XML that is returned.

2. The HTTP request is set up as the XML MIME type.

3. The HTTP request is made asynchronously. A callback is set up so that when data returns from the web service, a method is called to handle the returned data.

4. The `ProcessRestXmlLINQHttpResponse` method takes the result that is returned from the web service.

5. Within the `ProcessRestXmlLINQHttpResponse` callback method (Listing 5-14) are two things to note:

> ➤ XML serialization into a LIST of objects is performed using LINQ.

> ➤ It is important to close `HttpWebResponse` after data has been retrieved.

Now that the callback has been processed, you have a set of objects you can work with. Although this code just outputs to the Mono debugger that a set of objects has been returned, it is possible to save the data in another format, such as SQLite, present it to the user, or process it in any number of ways.

USING WEB SERVICES RESPONSIBLY

Now that you have learned how to use web services in various forms in Mono for Android, let's look at some issues. Web services are great tools for the following tasks:

> ➤ Building apps that run over the Internet. Because they run over port 80, there is a very small chance that the communication will be blocked.

> ➤ Keeping information centralized.

> ➤ Easily allowing disparate systems to communicate.

At the same time, web services over wireless have some drawbacks:

> ➤ Web services tend to be slow. Sending information over a textual format, such as JSON or XML, can be slower than sending the same information over a binary/compressed protocol.

> ➤ Wireless communications tend to be unreliable.

> ➤ Sending data over numerous networks, which the Internet is, tends to be unreliable.

As a result, it is important to remember to use web services in a responsible manner:

> ➤ Be efficient with the amount of data that is sent to the web service and sent back to Android. There is no reason to overburden Android or the connection to the web service.

> ➤ Android waits for 20 seconds for user code to finish executing. After 20 seconds, the code that is being executed terminates. As a result, it makes sense to call web services asynchronously or in another thread.

WORKING WITH REMOTE SQL SERVER DATABASES

Companies live on data. Many corporations keep their data in private databases that are stored behind a corporate firewall. The last thing companies want is for their internal data to appear on mobile devices or to be exposed on the Internet in the form of some type of web service. The problem may be that they have security concerns or don't know how to securely expose their data over web services. Therefore, let's look at getting at data in a different way.

Many applications are internal to a business and are called "line of business" applications. These applications typically are unexciting and aren't sold in the Android Market, but they are important to an organization's day-to-day operations.

The data that powers these applications is not exposed to the outside world. It is available only behind the corporate firewall. This data might be customer information, a bill of materials for a set of products in a manufacturing environment, or hotel lodging information. This is information that doesn't necessarily make sense to expose to the general public but is important to a business. For developers in the .NET space, this information is stored in a database such as SQL Server, Oracle, MySQL, or another server-based database.

Thankfully, Mono for Android contains the `Mono.Data.Tds.dll` assembly. This assembly and associated namespace support communicating with databases through the tabular data stream protocol. This means that you can connect from a Mono for Android application to a SQL Server database. This communication is done directly over the Tabular Data Stream (TDS) application layer protocol. This database includes support for connection, command, data adapter, and data set objects that .NET developers are familiar with.

Listing 5-15 shows some sample code making a query against a SQL Server database that is available to an Android device.

Available for download on Wrox.com

LISTING 5-15: Performing SqlClient commands

```
System.Data.SqlClient.SqlConnection sqlCn =
        new System.Data.SqlClient.SqlConnection();
System.Data.SqlClient.SqlCommand sqlCm =
        new System.Data.SqlClient.SqlCommand();
System.Data.SqlClient.SqlDataAdapter sqlDa =
        new System.Data.SqlClient.SqlDataAdapter();
DataTable dt = new DataTable();
string strSql = "select * from table";
string strCn = "...........";
sqlCn.ConnectionString = strCn;
sqlCm.CommandText = strSql;
sqlCm.CommandType = CommandType.Text;
sqlCm.Connection = sqlCn;
sqlDa.SelectCommand = sqlCm;
try
{
    sqlDa.Fill(dt);
    tv.Text = "Records returned: " + dt.Rows.Count.ToString();
}
catch (System.Exception sysExc)
{
    Console.WriteLine("Exc: " + sysExc.Message);
    tv.Text = "Exc: " + sysExc.Message;
}
finally
{
    if (sqlCn.State != ConnectionState.Closed)
    {
        sqlCn.Close();
    }
    sqlCn.Dispose();
    sqlCm.Dispose();
```

continues

LISTING 5-15 *(continued)*

```
        sqlDa.Dispose();
    }
}
```

This code is contained in \InternalNetworkData\InternalNetworkDataActivity1.cs

Figure 5-2 shows some output from a database query.

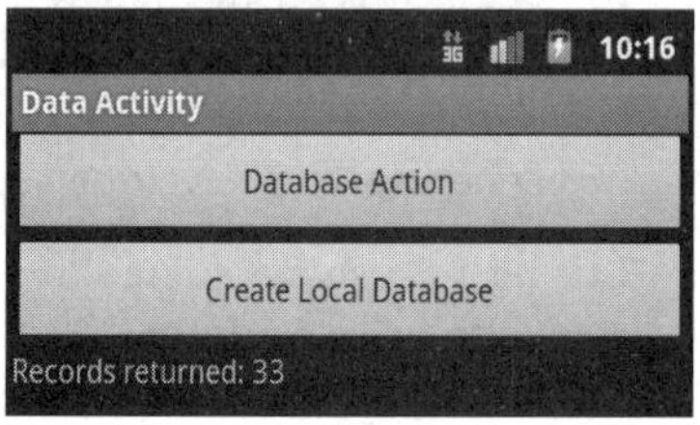

You should be aware of several important points with Mono TDS support:

➤ Currently, support for the TDS protocol from Mono for Android is experimental. Do not depend on it for too many advanced features.

➤ Mono TDS support works only across the ports it is allowed to work across. If a necessary port is blocked, the connection will not work properly. While this is most likely not a concern over a corporate intranet, this is a major concern over the public Internet, where ports may be blocked by a service provider.

➤ Very few Android devices have wired network ports. They typically communicate over Wi-Fi and mobile (3G/4G) networks. Opening up ports to work with SQL Server opens up attack surfaces. Unless taken with great caution and foresight into the issues that will come up, this opening of ports is generally frowned upon by corporate IT and security groups.

➤ Opening up ports beyond the standard HTTP (80), HTTPS (443), and VPN ports is generally a bad practice.

FIGURE 5-2

SUMMARY

This chapter looked at data strategies on Android. By using these technologies, developers can build native applications that run when a network connection is unavailable. You've learned how to do the following:

➤ Set up a local database in SQLite on Android

➤ Run commands against the SQLite database on Android

➤ Work with SOAP-based web services on Android

➤ Work with REST-based web services on Android

When they add the ability to call web services, Android developers and their applications can integrate with central data stores. This allows an application's users to interact with other users. For example, Twitter users can use Android to interact with other Twitter users without ever having to go to Twitter.com. Using Android, you can create applications that provide more features for users and that are more resistant to problems when connecting to the Internet and its data sources.

Binding Data to Controls

So far we have covered the basic components and processes involved in creating an Android/ Mono for Android application. We started with views and application life cycle events and then rounded out the tour of features by covering the different ways to access data. Now we can begin focusing on different ways to support interaction between these items to build feature-rich applications.

This chapter concentrates on utilizing the basic Android components to build data-driven interfaces for your app. The process of coupling a data set to a user interface is often called *databinding* or simply *binding*. Although the Android databinding mechanism differs a bit from other approaches (particularly those of ASP.NET), the Android platform has an elegant and simple way to quickly push rich data to a visual interface.

In addition to covering the basic concepts of the Android databinding story, we will walk through several different databinding scenarios. This is a common activity in any application, so we hope to provide a diverse exposure to the different tools that Mono for Android affords to help you develop your application. As with any programming language, there are many different ways to accomplish the databinding goal. Thus, this chapter will show not only what can be achieved, but also, given the many options, what method would work best for a given scenario.

This chapter assumes that you have a basic working knowledge of Android presentation mechanisms such as views, viewgroups, and layouts. In addition, this chapter uses different data sources, such as varying content providers. Since this chapter focuses on binding data, we will not spend much time reviewing how that data was generated. For more information on those subjects, refer to previous chapters, such as Chapter 5, or leverage the code downloads for this chapter to interact with the data-querying portions of the code examples.

 The term databinding *often has different connotations, depending on the environment in which you are working. It sometimes implies a tight integration between the UI and the data source, known as two-way binding. In this case, we are using the generic definition of databinding, which is simply a one-way binding of data to the UI.*

DATABINDING IN MONO FOR ANDROID

The databinding story in Mono for Android is actually quite simple. Databinding is achieved primarily through the use of three different components:

➤ **A basic view:** This view acts as the binding target, whose main responsibility is to carry the user interface layout for a single data entity within the data collection being bound. This will be the view that is repeated several times as the entire layout is generated.

➤ **Data adapter:** This serves as the control for managing the bridge between a data set and the adapter view. The data adapter accomplishes this by controlling the generation of the basic data item views for each entity within the data set.

➤ **Adapter view:** This is a type of viewgroup that supports the dynamic generation of child views for each data item contained within the bound data set. This view works like any other viewgroup in that it controls the layout and flow of the child controls. However, unlike a viewgroup, you cannot add or remove views directly.

If you're familiar with other databinding patterns, such as those in .NET, you might find this pattern to be overly complex, because the data adapter introduces a new layer of complexity. However, as you will see later, this additional complexity offers some great features that not only make your life easier, but also make your applications more stable.

What Is a Data Adapter?

As just stated, a data adapter is the channel by which data is bound and passed to the user interface controls. You can consider them the "man in the middle" for the databinding operation. The core function of a data adapter is to grab a requested data entity, bind it to the appropriate view item, and pass that view to the adapter view. In addition to this basic understanding, several other key facts about a data adapter are good to know:

> ➤ **Data adapters are responsible for generating the child views that belong within the context of the adapter view.** When you declare your data adapter, you need to pass in a reference to the view you want to use as your template for repeated items. The passed views can range from a large list of predefined Android views, controls such as buttons or images, or even a custom layout that you have defined yourself. It is up to the adapter to define the types of views it can support.

> ➤ **Data adapters are dynamic.** Rather than having to specify the number of items to display on the screen before binding, data adapters have a mechanism to allow the adapter view to determine how many elements it needs to fill its allocated space.

> ➤ **Data adapters can register observers to monitor your data for updates.** To handle cases in which bound data is changed after binding, you can register observers to monitor those changes and take appropriate action when the event occurs. Not all data adapters support this feature.

What Is an Adapter View?

An adapter view is a special type of viewgroup. As with other viewgroup types, its main purpose is to be a view that contains child views. As such, adapter views determine the presentation of the layout of its child views. In addition to this task, the adapter view plays a few other special roles in this relationship:

> ➤ **Adapter views control the number of items to display on the screen.** This is a key understanding. Whereas the adapter is in control of handing over databound views for the adapter to display, it is up to the adapter view to tell the adapter just how many views to generate. This aspect is critical in the databinding equation, because it allows for a wide variety of screen sizes and assists with memory management. We will cover this in more depth shortly.

> ➤ **Adapter views contain the events to respond to item selection as well as the mechanism to request the bound data entity.** When working with adapter views, you can easily build responsive layouts based on user interaction. In addition, it is a small matter to get access to the corresponding data item without having to go through extreme measures to find the original item.

> ➤ **Adapter views can support logic to animate their children.** When working with items such as a horizontal or vertical scrolling list, it is nice to be able to introduce smooth animations to improve the user experience. This handling is inherited from the `ViewGroup` class.

How Do These Items Relate to One Another?

Now that you have a basic understanding of the players in the databinding scenario, take a moment to understand how the databinding components interact with one another. Figure 6-1 shows the relationship between these three components.

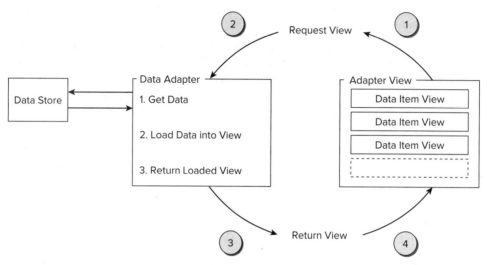

FIGURE 6-1

As you can see, the process of databinding begins with the adapter view. The view requests the next data item view from the data adapter. The data adapter, in turn, generates the appropriate view, using the bound data store to fill the appropriate data item view with data. Then the data adapter sends the data item view back to the adapter view to fill the next area in the window space.

This process continues iteratively until the visible area is filled with data item views. The adapter view is smart enough to detect when a view is no longer in the visible area and stops requesting new views from the data adapter.

Working with Adapter Views and Large Data Sets

When working with large data sets, developers are often hard pressed to find the perfect balance between managing the data set and providing a quick, responsive UI. Even simple, everyday screens, such as contact lists, browser bookmarks, and installed applications, can become cumbersome as the user begins adding more and more data to these items.

Imagine that you are creating a bookmark editor application. This bookmark editor uses the bookmarks data stored in the Android browser content provider. On load, the application needs to create a list of all the existing bookmarks. Once those initial items have loaded, the user may need to scroll down and up the list to view every possibility. Given your current understanding of how adapters work, you can make some assumptions about how your list view may work in this scenario. In particular, think about what will happen as the user begins to quickly scroll up and down this list. Figure 6-2 shows how this flow *could* work in Android.

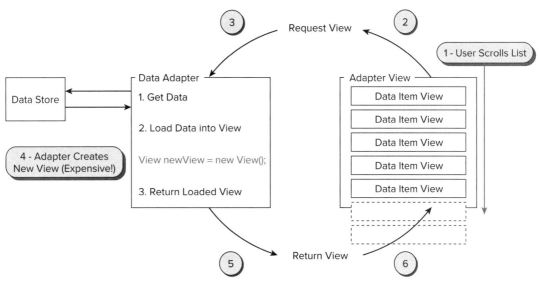

FIGURE 6-2

 This is not how the process works; it merely represents how you might assume the process would work. The key to this figure is to point out the flaw in this model.

As you can see from this example, the common assumption about how this application may work requires that a new view be created every time the user scrolls up or down the screen. This may be fine for a short list or a slow user, but what happens when you have 50 bookmarks? What about 100? What happens when the user quickly flicks the screen? Or when he or she quickly goes backward?

Additionally, with every move of the screen you are creating and destroying new views. The process of creating a view is one of the more expensive basic operations, particularly if you are inflating a custom layout.

Thankfully, this is not how the native Android adapters behave. When you create your own custom adapters, this is not how you should instruct those adapters to behave either. Rather than going through the process of creating a new view every time a user scrolls on the screen, why not recycle views that have scrolled off the screen and use them as the new view? Figure 6-3 depicts this model.

In this figure, the Android runtime uses something called *the recycler*. When you scroll down a list view, the biggest difference between one list item and the next is the data itself. Therefore, it makes little difference whether the data item view you are binding to is newly spun or one that you used previously, as long as you associate the appropriate data.

Native data adapters have the functionality to recycle view objects that pass out of a visible space. When they do so, the old view is "converted" into a new view by pushing in new data. This avoids the burden of having to create a new view object, which can *greatly* improve your adapter's performance!

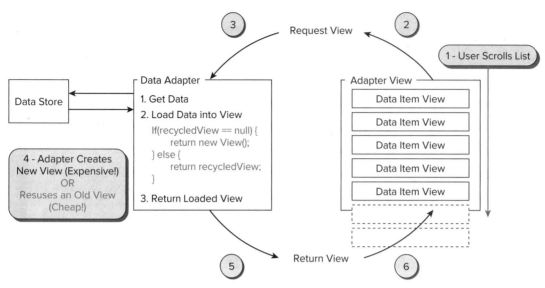

FIGURE 6-3

Want to test this functionality? You can do so easily. By overriding an adapter's `GetView()` *method, you can insert the logic to log times in which a view is recycled versus when it is created. In addition, you can even turn off recycling to gauge the difference in performance.*

The following code snippet contains the logic to log the recycling process of a list adapter:

```
    public int NewViewIter = 0;
public int RecycledViewIter = 0;

public override View GetView(int position, View convertView,
  ViewGroup parent)
{
    if (convertView == null)
    {
        NewViewIter++;
        Console.WriteLine(String.Format("New View #{0}",
          NewViewIter));

        var NewView = new View();
        // TODO:  Add implementation code here!
        return NewView;
    }
    else
    {
        RecycledViewIter++;
        Console.WriteLine(String.Format("Recycled View #{0}",
          RecycledViewIter));

        return (View)convertView;
    }
}
```

Exploring Adapters in Depth

At their core, adapters are pretty basic tools. Since they are essentially the middlemen between data sets and adapter views, most of their methods and functions pertain to that use. Functions such as `GetCount()`, `GetItem()`, and `IsEmpty()` are in place to ensure verbose communication channels.

Beyond these basic functions, adapters generally implement two other important functions/methods:

➤ `GetView()` is one of the most critical parts of the adapter. This method is called when the adapter view asks for the next view. In addition, this is where the adapter can decide whether to recycle a preexisting (but not visible) view object.

➤ `RegisterDataSetObserver()` allows your adapter to respond to times when the data set it is working with is either updated or invalidated.

Using Native Adapters

Because adapters play such an integral role in the databinding story, you will find occasion to use them in many different contexts. Although you have the option of rolling your own custom adapter, the Android runtime has several native adapters that cover a wide variety of different use cases. Table 6-1 describes many of the native adapters.

TABLE 6-1: Native Android Adapters

ADAPTER	DESCRIPTION
Base adapter	This is the adapter's common abstract class. It provides the framework for some native adapters, such as `ListAdapter` and `SpinnerAdapter`. In addition, this is a great place to start when considering creating your own custom adapter.
Simple adapter	The purpose of this adapter is to allow for easy binding between a static map of data and a view defined in an XML file. You should consider using this when you need to bind complex data objects to a view or data of any kind to a complex data item view.
Array adapter (generic)	This adapter can be used to bind an array of objects to `ListView`. Typically, the data item view involved in this relationship is a simple text view. However, you can use more complex views as a data item by directly mapping values to target IDs within the complex view via a different constructor.
Cursor adapter	A cursor adapter has two different types, `CursorAdapter` and `SimpleCursorAdapter`. A cursor adapter is used to bridge data between a cursor and an adapter view such as the `ListView`. All items returned by a cursor are accessed through an ID field, which acts much like a primary key in a database. A `SimpleCursorAdapter` can be used to quickly map cursor columns to different view types, such as `TextView`s or even `ImageView`s. These adapters require fewer steps to bind to an adapter view but do not have the same amount of flexibility.

continues

TABLE 6-1 *(continued)*

ADAPTER	DESCRIPTION
Head view list adapter	This type of adapter can be used when you have a `ListView` that has not only data item views but also header and footer views. Rather than trying to manage a complex UI hierarchy when trying to group data visually, you can use this adapter to manage that for you on a simple `ListView`.
Resource cursor adapter	This is a simple adapter used to directly bind cursor data to XML layouts defined in your `Resource` directory.
Spinner adapter	This adapter is created to specifically handle the binding of data to a `Spinner`.
Wrapper list adapter	This is for times when you need nested `ListAdapters`. A `WrapperListAdapter` wraps another `ListAdapter` and contains the logic to call the inner adapter via its `GetWrappedAdapter()` method.

Exploring Adapter Views in Depth

Adapter views are interesting objects to work with. Although they act like a viewgroup in many ways, adapter views have a bit more intelligence built into them. One of their main roles is to let the adapter know when the adapter view needs another item in its list. The adapter implements a couple of functions to assist this process:

➤   `GetFirstVisiblePosition()`

➤   `GetLastVisiblePosition()`

These self-explanatory methods enable the adapter view to know when to communicate with the adapter. In particular, they are essential when you consider recycling views.

Even though the adapter view inherits from the `ViewGroup` class, it is important to note that it does not support many of the common `ViewGroup` methods. In particular, most methods of the `ViewGroup` class that add or remove child views from the adapter throw an `UnsupportedOperationException`. Typically, the best way to add a data item or view to the UI is to add it at the data set level, rather than at the `AdapterView`. In cases in which you need to introduce headers, footers, or line breaks, be sure to use the corresponding native adapters and views, rather than trying to inject additional list items to serve as headers on the `AdapterView` level.

Finally, the adapter view does have one other method to allow you to manipulate the view data items as they are presented. By using the `SetEmptyView()` method, you can specify a view to display in cases in which the bound adapter is empty. For instance, if you had an `AdapterView` that listed search results, this gives you the functionality to return a `No Results Found` message rather than a blank screen.

Using Native Adapter Views

As with adapters, the Android platform exposes several different native adapter views. Since the main purpose of adapter views is to define the layout of their child views, most of these different adapter views vary on that point alone. Table 6-2 lists the common adapter views and describes their purpose.

TABLE 6-2: Native Adapter Views

ADAPTER	DESCRIPTION
ListView	Aside from the Spinner, this is probably the most commonly used adapter view because it is one of the most versatile. This adapter view is meant to show items in a vertical or horizontal list.
Gallery	The purpose of this view is to display items in a center-focused, horizontal, scrolling list. As the name suggests, it is a great tool for showcasing lines of images or visual-based views.
GridView	You can consider this view a hybrid of the Gallery and the ListView in that it can contain repeating items both horizontally and vertically.
Spinner	This is a special kind of view, created to mimic the common drop-down list or selection box. Although the spinner has some limitations, it's a great way to provide the user with a set of choices from which they can choose with ease.

WORKING WITH CURSORS

When working with content providers or anything that uses a SQLite storage system, you need to work with cursors. In Mono for Android, the cursor object is represented by the ICursor interface, which exposes all the methods necessary to work through the resulting data set. This is a direct adaptation of the Cursor interface found in the Android platform.

Cursors provide access to query results while providing many different ways to access them. Data is accessed from a cursor by moving the cursor to the appropriate position and then requesting a data type from the appropriate column index. The process of handling cursors has been covered in Chapter 3, but it is important to note that cursors should be treated as a sensitive resource. They should be closed when no longer in use or tied to the activity's life cycle via the activity's ManagedQuery() method.

The following examples explore the use of cursors when binding to two different types of adapter views.

Using a Cursor to Populate a Spinner

This next example looks at the process of binding a cursor to a simple spinner. Although this is a pretty cut-and-dried example, it is important to have a good foundational understanding of working with the ICursor interface. At the time of this writing, documentation for both the spinner and the Cursor in Android (or ICursor in Mono for Android) is not stellar. Hopefully this section can either enhance or plug existing gaps in the documented functionality.

Say that you are tasked with creating an application that allows the user to view all the current bookmarks on his device. This application simply has to list all the user's bookmarks and allow him to select one from the list. After thinking over this task, you decide to attempt the following steps to get your application working:

1. **Use the browser content provider to query for bookmarks.** This content provider allows you to access the device's browser settings, such as history and bookmarks.

2. **Add a `Spinner` control to your activity to list the device's bookmarks.** You do this by linking the browser query data to the `Spinner` control via a `SpinnerAdapter`.

Setting Up the Spinner and Data Source

You can set this process up by completing the following steps:

1. Create a new Mono for Android project called SpinnerExample. Within that, rename the label for the default activity Spinner Example. Also, it would be a good idea to rename the class `SpinnerExample`, rather than the generic `Activity1`.

2. Next, add the markup for the `Spinner` control in the `Main` layout. Within the `Layout` directory, open the `Main.axml` file and add the markup for a `Spinner` control. You may want to add a `TextView` describing the use of your `Spinner` control as well. Listing 6-1 shows what your `Main.axml` file should resemble.

LISTING 6-1: Adding a spinner to the Main.axml layout

```xml
<?xml version="1.0" encoding="utf-8"?>
<LinearLayout xmlns:android="http://schemas.android.com/apk/res/android"
        android:orientation="vertical"
        android:layout_width="fill_parent"
        android:layout_height="fill_parent">

    <TextView android:id="@+id/tvHeading"
        android:layout_width="fill_parent"
        android:layout_height="wrap_content"
        android:text="Welcome to the Spinner Example! Please select a
        bookmark!" />

    <Spinner android:id="@+id/spinner"
        android:layout_width="fill_parent"
        android:layout_height="wrap_content" />

</LinearLayout>
```

Databinding_SpinnerCursor\Databinding_Cursor\Resources\Layout\Resources\Layout\Main.axml

3. With that in place, open the default activity class you just renamed `SpinnerExample`. Within this class, add a method called `CreateSpinner()`. In this method, you will implement the actions necessary to databind your `Spinner`. For the time being, leave the contents of that method empty. You will focus on adding the appropriate logic after you finish setting up the project.

4. Now, add a call to your newly created `CreateSpinner()` method in the activity's `OnCreate()` event. When you are done, your additions should look like Listing 6-2. As you

can see, this is set up so that the spinner is created and databound as soon as the Activity's
OnCreate() event fires.

LISTING 6-2: Setting up the spinner create method

```
protected override void OnCreate(Bundle bundle)
{
    base.OnCreate(bundle);
    SetContentView(Resource.Layout.Main);

    CreateSpinner();
}

public void CreateSpinner()
{
    //TODO:  Add implementation code...
}
```

Databinding_SpinnerCursor\Databinding_Cursor\SpinnerSample.cs

5. With that in place, begin setting up the data source from which the application will
query. In this case, create a property called BookmarkCursor. This property will be used
to lazy-load the ICursor object upon request. As for the actual query, create a function called GetBookmarkCursor(), and set it to return an ICursor object. Within this
method, add the appropriate logic to acquire a cursor object filled with the browser's
bookmarks.

6. Finally, within the Get method of your property, check for a null value. If one is found, call
the GetBookmarkCursor() function, setting the private _BookmarkCursor in the process.
Listing 6-3 exemplifies this setup.

LISTING 6-3: Setting up the browser bookmark cursor

```
private ICursor _BookmarkCursor;
public ICursor BookmarkCursor
{
    get {
        if (_BookmarkCursor == null)
        {
            _BookmarkCursor = GetBookmarkCursor();
        }
        return _BookmarkCursor;
    }
    set { _BookmarkCursor = value; }
}

public ICursor GetBookmarkCursor()
{
    return ManagedQuery(Browser.BookmarksUri,
```

continues

LISTING 6-3 *(continued)*

```
        new String[] { Browser.BookmarkColumns.Title, Browser.BookmarkColumns
          .Url, Browser.BookmarkColumns.InterfaceConstants.ID },
        null, null, null);
    }
}
```

Databinding_SpinnerCursor\Databinding_Cursor\SpinnerSample.cs

Within the `GetBookmarkCursor()` method, the query for requesting the browser bookmarks has been added. Since using content providers was covered in Chapter 3, we will not go into too much depth here. But it is important to note that you are requesting all bookmarks from the device and placing their `Url`, `ID`, and `Title` attributes into the `String` projection. With this in place, the `BookmarkCursor` property enables access for the `ICursor` object at any point within the activity.

Finally, one last step is needed before you can begin using the `ICursor` object. To query from the browser content provider, you need to add the appropriate `uses-permission` node to the Android manifest. This can be accomplished easily by using the Visual Studio tooling:

1. Right-click the project within the Solution Explorer and select Properties.

2. Select the Android Manifest tab, as shown in Figure 6-4.

3. In the Required permissions box, check the READ_HISTORY_BOOKMARKS permission.

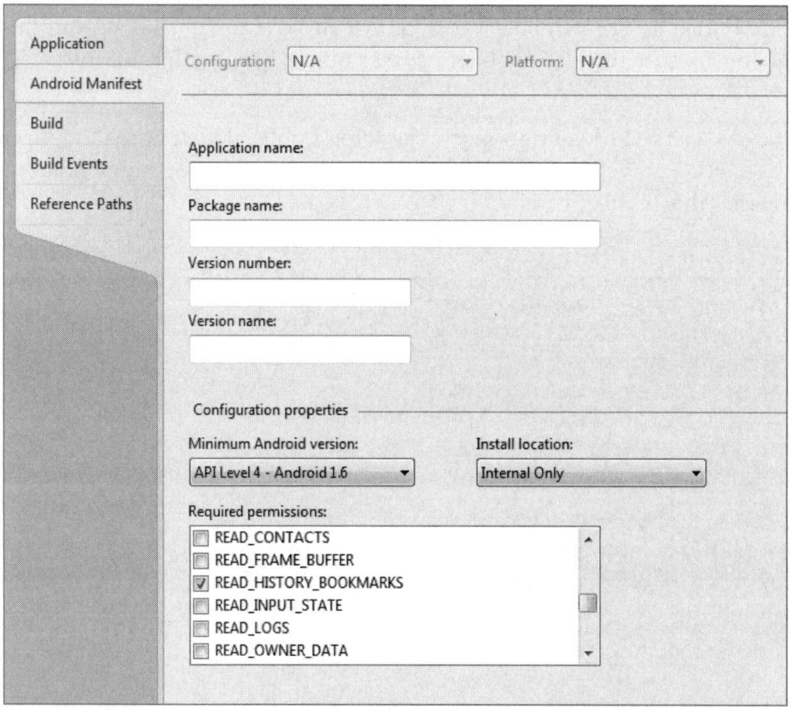

FIGURE 6-4

Using a Spinner Adapter

With the project properly set up and the data source ready for use, the CreateSpinner() method can be implemented. This particular project has quite a few different objects working within it, but they can be broken into three main parts:

➤ **The target spinner** is accomplished using the FindViewByID() method. It is a reference to the Spinner control added to the Main.axml file earlier in this section.

➤ **An instance of a SpinnerCursorAdapter** acts as the bridge between the target spinner and our cursor.

➤ **A data item view to repeat within the spinner** comes from one of the default layouts defined in the Android platform.

Using these three items, we can write the code necessary to bind our spinner, as shown in Listing 6-4.

LISTING 6-4: Implementing the CreateSpinner() method

```
public void CreateSpinner()
{
    var targetSpinner = FindViewById<Spinner>(Resource.Id.spinner);
    SimpleCursorAdapter SpinnerAdapter = new SimpleCursorAdapter(
        this,
        Android.Resource.Layout.SimpleSpinnerItem,
        BookmarkCursor,
        new string[] { Browser.BookmarkColumns.Title },
        new int[] { Android.Resource.Id.Text1 });

    SpinnerAdapter.SetDropDownViewResource(
        Android.Resource.Layout.SimpleSpinnerDropDownItem);
    targetSpinner.Adapter = SpinnerAdapter;
    targetSpinner.Prompt = "Select...";
}
```

Databinding_SpinnerCursor\Databinding_Cursor\SpinnerSample.cs

In this example, we acquire a reference to the Spinner control via the targetSpinner object. Using a new instance of a SimpleCursorAdapter, the BookmarkCursor object is bound to the adapter. In particular, a default Android view, Android.Resource.Layout.SimpleSpinnerItem, is used as a data item view. To databind the Title column in the BookmarkCursor to the data item view, use its child control with an ID of Text1.

Finally, we can set the target resource to use for the spinner's drop-down view. After we set the spinner's adapter equal to a reference to our newly created SpinnerAdapter, the databinding process is complete.

While looking at this example, you may wonder how we knew to bind the data value to the Android.Resource.Id.Text1 *control. When using the default Android views, you need to ascertain what child controls they contain, as well as what IDs those controls have within the Android documentation, to bind data to those controls.*

The Android.Resource.Id *namespace contains hints about what possible child controls may exist within the native layouts. Currently the process can involve a bit of trial and error, although many working examples utilize these default views.*

With all this code in place, launch the application with the debugger. Assuming that all goes well, you should see the screens shown in Figure 6-5.

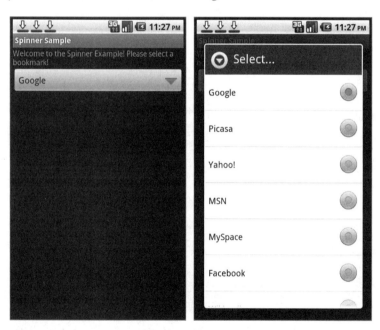

FIGURE 6-5

Adding a Listener Event for a Spinner

Suppose that, after getting your example up and running, you decide it would be handy to be able to click one of the listed bookmarks and open its URL in the Android browser. You can do this by using the spinner's ItemSelected event.

Spinners are great controls for many tasks, but they also make poor controls in some situations. Therefore, before we get into the code, two things need to be noted.

> ➤ Although they can be thought of as a drop-down list, spinners lack one of the major features of a drop-down list: *they do not have an unselected state.* Whenever a spinner is bound, it

automatically selects the first item in the binding collection. Not only does this mean that a spinner always displays a selection, but it also means that the first item in a spinner list cannot trigger the ItemSelected event when the spinner is first loaded, because it is already selected. This assumes that you did not manually change the selected index.

➤ This brings us to another large drawback of spinners. Since the first item is always selected when bound, the spinner calls the ItemSelected event before the view is presented to the user. Whatever events you set up in the ItemSelected event trigger before your activity view ever makes it to the user.

In this example, this means that the application would launch, the spinner would be bound, and then the Android browser would be launched with the URL of the first item in the list. Rather than seeing the activity, the user sees a browser window. This is a known behavior of the spinner and can be frustrating to deal with. In order to work around this issue, we will use a local variable to track the spinner's state and determine whether we want to launch our event.

After reading about the drawbacks of using spinners, you might question whether a spinner is the ideal control for the task we want to accomplish. This is a valid concern.

Typically, spinners are not a good tool to use when you need to respond to click events on an item list that does not have a preset value. In these cases, ListViews and other adapter views are much better tools.

For the sake of demonstration, however, we are extending our spinner example to handle this kind of scenario even though it is not quite the superior approach to this problem. When choosing an adapter view for a project, it is always a good idea to consider the drawbacks of every option to limit surprises that views such as a spinner may cause.

Adding a listener event for the spinner requires several steps.

1. First, create a local variable to track the spinner state. To do this, add a private integer field called LastSpinnerSelectedPosition. At the beginning of the Create spinner method, set this variable's value to 0. This way, every time the Spinner control is re-created, the selected position always reflects the databound state.

2. Next, add an event handler to the targetSpinner within the CreateSpinner() method. Be sure to do this as the last step in the method. At this point, your code should closely resemble Listing 6-5.

LISTING 6-5: Adding an ItemSelected event to the CreateSpinner() method

```
int LastSpinnerSelectedPosition;

public void CreateSpinner()
{
    // Since the spinner is just being created, set this
```

continues

LISTING 6-5 *(continued)*

```
        // tracking var to 0.
        LastSpinnerSelectedPosition = 0;

        // ...  targetSpinner binding logic as previously covered  ...

        targetSpinner.ItemSelected +=
            new EventHandler<ItemEventArgs>(SpinnerItemSelected);
    }
```

Databinding_SpinnerCursor\Databinding_Cursor\SpinnerSample.cs

3. Finally, add a method called `SpinnerItemSelected()` as the target event handler, accepting an object and `ItemEventArgs` as parameters. Within this method, we check to see if a new item has been selected. If it has, we get the URL for the target spinner item and launch a new activity to bring up the browser window. This is accomplished in Listing 6-6.

LISTING 6-6: Implementing the ItemSelected() event

```
public void SpinnerItemSelected(object sender, ItemEventArgs e)
{
        var CurrentSpinner = ((Spinner)sender);
        var CurrentSelectedIndex = CurrentSpinner.SelectedItemPosition;

        if (CurrentSelectedIndex != LastSpinnerSelectedPosition)
        {
            // The Selected item in a spinner is actually the
            // underlying cursor object w/ the position set to the
            // appropriate index.  Cast to ICursor to access.
            ICursor selectedItem = (ICursor)CurrentSpinner.SelectedItem;

            var URLColumnIndex = selectedItem.GetColumnIndex(
                Browser.BookmarkColumns.Url);
            var URL = selectedItem.GetString(URLColumnIndex);

            // In order to open a new browser, we need to create the appropriate
            // intent and then start a new activity using that intent.
            Intent BrowserIntent = new Intent(Intent.ActionView);
            BrowserIntent.SetData(Android.Net.Uri.Parse(URL));

            StartActivity(BrowserIntent);

            LastSpinnerSelectedPosition = CurrentSelectedIndex;
        }
    }
```

Databinding_SpinnerCursor\Databinding_Cursor\SpinnerSample.cs

Within this method, initially check to make sure that the spinner state is not the same as was initially set. This keeps the `OnCreate()` method from launching the selected item event prematurely. Next, find the URL value of the selected spinner item by using the spinner's `SelectedItem` property. This item represents the position in the `BookmarkCursor` that corresponds to the selected item.

Finally, we create `BrowserIntent` and set its data to our target URL. This allows us to create a new activity, which opens our browser application to the correct URL. With this code in place, you should be able to open your spinner example and watch it work, as shown in Figure 6-6.

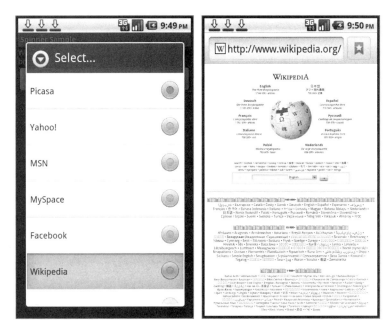

FIGURE 6-6

Using a Cursor with a Gallery

Now that you have seen a simple example of a cursor, you can look at an example that is a bit more complex. In this case, we create a `Gallery` view of images from an Android device. To accomplish this assignment, we will tackle the following tasks:

➤ **Use the media content provider to pull images from our device.** As you learned earlier in this book, media resources on Android can be universally accessed via this provider.

➤ **Add a Gallery view to the main activity, and bind our custom adapter to the Gallery.** This step doesn't vary much from the previous example because the Gallery view requires little setup.

➤ **Create a custom Image Adapter to handle the generation of Image Views.** Unlike the previous example, we won't simply rely on a predefined Android view to bind our images. By extending the `BaseAdapter` class, we have a bit more control over how we display our images.

Setting Up the Project

To get started, create a new Mono for Android project, renaming the activity label Gallery View Demo and also renaming the class `GalleryViewSample`. When this is done, set up the `Main` layout by adding a `Gallery` control. The markup for a `Gallery` control is straightforward, as shown in Listing 6-7.

LISTING 6-7: Adding a Gallery control to the Main.axml file

```xml
<?xml version="1.0" encoding="utf-8"?>
<LinearLayout xmlns:android="http://schemas.android.com/apk/res/android"
    android:orientation="vertical"
    android:layout_width="fill_parent"
    android:layout_height="fill_parent">

<TextView android:id="@+id/Welcome"
    android:layout_width="fill_parent"
    android:layout_height="wrap_content"
    android:text="Welcome to a Mono for Android Gallery"/>

<Gallery android:id="@+id/targetGallery"
    android:layout_width="fill_parent"
    android:layout_height="wrap_content"/>

</LinearLayout>
```

Databinding_GalleryView\Databinding_GalleryView\Resources\Layout\Main.axml

In this markup, the `Gallery` control has been added, giving it an ID of `targetGallery`. To add a little extra garnish to the layout, a `TextView` has been appended to describe the use of this control.

To set up the activity class to be used, a few methods need to be stubbed to prevent compile errors. These are as follows:

1. Within a new class file or just outside your activity class, create a new class called `ImageAdapter`. This `ImageAdapter` class needs to inherit from `BaseAdapter`. As discussed earlier in this chapter, `BaseAdapter` is an abstract class that contains many of the major tools you need to create a custom adapter.

2. Because `BaseAdapter` is abstract, several methods need to be implemented. You can add the appropriate methods by right-clicking the `BaseAdapter` class and choosing Implement Abstract Class. For the time being, do not worry about working with those generated methods. Once the activity class has been set up, our focus returns to those methods.

3. As a last step to set up the custom adapter, add a constructor that accepts a `Context` object as a parameter. Because this will be used throughout the custom adapter class, go ahead and make a field called `_Context` and assign its value to the parameter provided in the constructor of the class.

With everything in place, the skeleton of the `ImageAdapter` resembles Listing 6-8.

LISTING 6-8: Skeleton of the ImageAdapter class

```
public class ImageAdapter:BaseAdapter
{

    private Context _Context;

    public ImageAdapter(Context c)
    {
        _Context = c;
    }

    public override int  Count
    {
        get { throw new NotImplementedException(); }
    }

    public override Java.Lang.Object  GetItem(int position)
    {
        throw new NotImplementedException();
     }

    public override long  GetItemId(int position)
    {
        throw new NotImplementedException();
    }

    public override View  GetView(int position, View convertView,
    ViewGroup parent)
    {
        throw new NotImplementedException();
    }
}
```

Databinding_GalleryView\Databinding_GalleryView\GalleryViewSample.cs

This is all the information that needs to go into this class. When we begin implementing the adapter, we will work through setting up each method. Until then, the basic setup on our project can be completed by adding the logic to bind our new adapter to the Gallery control. Using the markup that was just added, set the adapter of the Gallery instance to the new instance of the ImageAdapter class, as shown in Listing 6-9.

LISTING 6-9: Setting the Gallery control's adapter to the ImageAdapter

```
[Activity(Label = "Gallery View Sample", MainLauncher = true)]
public class GalleryViewSample : Activity
{

    protected override void OnCreate(Bundle bundle)
    {
        base.OnCreate(bundle);
```

continues

LISTING 6-9 *(continued)*

```
        // Set our view from the "main" layout resource
        SetContentView(Resource.Layout.Main);
        CreateGallery();
    }

    private void CreateGallery()
    {
        Gallery g = FindViewById<Gallery>(Resource.Id.targetGallery);
        g.Adapter = new ImageAdapter (this);
    }
}
```

Databinding_GalleryView\Databinding_GalleryView\GalleryViewSample.cs

Unlike the spinner example, Listing 6-9 is a pretty cut-and-dried binding. To make the process of working with this Gallery a little easier down the road, the logic to create the Gallery has been broken out into a separate method, ingeniously named CreateGallery(). When creating a new instance of the ImageAdapter class, pass in a reference to the current activity by using the this keyword.

The project now is almost set up to begin focusing on your custom adapter. The one outstanding task is that you want to make sure that your target Android device actually has some images that the query can return. If you are using the emulator, you need to fire it up and download a few images. If you are using your own device in debug mode, you should have plenty of images already added.

To quickly find some images to add to your device for testing, go to Google image search (http://images.google.com). *Search for your favorite topic, and directly download the images from there. Any image downloaded in this fashion is automatically added to the media content provider. In order to continue with this example, it is important that you have at least a couple of images on your testing device. Otherwise the Gallery view will not function and will throw an exception.*

Adding the Cursor

With the framework of the project in place, we can begin focusing on fleshing out the ImageAdapter class. The main function of this class is to pass images from the Android device to the Gallery control. To do this, a data set needs to be generated by using a query against the media content provider. Once the data is in place, we use the acquired information to create new image views to pass to the Gallery upon request.

Because this project will interface with a content provider, the mode of getting data access will be via a `Cursor` object. Using a `Cursor` object was covered earlier in the chapter. The following steps outline the process of adding a cursor:

1. In the `ImageAdapter` class, create a private function called `GetImageCursor()`. This function handles the call to the media content provider and returns the type of `ICursor`.

2. To create an `ImageView`, use the cursor to get the ID of all the images on the Android device. Specifically, this example uses the image ID of the generated thumbnails of the images. Listing 6-10 provides an example of this process.

LISTING 6-10: Querying the media content provider

```
private ICursor GetImageCursor()
{
    string[] Projection = { MediaStore.Images.Thumbnails.ImageId };

    var ImageCursor = ((Activity)_Context).ManagedQuery(
        MediaStore.Images.Thumbnails.ExternalContentUri,
        Projection, null, null, null);

    return ImageCursor;
}
```

Databinding_GalleryView\Databinding_GalleryView\GalleryViewSample.cs

3. In this listing, a projection is created that contains the desired fields that need to be returned from the query. To make managing the cursor easier, use the `_Context` object to get an instance to the calling activity. After casting it back to an `Activity` type, this method will be able to utilize the `ManagedQuery()` function of the calling activity class, which allows the calling class to manage the life cycle of the `ICursor` object.

> *If you are querying from a physical Android device, you probably have many images on this device. To keep the return set to a manageable level, you may want to specify selection arguments in this query. Alternatively, you can force a limit in the* `GetView()` *method of this adapter after it is set up.*

4. With the cursor query in place, create a property within the `ImageAdapter` called `ImageCursor`. This will be used to manage the instance of the `ICursor` and will make it easier to leverage the cursor throughout the class. Since this is not something you would typically want to expose to the world, change the property protection level to `protected`. Listing 6-11 shows an example.

LISTING 6-11: Managing the ImageCursor instance

```
private ICursor _ImageCursor;
protected ICursor ImageCursor
{
    get {
        if (_ImageCursor == null)
        {
            _ImageCursor = GetImageCursor();
        }

        return _ImageCursor;
    }
    set { _ImageCursor = value; }
}
```

Databinding_GalleryView\Databinding_GalleryView\GalleryViewSample.cs

The `ImageAdapter` now has a complete data source that is lazy-loaded upon request. Now you can move on to the final steps of setting this adapter.

Completing the Custom Adapter

By inheriting from the `BaseAdapter` class, we have to override several methods to allow proper functionality of the adapter. Starting with the simplest methods, `Count()` and `GetItemId()`, let's begin supporting the binding operation.

1. As you might imagine, the `Count` class is used to return the total number of items within the cursor data set.

2. Next, the purpose of `GetItemId()` is to provide the actual ID of the data entity at the given index. Both of these methods can be supported by leveraging the `ImageAdapter` property that was just set up. Listing 6-12 demonstrates setting this up.

LISTING 6-12: Supporting the Count and GetItemID methods

```
public override int Count
{
    get { return ImageCursor.Count; }
}

public override long GetItemId(int position)
{
    ImageCursor.MoveToPosition(position);
    var ImageID = ImageCursor.GetString(0);

    return position;
}
```

Databinding_GalleryView\Databinding_GalleryView\GalleryViewSample.cs

You might have noticed that this example has a hard-coded index value at the following line:

```
ImageCursor.GetString(0);
```

This unwise setup is used so that the cursor returns only one field from the data source and for the sake of keeping the example simple. If needed, a more robust way to manage this would be to keep the right index for the right field value by creating a tracking field in the class. This is accomplished by using the cursor's GetColumnIndex() *function. In the case of this example, the code snippet looks like this:*

```
ImageCursor.GetColumnIndex(MediaStore.Images.Thumbnails.ImageId);
```

3. The next step is to set up the GetItem() function. For this one, either simply return null or return the same position integer that you were passed in the arguments. The purpose of this function is to allow the developer to call the GetItemAtPosition() function on the Gallery control. Currently we do not want to support this function.

It's up to you as the developer to decide what the GetItemAtPosition() *function will return. In some cases, this can be used to return the key to the appropriate entity on the data set. Other implementations actually return complex objects that contain the desired values. The use cases for each of these approaches depend on your needs and the type of data source you are using. Use your best judgment, and be sure to add appropriate documentation for this particular function.*

4. Finally, the GetView() function can be set up. As covered earlier in this chapter, this method needs to be able to either recycle previously populated views or create new views on demand. To do this, we can leverage the convertView variable and perform a null check. If the given view is null, generate a new ImageView based on the position integer that the Gallery provided. Otherwise, return the previously used view. Listing 6-13 does just this.

Available for download on Wrox.com

LISTING 6-13: The GetView function

```
public override View GetView(int position, View convertView, ViewGroup parent)
{
    if (convertView == null)
    {
        ImageView returnView = new ImageView(_Context);
        ImageCursor.MoveToPosition(position);

        var ImageID = ImageCursor.GetString(0);
```

continues

LISTING 6-13 *(continued)*

```
            returnView.SetImageURI(
                Android.Net.Uri.WithAppendedPath(
                    MediaStore.Images.Thumbnails.ExternalContentUri, ImageID));
            returnView.SetScaleType(ImageView.ScaleType.CenterCrop);
            return returnView;
        }
        else
        {
            return (ImageView)convertView;
        }
    }
}
```

Databinding_GalleryView\Databinding_GalleryView\GalleryViewSample.cs

Once your code is in place, the `Gallery` control should be ready for action. Launch the debugger and try it out. If all goes well, you should see a screen that looks like Figure 6-7.

FIGURE 6-7

WORKING WITH LISTS

Lists are an integral part of almost every modern mobile application. They provide a convenient way of displaying different types and amounts of data to users in a way that is easy to interact with.

Android's `ListView` is a row-based data display control, giving you ultimate flexibility over the data in each row and how it is displayed. You will also learn about the `GridView`, which is a row- and column-based data display control. It handles the layout of all the columns and rows.

On Android, `ListView` does a lot of the heavy lifting for you, including scrolling with inertia and displaying the appropriate rows at the right time. All you need to do is provide it with the layout and data for each row when asked. Android also handles different types of user interaction for you by raising events.

Lists are used throughout many Android applications. One of the most prominent uses is to display and edit user preferences. Other natural uses include RSS readers, Twitter clients, and media players. Figure 6-8 shows several different examples of applications using `ListView`, illustrating its power and flexibility.

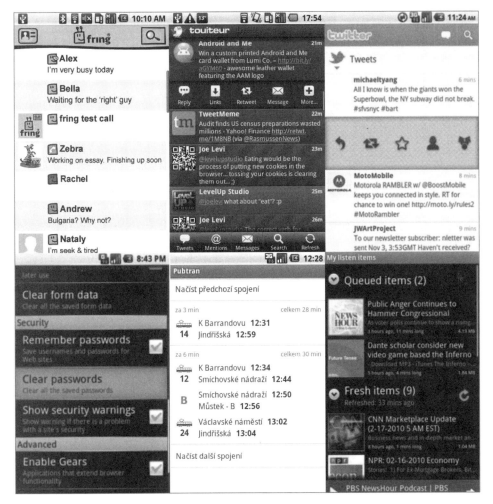

FIGURE 6-8

Displaying Simple Data in a List

In its simplest form, the main component required to display a list of data in Android is `ListActivity`. An `Activity` is a single focused screen that a user can work with, similar to an ASPX page or a WinForm. The `ListActivity` is a normal `Activity` that has a `ListView` filling the entire space of the

Activity's View, on the screen. It's a shortcut you can use if you don't want any other views displayed in the Activity. It doesn't require you to inflate a layout from an XML file or construct a layout programmatically. Of course, if you're so inclined, you can call SetContentView() in the OnCreate() override to inflate and use a custom layout which contains a ListView. Listing 6-14 shows what the layout XML file looks like for a ListActivity. This resource is contained within the Android framework.

LISTING 6-14: XML Layout resource

```xml
<?xml version="1.0" encoding="utf-8"?>
<LinearLayout
android:id="@+id/widget28"
android:layout_width="fill_parent"
android:layout_height="fill_parent"
android:orientation="vertical"
xmlns:android="http://schemas.android.com/apk/res/android"
>
    <ListView
    android:id="@+id/listView"
    android:layout_width="fill_parent"
    android:layout_height="fill_parent"
    >
    </ListView>
</LinearLayout>
```

Lists01\Resources\layout\ListActivity.axml

To create your first List, you should create a new activity and then change it to inherit from ListActivity instead of Activity. The base ListActivity automatically inflates the layout for you. Use the code sample shown in Listing 6-15 to implement these two key aspects of creating your first List:

➤ **Creating a data source to display:** This data can come from any source — the arrays.xml resource file, a hard-coded string array, a web service call, or a database.

➤ **Instantiating and assigning a list adapter to ListActivity's Adapter property:** This can be any type of list adapter — an ArrayAdapter, a SimpleAdapter, or a custom subclass of the BaseAdapter.

LISTING 6-15: Simple ListView with ListActivity

```csharp
using System;
using Android.App;
using Android.OS;
using Android.Widget;

namespace Lists01
{
    [Activity(MainLauncher = true, Label = "SimpleList",
            LaunchMode=Android.Content.PM.LaunchMode.SingleTask)]
    public class SimpleListActivity : ListActivity
```

```
{
    string[] items;

    protected override void OnCreate(Bundle bundle)
    {
        base.OnCreate(bundle);

        //Create a list of items to show
        items = new string[] {
            "Item One",
            "Second Item",
            "Number Three",
            "Fourth Option",
            "Fifth One",
            "Sixth Item",
            "Number Seven",
            "This is Eight",
            "Nine",
            "Ten Speed"
        };

        //Make an ArrayAdapter using the built in
        //SimpleListItem1 layout and our items array
        this.ListAdapter = new ArrayAdapter<string>(
            this,
            Android.Resource.Layout.SimpleListItem1,
            items);
    }
}
}
```

Lists01\SimpleListActivity.cs

You will notice that for the sample shown in Listing 6-15, the `Android.Resource.Layout.SimpleListItem1` layout is specified in the constructor of the `ArrayAdapter`. The list adapter is responsible for returning the view for each list item. This layout is another built-in Android resource. Listing 6-16 shows what the layout for `Android.Resource.Layout.SimpleListItem1` looks like.

LISTING 6-16: SimpleListItem1 source

```
<?xml version="1.0" encoding="utf-8"?>
<TextView xmlns:android="http://schemas.android.com/apk/res/android"
    android:id="@android:id/text1"
    android:layout_width="fill_parent"
    android:layout_height="wrap_content"
    android:textAppearance="?android:attr/textAppearanceLarge"
    android:gravity="center_vertical"
    android:paddingLeft="6dip"
    android:minHeight="?android:attr/listPreferredItemHeight"
/>
```

Lists01\Resources\layout\SimpleListItem1.axml

As you can see, the view for the `SimpleListItem1` is a simple, single `TextView` set to fill the width of the row, with a few other attributes set. It's not rocket science, but it is convenient not to have to produce that XML layout every time you want to display a simple list item with a single line of text.

A number of XML layouts come with Android. These layouts are included to provide a standardized look and feel across all applications. They also make your life as a developer a bit easier and keep you from constantly having to re-create the same XML layout files. Not surprisingly, a few layouts are specifically designed to be used with `ListView` items that come standard with Android (see Figure 6-9):

FIGURE 6-9

➤ `SimpleListItem1` is a `TextView` that displays one line of text.

➤ `SimpleListItem2` is a `TwoLineListItem` view with two `TextViews` (`Android.Resource. Id.Text1` and `Android.Resource.Id.Text2`) displayed one on top of the other in a Title/ Description configuration.

➤ `SimpleListItemChecked` is a single `TextView` with a check box on the right side of the list item.

➤ `SimpleListItemMultipleChoice` is a single `TextView` with a multiple-choice-style check box on the right side of the list item.

➤ `SimpleListItemSingleChoice` is a single `TextView` with a radio-button-style check box on the right side of the list item.

Working with Android's ListAdapters

Behind every great `ListView` is a great `ListAdapter`. The Android SDK provides some easy-to-use Adapters right out of the box.

`ArrayAdapter`, which derives from `BaseAdapter`, expects an enumerable set of strings, as well as a resource identifier for a layout and an optional field resource identifier. If only a resource identifier for the layout is provided, it must be that of a single `TextView` (such as `SimpleListItem1`).

You can specify a more complicated layout for your list item by using its resource identifier to indicate the parent view for each list item, as well as by specifying the identifier of the `TextView` field that is contained somewhere within that parent view. Either way, `ArrayAdapter` lets you pass in only a single array of values that get displayed in a `TextView` somewhere within the view of each list item. This is a great way to quickly display a collection of strings with little effort in a list form. You might consider using this method in conjunction with a LINQ query to get a list of names for all your objects to display. For example:

```
var adapter = new ArrayAdapter<string>(this,
Android.Resource.Layout.SimpleListItem1,
(from animal in this.Animals select animal.Name).ToArray());
```

The SimpleAdapter, shown in Listing 6-17, is a bit more advanced. It requires a List<T> of Dictionary<string, object>, where each Dictionary<string, object> represents a single list item. The Dictionary must contain a set of key/value pairs representing the various fields of data. The SimpleAdapter also requires a string[] array from, which is a list of fields in the Dictionary, and an int[] array to, which is a list of resource identifiers that correspond to the from array fields. The to and from arrays tell SimpleAdapter which fields from the Dictionary go in which views within the layout.

In Listing 6-17 the SimpleListItem2 that is built into the Android SDK is used. This is very similar to the SimpleListItem1 in Listing 6-16, except it has an additional TextView with an Id of Android.Resource.Id.Text2.

LISTING 6-17: SimpleAdapter usage

```
                              //Create our sample data
var items = new List<IDictionary<string, object>>();

var item1 = new Dictionary<string, object>();
item1.Add("simpleAdapterTitle", "First Title");
item1.Add("simpleAdapterDesc", "This is a Description");

var item2 = new Dictionary<string, object>();
item2.Add("simpleAdapterTitle", "Second Title");
item2.Add("simpleAdapterDesc", "Another Description");

items.Add(item1);
items.Add(item2);

//Create the Adapter from the sample data
var a = new SimpleAdapter(this,
    items,
        Android.Resource.Layout.SimpleListItem2,
    new string[]
    {
        "simpleAdapterTitle",
        "simpleAdapterDesc"
    },
    new int[]
    {
            Android.Resource.Id.Text1,
            Android.Resource.Id.Text2
    });

this.ListAdapter = a;
```

Lists01\SimpleAdapterActivity.cs

The SimpleAdapter gives you a lot more flexibility in your layout and what data you display for each list item. But it is still a bit clunky, coming from the .NET world. In a real use case, this would mean creating three different array objects just to map values from a list of data objects to a list item.

Customizing ListView with a Custom List Adapter

You've seen some of the Android SDK's built-in layouts for ListView items, classes for creating list adapters, and ListActivity for displaying a ListView. There's nothing wrong with using this functionality. However, at some point you may need to display your data in a ListView item in a specific way, different from what the default layouts allow. Or you may just find that using a SimpleListAdapter to display a collection of data objects is not as simple and elegant as it sounds. For these situations, you may be better off creating your own layout for your ListView items that uses your own custom list adapter subclassing the BaseAdapter class. It's a lot easier than it sounds, and it may just become your preferred way to create customized list displays!

The next example uses a list of Animal objects as the data source. You need to display the animal's name and description, as well as an image for each animal in a ListView. Listing 6-18 shows a simple class that holds the animal's name, description, and image. In this example Image refers to an image's resource ID, not an actual Image object itself, because that would be outside the scope of this example.

Available for download on Wrox.com

LISTING 6-18: Animal data object

```
public class Animal
{
    public string Name
    {
        get;
        set;
    }

    public string Description
    {
        get;
        set;
    }

    public int Image
    {
        get;
        set;
    }
}
```

Lists02\Animal.cs

Next, a layout is needed for each ListView item. A ListView item usually displays information for a single object from your data source. This example is no different. A single ListView item is responsible for displaying information for a single animal, including the name, description, and image.

More is going on in the XML layout shown in Listing 6-19 than in Android's built-in `SimpleListItem1`. A horizontal `LinearLayout` holds an `ImageView` for the animal's image, and a child vertical `LinearLayout` holds two `TextViews`: one for the animal's name, and another for the animal's description. This layout causes the image to appear on the left. To the right of the image are the name and, under that, the description.

LISTING 6-19: ListView item layout for Animal

```xml
<?xml version="1.0" encoding="utf-8"?>
<LinearLayout xmlns:android="http://schemas.android.com/apk/res/android"
    android:id="@+id/widget28"
    android:layout_width="fill_parent"
    android:layout_height="80px">
    <ImageView
    android:id="@+id/imageItem"
    android:layout_width="wrap_content"
    android:layout_height="wrap_content"
    android:layout_gravity="center_vertical">
    </ImageView>
    <LinearLayout
    android:id="@+id/linearText"
    android:layout_width="wrap_content"
    android:layout_height="fill_parent"
    android:orientation="vertical"
    android:layout_marginLeft="10px"
    android:layout_marginTop="10px">
        <TextView
        android:id="@+id/textTop"
        android:layout_width="wrap_content"
        android:layout_height="wrap_content"
        android:text="TextView">
        </TextView>
        <TextView
        android:id="@+id/textBottom"
        android:layout_width="wrap_content"
        android:layout_height="wrap_content"
        android:text="TextView">
        </TextView>
    </LinearLayout>
</LinearLayout>
```

Lists02\Resources\layout\AnimalItem.axml

It's important to take note of the IDs of the various views inside your layout for which you will want to set the data programmatically. In this case, you should take note of the IDs for the `ImageView` as well as both of the `TextViews`: `imageItem`, `textTop`, and `textBottom`. Mono for Android automatically makes these IDs available to you for referencing in the `Resource.Id` class. In Visual Studio, the `Resource.Designer.cs` is automatically generated based on the files in the Resources folder which have the `AndroidResource` set as their build action. It's important to remember that the `Resource.Id` class members are only regenerated whenever you build your project, and they will not show up in Intellisense until this time.

Assuming that your data source is some enumerable list, array, or other collection of `Animal` objects, it's pretty simple to build a custom `ListAdapter` that your `ListView` can use. One way to do this is to create a new class (call it `AnimalListAdapter`) and make it inherit the `BaseAdapter<T>` class (see Listing 6-20).

Inheriting from `BaseAdapter<T>` requires a method and a couple of properties to be implemented:

➤ `Count` property

➤ `Indexer this` property of type `T`

➤ `GetItemId` method

The `Count` property is obvious. It simply returns the number of items that should appear in your list. In most cases, this is the number of items in your data source.

The `Indexer` property should return the data object in your data source for a given index. In this case the property should return an `Animal` object type for the position being passed into the indexer.

The `GetItemId` method takes an int position value and returns a `long` value type. For the purposes of Mono, the actual number returned is not used by any critical underlying Android code. Just be sure to take care of what you return if you are going to be using the `ItemId` values anywhere else in your code. However, best practice would be to ensure that you return a unique value for every different position value passed into the method. An easy way to deal with this method is to simply return the `position` parameter directly. It should also be noted that the `ItemId` value does get passed to some `ListView` events, such as the `ItemClick` event, so it may be useful for you to pass a value that gives more meaning to identifying the actual data source object for the given position.

LISTING 6-20: AnimalListAdapter

```
using System;
using System.Collections.Generic;
using Android.App;
using Android.Views;
using Android.Widget;

namespace Lists02
{
    public class AnimalListAdapter : BaseAdapter<Animal>
    {
        Activity context;
        public List<Animal> Animals;

        public AnimalListAdapter(Activity context, List<Animal> animals)
            : base()
        {
```

```csharp
        this.context = context;
        this.Animals = animals;
    }

    public override int Count
    {
        get { return this.Animals.Count; }
    }

    public override Animal this[int position]
    {
        get { return this.Animals[position]; }
    }

    public override View GetView(int position, View convertView, ViewGroup
      parent)
    {
        //Get our object for this position
        var item = this.Animals[position];

        //Try to reuse convertView if it's not null, otherwise inflate it from
          our item layout
        // This gives us some performance gains by not always inflating a new
          view
        // This will sound familiar to MonoTouch developers with
          UITableViewCell.DequeueReusableCell()
        var view = convertView;

        if (convertView == null || !(convertView is LinearLayout))
            view = context.LayoutInflater.Inflate(Resource.Layout.AnimalItem,
              parent, false);

        //Find references to each subview in the list item's view
        var imageItem = view.FindViewById(Resource.Id.imageItem) as ImageView;
        var textTop = view.FindViewById(Resource.Id.textTop) as TextView;
        var textBottom = view.FindViewById(Resource.Id.textBottom) as TextView;

        //Assign this item's values to the various subviews
        imageItem.SetImageResource(item.Image);
        textTop.SetText(item.Name, TextView.BufferType.Normal);
        textBottom.SetText(item.Description, TextView.BufferType.Normal);

        //Finally return the view
        return view;
    }

    public long GetItemId(int position)
    {
        return position;
    }
    }
}
```

Lists02\AnimalListAdapter.cs

You may notice that the adapter's constructor expects an `Activity` to be passed into it. The adapter needs a reference to a context so that the layout and all the views within it can be created for the `ListView` items. Any time you create `view` objects, a context is required, so this is no exception. Typically you would pass into the constructor a reference to the `Activity` that is creating the custom `ListAdapter`.

The `GetView` method in the list adapter is responsible for returning a `View` that is the layout for a `ListView` item for the given position. The first thing the example does is get the `Animal` object for the given position from the data source (the `List<Animal> Animals` property).

> *If you've done any development for the iPhone, you may be familiar with the concept of reusing table cells in calls to the table adapter as a way to save memory resources and speed things up. The idea is the same on Android.*

Even though your list may have 500 items, only some of them (10, for example) can be displayed onscreen at any given time. Instead of making instances of your `ListView` item layout for all 500 items in the list, it is much more efficient to make only 10 instances for the items that can be shown onscreen at once. Then they can be recycled as items disappear from view and different items appear (see Figure 6-10).

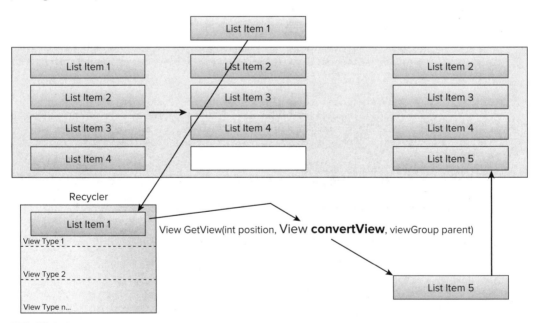

FIGURE 6-10

This is where the `convertView` parameter is useful. This parameter is null if there are no existing instances of your `ListView` item layouts to be recycled. In fact, the first 10 times that `GetView` is called, `convertView` is null. However, the 11th time (again assuming that only 10 items can fit on the screen at once) GetView is called, convertView contains the recycled instance of the ListView's item that just disappeared from the screen. It's important to note that the values of any TextViews, ImageViews, or any other subviews of convertView remain unchanged from what they were last set to be.

If convertView happens to be null, the code shown in Listing 6-20 uses a LayoutInflater to inflate a view from the layout you saw earlier. Otherwise, convertView can be reused, and no layout needs to be inflated.

If you are working with multiple types of layouts or views for different list items, you should override the ViewTypeCount property as well as the GetItemViewType(int position) method in your adapter. ListView calls the GetItemViewType method for each list item to ensure that it passes the proper type of recycled View for the contentView parameter in the GetView method. This also means that you may want to use the GetItemViewType method in your GetView method so that you know which type of view you are working with.

This example uses the View object to find all the subviews that need to have values set that correspond to the Animal instance being displayed. The view's FindViewById method works well to find references to the ImageView and two TextViews. As soon as you have those references, you can set the values for those subviews using the Animal instance of the row to be displayed. When all this is finished, the view is returned to be displayed for the row. You can think of this method as the Android version of ASP.NET's Control.FindControl method.

The last thing you need is an actual Activity to show your ListView. Listing 6-21 shows a simple use of ListActivity to show ListView with the custom list adapter.

LISTING 6-21: Activity to display the ListView

```
using System.Collections.Generic;
using Android.App;
using Android.OS;

namespace Lists02
{
    [Activity(Label = "Animal List", MainLauncher = true)]
    public class AnimalListActivity : ListActivity
    {
        protected override void OnCreate(Bundle savedInstanceState)
        {
            base.OnCreate(savedInstanceState);

            this.ListAdapter = new AnimalListAdapter(this,
                new List<Animal>() {
                    new Animal() { Name = "Elephant",
                        Description = "Big and Gray, but what the hey",
                        Image = Resource.Drawable.Elephant },
                    new Animal() { Name = "Chinchilla",
                        Description = "Little people of the andes",
                        Image = Resource.Drawable.Chinchilla },
                    new Animal() { Name = "Lion",
                        Description = "Cowardly lion, anyone?",
```

continues

LISTING 6-21 *(continued)*

```
                Image = Resource.Drawable.Lion },
            new Animal() { Name = "Skunk",
                Description = "Ello, baby. I am ze locksmith...",
                Image = Resource.Drawable.Skunk },
            new Animal() { Name = "Rhino",
                Description = "Most live to about 60!",
                Image = Resource.Drawable.Rhino },
            new Animal() { Name = "Zebra",
                Description = "Stripes, not so great for hiding"
                Image = Resource.Drawable.Zebra }

        });
      }
    }
  }
```

Lists02\AnimalListActivity.cs

Now you have all the components required to
display a custom list. You started with a custom
layout for your list items using multiple views,
you created a custom list adapter by overriding
the `BaseAdapter` class, and you created a
custom `ListActivity` with a data source to
display the `ListView` you wired to your
adapter. Your list should look something
like Figure 6-11.

Now you have seen a usable example for creating
your own customized lists using nondefault list
item layouts. This example also illustrates the

FIGURE 6-11

important real-world use case of incorporating your own custom data objects. You have taken the
most basic form of the list adapter by subclassing the `BaseAdapter`. From here, the sky's the limit!

Handling ListView Events

A `ListView` isn't very useful unless users can interact with it. `ListView` automatically gives you
scrolling and knows when to ask the list adapter for the right items to display. It even goes so far
as to recycle layouts for you with a little bit of knowledge implemented in your adapter. Luckily,
`ListView` also exposes a number of events for various types of interaction:

➤ `ItemClick` is raised whenever a user taps a list item once. This requires the user to touch the
list item and then lift while still in the area of the list item within a short period of time. On
some devices this event may also be fired when the Enter button is clicked.

➤ `ItemLongClick` is raised when a user taps and holds a list item for a longer period of time.
This could also include clicking and holding the Enter button on some devices.

➤ `ItemSelected` occurs when an item has been selected.

➤ `ItemCleared` is the opposite of `ItemSelected`. This is when the item's state is no longer selected.

➤ `CreateContextMenuEvent` is raised when a long click happens on a list item. This is a convenient way to know when to show a context menu rather than writing the code in the `ItemLongClick` event.

➤ `Touch` is a low-level event for touches that you can use to detect more complex touches.

➤ `Recycler` is raised with an instance to a view whenever a view is recycled for a list item.

Responding to one of these events is no different from any other .NET event, except that there is no design-time support in Visual Studio for wiring up events. You can wire up a delegate for it and have its code executed when the event fires. As with any other .NET event, you can use anonymous delegate methods or lambda expressions to make for some clean inline code. Listing 6-22 shows a few examples of wiring up `ListView` events to do something simple.

LISTING 6-22: Handling ListView events

```
using System;
using Android.App;
using Android.OS;
using Android.Widget;
using Android.Views;

namespace Lists03
{
    [Activity(Label = "Events List"), Mainlauncher=true)]
    public class EventsListActivity : ListActivity
    {
        private string[] items;

        protected override void OnCreate(Bundle bundle)
        {
            base.OnCreate(bundle);

            items = new string[] {"Item 1", "Item 2", "Item 3"};
            this.ListAdapter = new ArrayAdapter<string>(this,
                Android.Resource.Layout.SimpleListItem1, items);

            //Using an EventHandler
            this.ListView.ItemClick += new EventHandler<ItemEventArgs>(
                ListView_ItemClick);

            //Using an Anonymous Method
            this.ListView.ItemLongClick += delegate(object sender,
                Android.Widget.AdapterView.ItemLongClickEventArgs e)
            {
                Toast.MakeText(this,
                    "Long Click: " +
                    items[e.Position],
                        ToastLength.Short).Show();
            };

            //Using a Lambda Expression
            this.ListView.Recycler += (object sender,
```

continues

LISTING 6-22 *(continued)*

```
                               AbsListView.RecyclerEventArgs e) =>
            {
                Toast.MakeText(this, "Recycler!",
                    ToastLength.Short).Show();
            };
        }

        void ListView_ItemClick(object sender, ItemEventArgs e)
        {
            Toast.MakeText(this, "Click: " + items[e.Position],
                ToastLength.Short).Show();
        }
    }
}
```

Lists03\EventsListActivity.cs

Preferences Screen

You have many options for how your lists look and function; however, many times you may need to accomplish the same types of tasks with your lists. Preferences and settings, for example, often use the same types of list items to display and allow users to configure data. Android has some built-in functionality that specifically addresses the task of displaying preferences to users.

PreferenceActivity is another type of Activity designed specifically to display certain Preference list items with minimal effort. Most of the Preference list items allow you to define a key to access the values, as well as a title and description to display to the user:

➤ CheckBoxPreference is a simple on/off check box control.

➤ EditTextPreference displays a text box for editing in a dialog when the user taps the list item.

➤ ListPreference gives users a choice of items to select from a list. A default value can be set.

➤ PreferenceCategory displays a category title as a list item. This is for grouping Preference items in a logical and aesthetically pleasing way.

➤ PreferenceScreen is used as a placeholder to navigate to another list of preferences. The list items are obtained from the inner XML of the Preference screen in the layout file. You can nest several levels of preferences in the same XML file.

➤ RingtonePreference shows a list of ringtones for the user to pick from.

➤ PreferenceDialog is a base class that you can inherit from to display your own UI inside a dialog for a preference.

One of the nice things about this class is that it saves and loads preferences from a SharedPreference automatically. Then you can access those preferences by their key later using the Preference Manager's DefaultSharedPreferences. PreferenceActivity typically is constructed from an XML layout resource file. Listing 6-23 demonstrates a layout using many of the built-in preferences.

LISTING 6-23: Sample PreferenceActivity layout

```xml
<?xml version="1.0" encoding="utf-8"?>
<PreferenceScreen xmlns:android="http://schemas.android.com/apk/res/android">
    <PreferenceCategory android:title="First Category">
        <CheckBoxPreference
            android:key="chooseFromList"
            android:title="CheckBox Preference"
            android:defaultValue="true"
            android:summary="Do you want to Choose from the List?"
            />
        <ListPreference
            android:title="List Preference"
            android:summary=" Allows you to select an array item"
            android:dependency="chooseFromList"
            android:key="listChoice"
            android:defaultValue="1"
            android:entries="@array/listChoiceEntries"
            android:entryValues="@array/listChoiceEntryValues"
            />
    </PreferenceCategory>
    <PreferenceCategory android:title="Second Category">
        <PreferenceScreen android:title="Advanced Options">
            <CheckBoxPreference
                android:key="advancedOption"
                android:title="Advanced Option"
                android:defaultValue="true"
                android:summary="This is an Advanced Option"
                />
        </PreferenceScreen>
        <EditTextPreference android:dialogTitle="EditTextTitle"
            android:dialogMessage="Please enter your Text:"
            android:key="mainOption"
            android:title="Some Title"
            android:summary="This is an EditText Preference"
            android:defaultValue="Test"
            />
    </PreferenceCategory>
</PreferenceScreen>
```

Lists04\Resources\layout\Preferences.axml

Figure 6-12 shows what the XML layout from Listing 6-23 looks like after the layout is inflated. You can see how easy it is to create a rich set of `Preference` screens. Note that Second Category contains a `PreferenceScreen` with a `CheckBoxPreference` inside it. Nesting the `PreferenceScreen` in this way automatically creates the navigation between `PreferenceScreens`. When the user taps the Advanced Options list item, a `PreferenceScreen` with the Advanced Option check box is shown. You can easily nest multiple levels of `PreferenceScreen` layout items in this way to create multilevel navigable `Preferences` using a single `PreferenceActivity`.

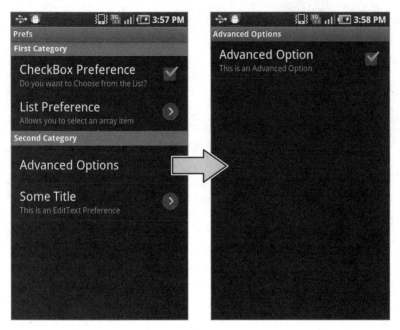

FIGURE 6-12

You can also create PreferenceScreens programmatically. Sometimes you need to use a combination of techniques. Normally, you would assign a resource identifier for the entries and entryVal-ues of a ListPreference in the XML layout file. The resource identifiers for these properties would be string arrays in your Resources\values\strings.xml file.

In practice, sometimes you don't know which values you want to use in your list until runtime. If you don't know what these entries and their values are at compile time, you can programmatically assign them to your PreferenceList item at runtime. Listing 6-24 shows one way you can accomplish this.

LISTING 6-24: Setting up ListPreference items at runtime

```
using System;
using Android.App;
using Android.Content;
using Android.OS;
using Android.Runtime;
using Android.Views;
using Android.Widget;
using Android.Preferences;

namespace Lists04
{
    [Activity(Label = "Prefs", MainLauncher=true)]
    public class Preferences : PreferenceActivity
    {
        protected override void OnCreate(Bundle bundle)
        {
            base.OnCreate(bundle);
```

```
        this.AddPreferencesFromResource(Resource.Layout.Preferences);

        var listPref = (this.FindPreference("listChoice") as ListPreference);

        listPref.SetEntries(new string[] { "Choice #1", "Option No. 2",
          "3rd" });
        listPref.SetEntryValues(new string[] { "1", "2", "3" });
      }
    }
  }
```

Lists04\PreferencesActivity.cs

In this example, the PreferenceActivity's layout is inflated from the preferences.xml layout by calling the method AddPreferencesFromResource. However, after the layout gets inflated, FindPreference is used to locate the instance of the ListPreference by the key specified in the layout resource XML file. Once you have a reference to the ListPreference, you can call the SetEntries and SetEntryValues methods to override whatever entries and values exist in the ListPreference, as assigned by the inflator.

If you look at Listing 6-23, you can see it is not necessary to specify the android:entries and android:entryValues properties in your layout XML file if you plan to manually assign entries and values at runtime. Figure 6-13 shows what the ListPreference looks like.

Nested Navigation

Lists are often used to navigate through an application. A user taps an item in a list, and then another list appears with more items to choose from. Using this type of navigation, users can drill down into an object's properties and subproperties.

FIGURE 6-13

Enabling this sort of functionality is simple in Android and uses the concepts you've learned in this chapter. All you need to do is wire up ListView's ItemClick event (see Listing 6-25) and start a new activity in the event handler. The Android Back button returns you to the previous ListActivity.

Don't forget that the same Activity life cycle applies here. It is possible that you could return to an Activity that has been unloaded. You should try to save and load states on an Activity-by-Activity basis wherever appropriate to avoid confusing the users and causing errors in your application. Please refer to Chapter 3 for more information about the life cycle of an Activity.

LISTING 6-25: Starting a nested activity

```
this.ListView.ItemClick += delegate
{
    StartActivity(typeof(SecondActivity));
};
```

Lists05\FirstActivity.cs

When dealing with nested lists, or nested activities of any type, you might need to pass data from one `Activity` to the next. The Android documentation suggests a couple of ways to do this:

➤ `Intent.PutExtra`: This method requires that you have instantiated your `Intent` to be used in the new `Activity` instead of just using a shortcut method such as `StartActivity(Type)`. With an `Intent` instance, calling `PutExtra` allows you to store simple data type values by key name, which can be retrieved in the new `Activity` by using one of the `Intent.GetTypeExtra` method variants. This is great for simple data types and arrays of simple data types (and, in some cases, complex data types) such as the following:

   ➤ `Bool`

   ➤ `Bool[]`

   ➤ `Bundle`: Just another key/value dictionary to store more simple data types. `PutExtra` uses a `Bundle` at the root level, so you can store `Bundles` within `Bundles` in this way.

   ➤ `byte[]`

   ➤ `char, char[]`

   ➤ `double, double[]`

   ➤ `float, float[]`

   ➤ `int, int[]`

   ➤ `sbyte`

   ➤ `short, short[]`

   ➤ `string, string[]`

   ➤ `Java.IO.Iserializable`: Any complex data type that implements this interface can be stored.

➤ **Static properties:** Creating a static property or variable is also an acceptable way of storing data to be passed between `Activities`. You could create a static property on either the `Activity` you are launching a new `Activity` from or the new `Activity` to be started. Just be aware that if you plan to use multiple instances of an `Activity`, they will all use the same static instance, which could cause problems.

Listing 6-26 shows how you can modify your code to start the next `Activity` by using the `PutExtra` method to pass in the selected value from the `ItemClick` event.

LISTING 6-26: Passing data to the nested activity

```
this.ListView.ItemLongClick += (sender, e) => {

    string sel = this.ListAdapter.GetItem(e.Position).ToString();

    var secondIntent = new Android.Content.Intent(this, typeof(SecondActivity));
    secondIntent.PutExtra("selected", sel + " was Selected!");
    StartActivity(secondIntent);

};
```

Lists05\FirstActivity.cs

Grouped Lists

Sometimes you may want to group items in your `ListView`. In the Preferences example, you used `PreferenceCategory` items to group different user preferences in a logical way. Unfortunately, Android does not yet provide a default way to do this `Category` grouping in a normal `ListView`. Only `PreferenceScreen` currently has this capability.

It is definitely possible to implement this style of grouped list, given the great flexibility that `ListView` gives you. One common way to implement this is to create a list adapter that displays a collection of list adapters — one for each group or section.

In this example you will create a list adapter called `SectionedAdapter`. You will use two different layouts for your list items. One layout is for the actual list items (in this example you will use an instance of an `ArrayAdapter` for each group), and the other is for the Group Name separator items. For the sake of simplicity, the sample uses the `SimpleListItem1` layout for the list items to be displayed from the `ArrayAdapters`. Listing 6-27 demonstrates a layout for the Group Name separator list item. The only unusual thing about the layout is the `style` property. It has a value of the built-in `listSeparatorTextViewStyle`, which produces a gray background with white text.

LISTING 6-27: Group Name separator list item layout

```
<TextView
xmlns:android="http://schemas.android.com/apk/res/android"
    android:id="@+id/separator"
    android:layout_width="fill_parent"
    android:layout_height="wrap_content"
    android:gravity="center"
    style="?android:attr/listSeparatorTextViewStyle" />
```

Lists06\Resources\layout\Separator.axml

`SectionedAdapter` is responsible for managing all the sections containing an instance of the `Section` property to be displayed. The `Section` object has a `Caption` property to store the section's displayable title, as well as a `BaseAdapter` property to keep a reference to the list adapter for the section. Listing 6-28 shows the code you need to create `SectionedAdapter`.

LISTING 6-28: SectionedAdapter

```csharp
using System;
using System.Collections.Generic;
using System.Linq;
using System.Text;
using Android.App;
using Android.Content;
using Android.OS;
using Android.Runtime;
using Android.Views;
using Android.Widget;

namespace Lists06
{
    public class SectionedAdapter : BaseAdapter<Section>
    {
        const int TYPE_SECTION_HEADER = 0;

        Context context;
        LayoutInflater inflater;

        public SectionedAdapter(Context context)
        {
            this.context = context;
            this.inflater = LayoutInflater.From(context);
            this.Sections = new List<Section>();
        }

        public List<Section> Sections
        {
            get;
            set;
        }

        public override int Count
        {
            get
            {
                int count = 0;

                //Get each adapter's count + 1 for the header
                foreach (var s in Sections)
                    count += s.Adapter.Count + 1;

                return count;
            }
        }

        public override int ViewTypeCount
        {
            get
            {
                //The headers count as a view type too
```

```csharp
        int viewTypeCount = 1;

        //Get each adapter's ViewTypeCount
        foreach (var s in Sections)
            viewTypeCount += s.Adapter.ViewTypeCount;

        return viewTypeCount;
    }
}

public override Section this[int position]
{
    get { return this.Sections[position]; }
}

public override bool AreAllItemsEnabled()
{
    return false;
}

public override int GetItemViewType(int position)
{
    // start counting from here
    int typeOffset = TYPE_SECTION_HEADER + 1;

    foreach (var s in Sections)
    {
        if (position == 0)
            return (TYPE_SECTION_HEADER);

        int size = s.Adapter.Count + 1;

        if (position < size)
            return (typeOffset + s.Adapter.GetItemViewType(position - 1));

        position -= size;
        typeOffset += s.Adapter.ViewTypeCount;
    }

    return -1;
}

public override long GetItemId(int position)
{
    return position;
}

public void AddSection(string caption, BaseAdapter adapter)
{
    this.Sections.Add(new Section() { Caption = caption, Adapter =
      adapter });
}

public override View GetView(int position, View convertView,
  ViewGroup parent)
```

continues

LISTING 6-28 *(continued)*

```
            {
                int sectionIndex = 0;

                foreach (var s in Sections)
                {
                    if (position == 0)
                    {
                        TextView separator = convertView as TextView;

                        if (separator == null)
                            inflater.Inflate(Resource.Layout.Separator, null) as
                                TextView;

                        separator.Text = s.Caption;

                        return separator;
                    }

                    int size = s.Adapter.Count + 1;

                    if (position < size)
                        return (s.Adapter.GetView(position - 1, convertView, parent));

                    position -= size;
                    sectionIndex++;
                }

                return null;
            }
        }
    }
```

Lists06\SectionedAdapter.cs

All the usual methods and properties for a derivative of `BaseAdapter` are overridden in `SectionedAdapter`. In the case of the `Count` property, the count becomes a `Sum` of the `Count` of each `Section`'s adapter, plus 1 for the header row for each `Section`. Similarly, `ViewTypeCount` is a `Sum` of `ViewTypeCounts` for each `Section`, plus 1 for the `Separator` view type.

`GetItemViewType` loops through all the `Sections` in order to find which type of view the given position is. In the case where the position is of a `Separator`, it returns the `VIEW_TYPE_HEADER` constant of 0. Otherwise, it calls the `GetItemViewType` on the `Adapter` containing the item at the specified position to get its view type directly from the `Adapter`. The view type returned is then added with the `typeOffset` value to ensure that no collisions occur in view types with other adapters.

`GetView` uses the separator layout to build a `View` for `Separator` title list item. This method calls on the adapter for the `Section` of the item in question, using the adapter's `GetView` method to pass along the `View` as the returned object.

Whereas you used an `ArrayAdapter` for both of the sections in your `SectionedAdapter` example, you can use the `SectionedAdapter` to display any type of list adapter you like. You can also mix and match different list adapters within a single `SectionedAdapter`. Each section can have its own list adapter type, as long as it derives from the `BaseAdapter` at some point. Your example should produce something similar to Figure 6-14.

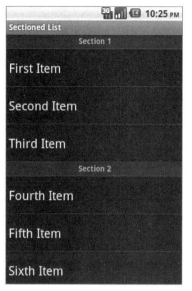

FIGURE 6-14

Displaying Data in a Grid

What if you wanted to display a grid of pictures in your application? You could use a `ListView` and divide each row into columns, managing each row yourself as actually being three separate items. This would be challenging, but you could create a subclass of `ListView` with this functionality, to be reused any time you need it.

Android has done this for you in the form of a `GridView`. `GridView` is ultimately derived from `ListView`, but instead of displaying one list item per row, it displays list items in rows as well as columns in a two-dimensional, scrollable grid. You can set the number of columns as well as the width of each column to display varying amounts of data.

No simple activity such as `ListActivity` can be used with `GridView`, so you must at the very least create a basic XML layout file with a `GridView` in it. Listing 6-29 shows a basic layout with a `GridView`. You need to be aware of a couple of attributes that are specific to `GridView`, in addition to the `ListView` attributes you are already familiar with:

➤ `numColumns` can be either an explicit number or `auto_fit`, which automatically shows as many columns in a row as can fit. This is useful in Landscape orientation, which, on most devices, can fit more columns than Portrait mode.

➤ `stretchMode` determines how to handle any extra space that is not taken up in a row by the columns that fit. If this value is set to `columnWidth`, any extra space is divided evenly between each column's width in the row. If this value is set to `spacingWidth`, the extra space is divided evenly between the white spaces between the columns in the row.

LISTING 6-29: GridView layout

```xml
<?xml version="1.0" encoding="utf-8"?>
<GridView xmlns:android="http://schemas.android.com/apk/res/android"
    android:id="@+id/gridview"
    android:layout_width="fill_parent"
    android:layout_height="fill_parent"
    android:columnWidth="90dp"
    android:numColumns="auto_fit"
    android:verticalSpacing="10dp"
```

continues

LISTING 6-29 *(continued)*

```
        android:horizontalSpacing="10dp"
        android:stretchMode="columnWidth"
        android:gravity="center"
    />
```

Lists07\Resources\layout\Gridview.axml

This `GridView` requires a `ListAdapter`, just like every `ListView`. This adapter could be an `ArrayAdapter`, a `SimpleAdapter`, or your own custom adapter derived from `BaseAdapter`, just like in the project you created earlier. Continuing with the example, you will create a new custom adapter called `ImageAdapter`, which will display one image per item. This is probably one of the more common uses for a `GridView`, but you certainly aren't limited to images. You can use Listing 6-30 to create your `ImageAdapter`.

LISTING 6-30: ImageAdapter

```
using System;
using System.Collections.Generic;
using System.Linq;
using System.Text;

using Android.App;
using Android.Content;
using Android.Graphics.Drawables;
using Android.OS;
using Android.Runtime;
using Android.Views;
using Android.Widget;

namespace Lists07
{
    public class ImageAdapter : BaseAdapter<Drawable>
    {
        Context context;

        public ImageAdapter(Context context)
        {
            this.context = context;
            this.Images = new List<Drawable>();
        }

        public List<Drawable> Images
        {
            get;
            set;
        }

        public override int Count
        {
```

```
            get { return this.Images.Count; }
        }

        public override Drawable this[int position]
        {
            get { return this.Images[position]; }
        }

        public override long GetItemId(int position)
        {
            return position;
        }


        public override View GetView(int position, View convertView, ViewGroup
            parent)
        {
            ImageView imageView;

            if (convertView == null)
                imageView = new ImageView(context);
            else
                imageView = (ImageView)convertView;

            imageView.SetImageDrawable(this.Images[position]);

            return imageView;
        }
    }
}
```

Lists07\ImageAdapter.cs

Notice that the `ImageAdapter` uses the `BaseAdapter<Drawable>` generic type, with a `Drawable` being an image to be displayed for each item. The `ImageAdapter` has a `List<Drawable>` property to store an instance of each image to be displayed in the `GridView`. The constructor requires a `Context` to be passed in so that you have a `Context` to use when creating `ImageViews` to be displayed in each list item.

Focusing on `GetView`, `convertView` is checked to see if it can be recycled. If it cannot, a new `ImageView` is created. In either case, the `imageView` reference is assigned a `Drawable` for the given position.

Next you need an `Activity` to show the `GridView`. Listing 6-31 shows an `Activity` using the XML layout from Listing 6-29.

LISTING 6-31: GridView Activity code

```
using System;
using Android.App;
using Android.Content;
using Android.Runtime;
using Android.Views;
```

continues

LISTING 6-31 *(continued)*

```
using Android.Widget;
using Android.OS;
using Android.Graphics.Drawables;

namespace Lists07
{
    [Activity(Label = "GridView", MainLauncher = true)]
    public class ImageGridViewActivity : Activity
    {
        protected override void OnCreate(Bundle bundle)
        {
            base.OnCreate(bundle);

            // Set our view from the "main" layout resource
            SetContentView(Resource.Layout.Gridview);

            // Get our button from the layout resource,
            // and attach an event to it
            var gridView = this.FindViewById<GridView>(Resource.Id.Gridview);

            var ia = new ImageAdapter(this);
            ia.Images.Add(Resources.GetDrawable(Resource.Drawable.Battery));
            ia.Images.Add(Resources.GetDrawable(Resource.Drawable.Computer));
            ia.Images.Add(Resources.GetDrawable(Resource.Drawable.DriveCDROM));
            ia.Images.Add(Resources.GetDrawable(Resource.Drawable.DriveHardDisk));
            ia.Images.Add(Resources.GetDrawable(Resource.Drawable.InputKeyboard));
            ia.Images.Add(Resources.GetDrawable(Resource.Drawable.InputMouse));
            ia.Images.Add(Resources.GetDrawable(Resource.Drawable.MediaCDROM));
            ia.Images.Add(Resources.GetDrawable(Resource.Drawable
                .MediaCDROMAudio));
            ia.Images.Add(Resources.GetDrawable(Resource.Drawable.MediaCDRW));
            ia.Images.Add(Resources.GetDrawable(Resource.Drawable.MediaDVD));
            ia.Images.Add(Resources.GetDrawable(Resource.Drawable.MediaDVDRW));
            ia.Images.Add(Resources.GetDrawable(Resource.Drawable.MediaFloppy));
            ia.Images.Add(Resources.GetDrawable(Resource.Drawable.Printer));
            ia.Images.Add(Resources.GetDrawable(Resource.Drawable.VideoDisplay));

            gridView.Adapter = ia;
        }
    }
}
```

Lists07\ImageGridViewActivity.cs

All the images used in your project must exist in the proper `Resources` folder structure and have the Build Action property set to `AndroidResource`. Figure 6-15 shows the Visual Studio Solution Explorer layout for the images.

When you compile and run your project, you see a `GridView` like the one shown in Figure 6-16. Notice how Portrait and Landscape modes hold a different number of columns. Because you did not specify a number of columns in the XML Layout Resource file, `GridView` automatically fits in as many columns as possible, based on their width.

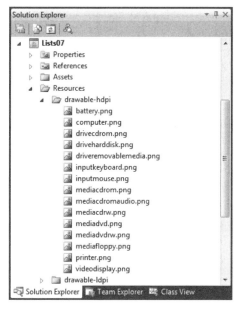

FIGURE 6-15

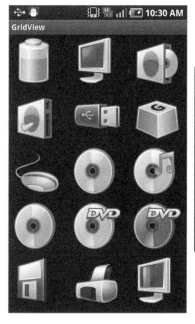
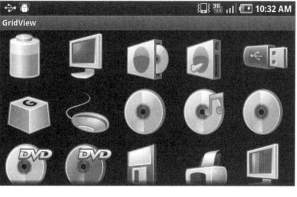

FIGURE 6-16

SUMMARY

As you have learned in this chapter, there are many different ways to bind data to controls in Android. First, you learned about data adapters and their relationship with adapter views. You learned in detail about the inner workings of an adapter and explored the various native adapters available in Android. Working with the SQLite storage system, you learned how to utilize cursors to populate a spinner, as well as how to handle events from the Spinner. You also created a gallery control with cursors and a custom `ImageAdapter` implementation.

Later in this chapter, you worked closely with the `ListView` and `ListActivity`. You built a basic `ListView` before creating a project using a Custom List Adapter to display `Animal` objects in the `ListView`. Using the `ListView` events, you learned how to create an application using nested navigation. You also explored the `PreferenceScreen` and different types of preference elements that can be used to easily create intuitive and stylish user input–driven lists. Next, you worked on a `SectionedAdapter` to create grouped lists. Finally, you used the `GridView` to display a grid of images.

Displaying data to users is an integral part of any application. With Android, displaying data most often follows the adapter powering a view pattern. This chapter has given you a close look at various techniques to present data to users in a meaningful way. Now you are one step closer to creating useful Android applications using Mono.

7

Working with the File System and Application Preferences

WHAT'S IN THIS CHAPTER?

➤ Reviewing the file system

➤ Reading and writing a file

➤ Creating and reading application shared preferences

➤ Processing an XML file

➤ Listening for preference changes

This chapter covers the file system, reading and writing files to the file system, and system and application preferences. The review of the file system covers the file system type and structure and gives examples of reading and writing text files from the application to the file system. For application preferences the chapter covers the API used for both shared and private preferences and preference change notification. The chapter also shows a program that uses the available preferences namespace to show a standard user preferences interface. Finally, the chapter shows how to process XML from an atom feed on the Internet.

User preferences are essential to providing a robust user experience, ensuring that users can tailor the software to their own liking. Also, in the context of Android, private preferences are important to maintaining user state in an environment where context changes can happen unexpectedly. For instance, if a user gets a call while keying data into your app, you want to be sure that when the user returns to the app, the input is still there. The samples in this chapter enable you to accomplish these tasks.

WORKING WITH THE FILE SYSTEM

As previously indicated, this chapter covers the file system and file I/O. It starts with a discussion of the file system type and structure and then moves to look at how you work with permissions and file access. Next it covers the file access API and wraps up with a sample program that reads and writes to and from a local XML file.

File System Type and Structure

The default file system for Android is YAFFS (Yet Another Flash File System). YAFFS is currently at version 2. It runs on top of the Linux operating system in Android and is also available for other OSs. YAFFS provides wear leveling to prolong the life of the Flash memory. It has built-in error correction for robustness in case of a power failure. It also provides fast boot-up, making it a solid file system for the Android platform.

 If you want a thorough review of YAFFS, go to `http://yaffs.net`. *In this chapter we will just cover some of the high points.*

The Linux operating system supports permissions to control the ability of the world, a group, or the owner of a file to read, write, list, or execute the file. Each process executed on the Linux system runs with a given set of user permissions. Each process running on Android is isolated. This is achieved partially by having each process run with its own unique user permissions.

So, what permissions can a file have in Android? The four modes of file accessibility are private, append, world-readable, and world-writeable. These modes are governed by the following constants:

➤   `FileCreationMode.Private`

➤   `FileCreationMode.Append`

➤   `FileCreationMode.WorldReadable`

➤   `FileCreationMode.WorldWriteable`

The names of these modes should be fairly obvious, but for clarity's sake:

➤   `Private` makes the file readable and writeable for the file owner and no one else.

➤   `Append` constrains a file to be written to in Append mode.

➤   `WorldReadable` allows any other process to read the file.

➤   `WorldWritable` allows any other process to read from or write to the file.

The following snippet shows how to read from a file. It comes from the longer QuickEdit example shown later in the chapter:

```
byte[] content = new byte[1024];
try
{
FileInputStream fis = OpenFileInput(QUICKEDIT_FILENAME);
```

```
fis.Read(content);
fis.Close();
}
catch (FileNotFoundException e)
{
Log.Error(QUICKEDIT_TAG, e.Message);
}
catch (IOException e)
{
        Log.Error(QUICKEDIT_TAG, e.Message);
}
```

The file access functions are defined in the `Java.IO` namespace. Table 7-1 lists the key functions and exceptions.

TABLE 7-1: The Java.IO Namespace

TYPE	DESCRIPTION
BufferedReader	Provides buffered file input.
BufferedWriter	Provides buffered file output.
EOFException	This exception is thrown when a program encounters the end of a file or stream during an input operation.
File	This is the object that abstracts a file in the file system, and could be a directory or a file. Also note that although Java doesn't specify character encoding for filenames, on Android Java strings are converted into UTF-8 byte sequences when sending filenames to the operating system. Byte sequences returned by the operating system (from the various list methods) are converted to Java strings by decoding them as UTF-8 byte sequences.
FileInputStream	This is a specialized `Java.IO.InputStream` that is used to stream read a file from the file system.
FileNotFoundException	This exception is thrown when a file specified by a program cannot be found.
FileOutputStream	This is a specialized `Java.IO.OutputStream` that stream writes a file in the file system.
FilePermission	Object that contains the permission enums for a file. Also note that a `File.separatorChar` must be used in all pathnames when constructing a `FilePermission`.

continues

TABLE 7-1 *(continued)*

TYPE	DESCRIPTION
InputStream	This is an abstract class that is inherited by many specialized input streams for purposes such as reading from a file or a byte array.
IOException	This exception signals a general, I/O-related error.
NotSerializableException	This exception signals that an object that is not serializable has been passed into the `ObjectOutput.writeObject()` method.
OutputStream	This is an abstract class that is inherited by many specialized output streams for purposes such as writing to a file or a byte array.
PrintStream	Wraps an existing `Java.IO.OutputStream` and provides convenience methods for writing common data types in a human-readable format.
PrintWriter	Wraps either an existing `Java.IO.OutputStream` or an existing `Java.IO.Writer` and provides convenience methods for printing common data types in a human-readable format.
RandomAccessFile	Allows reading from and writing to a file in a random-access manner.
StringReader	This is a specialized `Java.IO.Reader` that reads characters from a `String` in a sequential manner.
StringWriter	This is a specialized `Java.IO.Writer` that writes characters to a `StringBuffer` sequentially, appending them in the process.
UnsupportedEncodingException	This exception is thrown when a program asks for a particular character converter that is unavailable.
UTFDataFormatException	This exception signals that an incorrectly encoded UTF-8 string has been encountered, most likely while reading a `DataInputStream`.

Aside from persistent files, your application might need to store cache data in a file. To do that, you would use `GetCacheDir()` along with a `File` object to open a file in the cache directory. Cache files are subject to removal by Android if the system runs low on internal storage space, but you should not count on the system's cleaning up these files for you. If your application is removed, the cache files it owns are removed also. But, as a good Android citizen you should remove any unused cache files.

In addition to file creation, file placement also occurs. Files can be placed in internal or external storage. Internal storage refers to the built-in device storage, and external storage refers to a media card that can be added to the device. The two systems are accessed in a slightly different manner.

For internal files, the following functions are used:

➤   `OpenFileInput` (*filename, operatingmode*)

➤   `OpenFileOutput` (*filename, operatingmode*)

These are for file input and output, respectively. In each case, the parameters are a filename and one of the operating context modes that were mentioned earlier.

For external storage the operation is different. First you must check to see if any external storage is available. If it is, you have to check to see if it is writable. After you have confirmed that external storage is available, you use `GetExternalFilesDir()` in conjunction with a standard `File()` object to create a file on the external storage medium.

This can all be done with the `ExternalStorageState` property, as shown in the following code snippet:

```
if (Android.OS.Environment.ExternalStorageState == Android.OS.Environment
  .MediaMounted)
                {
                      File dataDir = this.GetExternalFilesDir(Android.OS.Environment
                        .DataDirectory.Path);
                      FileOutputStream fos = OpenFileOutput(dataDir +
                        QUICKEDIT_FILENAME, FileCreationMode.Private);
                      UTF8Encoding enc = new UTF8Encoding();
                      fos.Write(enc.GetBytes(content));
                      fos.Close();
                }
```

In this example there is only one test, whether `ExternalStorageState` equals `MediaMounted`. If this is true, then the external media is available and in read-write mode — all is good. If this is not true, then there are other media states that could be tested to determine the exact status.

`GetExternalFilesDir` takes a parameter of type `string` that indicates the standard directory for any of the several standard file types shown in Table 7-2.

TABLE 7-2: Standard Directories Used by GetExternalFilesDir

DIRECTORY CONSTANT	DESCRIPTION
DirectoryAlarms	Standard directory in which to place any audio files that should be in the list of alarms that the user can select (not as regular music).
DirectoryDcim	Standard directory in which to place pictures and videos when mounting the device as a camera.

continues

TABLE 7-2 *(continued)*

DIRECTORY CONSTANT	DESCRIPTION
DirectoryDownloads	Standard directory in which to place files that the user has downloaded.
DirectoryMovies	Standard directory in which to place movies that are available to the user.
DirectoryMusic	Standard directory in which to place any audio files that should be in the list of regular music for the user.
DirectoryNotifications	Standard directory in which to place any audio files that should be in the list of notifications that the user can select (not as regular music).
DirectoryPictures	Standard directory in which to place pictures that are available to the user.
DirectoryPodcasts	Standard directory in which to place any audio files that should be in the list of podcasts that the user can select (not as regular music).
DirectoryRingtones	Standard directory in which to place any audio files that should be in the list of ringtones that the user can select (not as regular music).

If you pass in a null instead of one of the previous constants, GetExternalFilesDir returns the path to the root of the external storage medium.

Again, as with internal storage, you may create cache files on the external storage medium. This is done with the unsurprisingly named GetExternalCacheDir() and a File object.

How do you read a file? Files can be read from or written to in either a streaming or random-access fashion. The following snippet shows how to read bytes from a file:

```
byte[] content = new byte[1024];
FileInputStream fis = OpenFileInput(QUICKEDIT_FILENAME);
fis.Read(content);
fis.Close();
```

The following snippet shows how to write to a file. Here a string value is written to a text file through FileOutputStream. It's important to note that because a string is made up of characters and FileOutputStream writes bytes, the characters must be converted to bytes. Here UTF8Encoding is used to accomplish the task:

```
String content = "content";
FileOutputStream fos = OpenFileOutput("filename.txt",
 FileCreationMode.Private);
UTF8Encoding enc = new UTF8Encoding();
fos.Write(enc.GetBytes(content));
fos.Close();
```

QuickEdit Sample Program: Working with a File Storage Example

Having reviewed file storage, now you are going to take a look at a program that reads and writes text data from the display to the file system.

The first thing to do is create a new Android program and call it QuickEdit.

The next thing to do is to change the layout:

```xml
<?xml version="1.0" encoding="utf-8"?>
<LinearLayout xmlns:android="http://schemas.android.com/apk/res/android"
    android:orientation="vertical"
    android:layout_width="fill_parent"
    android:layout_height="fill_parent"
    >
<EditText
    android:id="@+id/fileEditor"
    android:layout_width="fill_parent"
    android:layout_height="fill_parent"
    android:text="@string/Hello"
    android:gravity="top"
    />
</LinearLayout>
```

QuickEdit snippets can be found in the QuickEdit folder.

Here you can see to replace the default "Hello World" button with an `EditText` element that fills the screen.

Next add some constants that you will use in the program above the `OnCreate` function:

```
const int MENU_GROUP = 0;
const int SAVE_FILE_MENU_ID = 1;
const int SAVE_FILE_MENU_ORDER = 1;

const string QUICKEDIT_TAG = "QUICKEDIT";
const string QUICKEDIT_FILENAME = "quickedit.txt";
```

These constants specify values to be used by the context menu, the tag you will use in the log messages generated by the program, and a filename for the notes you create. Of course, a more sophisticated program would give the user a dialog box in which to enter this value, but a single filename is fine for demonstration purposes.

Next, you add an `OpenFile` function:

```
void OpenFile()
{
    byte[] content = new byte[1024];
    try
    {
        Stream fis = OpenFileInput(QUICKEDIT_FILENAME);
        if ((fis.Read(content,0,content.Length)) > 0)
        {
```

```
            EditText editText = (EditText)FindViewById(Resource.Id.fileEditor);
            UTF8Encoding enc = new UTF8Encoding();
            char[] chars = enc.GetChars(content);
            int charLength = chars.Length;
            if (charLength>0) {
                editText.SetText(new string(chars),
                    Android.Widget.TextView.BufferType.Editable);
            }
        }
        fis.Close();
    }
    catch (Java.IO.FileNotFoundException e)
    {
        Log.Error(QUICKEDIT_TAG, e.Message);
    }
    catch (Java.IO.IOException e)
    {
        Log.Error(QUICKEDIT_TAG, e.Message);
    }
}
```

Here you call the `OpenFileInput` function to open the filename specified by the constant value. The file data is read into a byte array (limited in size to 1024 bytes for demonstration purposes), and then the file is closed. The `editText` view is retrieved. Finally, the file text is set into the edit text view while the bytes are converted into characters using UTF8 encoding.

After this, you define two functions to display and handle the context menu and its events:

```
public override bool OnCreateOptionsMenu ( IMenu menu )
{
    base.OnCreateOptionsMenu(menu);
    menu.Add(MENU_GROUP,
             SAVE_FILE_MENU_ID,
             SAVE_FILE_MENU_ORDER,
             Resource.String.Save);
    return true;
}

public override bool OnOptionsItemSelected(IMenuItem item)
{
    base.OnOptionsItemSelected(item);
    switch (item.ItemId)
    {
        case SAVE_FILE_MENU_ID:
        SaveFile();
        return true;
    }

    return false;
}
```

First you create the options menu in the `OnCreateOptionsMenu` handler. Then you handle the `OnOptionsItemSelected` event, where you call `SaveFile` if that option has been selected.

Finally, you define the `SaveFile` function:

```
void SaveFile()
    {
        EditText editText = (EditText)FindViewById(Resource.Id.fileEditor);
        String content = editText.Text;
        try
        {
            Stream fos = OpenFileOutput(QUICKEDIT_FILENAME,
                FileCreationMode.Private);
            UTF8Encoding enc = new UTF8Encoding();
            fos.Write(enc.GetBytes(content),0,enc.GetBytes(content).Length);
            fos.Close();
        }
        catch (Java.IO.FileNotFoundException e)
        {
            Log.Error(QUICKEDIT_TAG, e.Message);
        }
        catch (Java.IO.IOException e)
        {
            Log.Error(QUICKEDIT_TAG, e.Message);
        }
    }
```

Here you do the reverse of the `OpenFile` function, opening an output stream to the `quickedit.txt` file. Then you write the bytes to the output stream after converting them from UTF8 characters.

Finally, add a call to `OpenFile` in the `OnCreate` method:

```
OpenFile();
```

Listing 7-1 shows the final program:

LISTING 7-1: QuickEdit sample program

```
using System;

using Android.App;
using Android.Content;
using Android.Runtime;
using Android.Views;
using Android.Widget;
using Android.OS;
using Java.IO;
using Android.Util;
using System.Text;
using System.IO;

namespace QuickEdit
{
    [Activity(Label = "QuickEdit", MainLauncher = true)]
    public class QuickEdit : Activity
    {
        const int MENU_GROUP = 0;
```

continues

LISTING 7-1 *(continued)*

```
const int SAVE_FILE_MENU_ID = 1;
const int SAVE_FILE_MENU_ORDER = 1;

const string QUICKEDIT_TAG = "QUICKEDIT";
const string QUICKEDIT_FILENAME = "quickedit.txt";

protected override void OnCreate(Bundle bundle)
{
    base.OnCreate(bundle);

    // Set our view from the "main" layout resource
    SetContentView(Resource.Layout.Main);

    OpenFile();
}

public override bool OnCreateOptionsMenu ( IMenu menu )
{
    base.OnCreateOptionsMenu(menu);
    menu.Add(MENU_GROUP,
            SAVE_FILE_MENU_ID,
            SAVE_FILE_MENU_ORDER,
            Resource.String.Save);
    return true;
}

public override bool OnOptionsItemSelected(IMenuItem item)
{
    base.OnOptionsItemSelected(item);
    switch (item.ItemId)
    {
        case SAVE_FILE_MENU_ID:
            SaveFile();
            return true;
    }
    return false;
}

void SaveFile()
{
    EditText editText = (EditText)FindViewById(Resource.Id.fileEditor);
    String content = editText.Text;
    try
    {
        Stream fos = OpenFileOutput(QUICKEDIT_FILENAME,
            FileCreationMode.Private);
        UTF8Encoding enc = new UTF8Encoding();
        fos.Write(enc.GetBytes(content),0,enc.GetBytes(content).Length);
        fos.Close();
    }
    catch (Java.IO.FileNotFoundException e)
    {
        Log.Error(QUICKEDIT_TAG, e.Message);
```

```
        }
        catch (Java.IO.IOException e)
        {
            Log.Error(QUICKEDIT_TAG, e.Message);
        }
    }

    void SaveExternalFile()
    {
        EditText editText = (EditText)FindViewById(Resource.Id.fileEditor);
        String content = editText.Text.ToString();
        try
        {

            if (Android.OS.Environment.ExternalStorageState ==
                Android.OS.Environment.MediaMounted)
            {
                Java.IO.File dataDir = this.GetExternalFilesDir
                    (Android.OS.Environment.DataDirectory.Path);
                Stream fos = OpenFileOutput(dataDir + QUICKEDIT_FILENAME,
                    FileCreationMode.Private);
                UTF8Encoding enc = new UTF8Encoding();
                fos.Write(enc.GetBytes(content), 0,
                    enc.GetBytes(content).Length);
                fos.Close();
            }
        }
        catch (Java.IO.FileNotFoundException e)
        {
            Log.Error(QUICKEDIT_TAG, e.Message);
        }
        catch (Java.IO.IOException e)
        {
            Log.Error(QUICKEDIT_TAG, e.Message);
        }
    }

    void OpenFile()
    {
        byte[] content = new byte[1024];
        try
        {
            Stream fis = OpenFileInput(QUICKEDIT_FILENAME);
            if ((fis.Read(content,0,content.Length)) > 0)
            {
                EditText editText =
                    (EditText)FindViewById(Resource.Id.fileEditor);
                UTF8Encoding enc = new UTF8Encoding();
                char[] chars = enc.GetChars(content);
                int charLength = chars.Length;
                if (charLength>0) {
                    editText.SetText(new string(chars),
                        Android.Widget.TextView.BufferType.Editable);
                }
            }
            fis.Close();
```

continues

LISTING 7-1 *(continued)*

```
            }
            catch (Java.IO.FileNotFoundException e)
            {
                Log.Error(QUICKEDIT_TAG, e.Message);
            }
            catch (Java.IO.IOException e)
            {
                Log.Error(QUICKEDIT_TAG, e.Message);
            }
        }
    }
}
```

The QuickEdit sample program can be found in the QuickEdit folder.

If you run this program in your Android emulator, you should see the result shown in Figure 7-1.

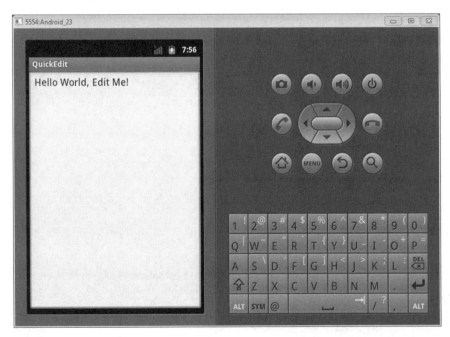

FIGURE 7-1

If you add some text and select Save from the menu, that text is saved and will be automatically loaded every time you reenter the program. To improve the program you should try a couple of things. Enhance the `OpenFile` function to be unlimited by the 1024-byte buffer. Also link `SaveFile` to a text-changed event so that the user does not need to remember to save his or her file.

WORKING WITH APPLICATION PREFERENCES

This section deals with application preferences. It starts by covering the types of application preferences and then discusses the preferences API. This section wraps up with a sample program that shows how to store and retrieve shared and private preferences and how to listen for preference changes.

Application Preference Types

Application preferences are simple maps of name-value pairs. Name-value pairs are stored through a key string and then one of a limited number of value types:

➤ Boolean

➤ Float

➤ Int

➤ Long

➤ String

The two types of preferences are private and shared. Private preferences are private to an activity within an application. Shared preferences are named and can be opened by any activity within the application. The function calls for each are as follows:

➤ GetPreferences(*mode*)

➤ GetSharedPreferences(*name, mode*)

Since private preferences are necessarily private and are inaccessible to any other activity, the call requires no name parameter — only an access mode. In fact, this function simply leverages the second function by calling it with the activity's class name as the *name* parameter.

GetSharedPreferences, however, requires two parameters. The first parameter is the name of the preferences file, and the second is the file access mode. These were mentioned in the previous section, but this time the available modes are limited to three:

➤ FileCreationMode.Private

➤ FileCreationMode.WorldReadable

➤ FileCreationMode.WorldWriteable

 You might ask, "What is the benefit of private preferences when you could simply have shared preferences in private mode?" The answer is simply convenience and a common scenario in Android. Given that activities in Android do not control their own life cycle and that users can navigate away at any time, you often need to save the activity state. So a quick call to GetPreferences(mode) *gives you a good object for storing partially entered text or other settings that have not yet been completed.*

Creating Your Own Application Preferences

So how do you create your own application preferences? There are a couple of ways. First you are going to look at some snippets of code that demonstrate how to manually create private and shared preferences. Then you are going to look at a sample program that uses a standard preferences screen to create preference values. Consider the following snippet:

```
ISharedPreferences p = GetPreferences(FileCreationMode.Private);
String value = p.GetString("MyTextValue", "");
```

The first line gets the private `ISharedPreferences` object. Again, it is important to note that both `GetPreferences()` and `GetSharedPreferences()` return an object of type `ISharedPreferences`. Then the second line retrieves the value stored under the key `"MyTextValue"`. If there is no value, it returns the second parameter — in this case, an empty string — as the default. There are six accessor methods:

➤   GetString

➤   GetFloat

➤   GetInt

➤   GetLong

➤   GetBoolean

➤   GetAll

The first five return a single value of the data type specified by the function. The last function returns a map of all the keys and values in the system.

Now that you have seen how to read values from a `ISharedPreferences` object, how do you change the values in this object? The answer is to use the `SharedPreferences.Editor` interface. You access this interface through a call to `p.Edit()` on the `ISharedPreferences` object. The following code snippet shows getting, editing, and storing the edited values:

```
ISharedPreferences p = GetPreferences(FileCreationMode.Private);
String value = p.GetString("MyTextValue", "");
value = "New Value";
ISharedPreferencesEditor e = p.Edit();
e.PutString("MyTextValue",value);
e.Commit();
```

Here you retrieve `ISharedPreferences` with a call to `GetPreferences()`. Then you retrieve whatever string is stored under the key `"MyTextValue"` or `""` if there is no value. The value string is then assigned `"New Value"`. A call to `p.Edit()` returns `ISharedPreferencesEditor`, which is used to store the string `"New Value"` into the key `"MyTextValue"`. Then a final call to `e.Commit()` writes the changes to disk.

Five functions are used to store values in `ISharedPreferencesEditor`:

➤   PutString(*string key, string value*)

➤   PutInt(*string key, int value*)

➤   PutLong(*string key*, *long value*)

➤   PutFloat(*string key*, *float value*)

➤   PutBoolean(*string key*, *boolean value*)

Two functions are used to remove keys:

➤   Remove(*string key*)

➤   Clear()

Remove removes the key-value pair specified by the key, and Clear removes all the key-value pairs.

Then it is important to note that all changes are batched and are not saved until the following function is called:

➤   Boolean Commit();

Commit() makes a synchronous call to write to storage immediately and provides a Boolean result to that call.

Preferences Program

This section shows you how to create a preferences screen and how to update preference values using that screen in a sample program. In this example you will use the objects in the preferences namespace, which are described in Table 7-3.

TABLE 7-3: Preferences Namespace

TYPE	DESCRIPTION
CheckBoxPreference	This preference stores a Boolean in SharedPreferences.
DialogPreference	This is a base class for Android.Preferences.Preference objects that are dialog box-based.
EditTextPreference	This preference allows an editable string to be stored into the preferences file.
ListPreference	This preference stores a string in SharedPreferences from a list of available strings.
Preference	This class contains a key that will be used as the key into Android.Content.ISharedPreferences.
PreferenceActivity	As a convenience, this activity implements a click listener for any preference in the current hierarchy.
PreferenceCategory	Used to group Android.Preferences.Preference objects and provide a disabled title above the group.

continues

TABLE 7-3 *(continued)*

TYPE	DESCRIPTION
PreferenceGroup	A container for multiple `Android.Preferences.Preference` objects.
PreferenceScreen	Used to group preferences onto another screen so that when the title is clicked, a new preference screen opens with the grouped preferences.
RingtonePreference	Allows the user to select a ringtone. If the user chooses the Default item, the saved string is one of `Android.Provider.Settings.System.DefaultRingtoneUri`, `Android.Provider.Settings.System.DefaultNotificationUri`, or `Android.Provider.Settings.System.DefaultAlarmAlertUri`.

Most of these objects don't need to be coded directly, but you will leverage them in a `PreferenceScreen` layout. So let's start. The first step is to create a new Android program. This time you will call it MonoForAndroidPreferences.

Once the new project is up and going, the next thing to do is add an `arrays.xml` file under `Resources/Values` with the following content:

```xml
<?xml version="1.0" encoding="utf-8" ?>
<resources>
  <string-array name="frequency_options">
    <item>Every Minute</item>
    <item>5 minutes</item>
    <item>10 minutes</item>
    <item>15 minutes</item>
    <item>Every Hour</item>
  </string-array>
  <string-array name="frequency_values">
    <item>1</item>
    <item>5</item>
    <item>10</item>
    <item>15</item>
    <item>60</item>
  </string-array>
  <string-array name="number_options">
    <item>3</item>
    <item>5</item>
    <item>6</item>
    <item>7</item>
    <item>8</item>
  </string-array>
  <string-array name="number_values">
    <item>3</item>
    <item>5</item>
    <item>6</item>
    <item>7</item>
    <item>8</item>
```

```
    </string-array>
</resources>
```

MonoForAndroidPreferences snippets can be found in the MonoForAndroidPreferences folder.

The layout uses these arrays to populate the preferences screen. The next thing to do is to create the following layout under the name userpreferences.xml in the Layouts folder.

```
<?xml version="1.0" encoding="utf-8" ?>
<PreferenceScreen
    xmlns:android="http://schemas.android.com/apk/res/android">
  <PreferenceCategory
            android:title="Category One"/>
  <CheckBoxPreference
        android:key="PREF_AUTO_UPDATE"
        android:title="Auto refresh"
        android:summary="Select to turn on automatic updating"
        android:defaultValue="true"
        />
  <ListPreference
        android:key="PREF_SIZE"
        android:title="Minimum size"
        android:summary="Select the minimum size"
        android:entries="@array/number_options"
        android:entryValues="@array/number_values"
        android:dialogTitle="Magnitude"
        android:defaultValue="3"
        />
  <ListPreference
        android:key="PREF_FREQUENCY"
        android:title="Refresh frequency"
        android:summary="Frequency at which to refresh"
        android:entries="@array/frequency_options"
        android:entryValues="@array/frequency_values"
        Android: dialogTitle="Refresh frequency"
        Android: defaultValue="60"
        />
  <PreferenceCategory
            Android:title="Category Two"/>
  <EditTextPreference
        android:name="EditText Preference"
        android:summary="This allows you to enter a string"
        android:defaultValue="Edit Me"
        android:title="Edit This Text"
        android:key="PREF_TEXT_1" />
  <PreferenceScreen
        android:key="SecondPrefScreen"
        android:title="Second PreferenceScreen"
        android:summary="This is a second PreferenceScreen">
    <EditTextPreference
```

```
        android:name="A second EditText Preference"
        android:summary="This is a preference in the second PreferenceScreen"
        android:title="Edit text"
        android:key="PREF_TEXT_2" />
    </PreferenceScreen>

  </PreferenceScreen>
```

A few items are worth noting in this piece of XML. The first is that the different preference objects such as ListPreference and EditTextPreference have android:key values. These refer to the keys that will be stored in the preferences file. The second thing to note is the reference to the arrays that we created under the list preferences. Finally, it is worth noting that you can embed one PreferenceScreen in another to automatically link to an extended set of preferences.

Next you want to make some quick changes to the Resources/Values strings.xml, setting the text to the following:

```
<resources>
    <string name="hello">Hello Preferences, Click Me!</string>
    <string name="app_name">MonoForAndroidPreferences</string>
</resources>
```

Next you want to move on to some actual code. So create a new class called UserPreferences and provide the following code:

```
namespace MonoForAndroidPreferences
{
    [Activity(Label = "User Preferences")]
    public class UserPreferences : PreferenceActivity
    {
        protected override void OnCreate(Bundle bundle)
        {
            base.OnCreate(bundle);

            // Create your application here
            this.AddPreferencesFromResource(Resource.Layout.userpreferences);
        }
    }
}
```

Notice that UserPreferences inherits from PreferenceActivity and that you call AddPreferencesFromResource referring to the previously created userpreferences layout.

Finally, return to the MonoForAndroidPreferences OnCreate handler to make the following changes:

```
namespace MonoForAndroidPreferences
{
    [Activity(Label = "Preferences", MainLauncher = true)]
    public class PreferencesDemo : Activity
    {
        int count = 1;

        protected override void OnCreate(Bundle bundle)
        {
            base.OnCreate(bundle);
```

```
            // Set our view from the "main" layout resource
            SetContentView(Resource.Layout.main);

            // Get our button from the layout resource,
            // and attach an event to it
            Button button = FindViewById<Button>(Resource.Id.myButton);

            button.Click += delegate {

                Intent i = new Intent(this, (Java.Lang.Class)(new
                UserPreferences().Class));
                this.StartActivityForResult(i, 0);
            };
        }
    }
}
```

Here you see the code changed for the button delegate. You create a new intent based on the UserPreferences class. Then, when the button is clicked, you fire off the activity using StartActivityForResult. This guarantees that you will return to this activity when you are through with your preference changes on the preference screens. Listing 7-2 presents a full listing of the code.

LISTING 7-2: MonoForAndroidPreferences sample program

```
namespace MonoForAndroidPreferences
{
    [Activity(Label = "Preferences", MainLauncher = true)]
    public class PreferencesDemo : Activity
    {
        int count = 1;

        protected override void OnCreate(Bundle bundle)
        {
            base.OnCreate(bundle);

            // Set our view from the "main" layout resource
            SetContentView(Resource.Layout.main);

            // Get our button from the layout resource,
            // and attach an event to it
            Button button = FindViewById<Button>(Resource.Id.myButton);

            button.Click += delegate {

                Intent i = new Intent(this, (Java.Lang.Class)(new
                UserPreferences().Class));
                this.StartActivityForResult(i, 0);
            };
        }
    }
}
```

continues

LISTING 7-2 *(continued)*

```
namespace MonoForAndroidPreferences
{
    [Activity(Label = "User Preferences")]
    public class UserPreferences : PreferenceActivity
    {
        protected override void OnCreate(Bundle bundle)
        {
            base.OnCreate(bundle);

            // Create your application here
            this.AddPreferencesFromResource(Resource.Layout.userpreferences);
        }
    }
}
```

The MonoForAndroidPreferences sample program can be found in the MonoForAndroidPreferences folder.

Figures 7-2 and 7-3 show the program running.

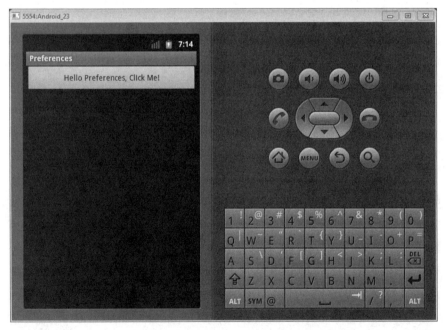

FIGURE 7-2

Listening for Preference Changes

One important aspect of preferences is to know when they change. This section looks at how to handle the change events that are generated by changes in shared preferences.

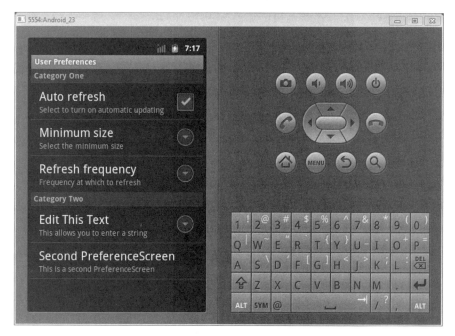

FIGURE 7-3

Two functions are important in this process — one for registering a change listener, and the other for unregistering it:

➤ RegisterOnSharedPreferenceChangeListener
(ISharedPreferencesOnSharedPreferenceChangeListener)

➤ UnregisterOnSharedPreferenceChangeListener
(ISharedPreferencesOnSharedPreferenceChangeListener)

The following code snippet shows these functions in action:

```
protected override void OnResume()
{
    base.OnResume();

    this.GetPreferences(FileCreationMode.Private)
        .RegisterOnSharedPreferenceChangeListener(this);
}

protected override void OnPause()
{
    base.OnPause();

    this.GetPreferences(FileCreationMode.Private)
        .UnregisterOnSharedPreferenceChangeListener(this);
}
```

```
public void OnSharedPreferenceChanged(ISharedPreferences prefs, string key)
{
    // Do something with the changed value pointed to by key
}
```

In this example the listener is registered during the `OnResume` process and is unregistered during the `OnPause` process. While the listener is active, whenever a preference changes, the `OnSharedPreferenceChanged` function is called, allowing the activity to react to the preference change.

Processing XML

Android provides access to three different XML parsers: the DOM parser, the SAX parser, and an XML pull parser. However, these have not all been exposed through the Mono for Android interface yet. Nevertheless, XML processing is available through the Linq XML namespace.

The following snippet shows how an Atom feed from `http://freshmeat.net`, a site focused on open source software, might be processed:

```
private void getFreshMeatFeed()
{
        WebClient client = new WebClient();
        client.DownloadStringAsync(new
        Uri("http://freshmeat.net/?format=atom"));
        client.DownloadStringCompleted += new
        DownloadStringCompletedEventHandler(client_DownloadStringCompleted);
}

private void client_DownloadStringCompleted(object sender,
    DownloadStringCompletedEventArgs e)
        {
        if (e.Error == null)
        {
            XDocument xml = XDocument.Parse(e.Result);
            XNamespace atomNS = "http://www.w3.org/2005/Atom";

            System.Collections.Generic.IEnumerable<AtomEntry> list = (from
                entry in xml.Descendants(atomNS + "entry")
            select new AtomEntry()
            {
                ID = entry.Element(atomNS + "id").Value,
                Title = entry.Element(atomNS + "title").Value,
                Content = entry.Element(atomNS + "content").Value,
                Published = DateTime.Parse(entry.Element(atomNS +
                    "published").Value),
                Updated = DateTime.Parse(entry.Element(atomNS +
                    "updated").Value)
            });

            ArrayList titles = new ArrayList();
            foreach (AtomEntry atomEntry in list) {
```

```
                    titles.Add(atomEntry.Title);
            }

            this.RunOnUiThread(() =>
            {
                Java.Lang.Object[] test = list.ToArray();
                ArrayAdapter aao = new ArrayAdapter<Java.Lang.Object>(this,
    Android.Resource.Layout.SimpleListItem1,test);
                ((ListView)this.FindViewById(Resource.Id.FMListView)).Adapter
    = aao;
            });
        }
    }
```

Code for this sample can be found in this chapter's download in the FreshMeat2 folder.

Here we see a couple of things going on. First, in the function `getFreshMeatFeed`, you create a `WebClient` object to make the call to the feed on the Internet. When the client download is finished, `client_DownloadStringCompleted` is called. After checking for any errors, the download result is parsed into an `XDocument` object. Then a list of `AtomEntry` objects is created by searching on "entry" descendants and parsing the contents of each entry.

Although this is only a snippet, it represents a common pattern for processing XML into a list. And although this XML comes from an Internet feed, it could have just as well come from a local file. And, once the list is in place, it could be iterated to display information, or it could be connected to a `ListAdapter` for display.

SUMMARY

This chapter started with program preferences. You saw that an activity can have private preferences accessible to only that activity, or an activity can access shared preferences that are available to multiple activities as long as they have the same process ID.

You also saw how to create, read from, and write to files on the file system. Files can have three different permission settings that cause them to be private, world-readable, or world-writeable. Files that are created directly can be either text or binary and can be accessed randomly or in a streaming mode.

Finally, we wrapped up with a couple of additional code snippets. One demonstrated how to register and unregister a shared preference change listener and receive and react to those events. The final code snippet showed how to use the `Linq.xml` namespace to parse the XML in an Atom feed from FreshMeat.

Now you should be able to create preferences for your users that add robustness to your app. Going forward, your activities will be able to maintain state despite losing focus, your program settings will be durable between usages, and data can be stored to files for later usage.

8

Programming with the Device Hardware

WHAT'S IN THIS CHAPTER?

➤ Using the sensor API

➤ Programming accelerometer, device orientation, and proximity detection support

➤ Supporting networking

➤ Bluetooth programming

Android contains a vast amount of exciting hardware. This hardware in and of itself doesn't interest users; the excitement occurs when the application presents the users with information in a way that makes sense to them. This hardware is very interesting to developers building apps because it allows applications to provide extraordinary features based on it. This chapter looks at the sensor API, accelerometer, device orientation, proximity detection, networking, and Bluetooth. Here are some sample uses of this hardware:

➤ A program can test whether a network is available over any connection (WiFi, 3G, or EDGE). If a connection does not exist, instead of seeing an error message when attempting to upload information, the user can be notified that there is no connection to a service.

➤ The accelerometer can be used to pull random data from a data source. When the device is shaken, the application can respond by reading random data from a data source.

➤ When the user changes the device from portrait to landscape, the application can change how it displays content to the user.

WORKING WITH SENSORS

Android devices come with all types of exciting features, including accelerometers, compasses, microphones, gyroscopes, and other nifty hardware. This hardware allows devices to detect what is happening around you. With the hardware in the device, applications and user interfaces can better provide user inputs based on the environment around them.

Android's `Sensor` class abstracts the actual implementation of sensors on each device. The `Sensor` class can then be used to obtain the properties of the hardware sensor, including the manufacturer, name, accuracy, range, and type of sensor.

Referencing the Sensor Manager

The first step in using sensors is to work with the Android Sensor Manager. The Sensor Manager is how you access the sensors on a particular device. This code provides a reference to the Sensor Manager:

```
String service_name = Context.SensorService;
sensManager = (SensorManager)GetSystemService(service_name);
```

Sensor Support

The `Sensor` class includes a set of constants that describe the type of sensor that is being used by a `Sensor` object. The following sensor types are currently supported, can be accessed through the `Android.Hardware.SensorType` enumeration, and can be programmed with:

➤ `Accelerometer` returns acceleration information in the x-, y-, and z-axes in meters per second squared.

➤ `Gyroscope` returns the device's current orientation in three axes in degrees.

➤ `Light` is a single value that is the illumination in lux. This sensor type can be used to set the screen's brightness based on the available light.

➤ `MagneticField` determines the magnetic field that the device is in. The magnetic field is measured in three axes and is returned in microteslas.

➤ `Orientation` determines the device orientation in three axes in degrees.

➤ `Pressure` returns the pressure on the current device in hPa.

➤ `Proximity` determines the distance between a device and a target object in centimeters. Typically, the proximity detector is used to determine if the phone is being held to the user's ear. This allows the device to listen for a voice command or to turn off the screen, since the screen is not needed for input when it's against the user's ear. The selection of the target object and the distances that are supported depend greatly on the hardware used within the proximity detector.

➤ `Temperature` determines the device's temperature in Celsius. The type of temperature returned varies depending on the hardware used to detect the temperature.

➤ `All` returns all the sensors on the host platform.

Accessing Sensors

There are two ways to obtain a sensor with the `Sensor` class. The first way is to obtain the default sensor corresponding to a given sensor type. This is done by calling the following:

```
defSensor = sensManager.GetDefaultSensor(SensorType.Accelerometer);
```

In this case, the code returns the default sensor for the accelerometer.

The other way is to obtain all the sensors associated with a given sensor type. This is done by calling the following:

```
IList<Sensor> accSensors = sensorManager.GetSensorList(SensorType.Accelerometer);
```

The result is a list of type `sensor` that a program can iterate through. This could be useful if a program needs to get all the sensors for a type on a device and allow a user to select a specific sensor.

Using Sensors

After you decide which sensor to use, the process of setting up the code involves three additional steps:

➤ **Registration:** The application must register that it is listening for updates from the hardware. This is accomplished with the following code:

```
sensManager.RegisterListener(this, defSensor, SensorDelay.Ui);
```

➤ **Processing:** The interfaces for `ISensorEventListener` must be implemented to process sensor values.

➤ **Unregistration.**

The registration of the listener takes multiple parameters. The first parameter is the class that processes the sensor's changes. The second parameter is the sensor that sends the change. The final parameter is the desired rate of getting an update from the sensor. The rate that is selected is not definite. Updates tend to be faster. To minimize usage of the battery, an application should use the slowest suitable rate. The `SensorDelay` enum has the following properties:

➤ `Fastest` is the fastest update value for the hardware.

➤ `Game` is an update rate suitable for games.

➤ `Normal` represents the default update rate for the hardware sensor.

➤ `Ui` represents a rate suitable for updating UI elements.

The class that listens for sensor updates must implement the `Android.Hardware.ISensorEventListener` interface. In the case of the example in this chapter, the activity implements the interface with the following code:

```
public class Activity1 : Activity, Android.Hardware.ISensorEventListener
```

The `ISensorEventListener` interface requires that the methods `OnSensorChanged` and `OnAccuracyChanged` be implemented. Listing 8-1 implements these two methods. One of the key things to notice in the `OnSensorChanged` method is that a check is done for the sensor type. This check allows a class to listen for multiple sensor changes.

LISTING 8-1: Processing Sensors using the Accelerometer

```
public void ISensorEventListener.OnSensorChanged(SensorEvent e)
{
    if ( e.Sensor.Type == SensorType.Accelerometer){
    var calibrationValue = SensorManager.StandardGravity;
    var mVals = e.Values;
    var x = mVals[0];
    var y = mVals[1];
    var z = mVals[2];
    var SumOfSq = Math.Pow(x, 2) + Math.Pow(y, 2) + Math.Pow(z, 2);
        var mag = Math.Pow(SumOfSq, .5) - calibrationValue;
        RunOnUiThread(() =>
            tv.Text = "Acceleration (g): " + mag.ToString()
        );
    }
}
public void ISensorEventListener.OnAccuracyChanged(Sensor sensor, int accuracy)
{
    if (sensor.Type == Android.Hardware.SensorType.Accelerometer)
    {
        if (Android.Hardware.SensorStatus.AccuracyHigh ==
    (Android.Hardware.SensorStatus)accuracy)
        {

        }
    }
}
```

This code is contained in Acceleration\Activity1.cs

 Objects on the Earth are always experiencing acceleration. Fortunately, the Android Sensor Manager provides a value representing the Earth's standard gravity.

Another item to remember is that Visual Studio can automatically cre-ate the necessary interface methods. Visual Studio will automatically put a NotImplementedException *within the method, so you will want to remove that exception.*

The OnAccuracyChanged event has an enum that can be used to determine the sensor's new accuracy. The enum is within Android.Hardware.SensorStatus.Accuracy. The values are as follows:

➤ AccuracyLow indicates that the hardware sensor's accuracy is low and that it may need calibration.

➤ AccuracyMedium indicates that the hardware sensor's accuracy is moderate. Calibrating the sensor may help improve the accuracy.

➤ `AccuracyHigh` indicates that the hardware sensor's accuracy is the best that it will be.

➤ `Unreliable` indicates that the data returned from the hardware sensor is unreliable. This can mean that the values returned are not possible or that the sensor must be calibrated.

The final operation to perform is to unregister sensor listening when the application no longer needs to receive updates. This is handled by calling the Sensor Manager's `.UnregisterListener` method:

```
sensManager.UnregisterListener(this, defSensor);
```

Understanding the Sensor Type Values

The following section describes the values that are returned from the various sensor types that are monitored.

➤ **Accelerometer:** The accelerometer returns three values — acceleration along three axes in meters per second squared:

  ➤ `value[0]`: Lateral (x direction)

  ➤ `value[1]`: Longitudinal (z direction)

  ➤ `value[2]`: Vertical (y direction)

The Sensor Manager includes a set of gravity constants of the form `SensorManager` `.GRAVITY*` that represent the gravity of various bodies in the solar system. This is helpful for those really long-distance trips.

Because there is always confusion on this subject, this is a good place to mention that a device only has zero acceleration in two places, when it is in free fall and when it is floating in a zero gravity/outer space environment. Because of this, a program will need to take this into account by using the standard gravity constants to pull out the constant acceleration due to gravity.

➤ **Gyroscope:** The gyroscope returns three values — device orientation in degrees along three axes:

  ➤ `value[0]`: Azimuth

  ➤ `value[1]`: Pitch

  ➤ `value[2]`: Roll

This is useful in games where the Android device is used as a game controller. For example, the phone could be rotated to simulate a turn on a steering wheel in a racing game.

➤ **Light:** The light sensor returns the measurement of illumination. Only one value is returned. It is obtained by `value[0]`. The illumination is measured in lux. The Sensor Manager includes a set of constants representing different standard illuminations of the form `SensorManager.LIGHT*`.

➤ **Magnetic Field:** The magnetic field that is returned is measured in three directions, and the values are in microteslas:

   ➤ `value[0]` : Lateral (x direction)

   ➤ `value[1]` : Longitudinal (z direction)

   ➤ `value[2]` : Vertical (y direction)

The Sensor Manager includes several values representing the minimum and maximum values of the magnetic field on the Earth.

Detecting a magnetic field on a phone sounds exceedingly boring. Who besides an engineer working in a power plant would care about this? However, detecting the intensity of a magnetic field does have a practical use. Suppose you're in your car, and you want to use your phone to get driving directions. You place your phone against the holding clamp with the magnet in it. When your phone adheres to the plate, it detects a significant increase in the magnetic field intensity and opens the turn by turn directions. An example later in this chapter combines a magnetic field and voice recognition.

➤ **Orientation:** The device's orientation is returned in degrees along three axes based on the following values:

   ➤ `value[0]`: Azimuth

   ➤ `value[1]`: Roll

   ➤ `value[2]`: Pitch

➤ **Pressure:** The pressure is returned in `value[0]`. This would be useful in an engineering scenario. The pressure is measured in hPa.

➤ **Proximity:** The proximity is measured in centimeters and is returned in `value[0]`.

➤ **Temperature:** The temperature is measured in Celsius and is returned in `value[0]`. This could be useful in a weather scenario. Imagine that an application needs to track the temperature for an amateur storm chaser.

RESPONDING TO ACCELERATION

The accelerometer is one of Android's more interesting features. It has many uses from a user interface standpoint. The UrbanSpoon.com app is a great example of using acceleration to return random restaurant data. With that app, you shake Android, and the app finds a good nearby restaurant for you. Another use I have found for acceleration is entertaining children. Imagine that you are at a restaurant, and your kids are bored. You can create an app that will record the maximum acceleration that your phone has been subjected to. Give the kids your phone, and they will entertain themselves seeing who can shake the device the fastest.

 When you give your phone to your kids to entertain them, be sure to tell them to keep a firm grip on it. If they don't, your phone may land on someone else's table. Please learn from my experience.

In general, an accelerometer measures the device's acceleration relative to free fall. Android's accelerometer detects changes in the XYZ axis, allowing a program to figure out the device's orientation and movement. Because the changes are provided in the XYZ axis, the acceleration can be calculated in a vector.

The Mono for Android framework makes it easy to access the accelerometer via the sensor API, as was discussed earlier.

Using the XYZ Coordinate System

Understanding how data is returned from the accelerometer is important. Multiple coordinate systems can be used. Android has implemented the XYZ coordinate system to provide acceleration information. Figure 8-1 shows Android within the coordinate system.

Assuming that the user is along the z-axis, if Android is moved toward or away from the user, acceleration occurs along the z-axis. If Android is moved left or right, acceleration occurs along the x-axis. If Android is moved up or down, acceleration occurs along the y-axis. The acceleration values can be determined along each axis. With each value known along an axis and the help of some math, the total magnitude of acceleration can be calculated, as well as the direction of that acceleration at any given time.

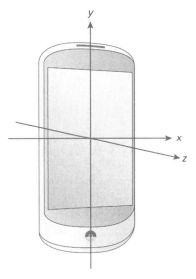

FIGURE 8-1

Coding with the Accelerometer

The accelerometer allows a program to read when Android is moving and to return data about the device's movement. This can also be used to keep kids at a restaurant entertained, as they will compete against each other to shake the device faster than others. Listing 8-2 shows how to handle acceleration events and display that information to the user.

LISTING 8-2: Processing acceleration changes

```
public void ISensorEventListener.OnSensorChanged(SensorEvent e)
{
    if ( e.Sensor.Type == SensorType.Accelerometer){
        var mVals = e.Values;
        var x = mVals[0];
        var y = mVals[1];
        var z = mVals[2];
        var SumOfSq = Math.Pow(x, 2) + Math.Pow(y, 2) + Math.Pow(z, 2);
        var mag = Math.Pow(SumOfSq, .5) - SensorManager.StandardGravity
        if (MaxAccel == 0.0)
        {
            MaxAccel = mag;
        }
```

continues

LISTING 8-2 *(continued)*

```
            if (mag > MaxAccel)
            {
                MaxAccel = mag;
            }
            RunOnUiThread(() =>
                tv.Text = "Acceleration (m/s^2): " + MaxAccel.ToString()
            );
        }
    }
```

This code is contained in Acceleration\Activity1.cs

Figure 8-2 shows the result of shaking the device.

FIGURE 8-2

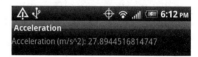

BUILDING A COMPASS

Location and direction are important in a mobile device. This section will build a compass so that direction can be determined. The sensor API is used to determine this direction. The top of the phone device is the heading that is used for the direction.

The first step is the XML for the UI (Listing 8-3). This code simply consists of a `LinearLayout` and a `TextView`.

LISTING 8-3: XML Layout for compass

Available for download on Wrox.com

```
<?xml version="1.0" encoding="utf-8"?>
<LinearLayout xmlns:android="http://schemas.android.com/apk/res/android"
 android:orientation="vertical"
 android:layout_width="fill_parent"
 android:layout_height="fill_parent"
 android:id="@+id/ll"
 >
  <TextView
   android:layout_width="fill_parent"
   android:layout_height="wrap_content"
   android:text="@string/display"
 />
</LinearLayout>
```

This code is contained in Compass\Compass\Resources\Layout\Main.axml

The next step is to create the class that will be used as the view to display the direction that a user is heading (see Listing 8-4).

LISTING 8-4: Custom view

```csharp
using System;
using System.Collections.Generic;
using System.Linq;
using System.Text;
using Android.App;
using Android.Content;
using Android.OS;
using Android.Runtime;
using Android.Util;
using Android.Views;
using Android.Widget;
using Android.Graphics;
namespace Compass
{
    public class CompassView : View
    {
        public CompassView(Context context)
            : base(context)
        {
            Initialize();
            init();
        }
        public CompassView(Context context, IAttributeSet attrs) :
            base(context, attrs)
        {
            Initialize();
            init();
        }
        public CompassView(Context context, IAttributeSet attrs, int defStyle) :
            base(context, attrs, defStyle)
        {
            Initialize();
            init();
        }

        private void Initialize()
        {
            init();
        }
        private float direction = 0;
        private Android.Graphics.Paint paint = new Paint(PaintFlags.AntiAlias);
        private bool firstDraw;
        private void init(){
            paint.SetStyle(Paint.Style.Stroke);
            paint.StrokeWidth = 3;
            paint.Color = Color.White;
            paint.TextSize = 30;
            firstDraw = true;
        }
```

continues

LISTING 8-4 *(continued)*

```
        protected override void OnMeasure(int widthMeasureSpec, int heightMeasureSpec) {
            SetMeasuredDimension(
                MeasureSpec.GetSize(widthMeasureSpec),
                MeasureSpec.GetSize(heightMeasureSpec));
        }
        protected override void OnDraw(Canvas canvas) {
            int cxCompass = MeasuredWidth/2;
            int cyCompass = MeasuredHeight/2;
            float radiusCompass;
            if(cxCompass > cyCompass){
              radiusCompass = (float) (cyCompass * 0.9);
            }
            else{
              radiusCompass = (float) (cxCompass * 0.9);
            }
            canvas.DrawCircle(cxCompass, cyCompass, radiusCompass, paint);
            canvas.DrawRect(0, 0, MeasuredWidth, MeasuredHeight, paint);

            if(!firstDraw){

              canvas.DrawLine(cxCompass, cyCompass,
                (float)(cxCompass +
                       radiusCompass * Math.Sin((double)(-direction) * 3.14/180)),
                (float)(cyCompass -
                       radiusCompass * Math.Cos((double)(-direction) * 3.14/180)),
                paint);
              canvas.DrawText(direction.ToString(), cxCompass, cyCompass, paint);
            }
        }
        public void updateDirection(float dir)
        {
            firstDraw = false;
            direction = dir;
            this.Invalidate();
        }
    }
  }
}
```

This code is contained in Compass\Compass\CompassView.cs

The final step in the process is to create the activity and to process the sensor events (Listing 8-5). The activity implements the ISensorEventListener interface. When a change is made in the Orientation SensorType, the change is sent to the activity and the activity will notify the control what the new orientation is. When the view receives the value, it performs a redraw of the control on the screen.

LISTING 8-5: Processing the activity

```
using System;
using System.Collections.Generic;
using Android.App;
```

```
using Android.Content;
using Android.Hardware;
using Android.Runtime;
using Android.Views;
using Android.Widget;
using Android.OS;
namespace Compass
{
    [Activity(Label = "Compass", MainLauncher = true,
        Icon = "@drawable/icon",
        ScreenOrientation=Android.Content.PM.ScreenOrientation.Portrait)]
    public class Activity1 : Activity, ISensorEventListener
    {
        int count = 1;
        private Android.Hardware.SensorManager sm;
        private bool sersorrunning;
        private CompassView compView;
        private Sensor s;

        protected override void OnCreate(Bundle bundle)
        {
            base.OnCreate(bundle);
            SetContentView(Resource.Layout.Main);
            var layout = FindViewById<LinearLayout>(Resource.Id.ll);
            var Params = new
                Android.Widget.LinearLayout.LayoutParams(ViewGroup.LayoutParams
                .FillParent, ViewGroup.LayoutParams.FillParent);
            compView = new CompassView(this, null);
            layout.AddView(compView, Params);
            sm = (Android.Hardware.SensorManager)GetSystemService
              (Context.SensorService);
            IList<Sensor> mySensors = sm.GetSensorList(SensorType.Orientation);
            if (mySensors.Count > 0)
            {
                s = mySensors[0];
                sm.RegisterListener(this, mySensors[0], SensorDelay.Normal);
                sersorrunning = true;
                Toast.MakeText(this, "Start ORIENTATION Sensor",
                        ToastLength.Long).Show();
            }
            else
            {
                Toast.MakeText(this, "No ORIENTATION Sensor", ToastLength.Long).Show();
                sersorrunning = false;
                Finish();
            }
        }

        public void ISensorEventListener.OnAccuracyChanged(Sensor sensor, int accuracy)
        {
        }

        public void ISensorEventListener.OnSensorChanged(SensorEvent e)
        {
            if (e.Sensor.Type == SensorType.Orientation)
```
continues

LISTING 8-5 *(continued)*

```
        {
            float dir = e.Values[0];
            compView.updateDirection(dir);
        }
    }

    protected override void OnPause()
    {
        base.OnPause();
        sm.UnregisterListener(this);
    }
    protected override void OnResume()
    {
        base.OnResume();
        sm.RegisterListener(this, s, SensorDelay.Normal);
    }
    protected override void OnDestroy()
    {
        sm.UnregisterListener(this);
    }
    }
}
```

This code is contained in Compass\Compass\Activity1.cs

Figure 8-3 shows the output of the compass.

VIBRATION

Vibration is commonly used to provide feedback to the user. For example, when the user selects a keyboard element on an HTC EVO 4G, the phone vibrates for about 50 milliseconds, telling the user that a letter has been selected. Another use of vibration is to notify the user that he or she has something to do on the device. This vibration could mean that an e-mail has arrived, someone is calling the user, or a similar event has occurred.

Mono for Android has the class `Android.OS.Vibrator`, which allows a developer to access a device's vibration hardware. Using the `Vibrator` class is a two-step process.

1. The first step is to set the appropriate permission in the `AndroidManifest.xml` file:

   ```
   <uses-permission android:name="android
   .permission.VIBRATE" />
   ```

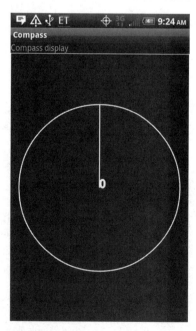

FIGURE 8-3

2. The second step is to program against the `Vibrator` class:

```
Vibrator vibrator = (Vibrator)GetSystemService(Context.VibratorService);
vibrator.Vibrate(pattern, -1);
```

Note two interesting things in this code:

➤ The `Vibrator` class is instantiated by getting a reference to the vibration service on the device.

➤ The `.Vibrate()` method can be called in two different ways. One overload takes the number of milliseconds that the device will be called for. The second overload takes an array of type `long` as well as a parameter indicating whether the vibration should be repeated.

NETWORKING CONNECTIVITY

The past few years have seen tremendous growth in wired, WiFi, and mobile Internet connectivity. Mobile broadband connectivity is quickly becoming a staple for wireless consumers. This wireless connectivity could take many forms, including EDGE, various flavors of 3G over GSM and CDMA, WiFi over various hotspots, and other data options. Given the options, it becomes important for an application to be able to provide connectivity and to be able to switch to a different connectivity option as necessary.

With Android, users can specify connectivity preferences. As connectivity options change, Android also provides the ability to broadcast intents describing the changes in network connectivity options.

ConnectivityManager

Android network connectivity is handled by the ConnectivityManager, a service that runs in the background. It allows a program to monitor the state of a preferred network connection and the network connectivity state and perform any network connectivity changes that need to happen.

The ConnectivityManager monitors the device's network state, controls network radios in the device, and makes any necessary changes regarding the current network connection.

The first step in accessing the ConnectivityManager is to get the appropriate permission. This is accomplished by adding the following permissions to the `AndroidManifest.xml` file:

```
<uses-permission android:name="android.permission.ACCESS_NETWORK_STATE" />
<uses-permission android:name="android.permission.CHANGE_NETWORK_STATE" />
```

The next step is to get a reference to ConnectivityManager. The ConnectivityManager is a system service and can be obtained by calling `GetSystemService`:

```
var cm = Context.ConnectivityService;
var cmMgr = (Android.Net.ConnectivityManager)GetSystemService(cm);
```

Checking User Communication Preferences

Once a program has a reference to the ConnectivityManager, the next step is to check the user preferences for whether background communications should be performed. The option for background communication is set in the Settings ⇨ Accounts & sync option, as shown in Figure 8-4.

The application reads this value to determine if background processing should be performed. If the background setting is not checked, an application should communicate off-device only when the application is in the foreground. Unfortunately, the developer is responsible for obeying this setting, and you know how easy it is to miss details.

This setting for background communications is done based on the following call:

```
bool bckgrnd = cmMgr.BackgroundDataSetting;
```

Checking for Changes to BackgroundDataSetting

Checking the background data setting is sufficient for most situations. However, what happens when a user changes that setting? An application should determine that this value has changed and act accordingly (see Listing 8-6):

FIGURE 8-4

Available for download on Wrox.com

LISTING 8-6: Listening to network changes

```
[BroadcastReceiver]
[IntentFilter(new[] { Android.Net.ConnectivityManager
  .ActionBackgroundDataSettingChanged },
    Categories = new[] { Android.Content.Intent.CategoryDefault })]
public class Receiver1 : BroadcastReceiver
{
    public override void OnReceive(Context context, Intent intent)
    {
        if ((intent != null) &&
            (intent.Action == Android.Net.ConnectivityManager
              .ActionBackgroundDataSettingChanged))
        {

        }
    }
}
```

This code is contained in Wifi\WifiManagement\Receiver1.cs

You check for a change in the background setting by creating a BroadcastReceiver and then listening for the ConnectivityManager.ActionBackgroundDataSettingChanged intent. After receiving the message that a change has occurred, your application should read the change and act accordingly.

Checking Current Network Configuration

Customers throughout the world have varying levels of network connectivity. Some have only local WiFi, others have wireless, and still others have only strings and tin cans. All of this depends on your location at any particular moment. Thankfully, the ConnectivityManager lets you find the current network interface and set your preferred network interface.

Creating Network Connectivity Notifications

The ConnectivityManager can notify an application that network connectivity has changed. This takes place through a broadcast receiver that listens for `ConnectionManager.ConnectionAction` intents. These intents have extra information about the state of the network connection. These nuggets of information can be obtained by calling `.Extra(...)` with a param to obtain the value. The ConnectivityManager contains a set of static string values that can be used to obtain these values:

➤ `ExtraIsFailover` is a Boolean. If the value is true, the current network is a failover from a preferred network.

➤ `ExtraNoConnectivity` is a Boolean. If the value is true, the device is not currently connected to a network.

➤ `ExtraReason` is a string. If the intent represents a connectivity failure, the reason is passed back.

➤ `ExtraNetworkInfo` is a `NetworkInfo` object. This object contains additional information about the network represented in the current intent.

➤ `ExtraOtherNetworkInfo` is a `NetworkInfo` object. This object represents network information about a failover network connection.

➤ `ExtraExtraInfo` contains additional connection details.

This network information could be used by an application to determine if network connectivity exists. If so, the application could go ahead and process the operation back on a remote server; otherwise, the data could be stored locally and sent to a central server once a connection is available.

WifiManager

Android contains the WifiManager. This class is a reference to the Android WiFi Connectivity Service. The WifiManager can be used to

➤ Configure WiFi connections

➤ Manage the current WiFi connection

➤ Scan the area for access points

➤ Monitor changes in a device's WiFi connectivity

To access and use the WifiManager, the first step is to request permission in the AndroidManifest
.xml file via these settings:

```
<uses-permission android:name="android.permission.ACCESS_WIFI_STATE" />
<uses-permission android:name="android.permission.CHANGE_WIFI_STATE" />
```

The final step (Listing 8-7) is to scan for networks and output the results (see Figure 8-5).

LISTING 8-7: Identifying WiFi networks

```
wifiMgr.StartScan(); // this is an async startup call
var wifiR = wifiMgr.ScanResults;
for (int i = 0; i < wifiR.Count; i++)
{
    tv.Text += wifiR[i].Ssid + System.Environment.NewLine;
using System;
using Android.App;
using Android.Content;
using Android.Runtime;
using Android.Views;
using Android.Widget;
using Android.OS;
using Android.Net.Wifi;
using Android.Net;

namespace WifiManagement
{
    [Activity(Label = "WifiManagement", MainLauncher = true)]
    public class Activity1 : Activity
    {
        public TextView _tv;
        public Button _button;
        WifiManager _wifiMgr;
        ScanResultBroadcastReceiver _scanResultBroadcastReceiver;

        protected override void OnCreate(Bundle bundle)
        {
            base.OnCreate(bundle);

            // Set our view from the "main" layout resource
            SetContentView(Resource.Layout.Main);

            // Get our button from the layout resource, and attach an event to it
            _button = FindViewById<Button>(Resource.Id.MyButton);
            _tv = FindViewById<TextView>(Resource.Id.tv);
            _wifiMgr = (Android.Net.Wifi.WifiManager)GetSystemService(
                    Context.WifiService);
            _button.Text = String.Format("wifi state: {0}", _wifiMgr.WifiState);

            // Define our receiver here so that we can update our UI
            _scanResultBroadcastReceiver = new ScanResultBroadcastReceiver();
            _scanResultBroadcastReceiver.Receive += (Context context,
                    Intent intent) =>
```

```
    {
        _button.Text = String.Format("wifi state: {0}",
            _wifiMgr.WifiState);
        var wifiR = _wifiMgr.ScanResults;
        _tv.Text = String.Empty;
        for (int i = 0; i < wifiR.Count; i++)
        {
            _tv.Text += wifiR[i].Ssid + System.Environment.NewLine;
        }
    };

    _button.Click += delegate
    {
        _button.Text = String.Format("wifi state: {0}",
            _wifiMgr.WifiState);

        if (_wifiMgr.WifiState == WifiState.Enabled)
        {
            _wifiMgr.StartScan();
        }
        else
        {
            // If WiFi is disabled, prompt the user to enable it
            new AlertDialog.Builder(this)
            .SetTitle("Alert!")
            .SetMessage("Enable WiFi?")
            .SetPositiveButton("Yes", delegate
            {
                // Enable WiFi and perform the scan.
                _button.Text = String.Format("wifi state: {0}",
                    "enabling..");
                _wifiMgr.SetWifiEnabled(true);
                _wifiMgr.StartScan();
            })
            .SetNegativeButton("No", delegate
            {
                // Do nothing
            })
            .Show();
        }
    };
}

protected override void OnResume()
{
    base.OnResume();

    RegisterReceiver(_scanResultBroadcastReceiver,
      new IntentFilter(Android.Net.Wifi.WifiManager.
      ScanResultsAvailableAction));
}

protected override void OnPause()
{
```

continues

LISTING 8-7 *(continued)*

```
            UnregisterReceiver(_scanResultBroadcastReceiver);

            base.OnPause();
        }

        public class ScanResultBroadcastReceiver : BroadcastReceiver
        {
            public event Action<Context, Intent> Receive;
            public override void OnReceive(Context context, Intent intent)
            {
                if (this.Receive != null && intent != null &&
                    intent.Action == "android.net.wifi.SCAN_RESULTS")
                {
                    this.Receive(context, intent);
                }
            }
        }
    }
}
}
```

This code is contained in Wifi\WifiManagement\Activity1.cs

WiFi States

Now that you have looked at the WifiManager, a couple of additional items may be important as you deal with developing apps with WiFi:

➤   .IsWifiEnabled is a Boolean property that can allow a program to determine if the WiFi is enabled on the device.

➤   .SetWifiEnabled(bool) is a method that enables /disables WiFi on the device.

FIGURE 8-5

➤   .WifiState is a property that returns the current WiFi state.

Along with these properties and methods, the WifiManager's .WifiState can be compared against the Android.Net.WifiState enum to determine the device's current WiFi state. The values are as follows:

➤   .Disabled means that WiFi is currently disabled.

➤   .Disabling means that WiFi is currently in the process of being disabled.

➤   .Enabled means that WiFi is currently enabled.

➤   .Enabling means that WiFi is currently in the process of being enabled.

➤   .Unknown means the WiFi state cannot be determined.

Developers of applications may find all this useful for certain types of applications that need higher bandwidth or a more reliable type of connection than a 3G using WiFi.

WiFi Changes

The WifiManager broadcasts intents when the network's connection state changes. Your program can register for these intents and then make changes as appropriate. This information may be valuable if a program needs to make changes to the way it communicates based on changes in the WiFi networks that a device encounters, as well as changes in WiFi states. For example, this could be used when an application wants to offer functionality only over a WiFi connection or over a specific WiFi connection.

The WifiManager has the following intents:

➤ `ActionPickWifiNetwork` is an intent that a program can start.

➤ `NetworkIdsChangedAction` means that the network IDs of the configured networks may have changed.

➤ `NetworkStateChangedAction` is fired when the state of the WiFi connection changes. The `ExtraNetworkInfo` key returns a `NetworkInfo` object that details the current network state. The `ExtraBssid` key returns the `Bssid` of the access point that the device has connected to.

➤ `RssiChangedAction` allows a program to check the changing signal strength of the WiFi connection. The `ExtraNewRssi` key returns an integer that represents the current signal strength. The integer can then be handed into the static method `CalculateSignalLevel` on the WifiManager.

➤ `ScanResultsAvailableAction` means that an access point scan has been completed.

➤ `SupplicantConnectionChangeAction` has the extra keys `ExtraSupplicantConnected` and `ExtraSupplicantError`. `ExtraSupplicantConnected` returns a Boolean that represents whether the supplicant connection has been gained or lost. `ExtraSupplicantError` returns supplicant error information.

➤ `SupplicantStateChangedAction` is a broadcast intent that reports that the state of the established connection to an access point has changed. The `ExtraNewState` key returns the new supplicant state. `ExtraSupplicantError` returns an error if it is reported.

➤ `WifiStateChangedAction` has the extra keys `ExtraWifiState` and `ExtraPreviousWifiState`. `ExtraWifiState` provides information about the new WiFi connection. `ExtraPreviousWifiState` provides information about the previous WiFi connection.

BLUETOOTH MANAGER

Bluetooth is a wireless technology standard that connects devices over relatively short distances. Bluetooth is managed by the Bluetooth Special Interest Group. Bluetooth in mobile phones is most often used to connect a phone with an earpiece that enables wireless and hands-free use of the phone.

Android supports Bluetooth in the following classes in the `Android.Bluetooth` namespace:

- ➤ `BluetoothAdapter`: The Bluetooth Adapter is the Android device that has an application running on it.

- ➤ `BluetoothDevice`: A Bluetooth device is a remote device that an Android device is connected to.

- ➤ `BluetoothSocket`: A Bluetooth socket is a mechanism to communicate with a device.

- ➤ `BluetoothServerSocket`: A Bluetooth server socket is a mechanism to listen for incoming connection requests from a Bluetooth socket on another device.

The first step in accessing the Bluetooth hardware is to obtain permission to use the Bluetooth hardware. This is obtained via the `BLUETOOTH` and `BLUETOOTH_ADMIN` privileges in the `AndroidManifest.xml` file:

```
<uses-permission android:name="android.permission.BLUETOOTH" />
<uses-permission android:name="android.permission.BLUETOOTH_ADMIN" />
```

The next step is to get a reference to the Bluetooth adapter on the host device:

```
BluetoothAdapter defaultAdapter = BluetoothAdapter.DefaultAdapter;
```

Working with Bluetooth State

`BluetoothAdapter` provides an array of methods and properties for interacting with Bluetooth on your Android device. These properties and methods allow an application to turn on Bluetooth and interact with it. Listing 8-8 shows the application querying for information regarding the Bluetooth:

LISTING 8-8: Getting Bluetooth-bound devices

Available for
download on
Wrox.com

```
string Output, AdapterAddress, AdapterName, AdapterBoundDevices = String.Empty;
BluetoothAdapter defaultAdapter = BluetoothAdapter.DefaultAdapter;
Android.Bluetooth.State AdapterState;
if (defaultAdapter.IsEnabled)
{
    AdapterAddress = defaultAdapter.Address;
    AdapterName = defaultAdapter.Name;
    var bd = defaultAdapter.BondedDevices;
    foreach (var dev in bd)
    {
        if (!String.IsNullOrEmpty(AdapterBoundDevices))
        {
            AdapterBoundDevices += ",";
        }
        AdapterBoundDevices += dev.Name;
    }
    AdapterState = defaultAdapter.State;
    Output = String.Format("{0}:{1}:{2}:State-{3}",
```

```
        AdapterName, AdapterAddress,
        AdapterBoundDevices, AdapterState);
      Toast.MakeText(this, Output, ToastLength.Long).Show();
  }
```

This code is contained in BlueToothAdapter\BlueTooth\Activity1.cs

In this code sample, a check is performed to verify that the Bluetooth adapter is enabled. After this is done, the name of the device, its address, and the names of the currently bound devices are obtained. This information is then sent to the user through a toast. The output is shown in Figure 8-6.

FIGURE 8-6

The BluetoothAdapter's .State property has four possible values, which are part of the Android.Bluetooth.State enum: OFF, TURNINGOFF, ON, and TURNINGON.

If the Bluetooth Adapter needs to be turned on, this can be accomplished as follows:

```
StartActivityForResult(new Intent(Android.Bluetooth.BluetoothAdapter
  .ActionRequestEnable), 0);
```

This line of code presents the user with the message shown in Figure 8-7, asking the user if he or she wants to turn on the Bluetooth adapter in the device.

Figure 8-8 tells the user that the Bluetooth adapter is being turned on.

FIGURE 8-7

FIGURE 8-8

 Depending on the device, these messages may be slightly different.

ENABLING VOICE RECOGNITION IN YOUR APP

Who doesn't want to just talk into their phone and have the phone perform the operation? This occurs through a technique known as voice recognition. With voice recognition, the user's voice goes into the microphone and is translated into a set of bits that looks like a wave. The waveform can then be translated into letters, words, and phrases with varying degrees of accuracy.

Starting with Android 1.5, Android supports voice recognition for input. The first step is to query the device to determine if it can perform speech recognition. This query doesn't necessarily test to see if the device has the necessary hardware. Instead, the query determines if the necessary activity is installed:

```
// Check to see if a recognition activity is present
PackageManager pm = PackageManager;
IList<ResolveInfo> activities = pm.QueryIntentActivities (new Intent
  (RecognizerIntent.ActionRecognizeSpeech), 0);
```

If one or more activities are present, the program can allow the user to perform voice recognition:

```
Intent intent = new Intent (RecognizerIntent.ActionRecognizeSpeech);
intent.PutExtra (RecognizerIntent.ExtraLanguageModel,
  RecognizerIntent.LanguageModelFreeForm);
intent.PutExtra (RecognizerIntent.ExtraPrompt, "Voice Recognition Demo");
StartActivityForResult (intent, VOICE_RECOGNITION_REQUEST_CODE);
```

With this code, an intent is created and an activity is started. The user is then handed to the speech recognition activity. When the speech recognition activity returns to the code, data is returned to the activity through the OnActivityResult method (Listing 8-9):

LISTING 8-9: Using voice recognition

Available for
download on
Wrox.com

```
protected override void OnActivityResult (int requestCode, Result resultCode,
Intent data)
{
    base.OnActivityResult (requestCode, resultCode, data);
    if ((requestCode == VOICE_RECOGNITION_REQUEST_CODE) &&
(resultCode == Result.Ok))
{
        // Fill the list view with the strings the recognizer
            thought it could have heard
        IList<String> matches = data.GetStringArrayListExtra
            (RecognizerIntent.ExtraResults);
        voice_list.Adapter = new ArrayAdapter<String> (this,
            Android.Resource.Layout.SimpleListItem1, matches);
    }
}
```

This code is contained in VoiceRecognition\VoiceRecognition\VoiceRecognition.cs

When voice recognition returns, the array adapter is filled with the possible phrases that the voice recognition applet returned. This is then presented to the user in a list view in this example.

> *Integrating voice recognition into your apps is also discussed in Chapter 9.*
>
> *If you have a custom ROM and do not have voice capabilities, you may need to install Google Voice from the Android Market.*

GETTING TURN-BY-TURN DIRECTIONS

I'm sure that by now, you are thinking that Android has great features in the operating system, and you are ready to start using them. So, let's take two features presented in the chapter, voice recognition and the sensors, to produce a turn-by-turn set of driving directions, or navigation from the current point.

One of the great features of mobile devices is that they are, in fact, mobile. This opens myriad options. Imagine that the user is getting into his or her car. You want the phone to provide a set of turn-by-turn directions, but only once the device is on a magnetic plate in the user's car. Once the device is placed on that magnetic plate, the user is presented with driving directions to the location from the current location.

> *If you decide to try this and you crash your car or end up at the wrong location, it's your fault, not mine.*
>
> *You will need to make sure that location services is available on your test system and is working properly.*

The first step is to present the user with a voice recognition input by starting the voice recognition intent (Listing 8-10).

LISTING 8-10: Opening the voice recognition applet

```
private void SetupVoice()
{
    // Check to see if a recognition activity is present
    PackageManager pm = PackageManager;
    IList<ResolveInfo> activities = pm.QueryIntentActivities(new
Intent(RecognizerIntent.ActionRecognizeSpeech), 0);
    if (activities.Count > 0)
    {
        Intent intent = new Intent(RecognizerIntent.ActionRecognizeSpeech);
        intent.PutExtra(RecognizerIntent.ExtraLanguageModel,
RecognizerIntent.LanguageModelFreeForm);
        intent.PutExtra(RecognizerIntent.ExtraPrompt, "Where do you want to go?");
        StartActivityForResult(intent, VOICE_RECOGNITION_REQUEST_CODE);
    }
}
```

This code is contained in MagneticSensors\MagneticSensors\Activity1.cs

This code opens the voice recognition activity asking the user where he or she wants to go, as shown in Figure 8-9.

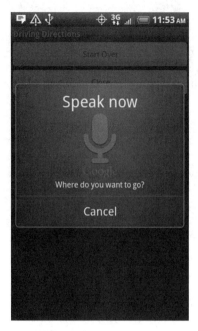

FIGURE 8-9

After the program knows where the user wants to go, the next step is to make it so the app recognizes when the device is attached to a magnetic plate. The magnetic field sensor can detect a change or increase in the magnetic field around the device. The sensor API will be presented with these changes (Listing 8-11).

LISTING 8-11: Detecting magnetic fields

```
public void OnSensorChanged(SensorEvent e)
{
    if ((e.Sensor.Type == SensorType.MagneticField) &&
        (lat.HasValue) && (lon.HasValue))
    {
        var mVals = e.Values;
        var x = mVals[0];
        var y = mVals[1];
        var z = mVals[2];
        var SumOfSq = Math.Pow(x, 2) + Math.Pow(y, 2) + Math.Pow(z, 2);
        var mag = Math.Pow(SumOfSq, .5);
        if ((mag > Threshold) && (!String.IsNullOrEmpty(dAddr)))
        {
            sensManager.UnregisterListener(this, magSensor);
            String url = String.Format("http://maps.google.com/maps?saddr={0},
                {1}&daddr={2}", lat, lon, dAddr);
            Intent intent = new Intent(Android.Content.Intent.ActionView,
                Android.Net.Uri.Parse(url));
            StartActivity(intent);
            count++;
```

```
        }
        if (count > 1)
        {
            sensManager.UnregisterListener(this, magSensor);
        }
    }
}
```

This code is contained in MagneticSensors\MagneticSensors\Activity1.cs

When the magnetic field intensity reaches a certain level, the program opens the driving directions, as shown in the preceding code. One interesting point that I have found while developing this application is that because the magnetic field sensor detects a large number of changes, there needs to be some check to keep from overloading the system with calls to the mapping activity while the application is displaying the directions. If the mapping intent is running and it receives additional information via the sensor event listener, this tends to cause problems and overload the mapping application. So, once the mapping intent is started, the application stops listening for the magnetic field changes.

Listing 8-12 shows the rest of the code.

LISTING 8-12: Driving directions from the current location

```
using System;
using System.Collections.Generic;
using Android.App;
using Android.Content;
using Android.Content.PM;
using Android.Runtime;
using Android.Views;
using Android.Widget;
using Android.OS;
using Android.Net;
using Android.Hardware;
using Android.Locations;
using Android.Speech;

namespace MagneticSensors
{
    [Activity(Label = "Driving Directions", MainLauncher = true)]
    public class Activity1 : Activity,
        ISensorEventListener, ILocationListener
    {
        int count = 1;
        double Threshold = 50.0;
        Sensor magSensor;
        SensorManager sensManager;
        string dAddr = String.Empty;
        double? lat, lon;
        LocationManager lm;
```

continues

LISTING 8-12 *(continued)*

```csharp
private const int VOICE_RECOGNITION_REQUEST_CODE = 1234;

protected override void OnCreate(Bundle bundle)
{
    base.OnCreate(bundle);

    // Set our view from the "main" layout resource
    SetContentView(Resource.Layout.Main);
    Button btn = FindViewById<Button>(Resource.Id.MyButton);
    btn.Click += new EventHandler(btn_Click);
    Button so = FindViewById<Button>(Resource.Id.StartOver);
    so.Click += new EventHandler(so_Click);
    SetupForLookup();
}

void so_Click(object sender, EventArgs e)
{
    count = 1;
    SetupVoice();
}

private void SetupForLookup()
{
    SetupSensorAndLocation();
    SetupVoice();
}

private void SetupVoice()
{
    // Check to see if a recognition activity is present
    PackageManager pm = PackageManager;
    IList<ResolveInfo> activities = pm.QueryIntentActivities(
     new Intent(RecognizerIntent.ActionRecognizeSpeech), 0);
    if (activities.Count > 0)
    {
        Intent intent = new Intent(
            RecognizerIntent.ActionRecognizeSpeech);
        intent.PutExtra(RecognizerIntent.ExtraLanguageModel,
            RecognizerIntent.LanguageModelFreeForm);
        intent.PutExtra(RecognizerIntent.ExtraPrompt,
            "Where do you want to go?");
        StartActivityForResult(intent, VOICE_RECOGNITION_REQUEST_CODE);
    }
}

private void SetupSensorAndLocation()
{
    String service_name = Context.SensorService;
    sensManager = (SensorManager)GetSystemService(service_name);
    magSensor = sensManager.GetDefaultSensor(SensorType.MagneticField);
    Criteria cr = new Criteria();
```

```
        cr.Accuracy = Accuracy.Coarse;
        cr.PowerRequirement = Power.Low;
        cr.AltitudeRequired = false;
        cr.BearingRequired = false;
        cr.SpeedRequired = false;
        cr.CostAllowed = true;
        String serviceString = Context.LocationService;
        lm = (LocationManager)GetSystemService(serviceString);
        string bestProvider = lm.GetBestProvider(cr, false);
        Location l = lm.GetLastKnownLocation(bestProvider);
        lat = l.Latitude;
        lon = l.Longitude;
        lm.RequestLocationUpdates(bestProvider, 5000, 10f, this);
    }

    void btn_Click(object sender, EventArgs e)
    {
        this.Finish();
    }

    protected override void OnDestroy()
    {
        base.OnDestroy();
        sensManager.UnregisterListener(this, magSensor);
        lm.RemoveUpdates(this);
    }
    public void OnAccuracyChanged(Sensor sensor, int accuracy)
    {
        //throw new NotImplementedException();
    }

    protected override void OnActivityResult(int requestCode,
        Result resultCode, Intent data)
    {
        if (requestCode == VOICE_RECOGNITION_REQUEST_CODE &&
          resultCode == Result.Ok)
        {
            IList<String> matches = data.GetStringArrayListExtra(
                RecognizerIntent.ExtraResults);
            if ( matches.Count > 0 ) {
                dAddr = matches[0];
                sensManager.RegisterListener(this, magSensor, SensorDelay.Ui);
            }
        }
        base.OnActivityResult(requestCode, resultCode, data);
    }

    public void OnSensorChanged(SensorEvent e)
    {
        if ((e.Sensor.Type == SensorType.MagneticField) &&
            (lat.HasValue) && (lon.HasValue))
        {
            var mVals = e.Values;
            var x = mVals[0];
```

continues

LISTING 8-12 *(continued)*

```
                var y = mVals[1];
                var z = mVals[2];
                var SumOfSq = Math.Pow(x, 2) + Math.Pow(y, 2) + Math.Pow(z, 2);
                var mag = Math.Pow(SumOfSq, .5);
                if ((mag > Threshold) && (!String.IsNullOrEmpty(dAddr)))
                {
                    sensManager.UnregisterListener(this, magSensor);
                    String url = String.Format(
                            "http://maps.google.com/maps?saddr={0},{1}&daddr={2}"
                            , lat, lon, dAddr);
                    Intent intent = new Intent(Android.Content.Intent.
                            ActionView, Android.Net.Uri.Parse(url));
                    StartActivity(intent);
                    count++;
                }
                if (count > 1)
                {
                    sensManager.UnregisterListener(this, magSensor);
                }
            }
        }

        public void OnLocationChanged(Location location)
        {
            lat = location.Latitude;
            lon = location.Longitude;
        }

        public void OnProviderDisabled(string provider)
        { }

        public void OnProviderEnabled(string provider)
        { }

        public void OnStatusChanged(string provider, Availability status,
                Bundle extras)
        { }
    }
}
```

This code is contained in MagneticSensors\MagneticSensors\Activity1.cs

Figure 8-10 shows the driving directions from my office in Knoxville, Tennessee, to Atlanta, Georgia.

You might be wondering what happens when the phone doesn't understand the address. Thankfully, by using the built-in activity, you have this situation taken care of for the program. The built-in map activity provides the user with a choice of addresses that might be the destination, as shown in Figure 8-11.

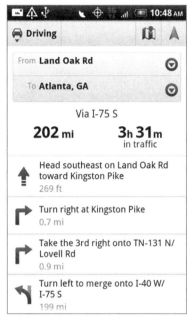

FIGURE 8-10

FIGURE 8-11

SUMMARY

This chapter has looked at integrating with various features in a device. These features can be used to present the users with information about their surroundings as well as provide information to the users in unique and very useful ways. Hopefully, developers will be able to use these and other features of the devices to create engaging applications. Some of the device features that have been demonstrated are:

➤ **Sensors** help the user determine acceleration on a device, heading, orientation, and other pieces of information that are particular to the device's environment.

➤ **Vibration** tells the user that an event has occurred on the device.

➤ **Network connectivity** is performed with Bluetooth and WiFi.

➤ **Voice recognition** allows the user to perform an operation based on voice input. This was used with the sensor magnetometer to provide the user with turn-by-turn driving directions.

Using Multimedia — Audio, Video, and the Camera

WHAT'S IN THIS CHAPTER?

➤ Playing audio and video

➤ SurfaceView and video playback

➤ Recording audio and video

➤ Recording video and taking pictures

➤ Reading and modifying image exif data

➤ Adding media to the media store

➤ Using voice recognition

Multimedia generally encompasses all the fun, non-text content: pictures, sound, video, and the like. This chapter shows you how to deal with this content in Mono for Android. Android takes its open philosophy into the realm of multimedia and has no bias for media providers. This ensures a broad range of support for image, audio, and video formats, which can be accessed locally or streamed to the device.

This chapter focuses on playing and recording audio and video using the available APIs. This chapter also covers voice input for your applications.

To effectively run the sample code in this chapter, you will need to use an actual Android device, as the emulator does not support the camera and those examples that use the camera will fail.

ANDROID MEDIA CLASSES

The following table provides a list of the Android media classes that are wrapped by Mono for Android to perform the magic in this chapter. Also, you will use the `MediaPlayer` and `MediaRecorder` along with the `ExifInterface` in examples in this chapter.

TABLE 9.1: Android Media Classes

CLASS	DESCRIPTION
AsyncPlayer	Plays an audio URI, but loading and preparing the audio is done on a background thread to prevent the foreground thread from blocking and performing slowly.
AudioFormat	Provides access to a number of audio format and channel configuration constants.
AudioManager	Provides access to volume and ringer mode control.
AudioRecord	Manages the audio resources for Java applications to record audio from the platform's audio input hardware.
AudioTrack	Manages and plays a single audio resource for Java applications.
CamcorderProfile	Retrieves the predefined camcorder profile settings for camcorder applications.
CameraProfile	Retrieves the predefined still image capture (JPEG) quality levels (0 to 100) used for low, medium, and high quality settings in the Camera application.
ExifInterface	Reads and writes exchangeable image file format (exif) tags in a JPEG file.
FaceDetector	Identifies the faces of people in a bitmap graphic object.
FaceDetector.Face	Contains all the information identifying the location of a face in a bitmap.
JetPlayer	Provides access to JET content playback and control.
MediaMetadataRetriever	Provides a unified interface for retrieving frame data and metadata from an input media file.
MediaPlayer	Controls playback of audio/video files and streams.
MediaRecorder	Records audio and video.
MediaRecorder.AudioEncoder	Defines the audio encoding used by the `MediaRecorder`.

CLASS	DESCRIPTION
`MediaRecorder.AudioSource`	Defines the audio source used by the `MediaRecorder`.
`MediaRecorder.OutputFormat`	Defines the output format used by the `MediaRecorder`.
`MediaRecorder.VideoEncoder`	Defines the video encoding used by the `MediaRecorder`.
`MediaRecorder.VideoSource`	Defines the video source used by the `MediaRecorder`.
`MediaScannerConnection`	Provides a way for applications to pass a newly created or downloaded media file to the media scanner service.
`Ringtone`	Provides a quick way to play a ringtone, notification, or similar types of sounds.
`RingtoneManager`	Provides access to ringtones, notifications, and other types of sounds.
`SoundPool`	Manages and plays audio resources for applications.
`ThumbnailUtils`	Generates routines for the media provider.
`ToneGenerator`	Provides methods to play DTMF tones (ITU-T Recommendation Q.23), call supervisory tones (3GPP TS 22.001, CEPT), and proprietary tones (3GPP TS 31.111).

Android Online Documentation

PLAYING AUDIO AND VIDEO

Playing audio and video is handled by the `MediaPlayer` object. This object conveniently abstracts the handling of specific media types from the developer. This section investigates the media player, the formats it supports, and how it is controlled.

Media Player Supported Formats

So, what is the media player, and how do you control it?

The media player supports the following formats:

➤ Audio

  ➤ AAC LC/LTP

  ➤ HE-AACv1 (AAC+)

  ➤ HE-AACv2 (Enhanced AAC+)

  ➤ AMR-NB

  ➤ AMR-WB

> MP3

> MIDI

> Ogg Vorbis

> PCM/WAVE

> FLAC (as of Android 3.1)

> Video

> H.263

> H.264 AVC

> MPEG-4 SP

> VP8

Playing back any of this media with the `MediaPlayer` object is a five-step process:

1. Initialize a `MediaPlayer` object.

2. Prepare the media player for playback.

3. Start the playback.

4. Optionally pause or stop the playback before completion.

5. Complete the playback.

 For a more detailed review of the `MediaPlayer` *object, refer to the Android documentation at* `http://developer.android.com/reference/android/media/MediaPlayer.html`.

Programming Audio Playback

So, how do you play back audio? As shown in the following code snippet, there are four ways to instantiate a new player object:

```
Context appContext = this;
MediaPlayer resourcePlayer = MediaPlayer.Create(appContext,
Resources.Raw.my_audio);
MediaPlayer filePlayer = MediaPlayer.Create(appContext,
Android.Net.Uri.parse("file://"+ Android.OS.Environment.ExternalStorageDirectory
    +"/localfile.mp3"));
MediaPlayer urlPlayer = MediaPlayer.Create(appContext,
Android.Net.Uri.parse("http://site.com/audio/audio.mp3"));
MediaPlayer contentPlayer = MediaPlayer.Create(appContext,
Settings.System.DefaultRingtoneUri);
```

You can see from this snippet that the four ways to instantiate a `MediaPlayer` object are to use the static `Create` function and pass in the application context and one of the following additional parameters:

➤ A resource identifier (`Resources.Raw.my_audio`)

➤ A URI to a local file using the `file://` schema (`"file://"`+ Android.OS.Environment .ExternalStorageDirectory +`"/localfile.mp3"`)

➤ A URI to an online audio resource as a URL (`http://site.com/audio/audio.mp3`)

➤ A URI to a local content provider row (`Settings.System.DefaultRingtoneUri`)

The following program illustrates how to play back audio using each of these four techniques. First, create a new default project using `SimpleAudioPlayback` as the project name and solution name. After creating the new project, edit the strings resources as follows:

```xml
<?xml version="1.0" encoding="utf-8"?>
<resources>
    <string name="PlayFromId">Play Music with Resource Id</string>
    <string name="PlayFromNet">Play Music from Internet</string>
    <string name="PlayFromFile">Play Music from File</string>
    <string name="PlayFromProvider">Play Music from Content Provider</string>
    <string name="ApplicationName">SimpleAudioPlayback</string>
</resources>
```

SimpleAudioPlayback program code snippets are in the SimpleAudioPlayback folder.

Having edited the strings, open `main.axml` and change the layout to the following:

```xml
<?xml version="1.0" encoding="utf-8"?>
<LinearLayout xmlns:android="http://schemas.android.com/apk/res/android"
    android:orientation="vertical"
    android:layout_width="fill_parent"
    android:layout_height="fill_parent"
    >
<Button
    android:id="@+id/PlayFromIdButton"
    android:layout_width="fill_parent"
    android:layout_height="wrap_content"
    android:text="@string/PlayFromId"
    />
<Button
    android:id="@+id/PlayFromNetButton"
    android:layout_width="fill_parent"
    android:layout_height="wrap_content"
    android:text="@string/PlayFromNet"
    />
<Button
    android:id="@+id/PlayFromFileButton"
    android:layout_width="fill_parent"
    android:layout_height="wrap_content"
    android:text="@string/PlayFromFile"
    />
<Button
    android:id="@+id/PlayFromProviderButton"
    android:layout_width="fill_parent"
```

```
                android:layout_height="wrap_content"
                android:text="@string/PlayFromProvider"
          />
    </LinearLayout>
```

Change the body of `Activity1` to the following:

```
protected override void OnCreate(Bundle bundle)
          {
              base.OnCreate(bundle);

              // Set our view from the "main" layout resource
              SetContentView(Resource.Layout.Main);

              // Get our button from the layout resource,
              // and attach an event to it
              Button playFromIdButton =
                  FindViewById<Button>(Resource.Id.PlayFromIdButton);
              Button playFromNetButton =
                  FindViewById<Button>(Resource.Id.PlayFromNetButton);
              Button playFromFileButton =
                  FindViewById<Button>(Resource.Id.PlayFromFileButton);
              Button playFromProviderButton =
                  FindViewById<Button>(Resource.Id.PlayFromProviderButton);

              playFromIdButton.Click += delegate
              {
                  MediaPlayer idPlayer = new MediaPlayer();
                  if (idPlayer != null) {
                      idPlayer.SetDataSource(this.Resources.OpenRawResourceFd
                          (Resource.Raw.monoforandroid).FileDescriptor);
                      idPlayer.SetOnCompletionListener(this);
                      idPlayer.Prepare();
                      idPlayer.Start();
                  }
              };

              playFromNetButton.Click += delegate
              {
                  Android.Net.Uri uri = Android.Net.Uri.Parse
      ("http://www.aspnetpodcast.com/PodcastFiles/MonoforAndroid.mp3");
                  MediaPlayer netPlayer = new MediaPlayer();
                  if (netPlayer != null) {
                      netPlayer.SetDataSource(this, uri);
                      netPlayer.SetOnCompletionListener(this);
                      netPlayer.Prepare();
                      netPlayer.Start();
                  }
              };

              playFromFileButton.Click += delegate
              {
                  Android.Net.Uri uri = Android.Net.Uri.Parse("file://"
                      + Android.OS.Environment.ExternalStorageDirectory
```

```
                        + "/monoforandroid.mp3");
                MediaPlayer filePlayer = new MediaPlayer();
                if (filePlayer != null) {
                    filePlayer.SetDataSource(this, uri);
                    filePlayer.SetOnCompletionListener(this);
                    filePlayer.Prepare();
                    filePlayer.Start();
                }
            };

            playFromProviderButton.Click += delegate
            {
                MediaPlayer player = new MediaPlayer();
                if (player != null ) {
    player.SetDataSource(this,Settings.System.DefaultRingtoneUri);
                    player.SetOnCompletionListener(this);
                    player.Prepare();
                    player.Start();
                }
            };
        }
    public void OnCompletion ( MediaPlayer player )
    {
        player.Stop();
        player.Release();
    }
```

Finally, change the declaration of `Activity1` to the following:

```
[Activity(Label = "Simple Audio Playback", MainLauncher = true)]
public class Activity1 : Activity, MediaPlayer.IOnCompletionListener
```

In this straightforward example, the layout is changed to have four buttons, one for each playback type. `Activity1` implements `IOnCompletionListener` so that when a player completes, `OnCompletion` is called, and the resources are released for the player.

There are some points to note before executing this code related to the playback from web, playback from file, and playback ringtone. If the file on the web is not available at the specified URL, then playback will not occur. In the play from file example you have to copy the file to `/sdcard` for the example to work. And in the playback ringtone example, some phones may loop forever, and the `OnCompletion` callback will never be called, which is a minor annoyance.

A couple more points are worth mentioning. One is that the `Prepare` function blocks while the media player is preparing content. This may not be significant for local content, but it could be when getting content from the web.

The solution is to use `PrepareAsync`, which asynchronously prepares the content and then calls the `Prepared` event handler when the content is ready. The handler could then call `Start` to play the audio as soon as it's ready. The following code snippet illustrates this:

```
mediaPlayer.Prepared += new EventHandler(mediaPlayer_Prepared);
mediaPlayer.PrepareAsync();
```

Then, in `mediaPlayer_Prepared`, the following code executes:

```
mediaPlayer.start();
```

Another point is that instead of using the static `MediaPlayer.Create` function to instantiate the media player, you could use the `new` operator to create a new `MediaPlayer` object and then assign the related values to the `MediaPlayer` object. The following snippet shows this methodology:

```
mediaPlayer = new MediaPlayer();
mediaPlayer.SetDataSource("http://site.com/androidaudio.mp3");
mediaPlayer.Prepare();
mediaPlayer.Start();
```

Which format you use is simply a matter of personal preference.

Programming Video Playback

Displaying video is slightly more complicated than playing back audio because video requires a display surface. This display surface is commonly acquired via the `SurfaceView` component, but you may also configure a custom surface and link to your own custom controls to manage the video. Here you will use the `SurfaceView`.

The `SurfaceView` object is the simplest means of playing back video. After you have instantiated the object, you call one function to initialize playback:

```
mediaPlayer.SetDataSource("http://www.aspnetpodcast.com/VideoFiles/
VideoTestForMonoForAndroid.mp4");
```

This function takes a URI, which could be directed at either a local provider or a remote source. The following program demonstrates how the media player and the `SurfaceView` component work together to display video.

The program, SimpleVideoPlayback, starts from the default program, as before. Then you change the string resources to the following:

```
<?xml version="1.0" encoding="utf-8"?>
<resources>
    <string name="PlayButton">Play Video</string>
    <string name="ApplicationName">SimpleVideoPlayback</string>
</resources>
```

SimpleVideoPlayback program code snippets are in the SimpleVideoPlayback folder.

This time you will launch a second activity that contains the video layout, so create the video layout in a file called `Video.axml`:

```
<?xml version="1.0" encoding="utf-8"?>
<LinearLayout xmlns:android="http://schemas.android.com/apk/res/android"
    android:id="@+id/VideoLayout"
    android:orientation="vertical"
    android:layout_width="fill_parent"
    android:layout_height="fill_parent">
```

```
  <Button
    android:id="@+id/CloseButton"
    android:layout_width="fill_parent"
    android:layout_height="wrap_content"
    android:text="Close Window"
    />

  <SurfaceView
    android:id="@+id/VideoSurface"
    android:layout_width="wrap_content"
    android:layout_height="wrap_content"
    android:layout_gravity="center"
    />

</LinearLayout>
```

Here you have a simple layout for a button and a `SurfaceView` that will display the video. Here's the `Main.axml` layout:

```
<?xml version="1.0" encoding="utf-8"?>
<LinearLayout xmlns:android="http://schemas.android.com/apk/res/android"
    android:orientation="vertical"
    android:layout_width="fill_parent"
    android:layout_height="fill_parent"
    >
<Button
    android:id="@+id/PlayButton"
    android:layout_width="fill_parent"
    android:layout_height="wrap_content"
    android:text="@string/PlayButton"
    />
</LinearLayout>
```

This is also a simple layout with just a play button that will be used to launch your video activity, the code for which is shown here:

```
[Activity(Label = "Video Activity")]
public class VideoActivity : Activity, ISurfaceHolderCallback
{
    MediaPlayer mediaPlayer;

    protected override void OnCreate(Bundle bundle)
    {
        base.OnCreate(bundle);

        // Create your application here
        SetContentView(Resource.Layout.Video);

        mediaPlayer = new Android.Media.MediaPlayer();
        SurfaceView surface = (SurfaceView)FindViewById(Resource.Id.VideoSurface);
        var holder = surface.Holder;
        holder.AddCallback(this);
        holder.SetType(Android.Views.SurfaceType.PushBuffers);
```

```
        holder.SetFixedSize(300, 200);
        Button closeButton = FindViewById<Button>(Resource.Id.CloseButton);
        closeButton.Click += new EventHandler(closeButton_Click);
    }

    void closeButton_Click(object sender, EventArgs e)
    {
        this.Finish();
    }

    public void SurfaceCreated(ISurfaceHolder holder)
    {
        try
        {
            mediaPlayer.SetDisplay(holder);
mediaPlayer.SetDataSource("http://www.aspnetpodcast.com/VideoFiles/
VideoTestForMonoForAndroid.mp4");
            mediaPlayer.Prepared += new EventHandler(mediaPlayer_Prepared);
            mediaPlayer.PrepareAsync();
        }
        catch (System.Exception e)
        {
            Android.Util.Log.Debug("MEDIA_PLAYER", e.Message);
            Toast.MakeText(this, e.Message, ToastLength.Short).Show();
        }
    }

    void mediaPlayer_Prepared(object sender, EventArgs e)
    {
        mediaPlayer.Start();
    }

    public void SurfaceDestroyed(ISurfaceHolder holder)
    {
        mediaPlayer.Release();
    }

    public void SurfaceChanged(ISurfaceHolder holder, int i, int j, int k) { }
}
```

Here the activity creates the video layout and gets the `SurfaceView` from that layout. Also, the activity implements the `ISurfaceHolderCallback` interface that allows you to react to changes in the surface and tie these changes to the behavior of the media player. So, you can see that as soon as the surface is created, the media player is configured, and when the surface is destroyed, the media player is released.

Following this you make some changes to `Activity1` that enable you to start playing the video:

```
[Activity(Label = "Simple Video Playback", MainLauncher = true)]
public class SimpleVideoActivity : Activity
{
    protected override void OnCreate(Bundle bundle)
    {
        base.OnCreate(bundle);
```

```
        // Set our view from the "main" layout resource
        SetContentView(Resource.Layout.Main);

        // Get our button from the layout resource,
        // and attach an event to it
        Button playButton = FindViewById<Button>(Resource.Id.PlayButton);
        playButton.Click += new EventHandler(playButton_Click);
    }

    void playButton_Click(object sender, EventArgs e)
    {
        Intent i = new Intent();
        i.SetClass(this, typeof(VideoActivity));
        i.AddFlags(ActivityFlags.NewTask);
        StartActivity(i);
    }
}
```

This is a simple implementation. Activity1 has been renamed SimpleVideoActivity, and in the OnCreate function you wire up the playButton_Click event. playButton_Click then launches VideoActivity. At this point you are ready to run.

Controlling Playback

Once the video is playing you can start and stop the video with the Start and Stop functions, but you can also control playback with the Pause and SeekTo functions.

The MediaPlayer provides the CurrentPosition and Duration properties to tell you where you are in the playback and how long the media is.

Managing Playback Output

There are three ways you can affect playback output:

➤ Looping: Looping is a bool and will determine whether the MediaPlayer will loop to the beginning when it reaches the end of the media.

➤ SetVolume: SetVolume takes a float between 0 and 1 to set the playback volume. Setting the volume to 0 would result in no sound, while setting the volume to 1 would result in maximum volume.

➤ SetScreenOnWhilePlaying: SetScreenOnWhilePlaying also takes a Boolean parameter and will prevent the screen from turning off for power savings while the media is playing back.

RECORDING AUDIO AND VIDEO

In this section you will learn how to record audio and video. We will discuss using intents to record video and see how to use the media recorder.

The easiest way to capture audio and video is to use intents to launch the video recorder. This method allows you to control the storage location along with the video recording quality, while still letting the native application handle all other controls for the video.

When you need more fine-grained control, the `MediaRecorder` object lets you control all aspects of the recording process.

Before any media can be recorded in Android, the following `uses-permissions` must be added to the program manifest:

```
<uses-permission android:name="android.permission.RECORD_AUDIO"/>
<uses-permission android:name="android.permission.RECORD_VIDEO"/>
```

Using Intents to Record Video

As mentioned previously, using an intent to launch the built-in video recorder is the easiest way to record video. The media recorder also can be used, as described in the next section. But if all you want to do is grab some moving pictures, there is no need to reinvent the wheel.

The following example extends the `SimpleVideoPlayback` program to record video. You start by adding a new `VideoRecordLayout`:

```xml
<?xml version="1.0" encoding="utf-8"?>
<LinearLayout xmlns:android="http://schemas.android.com/apk/res/android"
    android:id="@+id/VideoRecordLayout"
    android:orientation="vertical"
    android:layout_width="fill_parent"
    android:layout_height="fill_parent">

  <Button
    android:id="@+id/CloseButton"
    android:layout_width="fill_parent"
    android:layout_height="wrap_content"
    android:text="Close Window"
    />

</LinearLayout>
```

Code for this example of video recording is in the SimpleVideoPlayback folder.

Also, you change the main layout to have another button to call your new `VideoRecord` activity:

```xml
<?xml version="1.0" encoding="utf-8"?>
<LinearLayout xmlns:android="http://schemas.android.com/apk/res/android"
    android:orientation="vertical"
    android:layout_width="fill_parent"
    android:layout_height="fill_parent"
    >
<Button
    android:id="@+id/PlayButton"
    android:layout_width="fill_parent"
```

```
        android:layout_height="wrap_content"
        android:text="@string/PlayButton"
        />
    <Button
        android:id="@+id/RecordButton"
        android:layout_width="fill_parent"
        android:layout_height="wrap_content"
        android:text="@string/RecordButton"
      />
    </LinearLayout>
```

In addition, you need to add the string value for the record button to `Strings.xml`:

```
<string name="RecordButton">Play Video</string>
```

You then add the new `VideoRecordActivity`:

```
[Activity(Label = "Video Record Activity")]
public class VideoRecordActivity : Activity
{
    private const int RECORDVIDEO = 1;
    private const int HIGHVIDEOQUALITY = 1;
    private const int MMSVIDEOQUALITY = 0;

    protected override void OnCreate(Bundle bundle)
    {
        base.OnCreate(bundle);
        SetContentView(Resource.Layout.VideoRecord);

        // Create your application here
        Button closeButton = FindViewById<Button>(Resource.Id.CloseButton);
        closeButton.Click += new EventHandler(closeButton_Click);
        RecordVideo(null);
    }

    void closeButton_Click(object sender, EventArgs e)
    {
        this.Finish();
    }

    private void RecordVideo(Uri outputpath)
    {
        Intent intent =
 new Intent(Android.Provider.MediaStore.IntentActionVideoCamera);
        if (outputpath != null)
            intent.PutExtra(Android.Provider.MediaStore.ExtraOutput,
 outputpath.LocalPath);

        intent.PutExtra(Android.Provider.MediaStore.ExtraVideoQuality,
 HIGHVIDEOQUALITY);
        StartActivityForResult(intent, RECORDVIDEO);
    }

    protected override void OnActivityResult(int requestCode,
 Result resultCode, Intent data)
```

```
    {
        base.OnActivityResult(requestCode, resultCode, data);
        if (requestCode == RECORDVIDEO)
        {
            if ((data != null) && (data.Data != null))
            {
                Android.Net.Uri recordedVideo = data.Data;
                // TODO Do something with the recorded video
            }
        }
    }
}
```

> *Before we move on, we should note that the code above relies on the default video recorder having a button to indicate that recording is complete. If you have to use the back button to exit your video recording session, the* ResultCode *will be "Cancelled" and no data will be returned.*

Finally, you need to wire up the new button on the main activity to launch your new activity:

```
[Activity(Label = "Simple Video Playback", MainLauncher = true)]
public class SimpleVideoActivity : Activity
{
    protected override void OnCreate(Bundle bundle)
    {
        base.OnCreate(bundle);

        // Set our view from the "main" layout resource
        SetContentView(Resource.Layout.Main);

        // Get our button from the layout resource,
        // and attach an event to it
        Button playButton = FindViewById<Button>(Resource.Id.PlayButton);
        playButton.Click += new EventHandler(playButton_Click);

        Button recordButton = FindViewById<Button>(Resource.Id.RecordButton);
        recordButton.Click += new EventHandler(recordButton_Click);
    }

    void playButton_Click(object sender, EventArgs e)
    {
        Intent i = new Intent();
        i.SetClass(this, typeof(VideoActivity));
        i.AddFlags(ActivityFlags.NewTask);
        StartActivity(i);
    }

    void recordButton_Click(object sender, EventArgs e)
    {
        Intent i = new Intent();
        i.SetClass(this, typeof(VideoRecordActivity));
```

```
            i.AddFlags(ActivityFlags.NewTask);
            StartActivity(i);
        }
    }
```

Now when you run and select the record button, you begin recording video.

Using the Media Recorder

This section examines how to use the `MediaRecorder` object instead of an intent to record video.

Configuring Video Recording

The following snippet comes from the SimpleMediaRecorder application, which is available for download.

```
mediaRecorder = new MediaRecorder();

// Set input sources
mediaRecorder.SetAudioSource(AudioSource.Mic);
mediaRecorder.SetVideoSource(VideoSource.Camera);

// Set output format
mediaRecorder.SetOutputFormat(OutputFormat.Default);

// Set audio and video encoding
mediaRecorder.SetAudioEncoder(AudioEncoder.Default);
mediaRecorder.SetVideoEncoder(VideoEncoder.Default);

var outputFile = System.IO.Path.Combine
    (Android.OS.Environment.ExternalStorageDirectory.ToString(),
     "myvideooutputfile.mp4");
if (System.IO.File.Exists(outputFile))
    System.IO.File.Delete(outputFile);
System.IO.File.Create(outputFile);

// Set the output file
mediaRecorder.SetOutputFile(outputFile);


// Prepare
mediaRecorder.Prepare();
```

The MediaRecorder example code is in the SimpleMediaRecorder folder.

As you can see, the first line instantiates a new `MediaRecorder`. Then you set the audio and video sources, which here are set to the built-in mic and camera. Here the output format is set to the default along with the audio and video encoding.

Then the output file is set. Here it is hard-coded, but in your application, it would be useful to provide the user an input for a file name. Finally, the media recorder is prepared with all of the prior settings and recording begins with the call to start.

The following snippet shows how to terminate recording and release the `MediaRecorder` resources.

```
// Stop
mediaRecorder.Stop();

// Release resources
mediaRecorder.Release();
```

Previewing Video Recording

While the previous example works, one thing you probably noticed is that there is no running preview of the images that are captured. So how do you enhance the application to show a preview of the frames as they are captured?

First you add the following `SurfaceView` to the `main.axml` layout.

```
<SurfaceView
    android:id="@+id/Surface"
    android:layout_width="wrap_content"
    android:layout_height="wrap_content"
    android:layout_gravity="center" />
```

Then in the `OnCreate` function you add the following code to initialize the `SurfaceView`.

```
// Initialize the surface view
SurfaceView surface = (SurfaceView)FindViewById(Resource.Id.Surface);
var holder = surface.Holder;
holder.AddCallback(this);
holder.SetType(Android.Views.SurfaceType.PushBuffers);
holder.SetFixedSize(300, 200);
```

Notice the call to `AddCallback`. You will add the `ISurfaceHolderCallback` interface to the `MediaRecorderActivity` as follows:

```
public class MediaRecorderActivity : Activity, ISurfaceHolderCallback
```

Then you will need to implement three functions to fulfill the contract on `ISurfaceHolderCallback`.

```
public void SurfaceCreated(ISurfaceHolder holder)
{
    if (mediaRecorder == null)
    {
        mediaRecorder = new MediaRecorder();

        // Set input sources
        mediaRecorder.SetAudioSource(AudioSource.Mic);
        mediaRecorder.SetVideoSource(VideoSource.Camera);

        // Set output format
```

```
            mediaRecorder.SetOutputFormat(OutputFormat.Default);

            // Set audio and video encoding
            mediaRecorder.SetAudioEncoder(AudioEncoder.Default);
            mediaRecorder.SetVideoEncoder(VideoEncoder.Default);

            // Set the output file
            mediaRecorder.SetOutputFile(Android.OS.Environment
              .ExternalStorageDirectory + "/myoutputfile.mp4");

            // Set preview display
            mediaRecorder.SetPreviewDisplay(holder.Surface);

            // Prepare
            mediaRecorder.Prepare();
        }
    }

    public void SurfaceDestroyed(ISurfaceHolder holder)
    {
        mediaRecorder.Release();
    }

    public void SurfaceChanged(ISurfaceHolder holder, int i, int j, int k) { }
```

And finally you need to update the button to allow for starting and stopping the recording.

```
            button.Click += delegate { if (!recording) StartRecording(); else
                StopRecording(); };
```

Where StartRecording and StopRecording are defined as follows:

```
    void StartRecording()
    {
        // Start
        mediaRecorder.Start();
        recording = true;
    }

    void StopRecording()
    {
        // Stop
        mediaRecorder.Stop();
        recording = false;
    }
```

And with that you can record video with a preview window.

Audio Recording

While the example in the previous section recorded both audio and video at once, you can actually use the MediaRecorder to record one or the other separately. So, if you set an audio source and don't set a video source the MediaRecorder will simply record audio.

To play back the recorded audio you use the same techniques that were illustrated with the `MediaPlayer` object.

IMAGES AND USING THE CAMERA

This section investigates the use and control of the camera. It also reviews the image support built into Android. Android supports these image formats:

- JPEG
- GIF
- PNG
- BMP

Using Intents to Take Pictures

As with video, the simplest way to take a picture with the camera is to fire an intent to launch the default camera activity. You will continue to use the `SimpleVideoPlayback` program as an example to demonstrate this functionality.

You start by adding a new `Photo.axml` layout:

```xml
<?xml version="1.0" encoding="utf-8"?>
<LinearLayout xmlns:android="http://schemas.android.com/apk/res/android"
    android:id="@+id/VideoRecordLayout"
    android:orientation="vertical"
    android:layout_width="fill_parent"
    android:layout_height="fill_parent">

  <Button
    android:id="@+id/PhotoCloseButton"
    android:layout_width="fill_parent"
    android:layout_height="wrap_content"
    android:text="Close Window"
    />

</LinearLayout>
```

Code for this example of taking pictures is in the SimpleCamera folder.

Then you add a new string value:

```xml
<string name="PhotoButton">Photograph</string>
```

Then you add a new button to the `Main.axml` layout:

```xml
<Button
    android:id="@+id/PhotoButton"
```

```
        android:layout_width="fill_parent"
        android:layout_height="wrap_content"
        android:text="@string/PhotoButton"
    />
```

Then you create your new PhotoActivity:

```
[Activity(Label = "Photo Activity")]
public class PhotoActivity : Activity
{
    private static int TAKE_PICTURE = 1;
    private Uri outputFileUri;

    protected override void OnCreate(Bundle bundle)
    {
        base.OnCreate(bundle);

        // Create your application here
        SetContentView(Resource.Layout.Photo);
        Button closeButton = FindViewById<Button>(Resource.Id.PhotoCloseButton);
        closeButton.Click += new EventHandler(closeButton_Click);
        saveFullImage();
    }

    void closeButton_Click(object sender, EventArgs e)
    {
        this.Finish();
    }

    private void getThumbailPicture()
    {
        Intent intent = new Intent(Android.Provider.MediaStore.ActionImageCapture);
        StartActivityForResult(intent, TAKE_PICTURE);
    }

    private void saveFullImage()
    {
        Intent intent = new Intent(Android.Provider.MediaStore.ActionImageCapture);

        string file =
System.IO.Path.Combine(Android.OS.Environment.ExternalStorageDirectory.ToString(),
    Android.OS.Environment.DirectoryDcim.ToString(),
"test.jpg");

        outputFileUri = Android.Net.Uri.Parse(file);
        intent.PutExtra(Android.Provider.MediaStore.ExtraOutput, outputFileUri);
        StartActivityForResult(intent, TAKE_PICTURE);
    }

        protected override void OnActivityResult(int requestCode, Result
            resultCode, Intent data)
        {
            base.OnActivityResult(requestCode, resultCode, data);
            if ((requestCode == TAKE_PICTURE) && (resultCode == Result.Ok))
```

```
            {
                // Check if the result includes a thumbnail Bitmap
                if (data != null)
                {
                    if (data.HasExtra("data"))
                    {
                        var thumbnail = data.GetParcelableArrayExtra("data");
                        // TODO Do something with the thumbnail
                    }
                    else
                    {
                        // TODO Do something with the full image stored
                        // in outputFileUri
                    }
                }
            }
        }
    }
```

So, what you have done so far is three things. First, you created a layout for the new PhotoActivity. Second, you added a button to the main layout that you will use to launch the PhotoActivity. Finally, you defined the PhotoActivity itself, which displays the layout and handles the intents to take a picture.

So now, you wire up the photo button in the Main.axml layout:

```
[Activity(Label = "Simple Video Playback", MainLauncher = true)]
public class SimpleVideoActivity : Activity
{
    protected override void OnCreate(Bundle bundle)
    {
        base.OnCreate(bundle);

        // Set our view from the "main" layout resource
        SetContentView(Resource.Layout.Main);

        // Get our button from the layout resource,
        // and attach an event to it
        Button playButton = FindViewById<Button>(Resource.Id.PlayButton);
        playButton.Click += new EventHandler(playButton_Click);

        Button recordButton = FindViewById<Button>(Resource.Id.RecordButton);
        recordButton.Click += new EventHandler(recordButton_Click);

        Button photoButton = FindViewById<Button>(Resource.Id.PhotoButton);
        photoButton.Click += new EventHandler(photoButton_Click);
    }

    void playButton_Click(object sender, EventArgs e)
    {
        Intent i = new Intent();
        i.SetClass(this, typeof(VideoActivity));
        i.AddFlags(ActivityFlags.NewTask);
```

```
        StartActivity(i);
    }

    void recordButton_Click(object sender, EventArgs e)
    {
        Intent i = new Intent();
        i.SetClass(this, typeof(VideoRecordActivity));
        i.AddFlags(ActivityFlags.NewTask);
        StartActivity(i);
    }

    void photoButton_Click(object sender, EventArgs e)
    {
        Intent i = new Intent();
        i.SetClass(this, typeof(PhotoActivity));
        i.AddFlags(ActivityFlags.NewTask);
        StartActivity(i);
    }
```

You have now done two simple things: you added an event handler to handle the click event for the button that will launch the `PhotoActivity`, and you defined the `photoButton_Click` function, which is the target of the event handler.

Now you've added picture-taking to your repertoire.

Controlling the Camera

If you want to control the camera directly, you can do so with the use of the `Camera` class, which is found in `Android.Hardware`. It provides direct control over all aspects of the hardware available on the device. To get the camera you make a call to `Camera.Open`:

```
Camera camera = Camera.Open();
```

You can then interrogate and control the camera until you are done, at which point you should call `camera.Release();` to release the camera resources.

Managing Camera Settings and Picture Options

This section dives into the camera settings and picture options and how to control them. To change the camera's parameters you use the `Camera.Parameters` object, as shown in the following snippet:

```
Camera camera = Camera.Open();
Camera.Parameters parameters = camera.GetParameters();
ArrayList whiteBalanceModes = (ArrayList)parameters.SupportedWhiteBalance;
camera.Release();
```

In this snippet the camera is opened and a call to `GetParameters` is made, which returns a `Camera.Parameters` object. In this case the supported white balance modes are found by referencing `SupportedWhiteBalance`. Given that different cameras may support different features, it is always a good policy to interrogate the hardware to discover what's supported before setting parameter values.

The following properties indicate the camera's supported features as of API version 9(2.3.3):

- SupportedWhiteBalance
- SupportedSceneModes
- SupportedPreviewSizes
- SupportedPreviewFrameRates
- SupportedPreviewFormats
- SupportedPictureSizes
- SupportedPictureFormats
- SupportedJpegThumbnailSizes
- SupportedFocusModes
- SupportedFlashModes
- SupportedColorEffects
- SupportedAntibanding

The following properties can be set on the `Camera.Properties` object:

- Antibanding
- ColorEffect
- ExposureCompensation
- ExposureCompensationStep
- FlashMode
- FocalLength
- FocusMode
- HorizontalViewAngle
- JpegQuality
- JpegThumbnailQuality
- JpegThumbnailSize
- MaxExposureCompensation
- MaxZoom
- MinExposureCompensation
- PictureFormat
- PictureSize
- PreviewFormat
- PreviewFrameRate
- PreviewSize
- SceneMode
- VerticalViewAngle
- WhiteBalance
- Zoom
- ZoomRatios

It's important to note that none of the settings will take effect until a call to `Camera.SetProperties` is made with the updated properties object.

The `Camera` object also supports a number of interface callbacks to allow for notification of events while the camera is in operation:

- Camera.IAutoFocusCallback
- Camera.IErrorCallback
- Camera.IOnZoomChangeListener
- Camera.IPictureCallback
- Camera.IPreviewCallback
- Camera.IShutterCallback

The following two sections look at code that shows how to use the callbacks to monitor autofocus and image preview.

Monitoring Autofocus

Monitoring the autofocus on the camera is pretty straightforward. You implement the
IAutoFocusCallback interface on the activity in question, and you receive autofocus notifications.
The following snippet shows how this is done:

```
[Activity(Label = "SimpleCamera", MainLauncher = true)]
public class SimpleCameraActivity : Activity,
    Android.Hardware.Camera.IAutoFocusCallback,
        Android.Hardware.Camera.IPictureCallback,
        Android.Hardware.Camera.IPreviewCallback,
        Android.Hardware.Camera.IShutterCallback,
        ISurfaceHolderCallback
{
    Android.Hardware.Camera camera;
        String PICTURE_FILENAME = "picture.jpg";

    protected override void OnCreate(Bundle bundle)
    {
        base.OnCreate(bundle);

        // Set our view from the "main" layout resource
        SetContentView(Resource.Layout.Main);

        SurfaceView surface = (SurfaceView)FindViewById(Resource.Id.Surface);
        var holder = surface.Holder;
        holder.AddCallback(this);
        holder.SetType(Android.Views.SurfaceType.PushBuffers);
        holder.SetFixedSize(300, 200);

        // Get our button from the layout resource,
        // and attach an event to it
        Button button = FindViewById<Button>(Resource.Id.MyButton);
        button.Click += delegate
        {
            Android.Hardware.Camera.Parameters p = camera.GetParameters();
            p.PictureFormat = (int)Format.Jpeg;
            camera.SetParameters(p);
            camera.TakePicture(this,this,this);
        };

    }

    public void OnAutoFocus(bool focused, Android.Hardware.Camera camera)
    {
        if (focused)
        {
            Toast.MakeText(this, "Focused", ToastLength.Short);
        }
    }
}
```

Code for this snippet is in the SimpleCamera folder.

In this code, `SimpleCameraActivity` implements the `IAutoFocusCallback` interface. After the camera is opened, `OnAutoFocus` is called. It's also worth noting that if the camera on the device does not have an autofocus, `OnAutoFocus` is called with the `focused` parameter set to `true`.

Using the Camera Preview

Using the camera preview is a somewhat more involved process. During previewing, a series of frames are sent to the callback function. To be of any use they need to be displayed on a surface, much like video.

So, continuing to work with the simple camera project used in the previous section of the chapter, you add a surface view to the main layout:

```
<SurfaceView
    android:id="@+id/Surface"
    android:layout_width="wrap_content"
    android:layout_height="wrap_content"
    android:layout_gravity="center" />
```

Then you make sure that the `SimpleCameraActivity` implements both `Camera.IPreviewCallback` and `ISurfaceHolderCallback`:

```
public class SimpleCameraActivity : Activity, Camera.IAutoFocusCallback,
    Camera.IPictureCallback, Camera.IPreviewCallback, ISurfaceHolderCallback
```

Next, in the `OnCreate` function you get hold of and initialize the `SurfaceView` object you added to the layout:

```
SurfaceView surface = (SurfaceView)FindViewById(Resource.Id.Surface);
var holder = surface.Holder;
holder.AddCallback(this);
holder.SetType(Android.Views.SurfaceType.PushBuffers);
holder.SetFixedSize(300, 200);
```

Finally, the functions required by both of the interfaces are implemented:

```
public void SurfaceCreated(ISurfaceHolder holder)
{
    try
    {
        camera = Android.Hardware.Camera.Open();
        Android.Hardware.Camera.Parameters p = camera.GetParameters();
        p.PictureFormat = (int)Format.Jpeg;
        camera.SetParameters(p);
        camera.AutoFocus(this);
        camera.SetPreviewCallback(this);
        camera.Lock();
```

```
            camera.SetPreviewDisplay(holder);
            camera.StartPreview();
        }
        catch (IOException e)
        {
            Android.Util.Log.Debug("SIMPLECAMERA", e.Message);
        }
    }

    public void SurfaceDestroyed(ISurfaceHolder holder)
    {
        camera.Unlock();
        camera.StopPreview();
        camera.Release();
    }

    public void SurfaceChanged(ISurfaceHolder holder, int i, int j, int k) { }

    public void OnPreviewFrame(byte[] data, Android.Hardware.Camera camera)
    {
        //TODO: Display preview
    }
```

Code for the snippets in this section are in the SimpleCamera folder.

Now, as soon as the surface is created, the camera is opened, and the preview frames are bound to the surface. On each preview frame, `OnPreviewFrame` is called. When the surface is destroyed, the camera stops previewing, and the resources for the camera are released.

Taking a Picture

To capture the picture that is taken, you implement the `IPictureCallback` interface:

Available for download on Wrox.com

```
    public void OnPictureTaken(byte[] data, Android.Hardware.Camera camera)
    {
        // Save the image JPEG data to the SD card
        FileOutputStream outStream = null;
        File dataDir = Android.OS.Environment.ExternalStorageDirectory;

        if (data!=null)
        {
    try
    {
        outStream = new FileOutputStream(dataDir + "/" + PICTURE_FILENAME);
        outStream.Write(data);
        outStream.Close();
    }
```

```
catch (FileNotFoundException e)
{
    Android.Util.Log.Debug("SIMPLECAMERA", e.Message);
}
catch (IOException e)
{
    Android.Util.Log.Debug("SIMPLECAMERA", e.Message);
}

File file = new File(dataDir + "/" + PICTURE_FILENAME);
try {

        ExifInterface exif = new ExifInterface(file.CanonicalPath);
        // Read the camera model and location attributes
        exif.GetAttribute(ExifInterface.TagModel);
        float[] latLng = new float[2];
        exif.GetLatLong(latLng);
        // Set the camera make
        exif.SetAttribute(ExifInterface.TagMake, "My Phone");
        exif.SetAttribute(ExifInterface.TagDatetime,
            System.DateTime.Now.ToString());
    }
    catch (IOException e) {

        Android.Util.Log.Debug("SIMPLECAMERA", e.Message);
    }
}
else
{
    Toast.MakeText(this, "No Image Captured", ToastLength.Long);
}
}
```

Code for this snippet is in the SimpleCamera folder.

This snippet contains the `OnPictureTaken` function, which is defined by `IPictureCallback`. When the picture is taken, the function is called, and the image data is written to storage. The data's format is controlled by the `ImageFormat` property in the `CameraProperties` object.

Reading and Writing JPEG Exif Values

Now that you are capturing the image from the camera, how do you go about adding information, such as the time or location of the picture, to the image itself? If the image is a JPEG, there is an interface with which to do exactly this.

`ExifInterface` allows you to change the exif (exchangeable image file format) data on a JPEG image. You can set a number of metadata tags; refer to the documentation for a full list. The following snippet shows how you can set the date and get the location where a picture was taken:

```
File file = new File(dataDir + "/" + PICTURE_FILENAME);
try {

    ExifInterface exif = new ExifInterface(file.CanonicalPath);
    // Read the camera model and location attributes
    exif.GetAttribute(ExifInterface.TagModel);
    float[] latLng = new float[2];
    exif.GetLatLong(latLng);
    // Set the camera make
    exif.SetAttribute(ExifInterface.TagMake, "My Phone");
    exif.SetAttribute(ExifInterface.TagDatetime, System.DateTime.Now.ToString());
}
catch (IOException e) {

    Android.Util.Log.Debug("SIMPLECAMERA", e.Message)
}
```

In this example, you have added the ability to tag JPEG images generated by the camera through the `ExifInterface`. While this example uses only `TagMake` and `TagDatetime`, you can experiment with other available tags like those for latitude and longitude.

ADDING NEW MEDIA TO THE MEDIA STORE

This section examines the media store and looks at how new content can be added to it. The media store provides metadata for all the available media on the device on both the internal and external storage. Any media created by your application is, by default, inaccessible to other apps, so it is a good idea to put your media into the store so that it will be available.

There are two ways to get data into the media store. The first is to let the media scanner automatically analyze your file and add it. The other method is to manually add a record to the proper content provider.

Using the Media Scanner

The media scanner scans a file for you to determine its mime type and add it to the media store. However, you don't use the media scanner directly; you obtain a connection to it using the `MediaScannerConnection` class.

The following snippet shows how `MediaScannerConnection` is opened with a call to `Connect`. Then the file is scanned with a call to `ScanFile`. Finally, when the scan is completed, the connection is closed with a call to `Disconnect`.

> *The calls to* `MediaScannerConnection` *are all asynchronous. So the activity implements the* `IMediaScannerConnectionClient` *interface for notification of when the connection is established and when the scans are complete.*

```
[Activity(Label = "MediaStoreExamples", MainLauncher = true)]
public class MediaStoreActivity : Activity,
   MediaScannerConnection.IMediaScannerConnectionClient
{
    MediaScannerConnection msc;

    protected override void OnCreate(Bundle bundle)
    {
        base.OnCreate(bundle);

        // Set our view from the "main" layout resource
        SetContentView(Resource.Layout.Main);
        msc = new MediaScannerConnection(this, this);

        // Get our button from the layout resource,
        // and attach an event to it
        Button button = FindViewById<Button>(Resource.Id.ScanButton);
        button.Click += delegate {
            msc.Connect();
        };
    }

    public void OnMediaScannerConnected()
    {
        msc.ScanFile(Android.OS.Environment.ExternalStorageDirectory +
            "/myoutputfile.mp4", null);
    }
    public void OnScanCompleted(string path, Android.Net.Uri uri)
    {
        msc.Disconnect();
    }
}
```

Code for this snippet is in the MediaStoreExamples folder.

Adding New Media to the Store

If you want to add more metadata, or you don't want to rely on the media scanner, you can add your content to the appropriate media store content provider yourself.

The following code snippet comes from the MediaStoreExamples download and shows how to add media to the store 'manually.'

```
Button addButton = FindViewById<Button>(Resource.Id.AddButton);
addButton.Click += delegate
{
    ContentValues values = new ContentValues();
    values.Put(MediaStore.MediaColumns.Title, "Hiking Notes");
    values.Put(MediaStore.MediaColumns.Data,
```

```
                    Android.OS.Environment.ExternalStorageDirectory +
                        "/myoutputfile.mp4");
                values.Put(MediaStore.Audio.Media.ContentType, "audio/amr");

                ContentResolver resolver = this.ContentResolver;
                Android.Net.Uri uri =
                    resolver.Insert(MediaStore.Audio.Media.ExternalContentUri, values);

                this.SendBroadcast(new Intent(Intent.ActionMediaScannerScanFile, uri));
            };
```

Here we see the `ContentValues` object populated with data relevant to the mp4 file that is about to
be added to the content resolver. Then the content resolver is retrieved and the values are inserted
into the resolver. Finally, a broadcast is sent notifying any potential receivers of the newly added file.

SPEECH RECOGNITION

This section covers how to integrate speech recognition into an application. Ever since Android 1.5
(API level 3), Android has supported voice input and speech recognition. The `RecognizerIntent`
class provides the API that makes this happen. Before running the following code, you need to
ensure that you have Google Voice Search installed.

To get input from the voice recognition system, you start a new activity for the result:

```
int VOICE_RECOGNITION = 0;

protected override void OnCreate(Bundle bundle)
{
    base.OnCreate(bundle);

    // Set our view from the "main" layout resource
    SetContentView(Resource.Layout.Main);

    // Get our button from the layout resource,
    // and attach an event to it
    Button button = FindViewById<Button>(Resource.Id.MyButton);

    button.Click += new EventHandler(button_Click);
}

void button_Click(object sender, EventArgs e)
{
    Intent intent = new Intent(RecognizerIntent.ActionRecognizeSpeech);

    // Specify free form input
    intent.PutExtra(RecognizerIntent.ExtraLanguageModel,
                    RecognizerIntent.LanguageModelFreeForm);
```

```
        intent.PutExtra(RecognizerIntent.ExtraPrompt,
                        "to see something cool");
        intent.PutExtra(RecognizerIntent.ExtraMaxResults, 1);
        intent.PutExtra(RecognizerIntent.ExtraLanguage, Locale.English);

        StartActivityForResult(intent, VOICE_RECOGNITION);
    }

    Protected override void OnActivityResult (int requestCode, int resultCode,
        Intent data) {

        if (requestCode == VOICE_RECOGNITION)
        {
            if (resultCode == Result.Ok) {

                Toast.MakeText(this, data.Extras.ToString(), ToastLength.Long).Show();
            }
        }
    }
}
```

Code for this snippet is in the SimpleVoiceRecognition folder.

In addition to creating the new intent of type `RecognizerIntent.ActionRecognizeSpeech`, a number of extras are added to the intent.

➤ `ExtraLanguage` specifies the locale for recognition. The recognition engine works on only a subset of locales, however.

➤ `ExtraMaxResults` limits the number of responses that the recognition engine returns.

➤ `ExtraPrompt` displays some additional text on the speech prompt screen.

➤ `ExtraLanguageModel` tells the recognition engine what model to use to parse the spoken text. Currently there are two models: one that is free-form (which we use here), and another for web search.

SUMMARY

In this chapter you have learned about the multimedia aspects of the Android phone and how to control the multimedia systems. We covered how to play audio and video. We showed how audio can be bundled with an application as part of the raw resources. We saw how to play back video using the `SurfaceView` and a custom video surface.

We also looked at recording audio and video. First we used intents to launch the built-in recording applications. Then we examined how to use the media recorder to accomplish the same goals. In addition, we looked at the camera and how to control it. First we used intents to launch the built-in camera for results. Then we looked at how the camera hardware can be directly controlled using the `Camera` object. Along the way we looked at how the exif data on a JPEG image captured with the camera can be examined or modified using the `ExifInterface` class.

Also covered was how to add any media created by your app to the media store by using the media scanner or by adding the information directly.

We wrapped up with a quick look at how to use voice recognition as an input into your applications.

Including multimedia in your application is something that often gives it polish. Going beyond simple keyboard input and including voice recognition, or enabling pictures for a note-taking application, will help give your applications that something extra. Hopefully, this chapter has assisted you in seeing beyond the virtual keyboard.

10

Talking to Other Applications and Libraries

WHAT'S IN THIS CHAPTER?

➤ Allowing Mono for Android to talk with other applications using intents

➤ Having your applications integrate with other third-party applications

➤ Accessing the Android Address Book

This chapter discusses the ways in which you can use Mono for Android to talk to other applications on the Android device, both those built into the device and those downloaded from the Android application stores. It also describes how to access the device's contacts and insert and edit contacts without having to rebuild a common UI.

The secret behind interfacing with any application on the device is the `Intent` method. This method handles where and what to open when you pass in an `Intent` and a `Type` or `URI` object for the method to know how to work with the intent. When the method is called, the app suspends in its normal fashion and carries out the appropriate action based on the information the intent has been passed.

ANDROID APPLICATION INTEGRATION

This section shows you how to integrate Android built-in applications into your own application.

Opening the Browser

Opening a webpage in the native browser is a good place to start. The most likely reason for you to close your app and open the browser is because you want a website to be displayed.

A user could then use the device's Back button to return to your application. As with most of the examples in this section, you can use this functionality by starting an intent as a new activity. The following code displays a website:

```
var intent = new Intent(Intent.ActionView);
intent.SetData(Android.Net.Uri.Parse("http://wrox.com"));
StartActivity(intent);
```

 You can download relevant code from this chapter at this book's website at www.wrox.com. *The Chapter10Examples project contains all the code snippets in this chapter and can be found at* Chapter10Examples\Chapter10Examples.sln *in this chapter's code download.*

The first line instantiates a new `Intent` object. You can see that the type of action you pass into the constructor is a `View`. This basically means to display whatever data is set for the intent. The second line sets the data value. The data property is of type `Android.Net.Uri`, which is similar to the .NET version. You can use the `Parse` method to return a `Uri` from the URL string.

The `Intent` constructor has an overload method, which you can use to pass in the "data" `Android.Net.Uri` so that you do not need to manually set the data. This makes your code look like the following:

```
var intent = new Intent(Intent.ActionView,
                        Android.Net.Uri.Parse("http://wrox.com"));
StartActivity(intent);
```

When this code runs, you should find that the application you were in has closed. You are taken to the Wrox website, as shown in Figure 10-1.

FIGURE 10-1

You can achieve a similar solution by using the `Android.Webkit.WebView` class to include websites directly within your application without the need for the app to close. To do this, you can simply add a `WebView` tag into your existing layout. To make this clearer in the example, a new activity called `WebActivity` is created to handle the new `WebView` code and a new layout called `WebView` is used. Listing 10-1 shows the new layout `WebView.axml`.

Available for download on Wrox.com

LISTING 10-1: Layout for WebView.axml

```xml
<?xml version="1.0" encoding="utf-8"?>

<LinearLayout
    xmlns:android="http://schemas.android.com/apk/res/android"
    android:orientation="vertical"
    android:layout_width="fill_parent"
    android:layout_height="fill_parent"
    >

    <WebView
        android:id="@+id/webView"
        android:layout_width="fill_parent"
        android:layout_height="fill_parent"
    />

</LinearLayout>
```

This code is contained in Chapter10Examples\Chapter10Examples\Resources\layout\WebView.xaml

From here, you can then hook up the `WebView` in the `WebActivity.cs` to load a new URL. One of the things that happens when you tell the `WebView` to load the URL is that it will create a new intent to do this. Since you want your application to handle the `WebView`, you will need to implement a `WebViewClient` to handle the `ShouldOverrideUrlLoading` method to prevent this by overriding its functionality. When this event gets fired, you can run the same `LoadUrl` method for the view and return `true` to indicate that you have handled the `UrlLoading` yourself.

When the `WebView` is displayed and you click to navigate to different pages, as you click the back button, the `WebView` disappears and returns back to the previous intent. You can override the `OnKeyDown` method on your activity and check to see if the button that was pressed was indeed the Back button and that the `WebView` can go back to previous pages. Listing 10-2 shows the `WebActivity` in full.

Available for download on Wrox.com

LISTING 10-2: Activity for handling a WebView

```
[Activity(Label = "Web Activity")]
public class WebActivity : Activity
{

    private WebView webView;

    protected override void OnCreate(Bundle bundle)
```

continues

```
    {
        base.OnCreate(bundle);

        // Set our view from the "main" layout resource
        SetContentView(Resource.Layout.WebView);

        webView = FindViewById<WebView>(Resource.Id.webView);
        webView.SetWebViewClient(new MyWebViewClient());
        webView.LoadUrl("http://www.wrox.com");

    }

    public override bool OnKeyDown(Keycode keyCode, KeyEvent e)
    {

        if (keyCode == Keycode.Back && webView.CanGoBack())
        {
            webView.GoBack();
            return true;
        }
        return base.OnKeyDown(keyCode, e);

    }

    public class MyWebViewClient : WebViewClient
    {

        public override bool ShouldOverrideUrlLoading(WebView view, string url)
        {

            view.LoadUrl(url);
            return true;

        }
    }
}
```

This code is contained in Chapter10Examples\Chapter10Examples\WebActivity.cs

Opening E-mail

Opening e-mail works much like you expect it to; you use the `mailto:` protocol.

```
var intent = new Intent(Intent.ActionView,
        Android.Net.Uri.Parse("mailto:chris@example.com"));
StartActivity(intent);
```

The emulator by default does not have any mail accounts configured. This causes a fallback message saying Unsupported action, That action is currently not supported *when you start an activity with this intent. To test this method, you can set up an e-mail account in the emulator. This lets you continue testing e-mail-based activities.*

As the `mailto:` protocol states, you can also pass in the commands `bcc`, `cc`, `subject`, and `body`. This populates the necessary fields in the standard mail template. The Android SDK ignores the `from` command normally used with the `mailto:` protocol, so it will not work. Here is an example of the extra commands being used:

```
var intent = new Intent(Intent.ActionView,
    Android.Net.Uri.Parse("mailto:chris@example.com?cc=other@example.com
                    &subject=Wrox&body=Mono for Android "));
StartActivity(intent);
```

As with the browser example, the application again closes, and an e-mail compose message is displayed, as shown in Figure 10-2.

Making a Telephone Call

Using the `tel:` protocol, you can use the built-in telephone functionality of an Android device by using the following `Intent` example. This example shows hyphens within the number. If you do not enter any hyphens, they are automatically added when the Android device parses the URI.

```
var intent = new Intent(Intent.ActionDial,
                Android.Net.Uri
.Parse("tel:1-408-867-5309"));
StartActivity(intent);
```

By using this method, you only prompt the user to dial a number, as shown in Figure 10-3. If you wanted to, you could set the intent action to `Intent.ActionCall`, which immediately calls the entered number. This would then get displayed to the user as Figure 10-4.

```
var intent = new Intent(Intent.ActionCall,
                Android.Net.Uri.Parse("tel:1-408-867-5309"));
StartActivity(intent);
```

FIGURE 10-2

FIGURE 10-3

FIGURE 10-4

Since this could cause a user to spend money on a call, the application must ask permission to perform this task with the CALL_PHONE permission. Make sure your application has the following permission added to the AndroidManifest.xml file:

```
<uses-permission android:name="android.permission.CALL_PHONE" />
```

Sending a Text/SMS Message

The sms: protocol enables you to open an SMS message activity to send an SMS message. Again, you can use a new intent and pass in the number that you want to send an SMS message to:

```
var intent = new Intent(Intent.ActionView,
                        Android.Net.Uri.Parse("sms:1-408-867-5309"));
StartActivity(intent);
```

This next example shows how to open a new text message with the passed-in number and the text you want to put into the message using the PutExtra method on the intent. Even though the sms: protocol says to use body to pass in body text to an SMS message, Android does not use this and instead uses sms_body to pass in the message body. Figure 10-5 displays the message after the intent has been used.

```
var intent = new Intent(Intent.ActionView,
                        Android.Net.Uri.Parse("sms:1-408-867-5309"));
intent.PutExtra("sms_body", "Message Body");
StartActivity(intent);
```

Whilst you can allow the user to explicitly send a text message, the Android platform allows you to send SMS messages directly from the application. This allows you to potentially build a replacement SMS application that can be tailored to your liking.

To programmatically send a SMS message, you can use the SMSManager class, which provides useful methods to send SMS/Text messages. Listing 10-3 shows the code to create a PendingIntent to pick up an event when the text message is sent and the code to initiate the sending of the text message. The pending intent class called SentSMS needs to be created as a broadcast receiver, so Listing 10-4 sets this receiver up.

FIGURE 10-5

Available for
download on
Wrox.com

LISTING 10-3: Sending a text message programmatically

```
PendingIntent sentPendingIntent = PendingIntent.GetBroadcast(this, 300, new
    Intent(this, typeof(SentSms)), 0);

var smsManager = SmsManager.Default;

smsManager.SendTextMessage("ATelephoneNumber", null, "This is an automated
    SMS", sentPendingIntent, null);
```

LISTING 10-4: Creating the SentSMS broadcast receiver

```
[BroadcastReceiver]
public class SentSms : BroadcastReceiver
{
    public override void OnReceive (Context context, Intent intent)
    {
        if(this.ResultCode == (int) Result.Ok)
        {
            Android.Util.Log.Debug("Mono for Android","Result OK");
        }
        else if (this.ResultCode == (int) SmsResultError.GenericFailure)
        {
            Android.Util.Log.Debug("Mono for Android", "Generic Failure");
        }
        else if (this.ResultCode == (int) SmsResultError.NoService)
```

continues

LISTING 10-4 *(continued)*

```
    {
        Android.Util.Log.Debug("Mono for Android", "No Service");
    }
    else if (this.ResultCode == (int) SmsResultError.NullPdu)
    {
        Android.Util.Log.Debug("Mono for Android", "Null Pdu");
    }
    else if (this.ResultCode == (int) SmsResultError.RadioOff)
    {
        Android.Util.Log.Debug("Mono for Android", "Radio Off");
    }
  }
}
```

This code is contained in Chapter10Examples\Chapter10Examples\Activity1.cs

 You need explicit permission to send a SMS message programmatically, as this may have an additional cost to the user running the application. To allow permission, make sure you add the following line in the `AndroidManifest.xml` *file:*

```
<uses-permission android:name="android.permission.SEND_SMS"/>
```

Opening a Location in the Maps Application

To load the Maps application from within a native Android app, you simply use a normal website link to Google Maps. You can use a few query string parameters when creating a Google Maps URL, such as q for a search query and saddr and daddr for the source and destination address, respectively. This example loads a map of Manchester, United Kingdom:

```
var intent = new Intent(Intent.ActionView,
        Android.Net.Uri.Parse("http://maps.google.com/maps?q=Manchester,UK"));
StartActivity(intent);
```

If you are running this in the emulator with the Google API add-on, you get a prompt to open the map in either the browser or the Maps application, as shown in Figure 10-6. This would be the same on a device that has the Google Maps application installed.

The ability to have maps within your own application without closing your application is also available with the Google APIs and Maps API within that. You will see how to use this in Chapter 13.

Opening a YouTube Video

As you saw previously with the Maps example, you just use a normal URL to open the Maps application; this principle is the same when you want to play a YouTube video. You can use either of the two YouTube URLs in the following example code. You need to use the video identifier to play the video. The variable in the following code snippet, youTubeUrl, is an example of the type of URL that will open a YouTube video. As with the Google Maps example, in the simulator the link opens the browser and plays the video, whereas on the device it opens the YouTube application. Of course, the Google YouTube application must be installed.

```
var videoId = "QHyOnBYwIKM";
var youTubeUrl = String.Format("http://youtube.com/watch?v={0}", videoId);
var url = Android.Net.Uri.Parse(youTubeUrl);
var intent = new Intent(Intent.ActionView, url);
StartActivity(intent);
```

FIGURE 10-6

Opening the Market

A great way to promote applications you have built is to allow a user to link directly to an app from one of your apps. To do this, you can use the market:// protocol, which allows you to search the store for different criteria and get detailed information about an application.

To display a list of applications by a certain developer, you can use the following code example to open the Android Market application and display a list of applications by that developer:

```
var publisher = "Google Inc.";
var url = Android.Net.Uri.Parse(
            String.Format("market://search?q=pub:{0}", publisher)
          );
var intent = new Intent(Intent.ActionView, url);
StartActivity(intent);
```

The publisher needs to be exact, because the search will not return partial results.

This example requires the Android Market application because you are using the features of the Android Market, the sample code will not work on the emulator. The emulator does not include the Android Market.

You can use the `market://search?q=pname:`*`package-name`* protocol to search for a package name; again, only exact matches will show up. Here is an example of searching for the Google Earth package name:

```
var packageName = "com.google.earth";
var url = Android.Net.Uri.Parse(
            String.Format("market://search?q=pname:{0}", packageName)
        );
var intent = new Intent(Intent.ActionView, url);
StartActivity(intent);
```

If you wanted to provide a way to search through the Market and allow for partial matches, you could use just the `q` query string variable. Here is an example of searching for Google on the Market:

```
var searchTerm = "Google";
var url = Android.Net.Uri.Parse(
            String.Format("market://search?q={0}", searchTerm)
        );

var intent = new Intent(Intent.ActionView, url);
StartActivity(intent);
```

If you know the full package name of the application you want to display, you can just show a detail page of the application straight from your application. Use `details` instead of `search`, and pass in the package name as the `id`. Here's an example:

```
var packageName = "com.google.earth";
var url = Android.Net.Uri.Parse(
            String.Format("market://details?id={0}", packageName)
        );
var intent = new Intent(Intent.ActionView, url);
StartActivity(intent);
```

APPLICATION INTEGRATION

In addition to opening native Android applications from your own app, you can open applications written by third-party companies. These third-party applications need to optionally expose a protocol so that they can interact with other applications (this method is explained in the next section). Because applications can pick and choose how to implement a protocol, they also need to provide documentation on how to use their protocols.

Finding a particular application's website and figuring out how to implement its protocol can be difficult. It is worth checking the application or developer's website to see if it offers any information on how to integrate with the application. One great example of how to do this comes from a Twitter application for Android called HootSuite.

Simple Integration with HootSuite and Other Twitter Applications

HootSuite is a popular Twitter and Facebook social network application for Android. Because of this, many users commonly use it as their method of sending tweets. You could spend a lot of time building Twitter integration directly into your application, but an easier way to do this is to integrate with a familiar app for the user instead.

HootSuite provides an intent that lets you send text to the application and then go on to send a tweet. To do this, you use the `ActionSend` intent action and type `"application/twitter"`. You then pass in the text you want to send as the tweet and start an activity with the `CreateChooser` method. This allows your application to pick up future applications that support Twitter. The following code shows how you would do this:

Available for download on Wrox.com

```
var intent = new Intent(Intent.ActionSend);
intent.PutExtra(Intent.ExtraText, "Sending a tweet to another application");
intent.SetType("application/twitter");
StartActivity(Intent.CreateChooser(intent, "Select Twitter application"));
```

This code is included in the Tweet Sender example application in TweetSender\TweetSender\TweetSenderActivity.cs

Enabling your application to open other applications can be useful, as can enabling your application to be opened by other applications.

Configuring Your Intent Filters

To enable your application — or, more specifically, your activity — to be opened by other applications, you need to configure intent filters. They allow other applications to use intents to launch activities that are exposed this way. This is similar to how you have been using these intents in the start of the chapter.

An intent filter is an attribute that you add to your activity and set different properties for. This attribute then gets converted into XML that is then merged into the `AndroidManifest.xml` file, which is traditionally where the intent filters are exposed in your application.

For this example, you want to create a Twitter application that accepts when people send text for a tweet and then sends that on to Twitter. The application will behave similarly to HootSuite in how it handles getting a new tweet. First, you want to add the intent filter attribute to the application's activity. Since you want the user to send a tweet through text, you want the application to be available only in that case. You can add the attribute like so:

Available for download on Wrox.com

```
[IntentFilter (new[]{Intent.ActionSend},
                  Categories=new[]{Intent.CategoryDefault})]
[Activity(Label = "Tweet Receiver", MainLauncher = true)]
public class TweetReceiverActivity : Activity {
    // Application code.
}
```

This code is included in the Tweet Receiver example application in TweetReceiver\TweetReceiver\TweetReceiverActivity.cs

The constructor for the `IntentFilter` attribute takes an array of actions that the application will listen for like a normal intent. Because you want the user to send the tweet, this action is set to `Intent.ActionSend`. When an intent is called to match a filter, the intent must match at least one of the set actions in the `IntentFilter`. The category is also set to Default; this is the category for when an intent is called. You also set the Data properties on the intent filter to further filter the intent.

Now that the intent filter is set up on the send action, you need to set up an application that can call into the application. Following the HootSuite example, this looks like the following:

```
var intent = new Intent(Intent.ActionSend);
intent.PutExtra(Intent.ExtraText, "Sending a tweet to another application");
StartActivity(Intent.CreateChooser(intent, "Select Twitter application"));
```

This code is included in the Tweet Sender example application in TweetSender\TweetSender\TweetSenderActivity.cs

Using the `CreateChooser` method allows other applications with the `ActionSend` method to match and optionally be chosen.

Handling Incoming Intent Requests

With the intent filter in place, you will want to handle incoming requests from these intents in the activity. Since you can set up multiple intent requests, you need to make sure that each request is handled correctly. When the intent request comes in, you can check the intent's action directly against an expected action. For this application, you can check if the action matches `Intent.ActionSend`.

If this matches, the intent contains a bundle, which contains extra information that was passed in with the intent that can be extracted. Since you should have received the `Intent.ExtraText` value, you get back the string from the bundle, and then you can use it in your application however you want. Putting together all this information, you should get something like the following:

```
var action = this.Intent.Action;
if(Intent.ActionSend == action)
{
    //We have text for a tweet.
    var sentText = this.Intent.Extras.GetString(Intent.ExtraText);
    Toast.MakeText(this, sentText, ToastLength.Long).Show();
}
```

This code is included in the Tweet Receiver example application in TweetReceiver\TweetReceiver\TweetReceiverActivity.cs

INTEGRATING WITH CONTACTS

Contacts are a key part of any device, and this is no different on Android devices. Accessing this information can be useful within your application. You may want to allow users to see a list of their friends so that they can send a link to your application, for example.

To get access to the Contacts list, you need to use the `ManagedQuery` method and the `ContactsContract.Contacts.ContentUri` URI to go through each of the contacts on the device (see Listing 10-5). From here you can use the `GetString` method and the `GetColumnIndex` method from the cursor index to display the user's name and ID using the `Log.Info` method.

> *You need explicit permission to read through the contact list. To allow permission, make sure you add the following line in the* `AndroidManifest.xml` *file:*
>
> `<uses-permission android:name="android.permission.READ_CONTACTS"/>`

LISTING 10-5: Accessing contacts

```
var uri = ContactsContract.Contacts.ContentUri;
var cursor = ManagedQuery(uri, null, null, null, null);
if(cursor.Count > 0)
{
    while(cursor.MoveToNext())
    {
        Log.Info("Mono for Android", "Id = {0}", cursor.GetString(
cursor.GetColumnIndex(BaseColumns.Id)));
        Log.Info("Mono for Android", "Name = {0}",cursor.GetString(
cursor.GetColumnIndex(ContactsContract.ContactsColumns.DisplayName)));
        Log.Info("Mono for Android", "==============");
    }
    cursor.Close();
}
```

This code is contained in ContactExample\ContactExample\Activity1.cs

> *When you start with Android development, the Android emulator contains no contacts. To make sure Listing 10-5 works, add at least one person to the emulator. You can do this by clicking the Contact icon in the Application list, clicking the menu button, and selecting New Contact.*

Since the Contacts API is really just a wrapper around a SQLite table, you need to use `ColumnIndex` to get back columns from the database. Since a user can have many phone numbers or e-mail addresses, these are stored in a separate table linked to the main contacts table. To display the extra information, you can use the provided content URIs to get it back, as shown in Listing 10-6. Since you need to know the ID of the current contact, the phone and e-mail information is extracted while the existing cursor iterates over each contact.

LISTING 10-6: Accessing phone and e-mail information

```
var uri = ContactsContract.Contacts.ContentUri;
var cursor = ManagedQuery(uri, null, null, null, null);
if(cursor.Count > 0)
{
    while(cursor.MoveToNext())
    {
        var contactId =
            cursor.GetString(cursor.GetColumnIndex(BaseColumns.Id));
        Log.Info("Mono for Android", "Id = {0}", contactId);
        Log.Info("Mono for Android", "Name = {0}", cursor.GetString(
cursor.GetColumnIndex(ContactsContract.ContactsColumns.DisplayName)));

        if(cursor.GetInt(cursor.GetColumnIndex(
            ContactsContract.ContactsColumns.HasPhoneNumber)) == 1)
        {
            var phoneCursor = ManagedQuery(
                    ContactsContract.CommonDataKinds.Phone.ContentUri,
                    null,
                    "CONTACT_ID" + " = " + contactId,
                    null,
                    null);

            while(phoneCursor.MoveToNext())
            {
                var number =  phoneCursor.GetString(
                        phoneCursor.GetColumnIndex(
                        ContactsContract.CommonDataKinds.Phone.Number));

                var type = (PhoneDataKind) phoneCursor.GetInt(
                        phoneCursor.GetColumnIndex("DATA2"));

                Log.Info("Mono for Android",
                        "Telephone: {0} - {1}", number, type.ToString());
            }
            phoneCursor.Close();
        }

        var emailCursor = ManagedQuery(
                    ContactsContract.CommonDataKinds.Email.ContentUri,
                    null,
                    "CONTACT_ID" + " = " + contactId,
                    null,
                    null);

        while(emailCursor.MoveToNext())
        {
            var email =  emailCursor.GetString(
                    emailCursor.GetColumnIndex("DATA1"));


            Log.Info("Mono for Android", "E-mail: {0}", email);
```

```
        }
        emailCursor.Close();
        Log.Info("Mono for Android", "===============");

    }
    cursor.Close();
}
else
{
    Toast.MakeText(this, "No contacts found", ToastLength.Long).Show();
}
```

This code is contained in ContactExample\ContactExample\Activity1.cs

If you wanted to search for a user with a certain name, you could use the `ContactsContract` `.Contacts.ContentFilterUri` URI and append the name you wanted to filter into your search query. The following code shows how you would use this to search for all the contacts that match the partial name of Fred:

Available for download on Wrox.com

```
var filterUri = ContactsContract.Contacts.ContentFilterUri;
var uri = Android.Net.Uri.WithAppendedPath(filterUri, "Fred");

var cursor = ManagedQuery(uri, null, null, null, null);
Toast.MakeText(this, "Found " + cursor.Count + " people with Fred in their
    name", ToastLength.Long).Show();
```

This code is contained in ContactExample\ContactExample\Activity1.cs

Accessing the contacts programmatically can be useful for the most part, but hand-cranking UI components on top of this takes a long time when you really just want the default behavior that users expect from their Android devices. Fortunately you can reuse your knowledge of intents to manipulate and view contact information.

Displaying Contact Details

To display a contact's detail from your application, you can use the `Intent` class and the content URIs provided by the `ContactsContract` class. To display a person when you know his or her ID, you just create a new intent pointing to the ID appended to the content URI. The following code shows how to create this intent. Figure 10-7 shows the contact's detail view. Make sure you have a contact with an ID of `"1"` in your contacts so that the sample will work:

Available for download on Wrox.com

```
// Display contact detail for ID 1
var contactUri = ContactsContract.Contacts.ContentUri;
var uri = Android.Net.Uri.WithAppendedPath(contactUri, "1");

var intent = new Intent(Intent.ActionView, uri);
StartActivity(intent);
```

This code is contained in ContactExample\ContactExample\Activity1.cs

FIGURE 10-7

FIGURE 10-8

Notice that you could continue to edit this contact because it is displaying part of the native Android device and not an activity in your application.

Picking a Contact

To allow users to select a particular contact from a list of all their contacts, you use the `Intent`
`.ActionPick` intent type. To allow the activity to pick up on the user who was picked, use the
`StartActivityForResult` method, and use a unique integer to resolve the result when you get back
the result. The following code uses `100` as this unique integer. When the picker is loaded, you see a
list of all users, similar to the list shown in the Contacts application (see Figure 10-8).

```
// Display contact picker
var intent = new Intent(Intent.ActionPick,
                        ContactsContract.Contacts.ContentUri);
this.StartActivityForResult(intent, 100);
```

This code is contained in ContactExample\ContactExample\Activity1.cs

Since the intent was set off from the `StartActivityForResult` method, you need to handle this by
overriding the `OnActivityResult` method. To do this, you can use the intent's data as the URI to
pass straight back into a `ManagedQuery` to get the selected contact:

```
protected override void OnActivityResult (int requestCode, Result resultCode,
  Intent data)
{
    if(requestCode == 100)
    {
        if (data != null)
```

```
    {
        var cursor = ManagedQuery(data.Data, null, null, null);
        if(cursor.Count > 0)
        {
            cursor.MoveToFirst();
            Toast.MakeText(this, "Got contact " +
                            cursor.GetString(
                            cursor.GetColumnIndex(
                    ContactsContract.ContactsColumns.DisplayName)
                        ), ToastLength.Long).Show();
        }
    }
    else
    {
        Toast.MakeText(this, "No contact picked", ToastLength.Long).Show();
    }
    }
}
```

This code is contained in ContactExample\ContactExample\Activity1.cs

Creating a New Contact

Adding a new contact into the device is fairly similar to the other ways of hooking into the contact functionality. This intent provides the same view that you would see in the Contacts app (see Figure 10-9).

FIGURE 10-9

Using the PutExtra methods and the ContactsContract.Intents.Insert properties on the intent, you can pass in extra information that you already know about the new contact (such as a name or e-mail address). It is worth noting that you can add only a first name to the contact. Due to Android limitations, you cannot set the first and last name using this method. You do this as follows:

```
// Insert a new contact
var intent = new Intent(Intent.ActionInsert,
                        ContactsContract.Contacts.ContentUri);
intent.PutExtra(ContactsContract.Intents.Insert.Name, "Chris Hardy");
intent.PutExtra(ContactsContract.Intents.Insert.Phone, "1-408-867-5309");
intent.PutExtra(ContactsContract.Intents.Insert.Email,
                                      "chrisntr@gmail.com");
this.StartActivityForResult(intent, 150);
```

This code is contained in ContactExample\ContactExample\Activity1.cs

You use the `StartActivityForResult` method to call this because you are only presenting a Create New Contact screen to the user. The user may choose not to add a new contact, so to programmatically find out if the user added a new contact, you use the `resultCode` to see if the user canceled the activity or the activity result returned an OK. The following code shows this in action:

```
protected override void OnActivityResult (int requestCode, Result resultCode,
 Intent data)
{
    if (resultCode == Result.Ok)
{
        // TODO: Handle successful contact being added.
    }
    else if (resultCode == Result.Canceled)
    {
        // TODO: Handle no new contact getting added.
    }
}
```

This code is contained in ContactExample\ContactExample\Activity1.cs

Creating a New Contact or Adding to an Existing Contact

Sometimes you may have some information that you want to associate with a contact that already exists in your contact list. Or maybe you want to create a new contact with this new information. You can modify the intent so that the type it expects is `ContactsContract.Contacts` `.ContentItemType`, and the intent action can be changed to `ActionInsertOrEdit`. Now when the user initiates the intent, he or she sees the screen shown in Figure 10-10.

This screen allows the user to either create a new contact or use the list to pick a contact to add the extra information to. If the user selects the New Contact button at the top, the experience is the same as if the user were creating a new contact, as shown earlier. If the user selects an existing contact, the information you passed in either gets added or overwrites the existing content. The user can then save or revert (cancel) this action and return to the application.

Available for
download on
Wrox.com

```
var intent = new Intent(Intent.ActionInsertOrEdit);
intent.SetType(ContactsContract.Contacts.ContentItemType);

intent.PutExtra(ContactsContract.Intents.Insert.Name, "Chris Hardy");
intent.PutExtra(ContactsContract.Intents.Insert.Phone, "1-408-867-5309");

intent.PutExtra(ContactsContract.Intents.Insert.Email,
                                        "chrisntr@gmail.com");
this.StartActivityForResult(intent, 150);
```

This code is contained in ContactExample\ContactExample\Activity1.cs

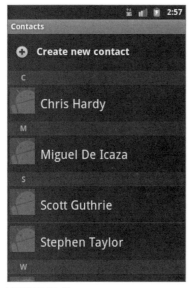

FIGURE 10-10

SUMMARY

Allowing native Android applications to talk to each other is a great way to create a consistent and intuitive user experience. Allowing access to the user's contact list can enable unique application experiences, can help your application make a much more personal connection with the user, and can give you access to key features of the phone such as calling a number or sending a text message — making your applications stand out from the rest.

11

Developing Background Services and Asynchronous Code

Unlike some other mobile operating systems, Android allows and even encourages the use of background processing using a variety of mechanisms to do things independently of a user interface. This allows applications to listen for broadcast intents from other applications or services, stay updated on location data, and even communicate over the Internet with other services, all without requiring the application's user interface to be running.

Separating the user interface from background processing is critical in creating efficient applications. There's no need to hold memory for a user interface when all your application is doing is polling a web service.

Android provides several mechanisms for processing in the background. Services don't even need to always be running. Android can wake up a service to do its processing in the background based on a scheduled time or interval, or when another thread or application broadcasts an intent in which the service is interested.

In this chapter you learn all about services and running code in the background, outside of the main application thread. You discover how to communicate updates from your background code to the user through notifications, as well as how to communicate with your activity user interface. You also explore efficient ways to make your background services poll at intervals with alarms. Finally, you will be introduced to Google's new Cloud to Device Messaging architecture for push notifications.

THE LIFE CYCLE OF A SERVICE

Since services are meant to be used as a mechanism for executing code without user interaction, it should be no surprise that they are considered more important than user interface activities that are not currently visible to the user. When the operating system needs to reclaim more memory, it kills services only in the most dire situations. Even then, it is possible to ask the operating system to restart your service if it needs to be temporarily killed.

A service can be started multiple times, once for each time `StartService` is called for a particular service. For each time a service is started, it passes an intent and a unique ID for the call to start it.

Creating Your First Service

Throughout this chapter, you will be working with different implementations of services and UIs that search Twitter for tweets containing the hash tag `#MonoDroid`. Listing 11-1 shows the simple `Tweet` and `Search` classes that will be referenced in each of the samples you work with. They are beyond the scope of this chapter, but it should not be difficult to become familiar with how they work at a basic level.

LISTING 11-1: Helper classes

```
using System;
using System.Collections.Generic;
using System.Linq;
using System.Net;
using System.Json;
using System.Web;

namespace Chapter11.Twitter
{
    public class Tweet
    {
        public long Id { get; set; }
        public string ProfileImgUrl { get; set; }
        public string Text { get; set; }
        public string FromUser { get; set; }
    }

    public class Search
    {
        public static List<Tweet> SearchTweets(long sinceId, params string[] terms)
```

```
        {
            var tweets = new List<Tweet>();

            var query = string.Format("{0}?q={1}&since_id={2}&lang=en",
                "http://search.twitter.com/search.json",
                HttpUtility.UrlEncode(string.Join(" OR ", terms)),
                sinceId);

            var data = (new WebClient()).DownloadString(query);

            var jsonObj = JsonObject.Parse(data) as JsonObject;
            var jsonResults = jsonObj["results"] as JsonArray;

            foreach (var jsonItem in jsonResults)
            {
                tweets.Add(new Tweet()
                {
                    Id = (long)jsonItem["id"],
                    ProfileImgUrl = jsonItem["profile_image_url"].ToString(),
                    Text = jsonItem["text"].ToString(),
                    FromUser = jsonItem["from_user"].ToString()
                });
            }

            return tweets;
        }
    }
}
```

This code is contained in Chapter11.Twitter\Search.cs

For your first service, you will create a straightforward service that simply searches for tweets each time it is started. This is done by subclassing the service class, as shown in Listing 11-2.

LISTING 11-2: Your first service

```
using System;
using System.Collections.Generic;
using System.Linq;
using System.Text;
using Android.App;
using Android.Content;
using Android.OS;
using Android.Runtime;
using Android.Views;
using Android.Widget;
using Chapter11.Twitter;

namespace Chapter11.FirstService
{
    [Service]
    public class FirstService : Service
```

continues

LISTING 11-2 *(continued)*

```
    {
        List<Tweet> tweets = new List<Tweet>();

        public override IBinder OnBind(Intent intent)
        {
            throw new NotImplementedException();
        }

        public override StartCommandResult OnStartCommand(Intent intent,
            StartCommandFlags flags, int startId)
        {
            var startCmdResult = base.OnStartCommand(intent, flags, startId);

            tweets = Search.SearchTweets(0, "#MonoDroid");

            foreach (var tweet in tweets)
                Android.Util.Log.Info("CHAPTER-11",
                    string.Format("{0} - {1}: {2}", tweet.Id,
                    tweet.FromUser, tweet.Text));
            Toast.MakeText(this, "Tweets Refreshed!", ToastLength.Short).Show();

            return startCmdResult;
        }
    }
}
```

This code is contained in Chapter11a.FirstService\FirstService.cs

 Throughout this chapter's code samples, you will see the Twitter hashtag #MonoDroid referenced. Mono for Android was initially known to the community as MonoDroid. Many references to it still use this name, such as IRC channels, open source projects, and tweets.

Subclassing the service class requires that you override the OnBind method (which you will learn about in the section "Communication with the UI: Using the Binder and service Connection Method"). In this example, you need not worry about what that method does, but your code will not compile without overriding this method. It wouldn't be very useful to have a service that didn't do anything, so you can see that OnStartCommand has been overridden as well. This is the main entry point for your service, and it is a method that may be called multiple times. The parameters include an intent that caused the service to start (it may contain relevant extras), a flag indicating if the service is being started as a Retry or Redelivery from a failed attempt, and a startId unique to the request to start.

The OnStartCommand method must return a StartCommandResult bitmask value. It tells the operating system how the service wants to be managed — specifically, if the service is killed by the operating system after it has been started (for example, in low-memory conditions). There are several possible `enum` flags:

➤ `NotSticky`: The service is taken out of started state, and no intents are redelivered if it is killed by the OS.

➤ `RedeliverIntent`: The service is scheduled for restart, and intents are redelivered if killed by the OS.

➤ `Sticky`: The service should be left in its started state, and no intents are redelivered if it is killed by the OS.

➤ `StickyCompatible`: Does not guarantee that service's start method will be called again if killed by the OS. This exists for compatibility with APIs older than Level 5 (Android 2.0).

➤ `ContinuationMask`: A bitmask of values returned. This value is not necessary for returning a `StartCommandResult`, but rather for reading different bitmasks from the returned value. You should not normally need to use this.

 Prior to API Level 5 (Android 2.0), `OnStart(Intent intent)` *was used instead of* `OnStartCommand`. *You should override both if you plan to support older platforms.*

Another important thing to note is the `[Service]` attribute decorating the class. If you've done any Java Android development, you might know that services need to be declared in the manifest file. Mono for Android automatically generates the correct service definitions in the manifest file if you use the `[Service]` attribute to decorate your service classes.

Prioritizing Services

Your service wants to keep running; it has inertia. services always have higher priority than activities, which are not visible to the user. If an activity is currently in use and is visible to the user (a foreground activity), it has the highest priority and should never be terminated. A service, then, has the next-highest priority.

Sometimes you might want your service to maintain a higher priority than its default, meaning that it should have the equivalent priority to a foreground activity. An example might be a VoIP application or a music player. You can start a service in the foreground (or move a running service to the foreground) status by using the `Service.StartForeground(int id, Notification n)` method. It expects, as parameters, a notification ID (unique within your application) and a `Notification` object (which should be an ongoing notification). This raises your service to foreground status and prevents it from being killed to free up memory except for the most dire low-memory conditions. Similarly, the `Service.StopForeground(bool removeNotification)` method is used to remove the service from foreground status, which expects a `bool` parameter indicating whether to remove the ongoing notification passed into the `StartForeground` call. Listing 11-3 shows how to prioritize a service.

Prior to API Level 5 (Android 2.0), you need to use `SetForeground(bool isForeground)` *to change the foreground status on your service.*

LISTING 11-3: Prioritizing a service

Available for download on Wrox.com

```
var notification = new Notification(
   Android.Resource.Drawable.SymActionEmail,
   "Prioritized Service!");
Notification.Flags = NotificationFlags.ForegroundService;

var pendingIntent = PendingIntent.GetActivity(this, 0,
   new Intent(this, typeof(MainActivity)),
   PendingIntentFlags.UpdateCurrent);

notification.SetLatestEventInfo(this, "Prioritized Service",
   "Prioritized Service running", pendingIntent);

StartForeground(1, notification);
NotificationManager.FromContext(this).Notify(0, notification);
```

This code is contained in Chapter11b.PrioritizingServices\PriorityService.cs

USING THREADS FOR ASYNCHRONOUS PROCESSING

It may not be immediately obvious, but the fact that services are running does not automatically mean that your code is running in the background. In fact, by default, the methods that your service overrides are executed on the main application thread. This means that if you call `StartService(...)` from your activity, your service's `OnStartCommand(...)` method is called, but your activity blocks calling this method on your service. If you're not careful, you could tie up your user interface while starting a service if you do a lot of processing in the `OnStartCommand(...)`. For this reason, it is important to move any lengthy processing routines to a different thread. There are several ways to accomplish this task in Mono for Android:

➤ **Manual threading:** Using the `System.Threading` namespace, you can spawn threads manually as needed to do background work.

➤ `System.Threading.Tasks`: Mono provides a namespace which abstracts threading, for executing code asynchronously, and in parallel.

➤ `IntentService`: This is a special subclass of `service` that does processing in the background whenever a new intent arrives. It starts and stops as required and handles the asynchronous plumbing for you.

Android contains a class called `AsyncTask` *that can also be used to execute code asynchronously. This class can also be used in Mono if it is necessary for interfacing with other Java methods. There are several .NET ways to accomplish asynchronous patterns, so the* `AsyncTask` *is not typically required.*

Threading Manually

If you are familiar with threading in .NET, the code shown in Listing 11-4 should make you feel right at home. It shows how you can use the `System.Threading.Thread` object to execute code in the background. The service utilizes a single `Thread` object. Each time the service is started, the thread instance is checked to see if it has been created or is still running. If it's not running, or has not yet been created, a new thread instance is generated and started. The thread executes the `serviceWorker()` method. If the thread is already running, no new thread is created.

LISTING 11-4: Using manual threading

```
using System;
using System.Threading;
using Android.App;
using Android.Content;
using Android.OS;
using Android.Runtime;
using Android.Views;
using Android.Widget;
using Chapter11.Twitter;

namespace Chapter11.ManualThreading
{
    [Service]
    public class ThreadedService : Service
    {
        int startCount = 0;
        Thread worker = null;
        Handler handler = new Handler();

        public override IBinder OnBind(Intent intent)
        {
            throw new NotImplementedException();
        }

        public override StartCommandResult OnStartCommand(Intent intent,
            StartCommandFlags flags, int startId)
        {
            var startCmdResult = base.OnStartCommand(intent, flags, startId);

            startCount++;
```

continues

LISTING 11-4 *(continued)*

```
        if (worker == null || !worker.IsAlive)
        {
            worker = new Thread(new ThreadStart(serviceWorker));
            worker.Start();
        }

        return startCmdResult;
    }

    void serviceWorker()
    {
        while (startCount > 0)
        {
            startCount--;

            var tweets = Search.SearchTweets(0, "#MonoDroid");

            foreach (var tweet in tweets)
                Android.Util.Log.Info("CHAPTER-11", string.Format(
                    "{0} - {1}: {2}", tweet.Id, tweet.FromUser, tweet.Text));

            handler.Post(() =>
            {
                Toast.MakeText(this, "Tweets Refreshed!",
                    ToastLength.Short).Show();
            });                      }

        this.StopSelf();
    }
}
}
```

This code is contained in Chapter11c.ManualThreading\ThreadedService.cs

This service has a single worker thread that is started if it's not already running, in the
OnStartCommand override, after startCount is incremented. The worker thread loops while
startCount is greater than 0 and decrements it after each iteration. If the service is already running, startCount is incremented so that the loop is run as many times as the service has been
requested to start.

You may have noticed the use of a Handler in Listing 11-4 to display a Toast. Since a Toast
causes a change in the UI, it needs to be displayed on the main application thread. The
TaskService uses a Task, which uses threading to refresh tweets without blocking the main application thread. (Remember that a service runs on the main application thread.) In an Activity
you would typically use RunOnUiThread() to interact with the UI from another thread. In a service, this method is not available, but a Handler instance can be used to Post() code to be run
on the main application thread. It is important to note that the Handler must be instantiated from
the main application thread.

Utilizing System.Threading.Tasks

One of the features that Mono brings to Android is the `System.Threading.Tasks` (formerly known as the Parallel Extensions) namespace. This namespace is designed to help execute code asynchronously, and in parallel. This has become important on personal computers with the advent of multiple core processors. This same pattern will also hold true for mobile devices, as more and more computers with multiple core processors are released. Using this namespace is an easy way to make your code execute asynchronously, as well as take advantage of multicore power in devices.

Listing 11-5 shows an example of using the `Task` pattern to execute code in a service asynchronously. It also uses the `Parallel.ForEach` pattern to iterate over the tweets returned from the search. If the device running the code has multiple cores, the loop is able to process multiple items at the same time, without any additional code on your part.

LISTING 11-5: Implementing System.Threading.Tasks

```
using System;
using System.Collections.Generic;
using System.Linq;
using System.Text;
using System.Threading.Tasks;

using Android.App;
using Android.Content;
using Android.OS;
using Android.Runtime;
using Android.Views;
using Android.Widget;

using Chapter11.Twitter;

namespace Chapter11.Tasks
{
    [Service]
    public class TaskService : Service
    {
        List<Tweet> tweets = new List<Tweet>();
        Handler handler = new Handler();

        public override IBinder OnBind(Intent intent)
        {
            return default(IBinder);
        }

        public override StartCommandResult OnStartCommand(Intent intent,
            StartCommandFlags flags, int startId)
        {
            var result = base.OnStartCommand(intent, flags, startId);

            Task.Factory.StartNew(() =>
            {
```

continues

LISTING 11-5 *(continued)*

```
                tweets = Search.SearchTweets(0, "#MonoDroid");

                Parallel.ForEach<Tweet>(tweets, (Tweet tweet) =>
                {
                    Android.Util.Log.Info("CHAPTER-11", string.Format(
                        "{0} - {1}: {2}", tweet.Id, tweet.FromUser, tweet.Text));
                });

                handler.Post(() =>
                {
                    Toast.MakeText(this, "Tweets Refreshed!",
                        ToastLength.Short).Show();
                });
            });

            return result;
        }
    }
}
```

This code is contained in Chapter11d.Tasks\TaskService.cs

Implicit Threading with the IntentService

Android has a class called `IntentService` that the previous listing mimics quite closely. It is a special type of service that moves processing to another thread. It also uses only a single thread that does all the processing of any intents queued from calls to the `OnStartCommand` method. When `IntentService` has no more work to do (no more queued intents), it stops itself and waits for the next time something calls for it to start. Listing 11-6 shows how you would implement `IntentService` to do the same job as the service shown in Listing 11-5.

LISTING 11-6: Implementing IntentService

```
using System;
using System.Collections.Generic;
using Android.App;
using Android.Content;
using Android.OS;
using Android.Runtime;
using Android.Views;
using Android.Widget;
using Chapter11.Twitter;

namespace Chapter11.IntentServiceSample
{
    [Service]
    public class IntentServiceSample : IntentService
    {
```

```
List<Tweet> tweets = new List<Tweet>();
Handler handler = new Handler();

protected override void OnHandleIntent(Intent intent)
{
    tweets = Search.SearchTweets(0, "#MonoDroid");
    foreach (var tweet in tweets)
        Android.Util.Log.Info("CHAPTER-11", string.Format(
            "{0} - {1}: {2}", tweet.Id, tweet.FromUser, tweet.Text));

    handler.Post(() =>
    {
        Toast.MakeText(this, "Tweets Refreshed!", ToastLength.Short)
            .Show();
    });
}
}
}
```

This code is contained in Chapter11e.IntentServiceSample\IntentServiceSample.cs

You can see that there's not much to implementing the `IntentService` and that it does a lot of heavy lifting. This is a great class, and you should use it whenever possible.

COMMUNICATING WITH THE UI

In most apps, a service isn't much use unless it can communicate with the user interface to let it know when changes or updates have occurred. With Android, you should consider that the user interface is responsible for communicating with the service, because at any given time your activity may not be in the foreground. Consider that your service may be running and have new data to share with an activity at any time, but it would be a waste of resources trying to update an activity if it's paused or has been destroyed. A number of methods can be used to communicate with services:

➤   Binding with the binder and service connection

➤   Using a broadcast receiver when the activity is active

➤   Registering for a static event in the activity

Using the Binder and Service Connection Method

The binder and service connection method is a standard Android way to obtain a reference to the actual instance of a service. With a reference to the service, you can call public methods, change properties, and register for instance events as a means of communicating with the service from an activity. To create a binding, your service must override and implement the `OnBind` method. It should return an instance of a class implementing `IBinder`. In Listing 11-7, you subclass the `Binder` class to simply store a strongly typed reference to the service itself.

On the activity side, you need to create an instance of a class implementing `IServiceConnection`, which requires `OnServiceConnected` and `OnServiceDisconnected` method implementations. In

Listing 11-7 you create an implementation that exposes a `Connected` event that passes along the binder instance. The activity registers for the connected event and, in that event, wires instance events on the service instance itself. Finally, the activity must bind to the service in the `OnResume` override and unbind on the `OnPause` override so that it does not maintain a connection to the service when it is not in the foreground. Since you used the `AutoCreate` bind flag, there is no need to explicitly start the service. This is done automatically if the service is not already running.

LISTING 11-7: Binding a service to an activity

```
using System;
using System.Collections.Generic;
using System.Linq;
using System.Text;
using Android.App;
using Android.Content;
using Android.OS;
using Android.Runtime;
using Android.Views;
using Android.Widget;

using Chapter11.Twitter;

namespace Chapter11.UICommunication
{
    [Service]
    public class BindingTweetService : IntentService
    {
        public event Action NewTweetsFound;

        public List<Tweet> Tweets { get; set; }
        public long LastSinceId { get; set; }

        private TweetServiceBinder binder;

        public BindingTweetService()
            : base()
        {
            this.Tweets = new List<Tweet>();
            this.LastSinceId = 0;

            this.binder = new TweetServiceBinder(this);
        }

        public override IBinder OnBind(Intent intent)
        {
            base.OnBind(intent);
            return binder;
        }

        protected override void OnHandleIntent(Intent intent)
        {
            this.Tweets = Search.SearchTweets(LastSinceId,
```

```
                "#MonoDroid");

        if (this.Tweets.Exists(t => t.Id > LastSinceId))
        {
            if (this.NewTweetsFound != null)
                this.NewTweetsFound();
        }
    }

    public class TweetServiceBinder : Binder
    {
        public TweetServiceBinder(BindingTweetService service)
        {
            this.ServiceInstance = service;
        }

        public BindingTweetService ServiceInstance
        {
            get;
            private set;
        }
    }

    public class TweetServiceConnection : Java.Lang.Object, IServiceConnection
    {
        public event Action<BindingTweetService> Connected;

        public event Action Disconnected;

        public void OnServiceConnected(ComponentName className,
            IBinder serviceBinder)
        {
            if (this.Connected != null)
                this.Connected((serviceBinder as
                    TweetServiceBinder).ServiceInstance);
        }

        public void OnServiceDisconnected(ComponentName className)
        {
            if (this.Disconnected != null)
                this.Disconnected();
        }
    }

    [Activity(Label = "CH11 Binding Service", MainLauncher=true,
        LaunchMode=Android.Content.PM.LaunchMode.SingleTask)]
    public class BindingActivity : Activity
    {
        TweetServiceConnection serviceConnection;

        protected override void OnCreate(Bundle bundle)
        {
            base.OnCreate(bundle);

            SetContentView(Resource.Layout.Main);
```

continues

LISTING 11-7 *(continued)*

```
Button button = FindViewById<Button>(Resource.Id.myButton);
button.Text = "Check Tweets via Service";

button.Click += delegate
{
    StartService(new Intent(this, typeof(BindingTweetService)));
};

serviceConnection = new TweetServiceConnection();
serviceConnection.Connected += (BindingTweetService svc) =>
{
    Toast.MakeText(this, "Bound to Service!",
        ToastLength.Short).Show();

    svc.NewTweetsFound += () =>
    {
        foreach (var tweet in svc.Tweets)
            Android.Util.Log.Info("CHAPTER-11", string.Format(
                "{0} - {1}: {2}", tweet.Id, tweet.FromUser,
                tweet.Text));
        RunOnUiThread(() =>
        {
            Toast.MakeText(this, "Tweets Refreshed!",
                ToastLength.Short).Show();
        });
    };
};
}

protected override void OnResume()
{
    base.OnResume();

    var serviceIntent = new Intent(this, typeof(BindingTweetService));
    BindService(serviceIntent, serviceConnection, Bind.AutoCreate);
}

protected override void OnPause()
{
    UnbindService(serviceConnection);

    base.OnPause();
}
}
}
}
```

This code is contained in Chapter11f.UICommunication\Binding.cs

As you can see, this is a fairly verbose way of talking to a service, but it does provide ultimate control since you eventually obtain a reference to the actual typed instance of the service.

The tricky part of binding a service is that you have no guarantee of when the binding will be completed. This is why you created the `Connected` event in the service connection class. With lambdas and anonymous methods, this pattern works quite well, since the service instance variable is in scope for the anonymous event handler for the `NewTweetsFound` event.

As you will see in Listings 11-8 and 11-9, this isn't the only way to accomplish communication between a service and a UI. However, since this is a built-in mechanism for such communication, you may find yourself needing to use it if you want to make your applications talk to services that you did not write yourself or that were not written using Mono for Android.

Using the Broadcast Receiver Method

Android applications can use another common method that involves a `BroadcastReceiver`. In C# you can take advantage of this mechanism by subclassing `BroadcastReceiver` to expose a `Receive` event. In the override for `OnReceive` in `BroadcastReceiver`, the `Receive` event is fired. The activity then registers for the `Receive` event and can do its UI updates when the event is raised. Listing 11-8 shows this technique in action.

LISTING 11-8: BroadcastReceiver in an activity

```csharp
using System;
using Android.App;
using Android.Content;
using Android.OS;
using Android.Runtime;
using Android.Views;
using Android.Widget;
using Android.Content.PM;

namespace Chapter11.UICommunication
{
    [Activity(Label = "CH11 UI Broadcast Rec", MainLauncher=true,
        LaunchMode=Android.Content.PM.LaunchMode.SingleTask)]
    public class BroadcastActivity : Activity
    {
        const string ACTION_NEW_TWEETS = "action.NEW_TWEETS";

        ActivityBroadcastReceiver broadcastReceiver;
        Button buttonNewestId;

        protected override void OnCreate(Bundle bundle)
        {
            base.OnCreate(bundle);

            SetContentView(Resource.Layout.Main);

            buttonNewestId = FindViewById<Button>(Resource.Id.myButton);
            buttonNewestId.Click += delegate
            {
                StartService(new Intent(this, typeof(BroadcastService)));
            };
            broadcastReceiver = new ActivityBroadcastReceiver();
```

continues

LISTING 11-8 *(continued)*

```
        broadcastReceiver.Receive += (Context context, Intent intent) =>
        {
            var lastSinceId = intent.GetLongExtra("oldSinceId", 0);
            var tweets = Twitter.Search.SearchTweets(lastSinceId,
                "#MonoDroid");

            foreach (var tweet in tweets)
                Android.Util.Log.Info("CHAPTER-11", string.Format(
                    "{0} - {1}: {2}", tweet.Id, tweet.FromUser, tweet.Text));
            Toast.MakeText(this, "Tweets Refreshed!", ToastLength.Short)
                .Show();
        };
    }

    protected override void OnResume()
    {
        base.OnResume();

        RegisterReceiver(broadcastReceiver,
            new IntentFilter(ACTION_NEW_TWEETS));
    }

    protected override void OnPause()
    {
        UnregisterReceiver(broadcastReceiver);

        base.OnPause();
    }
}

public class ActivityBroadcastReceiver : BroadcastReceiver
{
    public event Action<Context, Intent> Receive;

    public override void OnReceive(Context context, Intent intent)
    {
        if (this.Receive != null)
            this.Receive(context, intent);
    }
}
}
```

This code is contained in Chapter11f.UICommunication\BroadcastActivity.cs

You'll notice that the activity dynamically registers an `IntentFilter` for the broadcast receiver in the `OnResume` override. It also unregisters the receiver in the `OnPause` override. This ensures that no broadcasts are received as soon as the activity is paused, wasting resources.

On the service side, Listing 11-9 shows how to notify the broadcast receiver. To make this work, you need to define a common action: something the server can broadcast and that the broadcast receiver listens for.

LISTING 11-9: Sending broadcasts from a service

```
using System;
using System.Linq;
using Android.App;
using Android.Content;
using Android.OS;
using Android.Runtime;
using Android.Views;
using Android.Widget;
using Chapter11.Twitter;

namespace Chapter11.UICommunication
{
    [Service]
    public class BroadcastService : IntentService
    {
        public const string ACTION_NEW_TWEETS = "action.NEW_TWEETS";

        public long LastSinceId { get; set; }

        public BroadcastService() : base()
        {
            this.LastSinceId = 0;
        }

        protected override void OnHandleIntent(Intent intent)
        {
            var lastSinceId = this.LastSinceId;

            var tweets = Search.SearchTweets(lastSinceId, "#MonoDroid");

            this.LastSinceId = tweets.Max(t => t.Id);

            if (tweets.Exists(t => t.Id > lastSinceId))
            {
                var newTweetsIntent = new Intent(ACTION_NEW_TWEETS);
                newTweetsIntent.PutExtra("oldSinceId", lastSinceId);

                SendBroadcast(newTweetsIntent);
            }
        }
    }
}
```

This code is contained in Chapter11f.UICommunication\BroadcastService.cs

Using the Static Event Method

An alternative method of communicating is to use static events. This is a very .NET way of thinking, but it can work well. All you need to do is define a static event somewhere. You can do this for
both directions of communication: from the activity to the service, and vice versa, as shown
in Listing 11-10.

LISTING 11-10: Using static events for communication

```
using System;
using System.Collections.Generic;
using System.Linq;
using System.Text;
using Android.App;
using Android.Content;
using Android.OS;
using Android.Runtime;
using Android.Views;
using Android.Widget;
using Chapter11.Twitter;

namespace Chapter11.UICommunication
{
    [Service]
    public class StaticEventService : IntentService
    {
        public static event Action<List<Tweet>> NewTweetsFound;

        public long LastSinceId { get; set; }

        public StaticEventService()
            : base()
        {
            this.LastSinceId = 0;
        }

        protected override void OnHandleIntent(Intent intent)
        {
            var lastSinceId = this.LastSinceId;

            var tweets = Search.SearchTweets(LastSinceId, "#MonoDroid");
            this.LastSinceId = tweets.Max(t => t.Id);

            var newTweets = from t in tweets
                            where t.Id > lastSinceId
                            select t;

            if (newTweets != null && newTweets.Count() > 0 && NewTweetsFound !=
              null)
                NewTweetsFound(newTweets.ToList());
        }
    }

    [Activity(Label = "CH11 Static Events", MainLauncher=true,
        LaunchMode=Android.Content.PM.LaunchMode.SingleTask)]
    public class StaticEventActivity : Activity
    {
        Action<List<Tweet>> newTweetsAction;

        protected override void OnCreate(Bundle bundle)
        {
```

```
        base.OnCreate(bundle);

        SetContentView(Resource.Layout.Main);

        var button = FindViewById<Button>(Resource.Id.myButton);
        button.Text = "Refresh Tweets";

        button.Click += delegate
        {
            StartService(new Intent(this, typeof(StaticEventService)));
        };

        newTweetsAction = (List<Tweet> tweets) => {
            foreach (var tweet in tweets)
                Android.Util.Log.Info("CHAPTER-11", string.Format(
                    "{0} - {1}: {2}", tweet.Id, tweet.FromUser, tweet.Text));
            RunOnUiThread(() =>
            {
                Toast.MakeText(this, "Tweets Refreshed!",
                    ToastLength.Short).Show();
            });
        };
    }
    protected override void OnResume()
    {
        base.OnResume();

        StaticEventService.NewTweetsFound += newTweetsAction;
    }

    protected override void OnPause()
    {
        StaticEventService.NewTweetsFound -= newTweetsAction;

        base.OnPause();
    }
}
}
```

This code is contained in Chapter11f.UICommunication\StaticEvents.cs

This code sample includes a service and an activity. The service is a simple `IntentService` that exposes a static event called `NewTweetsFound`. Each time `OnHandleIntent` is called, the service looks for new tweets since the last ID. If it finds new tweets, it raises the `NewTweetsFound` event.

The activity defines an action in `OnCreate` for what it should do when it is notified of new tweets. In this example, it doesn't actually do anything with the information, but you could put code here to update your `ListAdapter` or display the newest tweet. The important part of this activity is in the `OnResume` and `OnPause` methods. In `OnResume`, the static event from the service is wired to the Action you previously created. In the `OnPause` override, the event is unregistered. This prevents the activity from receiving raised events when it is not in the foreground.

Static members are kept in memory for the entire life of the application. It is bad practice to store anything but references or primitive types in static variables.

NOTIFYING THE USER WITH NOTIFICATIONS

Now that you've learned how to use services and how to communicate between the UI and those services, a piece is still missing. What happens if your service has new information to share with your activity, but your activity is not the foreground activity?

It would be rude of you to demand that your activity of tweets show up without the user's asking to see it, just because you found new tweets. This is where Notifications are useful. Notifications provide a platform-standard way to unobtrusively notify the user when an application has a change in state. The user can choose when to address these notifications so that she isn't interrupted in her current task against her wishes.

In case you are unfamiliar with them, Notifications are what you see in the expanded status bar (when you swipe from the status bar at the top of your device's screen downward). You can set several properties of a Notification, including the following:

➤ `Sound`: The sound you want played on the device as soon as the notification is presented to the user.

➤ `Vibrate`: An array of type `long` indicating a succession of vibration lengths. For example, `long[] { 100, 100 }` would vibrate twice for 100 milliseconds. Using this requires the `Vibrate` permission in the Android Manifest, which can be selected in your project's properties in the Android Manifest section.

➤ `CaptionTitle`: Title text of the notification in the expanded status bar view.

➤ `CaptionDescription`: Description text of the notification in the expanded status bar view.

➤ `TickerText`: Text that is shown in a ticker style on the status bar when your notification first appears.

➤ `ContentIntent`: A `PendingIntent` that is run after the notification is tapped.

➤ `DeleteIntent`: A `PendingIntent` that is run after the notification is cleared from the expanded status bar.

➤ `ContentView`: The view for the notification in the expanded status bar.

➤ `LedARGB`: If the device supports it, the color of the LED to show when a notification has not been seen.

➤ `LedOnMS`: How long, in milliseconds, the LED should flash on for.

➤ `LedOffMS`: How long, in milliseconds, the LED should flash off for.

➤ `Icon`: The icon for the notification.

➤ `Number`: The number of events that a notification represents. This number is overlaid on the icon if it is more than 1.

➤ **When:** A timestamp for when the notification should be displayed. By default the timestamp is immediate.

➤ **Flags:** A bitmask of various options defining some additional characteristics of a notification for how it is displayed and what happens when a user taps the notification.

➤ `AutoCancel`: The notification is automatically canceled as soon as the user taps it in the expanded status bar.

➤ `ForegroundService`: Indicates that the notification represents a foreground service. This is set automatically on the notification when you use `StartForeground()`.

➤ `Insistent`: Causes the audio for the notification to be repeated until the notification is canceled or the expanded status bar is opened.

➤ `NoClear`: If set, the notification is not canceled if the user taps the Clear all button in the expanded status bar.

➤ `OngoingEvent`: Indicates an event that is ongoing, such as a telephone call.

➤ `OnlyAlertOnce`: Causes the sound, LED, and vibration to occur only once.

➤ `ShowLights`: Indicates that LED should be used, which means you should set values for `LedOnMS` and `LedOffMS`.

To create a notification, you need to create a new instance of the `Notification` class. In the constructor you specify the `Icon` and `TickerText`. Any time you make a change to a notification, you need to call the `Notification` object's `SetLatestEventInfo` method, passing in a context, title text, description, and `PendingIntent` to be used when the notification is tapped. You should also call `SetLatestEventInfo` before the first time you display it.

To display the notification, you need to use the `NotificationManager`. You can create notifications from anywhere you have a context, such as an activity or service. Listing 11-11 shows how to display a simple notification.

Available for download on Wrox.com

LISTING 11-11: Creating a simple notification

```
var notificationManager = NotificationManager.FromContext(this);

var notification = new Notification(Android.Resource.Drawable.SymActionEmail,
  "Notification ticker...");

notification.Vibrate = new long[] { 100, 200, 300 };
notification.Number = 2;
notification.LedOnMS = 1000;
notification.LedOffMS = 2000;
notification.Flags = NotificationFlags.AutoCancel | NotificationFlags.ShowLights;

var intent = new Intent(this, typeof(MyActivity));

var pendingIntent = PendingIntent.GetActivity(this,
  0, intent, PendingIntentFlags.CancelCurrent);
```

continues

LISTING 11-11 *(continued)*

```
notification.SetLatestEventInfo(this,
  "Notification Title",
  "Notification description...",
  pendingIntent);

notificationManager.Notify(Notify(1, notification);
```

This code is contained in Chapter11g.Notifications\MainActivity.cs

You will notice that the code creates a `PendingIntent`, using an intent that was previously created, to show an activity. It's also clear that you can pass data via the intent's extras. In this way, you could easily pass some data from a service to the activity displayed by `PendingIntent`.

Finally, to show the notification, you must use the `NotificationManager` instance's `Notify` method. This requires you to pass an identifier as well as your notification object. The identifier should be unique to your application, because you will need it if you want to explicitly change or update the notification later.

Scheduling Intents with Alarms and the IntentService

Suppose you want to poll the Twitter API every so often to check for new tweets. You could create a sticky service that has a thread constantly running, sleeping between times that it should check for updates. This would work, but it is not the most efficient way to get the job done. Android provides an alarm mechanism that allows you to schedule intents to be processed at a specific interval. This works well with the `IntentService` to process on demand, and it doesn't require that your service run constantly.

You can set alarms using the AlarmManager in three ways:

➤ `Set` schedules a one-time alarm.

➤ `SetRepeating` schedules an alarm that repeats.

➤ `SetInexactRepeating` schedules an alarm that repeats, but with inexact trigger time requirements. An example is an alarm that repeats every hour but doesn't have to occur at exactly the top of each hour.

Each kind of alarm requires similar parameters:

➤ `AlarmType` determines which clock is used to schedule the start of an alarm. The following types are available:

   ➤ `ElapsedRealtime` is the milliseconds since system boot. This type of alarm waits to go off until the next time the device is awake.

   ➤ `ElapsedRealtimeWakeup` is the milliseconds since system boot. It causes the device to wake up as soon as the alarm goes off.

➤   Rtc is the milliseconds in UTC time. This type of alarm waits to go off until the next time the device is awake.

➤   RtcWakeup is the milliseconds in UTC time. It causes the device to wake up as soon as the alarm goes off.

➤ TriggerAtTime is the time to trigger the alarm, based on the AlarmType.

➤ Interval is used only for repeating alarms. You can specify an exact interval or use one of the following constants from AlarmManager:

➤   IntervalDay

➤   IntervalHalfDay

➤   IntervalFifteenMinutes

➤   IntervalHalfHour

➤   IntervalHour

➤ PendingIntent is the pending intent that is run when the alarm goes off.

 If you use one of the AlarmManager interval constants to schedule your inexact repeating alarm, the operating system phase-aligns other alarms with similar intervals to reduce the number of times the device has to wake up. If you do not use one of the interval constants with SetInexactRepeating, the alarm is set as if you had called SetRepeating.

Typically, you would use an alarm to schedule a PendingIntent for a BroadcastReceiver or, in this case, an IntentService. Listing 11-12 shows how to set an inexact repeating alarm.

LISTING 11-12: Creating an inexact repeating alarm

```
var alarmManager = context.GetSystemService(Context.AlarmService) as AlarmManager;

var serviceIntent = new Intent(context, typeof(TweetSearchService));

alarmManager.SetInexactRepeating(AlarmType.Rtc,
    0, AlarmManager.IntervalFifteenMinutes,
    PendingIntent.GetService(context,
    0, serviceIntent, PendingIntentFlags.CancelCurrent));
```

This code is contained in Chapter11b.Alarms\MainActivity.cs

The AlarmManager is used to set an inexact repeating alarm using the real-time clock and a 0 value (meaning that the alarm should be set immediately). A PendingIntent is used to tell the alarm it should run the TweetSearchService at the scheduled interval of 15 minutes.

It is important to note that scheduled alarms are not persisted on rebooting a device. To schedule your alarm at boot time, you should register a `BroadcastReceiver` that has an `IntentFilter` for the action `android.intent.action.BOOT_COMPLETED`. Your `BroadcastReceiver` could set the alarm directly when it receives this intent, or it could pass the intent to a service that then schedules the alarm.

Push Notifications Using Cloud to Device Messaging (C2DM)

Push notifications are a necessity on the iOS platform, simply because developers do not have the option of running a background service. On Android, however, background services have been a big part of the architecture of an application since the first API release. So why did Google decide to create a push notification service for Froyo (API 8, Android 2.2)? There are at least a couple of scenarios where push notifications can be used to conserve battery life and system memory:

➤ **VoIP/instant messaging:** Typically, this type of application must run a service constantly to maintain a socket connection to the remote server. Usually these applications run as a foreground service, which means that they are always in memory, and always running, to avoid losing their critical connections to the Internet server. This is costly because it uses more CPU cycles and more memory, since the service is always running.

➤ **Polling:** Twitter clients and RSS feed readers may use a polling technique in which their service wakes up at a regular interval to contact a server to see if new data needs to be processed. This means that the application needs to wake up to look for new data even if none is available to be processed.

This wouldn't be so bad if you had just one or two of these types of applications running, but when you have more applications like these, you can see how this scenario quickly fails at scaling.

Instead, Google has designed a service called Cloud to Device Messaging (C2DM) that utilizes a single C2DM service running in the background. It maintains a single network connection to Google's servers but receives notifications for multiple applications. It wakes up these other applications when a new message arrives for them to process.

The benefit of using C2DM is that you incur the cost of maintaining only a single network connection and keeping a single service running for as many applications as can receive push notifications. Google achieves this by having third-party application servers funnel notifications through its C2DM servers using a simple web service API, as shown in Figure 11-1. Even in a polling scenario, it is conceivable that a third-party application server could do the polling work at a regular interval and send push notifications when the Android device has new data to process.

Of course, using C2DM for your application means that you need to set up and maintain your own application server(s). It also means that your Android application must include logic to register with C2DM and then send the registration to your application server so that it knows which devices to send push notifications to. Much more overhead occurs on the development side when using C2DM compared to putting the logic right in the Android application. But with more and more Internet-centric applications coming out, your users will thank you for saving them battery life and system resources!

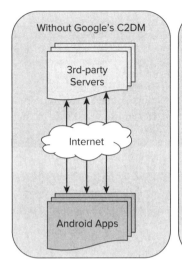
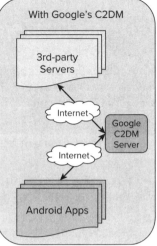

FIGURE 11-1

 It's important to remember that you must have a Google Apps–compatible device to be eligible to register for C2DM. This means that you must use a Google API when creating your emulator, or use a device with the Android Market on it to debug C2DM.

Listening for C2DM in Your Application

To receive C2DM messages, you need to register for a few permissions in your manifest file. Currently, some of these permissions can be set up via the project properties by checking off the appropriate permissions properties. However, you need to set up custom permissions by adding a manifest to your project, if you have not already done so, and then manually add these lines:

```
<permission android:name="__PackageName__.permission.C2D_MESSAGE"
  android:protectionLevel="signature" />
<uses-permission android:name="__PackageName__.permission.C2D_MESSAGE" />
```

Note that you must use your app's package name instead of __PackageName__. This listing demonstrates creating a custom permission, and declaring your application's use of it, so that only your application can receive C2DM messages intended for it.

To register for C2DM, you must start the C2DM service with an intent it can handle:

```
//Create our intent, with a pending intent to our app's broadcast
Intent registrationIntent = new Intent("com.google.android.c2dm.intent.REGISTER");
registrationIntent.PutExtra("app", PendingIntent.GetBroadcast(context, 0,
  new Intent(), 0));
```

```
registrationIntent.PutExtra("sender", senderIdEmail);

//Start intent
context.StartService(registrationIntent);
```

The intent uses a specific action defined by C2DM and adds an app extra referring to your application's PendingIntent. It also adds a sender string extra. This must be the sender ID e-mail (or role e-mail) you whitelisted with Google's C2DM servers. (You'll read more about this in the next section.)

Unregistering from C2DM is even easier. You create an intent with a specific action and the app extra parameter, as you did in registering:

```
Intent unregIntent = new Intent("com.google.android.c2dm.intent.UNREGISTER");
unregIntent.PutExtra("app", PendingIntent.GetBroadcast(context, 0, new Intent(),
    0));
context.StartService(unregIntent);
```

Next, to start receiving C2DM information, you need to create a BroadcastReceiver implementation. In Listing 11-13, the BroadcastReceiver implementation registers to receive intents for Registration and Message C2DM broadcasts. Then it passes them to an IntentService that handles the message differently, depending on the intent's action and extras.

LISTING 11-13: Receiving C2DM events

```
using System;
using Android.App;
using Android.Content;
using Android.OS;
using Android.Runtime;

namespace Chapter11.C2DM
{
    [BroadcastReceiver(Permission = "com.google.android.c2dm.permission.SEND")]
    [IntentFilter(new string[] { "com.google.android.c2dm.intent.RECEIVE" },
        Categories = new string[] { "chapter11i.c2dm" })]
    [IntentFilter(new string[] { "com.google.android.c2dm.intent.REGISTRATION" },
        Categories = new string[] { "chapter11i.c2dm" })]
    public class C2DMBroadcastReceiver : BroadcastReceiver
    {
        public override void OnReceive(Context context, Intent intent)
        {
            var svcIntent = new Intent(context, typeof(C2DMService));

            svcIntent.PutExtras(intent.Extras);
            svcIntent.PutExtra("c2dm_action", intent.Action);

            context.StartService(svcIntent);
        }
    }

    [Service]
```

```csharp
public class C2DMService : IntentService
{
    Handler handler;

    public override void OnCreate()
    {
        base.OnCreate();
        handler = new Handler();
    }

    protected override void OnHandleIntent(Intent intent)
    {
        var action = intent.GetStringExtra("c2dm_action");

        if (action == "com.google.android.c2dm.intent.REGISTRATION")
        {
            var unregistered = intent.GetStringExtra("unregistered");
            var error = intent.GetStringExtra("error");

            if (!string.IsNullOrEmpty(error))
                Error(intent.Extras);
            else if (string.IsNullOrEmpty(unregistered))
                Registered(intent.GetStringExtra("registration_id"));
            else
                Unregistered();

        }
        else if (action == "com.google.android.c2dm.intent.RECEIVE")
        {
            Message(intent.Extras);
        }
    }

    void Registered(string registrationId)
    {
        //Send the registration id to your server...
        handler.Post(() =>
        {
            Toast.MakeText(this, "C2DM - Registered - " + registrationId,
                ToastLength.Short).Show();
        });
    }

    void Unregistered()
    {
        //Tell your server to stop sending messages to this device
        handler.Post(() =>
        {
            Toast.MakeText(this, "C2DM - Unregistered",
                ToastLength.Short).Show();
        });
    }

    void Message(Bundle extras)
    {
```

continues

LISTING 11-13 *(continued)*

```
                //Create a Notification to alert the user
                handler.Post(() =>
                {
                    Toast.MakeText(this, "C2DM - Msg Received",
                        ToastLength.Short).Show();
                });
        }

        void Error(Bundle extras)
        {
            //Determine the error, and handle it
            handler.Post(() =>
            {
                Toast.MakeText(this, "C2DM - Error",
                    ToastLength.Short).Show();
            });
        }
    }
}
```

This code is contained in Chapter11i.C2DM\C2DMBroadcastReceiver.cs

Of course, this listing is incomplete, because it doesn't do anything to handle the incoming intents. When you receive a registration ID, you should notify your server that is responsible for sending C2DM messages about this update. You may want to store the registration ID in a preference or file for future reference at this point. You may also want to send the device ID along with the registration ID to your server. You should be prepared to do this whenever you receive this intent, because Google may choose to create a new registration ID occasionally, without explicitly asking for it!

Similarly, when you find out that unregistration has happened, you should tell your server to stop sending C2DM messages using that registration ID.

Several errors can happen during registration. You can retrieve the `"error"` string extra to get a description of the error. Here are the possible errors:

➤ SERVICE_NOT_AVAILABLE: The registration service cannot be reached, so you need to try again later.

➤ ACCOUNT_MISSING: No Google accounts are set up on the device. At least one Google account is required to be set up on the device. You should tell your user to set one up at this point.

➤ AUTHENTICATION_FAILED: The user should fix his or her Google account information, because the device failed to authenticate the account.

➤ TOO_MANY_REGISTRATIONS: The device has too many applications registered with C2DM. This should be rare, but you might consider asking the user to remove some applications with C2DM enabled in this case.

➤ `INVALID_SENDER`: The sender ID e-mail you specified in your registration request is invalid or has not been whitelisted with Google yet.

➤ `PHONE_REGISTRATION_ERROR`: The device does not support C2DM, such as a device without Android 2.2 or later.

Sending a C2DM Message from Your Server

Now that your application is set up to receive messages from the Google C2DM service, you need to set up a process on a server that sends messages. You need several critical pieces of information to be able to send C2DM messages.

First, go to Google's C2DM Registration site at `http://code.google.com/android/c2dm/signup.html` to get your application whitelisted for sending C2DM messages using Google's servers. This form has two critical pieces of information you should pay close attention to:

➤ **The name of your Android app or the Package Name** needs to be identical to the Package Name property in your Android Manifest — the same one you used in your `BroadcastReceiver`'s `IntentFilter` categories.

➤ **The role account e-mail** is a Google account e-mail address (such as a Gmail account) that you will use to send messages from the server. It is recommended that you create a new account for this.

 The role account e-mail is also called the sender ID. It is important not to use the same e-mail as the "receiver" e-mail account you test with on your device, or messages will not be received. The most foolproof method is to create an account specifically for the server to use.

After you have registered with Google, you are ready to start sending C2DM messages to the application you created earlier.

On your server, you can use any programming platform you want to send messages, because the mechanism to deliver these messages to Google's servers is simple HTTP protocol.

Sending a C2DM message to Google's servers requires a few steps:

1. You need to construct an HTTP post to the Client Login URL at `https://www.google.com/accounts/ClientLogin`. The HTTP response body will include a string containing the `AuthID` if you sent the proper data in your request. This request should contain the following post request variables:

➤ `Email` is the sender ID e-mail you whitelisted with Google.

➤ `Passwd` is the Google account password to log in to the sender ID e-mail account.

➤ `accountType` should be the value `GOOGLE_OR_HOSTED`.

> ➤ `service` should be the value `ac2dm`.

> ➤ `source` should be the application ID or Package Name you whitelisted with Google.

2. Using your `AuthID`, you need to construct another HTTP post for each C2DM message you want to send. This request should contain several pieces of information:

    HTTP request headers:

> ➤ `ContentType` is `application/x-www-form-urlencoded`.

> ➤ `UserAgent` is something to uniquely identify your server application to Google.

> ➤ `Authorization: GoogleLogin auth=<authID>` where `<authid>` is the `AuthID` you received in the response from the previous HTTP request.

    HTTP post request variables:

> ➤ `registration_id` is the registration ID for the device you want to send a message to.

> ➤ `collapse_key` is a value you can use to collapse messages that have the same key so that only the newest one is displayed. A value is required.

> ➤ `delay_while_idle`, if `true`, indicates that C2DM should deliver the message only when the device is not idle.

> ➤ `data.<any_name>`, where `<any_name>` specifies the key in a key/value pair that you intend to be passed as an extra in the intent received by your C2DM Android application. This is a way to pass small pieces of data to your application from the server.

You can find more information on the C2DM server protocol from Google's official C2DM documentation at `http://code.google.com/android/c2dm/index.html#server`.

 An open source project called C2DM-Sharp (`https://github.com/Redth/C2DM-Sharp`) contains libraries for both sending C2DM messages from a server and receiving messages in your Mono for Android app.

Listing 11-14 contains a complete code sample of how to send a C2DM message through Google's servers using C# code. You can run this sample from a server or your local machine; it does not need to be run on an Android device. This is how you would send notifications from your web service. If you use this sample, be sure to change the first four variables to reflect your own data. In particular, make sure your `registrationId` is a valid value returned from your Android application's successful registration with the C2DM servers.

LISTING 11-14: Sending a C2DM message

Available for download on Wrox.com

```
var googleSender = "sender@gmail.com";
var googlePassword = "password";
var registrationId = "registrationid";
```

```
var message = "Hello from C2DM!";

var authUrl = @"https://www.google.com/accounts/ClientLogin";
var c2dmUrl = @"https://android.apis.google.com/c2dm/send";

try
{
    // First, let's get the auth code - requires Google credentials
    var sb = new StringBuilder();
    var kvp = new NameValueCollection();
    kvp.Add("accountType", "GOOGLE");
    kvp.Add("Email", googleSender);
    kvp.Add("Passwd", googlePassword);
    kvp.Add("service", "ac2dm");
    kvp.Add("source", "long2know.chapter11.c2dm");

    foreach (string key in kvp.Keys)
        sb.Append(string.Format("{0}={1}&", key, kvp[key]));

    var encoding = new ASCIIEncoding();
    byte[] data = encoding.GetBytes(sb.ToString());

    var myRequest = (HttpWebRequest)WebRequest.Create(authUrl);
    myRequest.Method = "POST";
    myRequest.ContentType = "application/x-www-form-urlencoded";
    myRequest.ContentLength = data.Length;
    Stream newStream = myRequest.GetRequestStream();
    newStream.Write(data, 0, data.Length);
    newStream.Close();

    var sr = new StreamReader(myRequest.GetResponse().GetResponseStream());
    string readResponse = sr.ReadToEnd();

    // Parse Auth
    Regex regAuth = new Regex(@"Auth=(.+)", RegexOptions.IgnoreCase);

    Match matchAuth = regAuth.Match(readResponse);

    string auth = string.Empty;

    if (matchAuth.Success)
        auth = matchAuth.Groups[0].Value;
    else
    {
        throw new WebException("Could not authenticate.",
            new Exception("Failed to retrieve auth, sid, or lsid"));
    }

    // Ignore SSL exceptions at this point
    ServicePointManager.ServerCertificateValidationCallback +=
        new RemoteCertificateValidationCallback((sender, cert, chain, policyErr) =>
        {
            return true;
        });
```

continues

LISTING 11-14 *(continued)*

```
    // Finally, let's send the message
    sb = new StringBuilder();
    kvp = new NameValueCollection();
    kvp.Add("registration_id", HttpUtility.UrlEncode(registrationId));
    kvp.Add("delay_while_idle", "false");
    kvp.Add("collapse_key", "chapter11c2dm");
    kvp.Add("data.message", HttpUtility.UrlEncode(message));

    foreach (string key in kvp.Keys)
    {
        sb.Append(string.Format("{0}={1}&", key, kvp[key]));
    }

    data = encoding.GetBytes(sb.ToString());

    myRequest = (HttpWebRequest)WebRequest.Create(c2dmUrl);
    myRequest.Headers.Add(HttpRequestHeader.Authorization,
        string.Format("GoogleLogin {0}", auth));
    myRequest.Method = "POST";
    myRequest.ContentType = "application/x-www-form-urlencoded";
    myRequest.ContentLength = data.Length;
    newStream = myRequest.GetRequestStream();
    newStream.Write(data, 0, data.Length);
    newStream.Close();

    sr = new StreamReader(myRequest.GetResponse().GetResponseStream());
    readResponse = sr.ReadToEnd();

    string id = string.Empty;
    Regex regId = new Regex(@"id=(.+)", RegexOptions.IgnoreCase);
    Match matchId = regId.Match(readResponse);

    if (matchId.Success)
    {
        id = matchAuth.Groups[0].Value;

        Console.WriteLine(string.Format("Received response: {0}", id));
    }
    else
    {
        Console.WriteLine(string.Format("Invalid response received: {0}",
            readResponse));
    }
}
catch (WebException e)
{
    Console.WriteLine(string.Format("Web Exception: {0}", e.InnerException));
}
```

This code is contained in Chapter11j.C2DM.Sending\Program.cs

SUMMARY

In this chapter, you learned about the life cycle of a service and why services are crucial to the architecture of your applications. You learned how to create a simple service and saw that services are not inherently multithreaded, but simply classes. You worked with `System.Threading` and `System.Threading.Tasks` to make your services multithreaded. Learning how to implement `IntentService` enabled you to create multithreaded services with relative ease, handling intents received from `BroadcastReceivers`.

You covered creating notifications to interact with users, and you implemented communication between services and the UI via several methods. You also covered creating alarms that repeated with high efficiency to send intents at scheduled intervals to your `BroadcastReceivers` and services.

Finally, you were introduced to C2DM. You saw why it is important and how to use it in your applications. You should now feel confident in using services in your own applications. You have found out just how simple they are to use and how useful they are in providing a great experience to your applications' users.

12

Canvas and Drawables: Building Custom Android Graphics

WHAT'S IN THIS CHAPTER?

➤ Using the `Canvas` object

➤ Understanding the drawing process and players

➤ Creating, animating, and transforming custom graphics

➤ Optimizing performance via `SurfaceView`

➤ Understanding drawables

➤ Using drawables as XML resources

➤ Making basic shapes and colors

➤ Creating compound drawables

➤ Responding to events

This chapter dives deeply into the process of creating custom graphics using Mono for Android. In particular, we will delve into not only the different tools available to create custom graphics but also where and why to apply them.

At this point, you have covered many of the basic concepts regarding developing for Mono for Android. From using basic resources to understanding the application life cycle to using various views, you have all the pieces in place to create fully functional applications. With this understanding, you can use an amalgamation of these concepts to approach the finer details of creating custom graphics on the Android platform.

The focus of this chapter is to build on your foundational understanding of the Android platform to accomplish more advanced effects such as drawing graphics on the fly, creating animations, and making a more interactive interface. In particular, this chapter walks through the design and implementation of the drawable packages that are provided in Android. Finally, we will touch on a few different common yet advanced tasks that developers often face when working with animated graphics.

This chapter will help you achieve a clear understanding of the Android graphics model. In addition, this chapter covers the many ways to accomplish a single task and also why one of those approaches may be superior to the rest in terms of performance, maintainability, and overall flexibility of the toolset.

WORKING WITH GRAPHICS IN MONO FOR ANDROID

You have several options when working with graphics in Mono for Android. As with any approach, each option has its strengths and weaknesses and varies in complexity and flexibility:

➤ The first option is one that you should already be familiar with — working with view objects and application resources. Views such as the `ImageView` and `Gallery` allow a developer to quickly utilize graphic resources in an application at the expense of flexibility. Typically, this approach covers the majority of application use cases and enables you to go far into the process of developing an interactive and appealing application.

➤ The next option, the canvas approach, involves digging a bit deeper into the view objects and beginning to customize and extend the underlying logic of a view's `OnDraw()` method. In particular, this option requires a developer to have a basic understanding of utilizing the canvas, bitmaps, and different graphic primitives. In a way, you may think of this as the "low-level" approach, because you are responsible for precisely defining each aspect of your graphic as it gets passed to the UI. Granted, tools are available to assist you in this process, but it is up to the developer to make wise decisions about performance when creating or destroying graphic resources. Needless to say, performance is a large consideration when using this approach to create graphics. An experienced developer can create some stunning designs, but a less cautious developer can create huge performance issues, ruining the graphic appeal.

➤ The last approach to utilizing graphics is to use Android's built-in custom 2D graphics library via drawables. The purpose of this library is to increase the flexibility of the graphics controls while removing some of the complexity of having to directly manage the logic of writing the graphic to the screen.

When working with the canvas approach or using system drawables, you need to understand the strengths and weaknesses of each approach. Although they do have quite a bit of overlap in terms of functionality, their applications can be quite different from one another. For instance, the canvas approach is often the desired approach for video game designers or for applications that have very high graphics demands. By being able to control the creation, lifetime, and destruction of various resources, developers can push the Android device to its limits.

On the other hand, drawables are prevalent throughout the entire Mono for Android framework. Not only do they expose sets of methods for working with graphics themselves, but they also are accepted by many framework-level methods and processes. This makes drawables an efficient and convenient way to communicate graphic instructions throughout an application.

> *Although graphics are a core aspect of the Android library, the documentation on this topic is rather sparse. Several modifications and additions have been made to the graphics libraries between versions, which only exacerbates the issue.*
>
> *Of course, the key to dealing with this is having a good measure of patience, as well as having some great resources (such as this book!) at your disposal. In addition, graphics objects in Android work much like those found in HTML5, such as the HTML5 canvas. You can use the documentation in this case as well to help gain perspective on how these objects may work in Android, because Android follows many of the same naming conventions and general functionality.*

USING THE CANVAS OBJECT

One of the main options for working with graphics in Mono for Android is to work directly with the graphic output itself rather than relying on abstractions. This approach gives you a great deal of flexibility in terms of performance and usability. In addition, this approach is not overly complicated, assuming that you have a basic understanding of how graphics are rendered on the Android platform. With this understanding, and by following a few basic rules, developers can create amazing applications and games using the Canvas object.

Using the Canvas object to draw is dependent on the interactions of several key items. These combine to make a direct channel in which a developer can pipe instructions from the graphics classes directly to the Android device. These key items include the following:

- ➤ **Graphics primitives** are a basic type of object that can be used as a medium to express different types of graphical instructions. Whether they take the form of basic images such as PNG or JPG or point-by-point mappings via paths, these primitives give you great flexibility in defining shapes, colors, and other graphical features in a wide variety of methods.

- ➤ **The view object** acts as the medium by which a canvas can connect to the overall application life cycle. As with almost everything else in Android, the View object serves as a container for various events that can be triggered by the requesting application. When customizing a Canvas object, a view's OnDraw() method is used as the override for the view's drawing command.

- ➤ **The Canvas object** represents the interface through which you can pass instructions on how to draw the graphic. This object contains a variety of tools and properties to act as the link between graphic primitives and the underlying Bitmap object.

- ➤ **The Paint object** represents an abstracted definition of stylistic effects that can be applied across most graphic primitives. This effect can include color, border, and transparency.

- ➤ **The Bitmap object** is the underlying image on which the canvas draws. After the canvas has completed its work, the Bitmap object is presented to the UI in the appropriate scale for the user to experience.

It's important to understand the relationship between each of these items, because it is the foundation for almost all graphics work in Mono for Android. Figure 12-1 depicts this relationship.

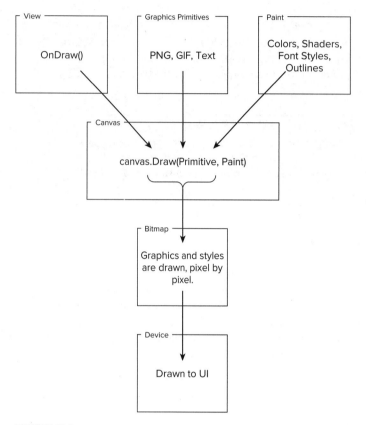

FIGURE 12-1

Graphics Primitives

Graphics primitives are a generic way to describe different formats or instructions for how to draw something. This is a rather loosely defined group of tools that are unified in their purpose, which is to draw. Within the framework are several different kinds of base primitives.

Table 12-1 lists many of the basic primitives. Although some of the uses are obvious, it is a good idea to have a working knowledge of each available option. You may find some overlap in functionality between items, such as a path and a shape. You could represent almost any shape via the `Path` object. But this would be much more work, and you would lose the advantage of all the additional transformation methods that a shape object would have at its disposal.

TABLE 12-1: Common Graphics Primitives

GENERAL NAME	DESCRIPTION
Shape objects	Shape objects include basic geometric shapes such as ovals, circles, and rectangles. These shapes can be defined using the `Canvas` object, but they should not be confused with the objects in the `Android.Graphics.Shapes` namespace, which is used with drawables.
Colors	Colors are represented in many ways throughout Mono for Android. In this instance, a color primitive usually refers to the color's integer value via alpha, red, green, blue (ARGB) values.
Images	When working with the `Canvas` object directly, image formats are ultimately expressed via the versatile bitmap image class. Using a `BitmapFactory` object, resources such as PNG and JPEG can be converted into the appropriate bitmap format.
Paths, points, arcs, and lines	Paths, points, arcs, and lines are objects that are defined by underlying coordinates. Using the provided points, the framework renders full shapes, affording you great flexibility in creating custom, scalable art.
Text	Although text may not seem to be a graphic primitive, text-as-art is one of the most-used drawing tasks. By using text as a graphic primitive, a developer can customize logos and text art with minimal effort, allowing for some unique interactions with different gradients or skew filters to create a unique text presentation.

Graphic primitives offer the greatest opportunity to make clean, high-performance code. The process of inflating or spinning up a graphic primitive is quite expensive and should always be handled with care. For example, keeping a graphic description in memory is much cheaper than re-creating it upon every request.

The Canvas Object

The canvas serves as the interface by which a developer can communicate graphic intentions to the underlying `Bitmap` object. Although this may sound like it could be a complex process, it is greatly simplified by the fact that the canvas exposes many different draw functions, each of which supports a different graphic primitive.

It is not by chance that a `Canvas` object is named so. The reason for this is that it helps to think of this object as an artist's canvas. With each `drawX()` call, the platform essentially creates another layer of paint on the canvas that will eventually be the application's background. The `draw` method can be called several times and with different primitives. This offers a great deal of flexibility, because you aren't restricted to a single primitive to express a graphic. Another good analogy for how the canvas works is to think of its being able to support multiple layers, as with different drawing applications such as GIMP, Paint.NET, and Photoshop.

The `Canvas` object also has two important functions: `Save()` and `Restore()`. The purpose of these functions is to create snapshots of the current canvas state to be accessed later. Essentially, a `Canvas` object can be saved with a set of drawings completed on it, and then altered as much as possible, and then fully reinstated to the previous saved state via the `Restore()` method. Although this may sound like a minor achievement, it is a great way to reduce code clutter and increase readability when working with repetitive patterns or colors. Finally, these methods can be used to increase application performance when used in the right context.

Finally, the `Canvas` object exposes some functionality to allow a developer to translate, skew, or adjust the graphic's underlying matrix. By using a canvas's `translate()` and `skew()` methods, you can reform and reshape a canvas drawing without incurring the overhead cost of creating a new `Canvas` object or graphic primitive. This too will be covered in more depth shortly.

When working with different advanced tactics with the `Canvas` *object, you need to be familiar with the* `Matrix` *object and how it relates to the canvas. The* `Matrix` *object represents a rectangular array or table of numbers (in the case of Mono for Android, it's a 3-by-3 matrix dimension). Matrices can be used for various tasks. It uses them to achieve exact transformations from one object to another by preserving the relative distance and colinearity between points on that shape. This is known as* affine transformation.

Using this technique, the framework can quickly apply many transformations to a single graphic, whether that transformation is to rotate, scale, clip, reflect, or skew. You can read more about matrices and affine transformations at:

➤ Wikipedia — transformation matrix:
  `http://en.wikipedia.org/wiki/Transformation_matrix`

➤ Wikipedia — affine transformation:
  `http://en.wikipedia.org/wiki/Affine_transformation`

Even if you do not have occasion to directly use a matrix with the `Canvas` *object, it is good to have a working understanding of what happens when the* `canvas .Translate()` *or other transformation methods are called.*

The Paint Object

The `Paint` object represents stylistic effects that can be applied to a graphic primitive. In a sense, the term *paint* is a great simplification of everything that the `Paint` class can do. At its most basic, the `Paint` class can be used to express a color. Building on that, paints can be used to express concepts such as shaders, transparency, strokes, antialiasing, masks, color filters, and many other effects.

When you use the `Paint` object in conjunction with the `Canvas` object, the `Paint` object is often treated as a resource separate from the `Shape` object it will apply to. The reason is that it allows for a significant separation of concerns. Also, a single `Paint` object can be used to help define an infinite number of different graphic primitives, whether they are text, images, or paths. In terms of HTML design, you could think of the canvas as the HTML markup and the `Paint` object as the CSS layout.

In addition to the `Paint` object's generic functionality, it has several handle methods pertaining to working with text-based primitives. The `Paint` object greatly expands the capabilities of producing text-as-art by providing quite a few tools to assist in the drawing, measuring, and styling of text.

When you are working with the `Paint` object, one of the most important choices is whether to use *antialiasing*. This is the process of "tricking" the eye into thinking that text or the edges of an image are smooth rather than being composed of hard, square edges. To achieve this, a system employs a number of techniques, such as sampling and blending or using slight color distortion. Although this greatly improves the graphic's overall quality (and readability in the case of text), it comes at the cost of performance. You should use antialiasing with care with many objects, although text-based graphics generally are a great target. Listing 12-1 is a basic example of how to use the `Paint` object to draw styles for a text blurb.

LISTING 12-1: Using the Paint object

```
Paint p = new Paint()
{
    AntiAlias = true,
    Color = Color.CornflowerBlue,
    TextSize = 20,
    UnderlineText = true
};

canvas.DrawText("Mono for Android is awesome!", 10, 10, p);
```

The Bitmap Object

If a canvas is the medium by which graphics are communicated, the `Bitmap` object is the final work of art that is born from that communication. When the drawing methods are complete, it is the `Bitmap` object that is ultimately presented to the user interface and, therefore, the end user. The `Bitmap` object is always a requirement when working with a canvas.

The difference between a bitmap graphic primitive and the `Bitmap` object that the `Canvas` object draws on can be confusing. In truth, there is no difference. The `Bitmap` object contains the tools necessary to write to each pixel within the final rendered image. As such, it is essentially the lowest common denominator between all graphics types.

For the most part, you probably won't need to work directly with a `Bitmap` object. However, if the need does arise, the tools are certainly there to manually tweak and configure the underlying bitmap for a canvas. This is achieved by creating a new `Bitmap` object, adjusting it according to the specifications, and then passing it as a primitive to the appropriate `Canvas` object. In addition, you can simply create a new `Canvas` object and pass the bitmap instance to it instead.

The bitmap lets you work directly with some pretty advanced topics, such as different compression techniques (.png/.jpg), directly requesting each byte or pixel in the bitmap, differing scaling scenarios, and a few other tools. As you might imagine, these tools are powerful, but their usage scenarios are beyond the scope of this chapter.

Bringing It All Together

Now that you understand the basic players, we can see them in action. Of course, the best way to understand the `Canvas` object and its associated pieces is to work with it. The following section does just that by presenting a use-case scenario and walking through the entire process of conceptualizing, creating, and completing a custom graphic.

A Path Primer

Before we walk through creating custom graphics, you should become familiar with the `Path` object. The following examples use the `Path` object as their primary graphic primitive. The reason for this is not only to expose one of the more complex graphic primitives but also to emulate the process of creating a graphic primitive at the lowest level. If you are already familiar with `Path`, feel free to skip to the next section.

Paths are simple geometric instructions that are built by defining a series of different points and then specifying either lines or curves to draw from one point to another. Each defined point represents a place on the graphic where the flow of the current line or curve is altered.

After the points have been selected, simple paths can be defined using `Path.LineTo(pointX, pointY)` to define in which direction and how far to draw the line. In Listing 12-2, the `Path` object is used to construct a simple square.

LISTING 12-2: Creating a basic shape using the Path object

Available for
download on
Wrox.com

```
public class Square:View
{
    public Square(Context context) : base(context) { }

    protected override void OnDraw(Canvas canvas)
    {
        Path SquarePath = new Path();

        SquarePath.LineTo(50, 0);
        SquarePath.LineTo(50, 50);
        SquarePath.LineTo(0, 50);

        SquarePath.Close();
```

```
        canvas.DrawPath(SquarePath, new Paint(){ Color = Color.CornflowerBlue});
    }
}
```

Graphics_Canvas\Graphics_Canvas\Square.cs

The first thing to note in this code is a class that inherits from the `View` class. Within the view, the `OnDraw()` method is overridden to take command of the canvas drawing method. Much of the time, this is the typical technique for drawing directly on the canvas. If this view were added to an application and loaded, you would see a small, simple square.

Looking at the `Path` object, several commands indicate movement, such as `LineTo()`, `MoveTo()`, `QuadTo()`, `CubicTo()`, and `ArcTo()`. Each of these actions represents a movement from the current point to the one specified. Unless it is changed, the `Path` object assumes that the drawing's initial point is at the canvas's origin, `Point(0,0)`.

The `Path.Close()` function is used to close the current contour. If the `Close()` method is not called on the origin point, a line is drawn between the closing point and the origin.

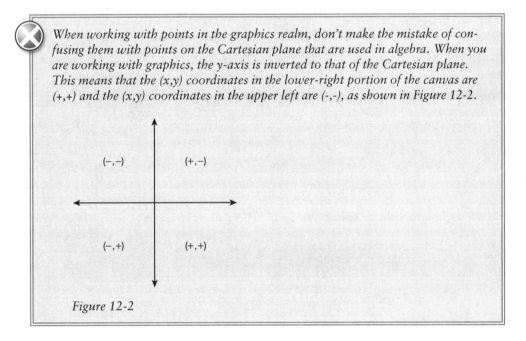

When working with points in the graphics realm, don't make the mistake of confusing them with points on the Cartesian plane that are used in algebra. When you are working with graphics, the y-axis is inverted to that of the Cartesian plane. This means that the (x,y) coordinates in the lower-right portion of the canvas are (+,+) and the (x,y) coordinates in the upper left are (-,-), as shown in Figure 12-2.

Figure 12-2

Case 1: Creating a Custom Graphic

Imagine that you were recently hired to work on the development team for the W3C (World Wide Web Consortium). Recently, many people have expressed interest in the upcoming HTML5 specification. In fact, your peers at the W3C have created a visually appealing graphic to represent HTML5 as a way to help spread the word about this new territory, as shown in Figure 12-3. As a way to assist in their efforts, you have been given the task of writing an app that uses the new HTML5 logo.

HTML5 LOGO BY THE
WORLD WIDE WEB CONSORTIUM:
www.w3.org

FIGURE 12-3

In a new Mono for Android project, add a new class called HTML5Logo. As with the previous square example, the HTML5Logo class needs to inherit from the View object to get access to the Canvas object to draw on. To complete the inheritance, add an appropriate constructor and override the OnDraw() method. When complete, the class should look like Listing 12-3.

LISTING 12-3: Creating a custom view for the HTML5 logo

```
public class HTML5Logo : View
{

    protected Context _context;

    public int Scale { get; set; }

    public HTML5Logo(Context context, int Scale): base(context)
    {
        this._context = context;
        this.Scale = Scale;
    }

    protected override void OnDraw(Canvas canvas)
    {
    }
}
```

Graphics_Canvas\Graphics_Canvas\HTML5Logo.cs

In addition to the default structure, properties were added for Scale and Context. Although you should be familiar with the process of saving the context state of an overridden view Context property, the Scale property acts as a multiplier for the overall dimensions of HTML5Logo to allow for a difference in scale of the object during initialization. Now it is time to begin creating the custom graphic.

Looking at the logo, consider the different types of graphic primitives you could leverage to express the graphic intention. At first glance, the logo can be broken into three separate sections: the background shield, the shield reflection, and the graphic 5 that overlies them both. Due to the simple, angular nature of this logo, the Path primitive would be an efficient tool to express the different parts of this graphic.

> *You might wonder why we don't just use an image rather than going to the trouble of making a* Path *object. In fact, the image approach would be the better choice in most cases. However, since we are focusing on creating custom graphics, this section uses the path approach to re-create this graphic from scratch.*

To keep things as simple as possible, the HTML5Logo will be divided into three distinct pieces that will be defined by three distinct Path objects. Although the entire graphic could be handled differently, this approach keeps everything clean and readable.

Begin by defining the HTML5Logo shield background. Create a method called DrawHTML5Background(), and accept a canvas as a parameter. This method encapsulates the process of drawing the shield background directly on the canvas. Listing 12-4 shows how this method should appear.

LISTING 12-4: Drawing the HTML5 background path

```
private void DrawHTML5Background(Canvas canvas)
{
    Path HTML5Background = new Path();

    HTML5Background.LineTo(Scale, 0);
    HTML5Background.LineTo((int)(Scale * .914), (int)(Scale * 1.015));
    HTML5Background.LineTo((int)(Scale / 2), (int)(Scale * 1.115));
    HTML5Background.LineTo((int)(Scale * .087), (int)(Scale * 1.015));
    HTML5Background.Close();

    var HTML5Paint = new Paint() { AntiAlias = true,
        StrokeWidth = 3, Color = new Color(228, 76, 39) };

    canvas.DrawPath(HTML5Background, HTML5Paint);
}
```

Graphics_Canvas\Graphics_Canvas\HTML5Logo.cs

In this method, a new Path object is created, and four points are added. In addition to the origin of (0,0), each of these points represents one of the corners of the background shield of the HTML5 logo. Notice that every point is based on a ratio of the point's coordinate according to the Scale value. The reason for this is that it allows the entire background to be quickly sized during initialization of the object. Looking at the points, you might wonder where the point values came from to define the shield. In this case, they were measured using a web measuring tool and roughly rounded to represent the right location.

Finally, the `Paint` object is created using the darker orange color, and the `Path` is added to the `Canvas` object. Since this image is more important than the others, antialiasing has been turned on.

The next piece to tackle is to add the appropriate calls to create the gleam overlay on the shield. Create a method called `DrawHTML5InnerBackground`, again accepting the `Canvas` object as the parameter. Listing 12-5 displays the appropriate code for this method.

LISTING 12-5: Drawing the HTML5 inner background path

```
private void DrawHTML5InnerBackground(Canvas canvas)
{
    Path HTML5InnerBackground = new Path();

    HTML5InnerBackground.MoveTo(Scale / 2, (int)(Scale * .078));

    HTML5InnerBackground.LineTo((int)(Scale * .915), (int)(Scale * .078));
    HTML5InnerBackground.LineTo((int)(Scale * .829), (int)(Scale * .948));
    HTML5InnerBackground.LineTo((int)(Scale / 2), (int)(Scale * 1.032));

    var HTML5Paint = new Paint() { AntiAlias = true,
        StrokeWidth = 3, Color = new Color(240, 101, 42) };

    canvas.DrawPath(HTML5InnerBackground, HTML5Paint);
}
```

Graphics_Canvas\Graphics_Canvas\HTML5Logo.cs

This method behaves much like the previous draw method. Notice that rather than starting at the origin, the `MoveTo()` function is used to start the `Path` at the appropriate point. Again, the `Scale` property is used to calculate all these points to allow for dynamic sizing.

The final portion of the custom graphic is the number 5 that will overlay the entire graphic. At first glance, this may seem to be a simple matter of overlaying a text primitive of the right scale onto the graphic. However, this is not quite so simple — for two main reasons. First, trying to find the corresponding font to match the logo precisely would be difficult. Second, the fact that the logo has a two-tone color means that paint objects will need to be applied to different sections of the text object. Again, we will turn to the `Path` object to solve this problem. Create a method called `DrawHTML5Text()`, accepting a canvas as a parameter. In this method, add the code shown in Listing 12-6 to the class.

LISTING 12-6: Drawing the HTML5 text path objects

```
private void DrawHTML5Text(Canvas canvas)
{
    //Set up our Paints, since these objects will be shared between quadrants.
    Paint White = new Paint() { AntiAlias = true, StrokeWidth = 3,
        Color = Color.White };
```

```
Paint OffWhite = new Paint { AntiAlias = true, StrokeWidth = 3,
    Color = new Color(235, 235, 235) };

//Quadrant #1
var Path_Q1 = new Path();
Path_Q1.MoveTo(Scale / 2, (int)(Scale * .212));
Path_Q1.LineTo((int)(Scale * .809), (int)(Scale * .212));
Path_Q1.LineTo((int)(Scale * .797), (int)(Scale * .326));
Path_Q1.LineTo((int)(Scale / 2), (int)(Scale * .326));

canvas.DrawPath(Path_Q1, White);

//Quadrant #2
var Path_Q2 = new Path();

Path_Q2.MoveTo((int)(Scale * .203), (int)(Scale * .212));
Path_Q2.LineTo((int)(Scale / 2), (int)(Scale * .212));
Path_Q2.LineTo((int)(Scale / 2), (int)(Scale * .326));
Path_Q2.LineTo((int)(Scale * .328), (int)(Scale * .326));
Path_Q2.LineTo((int)(Scale * .345), (int)(Scale * .472));
Path_Q2.LineTo((int)(Scale / 2), (int)(Scale * .472));
Path_Q2.LineTo((int)(Scale / 2), (int)(Scale * .591));
Path_Q2.LineTo((int)(Scale * .235), (int)(Scale * .591));

canvas.DrawPath(Path_Q2, OffWhite);

//Quadrant #3
var Path_Q3 = new Path();

Path_Q3.MoveTo((int)(Scale / 2), (int)(Scale * .472));
Path_Q3.LineTo((int)(Scale * .786), (int)(Scale * .472));
Path_Q3.LineTo((int)(Scale * .751), (int)(Scale * .852));
Path_Q3.LineTo((int)(Scale / 2), (int)(Scale * .899));
Path_Q3.LineTo((int)(Scale / 2), (int)(Scale * .783));
Path_Q3.LineTo((int)(Scale * .641), (int)(Scale * .754));
Path_Q3.LineTo((int)(Scale * .658), (int)(Scale * .591));
Path_Q3.LineTo((int)(Scale / 2), (int)(Scale * .591));

canvas.DrawPath(Path_Q3, White);

//Quadrant #4
var Path_Q4 = new Path();

Path_Q4.MoveTo((int)(Scale * .249), (int)(Scale * .646));
Path_Q4.LineTo((int)(Scale * .365), (int)(Scale * .646));
Path_Q4.LineTo((int)(Scale * .371), (int)(Scale * .754));
Path_Q4.LineTo((int)(Scale / 2), (int)(Scale * .783));
Path_Q4.LineTo((int)(Scale / 2), (int)(Scale * .899));
Path_Q4.LineTo((int)(Scale * .27), (int)(Scale * .852));

canvas.DrawPath(Path_Q4, OffWhite);
}
```

Graphics_Canvas\Graphics_Canvas\HTML5Logo.cs

Looking at this listing, it is pretty amazing how a simple number can take the most time to express via Path. However, do not feel too daunted, because it is really four simple Paths used to represent a whole. Since the number in the logo is two-toned, two different Paint objects are needed to express its colors. Initially in this method, the Paint objects are initialized and named White and Offwhite so that they can be reused in each section. Then the number graphic is separated into four quadrants based on color and location in the graphic. For each quadrant, a Path object is created. As each path is created, it is drawn on the Canvas object.

With those methods in place, modify the OnDraw() method so that it calls all three of these methods in the correct order. Listing 12-7 gives an example.

LISTING 12-7: Overriding the OnDraw() method for the HTML5 logo view

```
protected override void OnDraw(Canvas canvas)
{
        DrawHTML5Background(canvas);
        DrawHTML5InnerBackground(canvas);
        DrawHTML5Text(canvas);
}
```

Graphics_Canvas\Graphics_Canvas\HTML5Logo.cs

The HTML5Logo view is now complete. Within the startup activity of this project, create a new instance of HTML5Logo, and set it as your content view. The resulting OnCreate() method should resemble Listing 12-8.

LISTING 12-8: Overriding the OnCreate() method in the main activity

```
protected override void OnCreate(Bundle bundle)
{
        base.OnCreate(bundle);

        var targetView = new HTML5Logo(this, 100);
        SetContentView(targetView);
}
```

Graphics_Canvas\Graphics_Canvas\GraphicsCanvasDemo.cs

With this in place, run the project. Figure 12-4 displays the expected end result.

Case 2: Responding to Events

After you complete the new HTML5Logo view, your peers at the W3C have a new request. Although it is a nice-looking graphic sitting on your Android screen, they would like to be able to do something with it. They suggest making the graphic draggable so that you can move it about the screen with your finger.

In the same project that was used in the previous example, create a new class called HTML5Logo_Draggable. In this class, you will leverage your work from the previous example, inheriting from the HTML5Logo class (and thus inheriting from the View class as well).

The process of making a custom graphic draggable is not too complicated. Since the HTML5Logo_Draggable class already inherits from the View class, you can leverage the OnTouchEvent method of the View to listen for and respond to any touch events.

The OnTouchEvent method of the View class listens for any type of touch registered on the device. As a way to ascertain the type of touch that triggered the event, OnTouchEvent accesses a parameter of type MotionEvent. The class is the key component when working with touch events.

The MotionEvent class exposes several members that are key to being able to respond to a touch event on an Android device:

➤ The Action integer is used to describe the kind of action that took place using the values of the MotionEventAction enumeration. Using this enumeration, you can quickly determine if this was an initial press, a finger drag, and so on.

➤ The GetX() and GetY() functions return the exact coordinates where the user pressed initially. Also, there are several other variations of the *x*, *y* coordinate values, such as nonadjusted coordinates or historical coordinates.

➤ The Downtime value returns the total amount of time in milliseconds (ms) that has elapsed since the user initially pressed the device.

FIGURE 12-4

Finally, you may notice that the OnTouchEvent is a Boolean rather than a simple method. The reason for this is to enable other handlers to try to respond to this touch event if this handler fails to accommodate for it. If this returns true, no other handlers get the opportunity to respond to this touch event.

In addition to using OnTouchEvent, the new class needs a few tracking variables to help determine where the logo is currently located on the Android device's screen. Within your HTML5Logo_Draggable class, add four float fields named Current_X, Current_Y, Previous_X, and Previous_Y. These will be used to track positions.

Next, go ahead and override the OnTouchEvent of the underlying View class. Within this class, you will check the MotionEvent object to see how the view has been touched. Listing 12-9 details the code used to accomplish this.

LISTING 12-9: Setting up the HTML5Logo_Draggable class

```
public class HTML5Logo_Draggable : HTML5Logo
{
        private float Current_X;
        private float Current_Y;
```

continues

LISTING 12-9 *(continued)*

```
        private float Previous_X;
        private float Previous_Y;

        public HTML5Logo_Draggable(Context context, int Scale)
            : base(context, Scale)
        {
            this.Scale = Scale;
        }

        public override bool OnTouchEvent(MotionEvent e)
        {
            int Action = (int)e.Action;
            switch (Action)
            {
                case (int)MotionEventActions.Down:
                    Previous_X = e.GetX();
                    Previous_Y = e.GetY();
                    break;
                case (int)MotionEventActions.Move:
                    Current_X += e.GetX() - Previous_X;
                    Current_Y += e.GetY() - Previous_Y;

                    Previous_X = e.GetX();
                    Previous_Y = e.GetY();

                    Invalidate();
                    break;
            }

        return true;
        }
    }
```

Graphics_Canvas\Graphics_Canvas\HTML5Logo_Draggable.cs

Using the `Action` enumeration within the `MotionEvent` class, the `OnTouchEvent` method listens for two specific kinds of events:

➤ `MotionEventActions.Down` is triggered upon the first touch on the view. This is used to track the initial point at which the screen is touched.

➤ `MotionEventActions.Move` is used to express that the touch point has moved (that is, the touching finger has been dragged across the device's surface).

Using these two events, you can establish a baseline of when and where the first touch happens against where the next touch event occurs.

Using the `GetX()` and `GetY()` functions of the `MotionEvent` class, you can begin to adjust the graphic's position according to the user's finger strokes. Within the first `case` statement, the previous coordinates are updated to the initial touch point. Consider this as establishing a baseline for the overall motion consideration, because it gives you a marker to measure how far the user intends to drag the object. Within the second `case` statement, the system throws a `Move` event. To update the graphic's position, the function uses the last point coordinates (which represent the initial touch point) and updates the current point coordinates using the `GetX()` and `GetY()` functions of the `MotionEvent` class.

Finally, the `Invalidate()` function is called. It is used to force the view to redraw itself as soon as possible.

> *The `Invalidate()` call on a view does not behave quite as many new Android developers may expect. When the `Invalidate()` method is called, it essentially sends a request to the Android OS to redraw the screen as soon as possible. Typically, this means that the Android OS waits until the main application thread is idle before it attempts to redraw.*
>
> *The `Invalidate()` function is excellent for standard application needs. However, if you are creating a graphics-intensive or gaming application, there are better approaches than this, which will be partially covered in the next section.*

With these items in place, only one more item needs to be changed. Using the current position coordinates, you now know the point to which each `Move` event intends to move our graphics. Furthermore, you know that your `OnDraw()` event will be called by every touch event, due to the `Invalidate()` function's being added to the `OnTouchEvent()`. Now, you simply need to update the position of the item on every `OnDraw()` method to match the current coordinates. You can achieve this by overriding the `OnDraw()` event and using the `canvas.Translate()` method. Listing 12-10 shows how this is done.

LISTING 12-10: Translating a canvas's position

```
protected override void OnDraw(Canvas canvas)
{
        canvas.Translate(Current_X, Current_Y);
        base.OnDraw(canvas);
}
```

Graphics_Canvas\Graphics_Canvas\HTML5Logo_Draggable.cs

This example leverages the `Translate` method of the `Canvas` object to update the graphic's position. This method is used to move the origin of the `Canvas` object to another position in the screen's space. In this case, it updates the graphic's position to the user's expected position based on the distance of his or her touch drag.

If you were to run the emulator at this point, you would see a screen much like the previous demo. However, you will find that it moves across the screen as you drag your finger. Also note that, if you touch the center of the screen, far from the actual image, the image still drags at the same pace as you do. The reason is that the view currently fills the entire screen because the view bounds have no limits.

With the new application running, drag the logo wildly and quickly. Assuming that you are running on the emulator with approximately 512MB of allocated memory, you may find that the application quickly crashes with a random error, usually during the build methods of the HTML5Logo class. This occurs because you have made a poor performance decision in regards to your implementation of the OnDraw() method.

Within the current logic, this application re-creates the HTML5Logo graphic every time this graphic is drawn. Although this may be acceptable for stationary graphics, as seen in Case 1, it becomes a major performance hit when OnDraw() is called rapidly. The problem occurs because the OnDraw() event is wired to the OnTouchEvent method. In particular, as you begin to drag it more quickly and erratically, the device has to work much harder, creating a new graphic instance for every motion. Since the HTML5Logo graphic is static, it would be easier on the system if you saved a single instance of the graphic, rather than re-creating it upon every request.

To fix this issue, you will modify the underlying HTML5Logo class that your current class inherited from. Within this class you add a property called HTML5Bitmap and give it the type of Bitmap. This will be used to store the graphic in memory after it has been created for the first time.

Next, create a function called CreateHTML5Bitmap, giving it a return type of Bitmap. This function will be used to create an instance of our graphic on demand. Finally, you can refactor the OnDraw() event so that it checks to see if the HTML5Bitmap property is null and creates the new bitmap as needed. Listing 12-11 displays these adjustments.

LISTING 12-11: Saving an HTML5 Bitmap object in memory for better performance

```
public Bitmap HTML5Bitmap { get; set; }

protected override void OnDraw(Canvas canvas)
{
    if (HTML5Bitmap == null) HTML5Bitmap = CreateHTML5Bitmap();

    canvas.DrawBitmap(HTML5Bitmap, 0, 0, null);
}

protected Bitmap CreateHTML5Bitmap()
{
    var tempCanvas = new Canvas();
    var CurrentBitmap = Bitmap.CreateBitmap(Scale,
        (int)(Scale*1.115), Bitmap.Config.Argb8888);
    tempCanvas.SetBitmap(CurrentBitmap);

    DrawHTML5Background(tempCanvas);
    DrawHTML5InnerBackground(tempCanvas);
```

```
        DrawHTML5Text(tempCanvas);

        return CurrentBitmap;
    }
```

Graphics_Canvas\Graphics_Canvas\HTML5Logo.cs

Within the new `CreateHTML5Bitmap()` method, a new `Bitmap` object is created using the `CreateBitmap()` static function of the `Bitmap` class. As a part of this call, you must include the height, width, and configuration settings of the new `Bitmap`, which have already been figured out by the previous efforts. As with the other calls, the height and width are set according to the `Scale` property, ensuring that the created `Bitmap` is the same size as the target graphic. Also, the `Bitmap.Config` setting is used to specify the screen's pixel configuration.

> The `BitmapConfig` of `Argb8888` *(also known as* `Argb32`*) refers to the color and alpha capabilities of a particular image. Each 8 in the name represents the number of bits that this configuration uses to express the values for the color's alpha, red, green, and blue values. The higher the number of supported bits, the more color variations supported.*

In addition, this method creates a new `Canvas` object. Since you want to predraw the logo, a new `Canvas` object ensures that you do not alter the actual `Canvas` object in any way. By using the `SetBitmap()` method of the new `Canvas` object, the function ensures that all writes to this canvas go directly onto the target bitmap.

Finally, call the draw functions that were once in the `OnDraw()` method, thereby drawing the custom graphic on the target bitmap. By returning the instance of the `CurrentBitmap` object, you now have an in-memory `Bitmap` that you can use many times.

> The `CreateHTML5Bitmap()` *function initially may seem backwards, since it creates not only a new* `Bitmap` *object but also a new* `Canvas` *object. However, it is important to remember that a* `Canvas` *object is a communication channel by which developers can pass graphic instructions to a* `Bitmap`*.*
>
> *In this case, we are leveraging the toolset of a new* `Canvas` *object to make the creation of an in-memory* `Bitmap` *much simpler. Also, by using a new* `Canvas` *object, we can avoid skewing the actual* `Canvas` *object that the application is passing to us.*

With this modification in place, the application should run with much greater efficiency, and the random system errors should no longer be an issue. Run the project, and drag around the logo as erratically and quickly as you desire.

Case 3: Animating Custom Graphics

Finally, you complete the dragging demo for your peers at the W3C. Due to all the excitement about your awesome work, the big boss downloads your app and works with it himself. He likes what he sees, but then he has a stroke of genius. Rather than being draggable, he thinks it should bounce around the screen on its own. No one has done that before, so it will blow everyone away! You begin the process of animating the HTML5 logo so that it will bounce around the screen.

To accomplish this task, two different areas need to be adjusted:

➤ First, the HTML5 graphic needs a way to track its current location and also be able to move itself upon every update call via the view's Invalidate() method. This is similar to the work completed in the previous section when the user's drag motions were tracked.

➤ The second change is that the activity needs to create a timed loop to systematically call the Invalidate() method at correct intervals. This loop will be similar to the kind of loops needed for running gaming applications, in which a timed update needs to occur to simulate motion.

Tracking a Graphic's Location

In the same application that was used in the previous two examples, create a new class called HTML5Logo_Bouncing. In this class, inherit from the HTML5Logo class so that it can leverage the drawing optimizations that were implemented in the previous example.

Within this class, add several properties to help track the moving logo:

➤ A Point object called CurrentPosition: This field will store where the graphic is currently located on the field.

➤ A private Enum called AxisDirection: Within this enumeration, create two items called Positive and Negative. Set the Positive value to 0 and the Negative to 1. Although an enumeration is not essential, it's a nice, visual way to track the current direction in which the logo is moving.

➤ Two private AxisDirection enumerations called VerticalAxisDirection and HorizontalAxisDirection: The purpose of these variables is to track whether the graphics are moving in a positive or negative direction on each axis. Every time the graphic encounters a "bounce condition," the values are inverted, beginning motion in the opposite direction.

➤ A private int called Velocity: As can be inferred, this is used to control the speed at which the graphic moves. Specifically, it tells the graphic how far to move between each call to the OnDraw() method.

With those values in place, you need to override the OnDraw() function so that it handles the logo's motion. In addition to being in control of rendering the view, the OnDraw() method is used to move the object according to its velocity as well as handle any bounce conditions. This way, external calls only have to worry about calling the view's Invalidate function rather than dealing with other information.

Listing 12-12 displays all the appropriate modifications to the HTML5Logo_Bouncing class as well as the implementation of the bouncing logic in the OnDraw() override.

LISTING 12-12: Creating the HTML5Logo_Bouncing view

```
public class HTML5Logo_Bouncing : HTML5Logo
{
    private Point CurrentPosition = new Point(1, 1);

    private enum AxisDirection { Positive = 0, Negative = 1 };

    private AxisDirection VerticalAxisDirection = AxisDirection.Positive;
    private AxisDirection HorizontalDirection = AxisDirection.Positive;
    private int Velocity = 2;

    public HTML5Logo_Bouncing(Context context, int Scale)
        : base(context, Scale)
    {
        this.Scale = Scale;
        this._context = context;
    }

    protected override void OnDraw(Canvas canvas)
    {
        if (HTML5Bitmap == null) HTML5Bitmap = CreateHTML5Bitmap();

        //TODO:  Do not include in production code!!
        Console.WriteLine(String.Format(
            "Logging Message:  CanvasWidth: {0}, BitMapWidth: {1},
                Current X / Y: {2} / {3}",
        canvas.Width, HTML5Bitmap.Width, CurrentPosition.X, CurrentPosition.Y));

        //X-Axis
        if(CurrentPosition.X >= this.Width - HTML5Bitmap.GetScaledWidth(canvas))
        {
            HorizontalDirection = AxisDirection.Negative;
        } else if (CurrentPosition.X <= 0) {
            HorizontalDirection = AxisDirection.Positive;
        }

        if (HorizontalDirection == AxisDirection.Positive)
        {
            CurrentPosition.X += Velocity;
        } else {
            CurrentPosition.X -= Velocity;
        }

        //Y-Axis
        if (CurrentPosition.Y >= this.Height -
HTML5Bitmap.GetScaledHeight(canvas))
        {
```

continues

LISTING 12-12 *(continued)*

```
            VerticalAxisDirection = AxisDirection.Negative;
    }
    else if (CurrentPosition.Y <= 0)
    {
            VerticalAxisDirection = AxisDirection.Positive;
    }

    if (VerticalAxisDirection == AxisDirection.Positive)
    {
            CurrentPosition.Y += Velocity;
    }
    else
    {
            CurrentPosition.Y -= Velocity;
    }

    canvas.Translate(CurrentPosition.X, CurrentPosition.Y);
    canvas.DrawBitmap(HTML5Bitmap, 0, 0, null);
    }
}
```

Graphics_Canvas\Graphics_Canvas\HTML5Logo_Bouncing.cs

Within this listing, the OnDraw() method has several different key behaviors going on within it. As you may recognize from the last example, this function starts by checking to see if the underlying graphic has been drawn. Just as with the draggable demo, it is vital that this program tries to run as lean as possible, which means that you want to take this performance hit only once.

After that, a quick logging message writes some key values to the Console window. Because quite a few different variables move at once in this call, this will help you track the motion of the graphic as well as your underlying conditional logic. Even though we are not in the business of writing bugs, this is a great way to track them down if they occur.

Within the next section of the OnDraw() methods are two code blocks with comment labels of X-Axis and Y-Axis. These sections are used to track the current direction in which the bitmap should be moving, at both a horizontal and vertical level. Basically, these check to see if the graphic is in the bounds of the screen. If not, it reverses the direction in which the graphic is moving, which brings the graphic back into the screen bounds. Since the origin of this graphic is at (0,0), half the bounce condition checks to see if the graphic has moved below these values. The second bounce condition is the difference between the overall length of a canvas and the scaled length of the graphic. This way, the graphic bounces as soon as any point touches a screen edge, rather than just the origin point.

To get the graphic's height and width, this function uses the bitmap's GetScaledWidth() *and* GetScaledHeight() *functions. The purpose of using these functions is that they always return the bitmap's true size, even if the canvas or other method has applied a scaling effect to the graphic.*

In most cases, just about every graphic receives some kind of scaling effect as it is passed to the screen. Therefore, it is a good idea to use the scaled values.

Finally, the last section of the method offsets the corresponding location of the graphic, using the `AxisDirection` settings to determine whether to move it in a positive or negative direction. In these areas, the `Velocity` variable is used to know how many points to shift the graphic. Once the `CurrentPosition` point has been updated, use the `Translate()` method to move the canvas to the correct location. The `View` object now should be ready for action. This completes the first task.

Redrawing the Canvas at Regular Intervals

The second task is to adjust the activity so that it calls the view's `Invalidate()` function at regular intervals. This can be accomplished in a variety of ways, but the gist is to create a separate thread in the activity's `OnCreate()` function and call a looping function. Using `Thread.Sleep()`, update the `View` object at appropriate intervals. Listing 12-13 shows a basic implementation of this process.

LISTING 12-13: Creating an update loop for the HTML5Logo_Bouncing view

```
[Activity(Label = "Graphics_DemoTrials", MainLauncher = true)]
public class GraphicsSample : Activity
{
    protected override void OnCreate(Bundle bundle)
    {
    base.OnCreate(bundle);
        var targetView = new HTML5Logo_Bouncing(this, 100);

        SetContentView(targetView);
        ThreadPool.QueueUserWorkItem(o => RunLoop(targetView));
    }

    private void RunLoop(View TargetView)
    {
        while (true)
        {
            Thread.Sleep(10);
            RunOnUiThread(() => TargetView.Invalidate());
        }
    }
}
```

Graphics_Canvas\Graphics_Canvas\GraphicsCanvasDemo.cs

In this listing, a new method called `RunLoop()` has been created. Using an endless loop, this thread sleeps for 10 ms and then calls the `Invalidate()` function on the appropriate view. The `RunOnUiThread()` function is used for the `Invalidate()` function because this is a requirement for it to work as intended.

Now, run the application and view the results. Figure 12-5 outlines the logo's expected path. To adjust the speed of the logo's movement, adjust the `Thread.Sleep()` value or the `Velocity` variable within the `HTML5Logo_Bouncing` class. Remember that the `Invalidate()` call is more of a suggestion to redraw rather than a direct command. Therefore, speed and velocity settings may not be completely accurate, because the redraw depends on the Android OS to initiate.

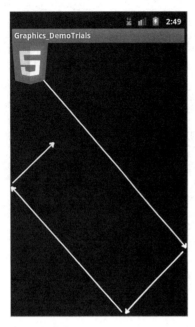

FIGURE 12-5

At this point, you should have a fully functioning application. Although it works as intended, one more task must be added. Since this is a constantly running loop, you should follow a few steps to make sure that it is a good citizen on the device. Specifically, the loop should stop trying to run anytime the application is moved into the background. This is achieved by adding a Boolean variable called IsRunning and by overriding the OnPause() and OnResume() methods. Listing 12-14 displays this technique.

LISTING 12-14: Managing the run loop

```
public Boolean IsRunning = true;

protected override void OnPause()
{
    IsRunning = false;
    base.OnPause();
}

protected override void OnResume()
{
    IsRunning = true;
    base.OnResume();
}

private void RunLoop(View TargetView)
{
    while (IsRunning)
```

```
        {
            Thread.Sleep(10);
            RunOnUiThread(() => TargetView.Invalidate());
        }
    }
```

In this example, the application has been given the ability to clean up its resource usage with just a few lines of code. The OnPause() and OnResume() functions are called when the application goes into and comes back from the background. Using the IsRunning Boolean, these two functions let the application track when it is in a running state. By replacing the true condition on the while loop with IsRunning, the application will no longer try to update the TargetView graphic when the application is moved into the background.

Case 4: Improving Performance Using SurfaceView

After setting up the bouncing image view, you feel that your job is complete, and you deploy the view to your testers. After a few days, you start to get complaints because the application seems randomly sluggish, especially when the users are working with other UI elements. You must figure out a better way to display this view that has faster performance.

Although using a custom view is an excellent way to draw graphics onto the device, this method has one major drawback. All typical views are drawn using the GUI thread. Even though you can handle much of the processing on a background thread, the final drawing function of a typical view cannot run on any other thread but the GUI. This is why the previous example needed to use the RunOnUiThread() call to start the view invalidation process.

When you are in a situation in which you are rapidly invalidating (updating) a custom view, this can begin to bog down the GUI thread. Also, if the view's OnDraw() method is particularly heavy or is trying to render animations, this greatly inhibits the performance of the GUI thread. Since the GUI thread is used for all user activities (finger presses, text entry, or accelerometer responses), this situation can lead to a bad user experience, because your graphic can become choppy or the interface can freeze.

Thankfully, there is a great way to work around this issue. Whereas typical views are forced to render on the UI thread, a special type of object called a SurfaceView can update on a background thread. The SurfaceView can accomplish this because it has a dedicated surface assigned to it within the view hierarchy. Using a SurfaceView, you can fully implement animations and graphics without impacting overall application interface responsiveness.

When using a SurfaceView, you need to keep a few key things in mind:

➤ A SurfaceView is not the perfect solution. Using a SurfaceView comes at a price — it requires additional memory consumption to function. Therefore, a developer needs to balance the cost versus the gain before moving to a SurfaceView.

➤ Sometimes it is better to try a custom view before moving to a SurfaceView. Since the setup and functionality of a SurfaceView is similar to that of a custom view, it is a small matter to convert a custom view into a SurfaceView. This will be demonstrated in a moment.

➤ When using a `SurfaceView`, you move fully into a threading situation. Make sure that any variable or state storage access is thread-safe.

➤ `SurfaceViews` are less forgiving of errors or memory leaks than their custom view cousins. Take great care to correctly set up and clean up `SurfaceView` implementations so that you do not inadvertently leave the surface in an unusable state.

The `SurfaceView` class contains all the methods and events needed to create a custom `SurfaceView` object. This view actually inherits from the `View` class but adds a couple of additional properties. Also within this class are methods to control the z-order of how the `SurfaceView` is placed within the view hierarchy. Similar to what you find with CSS style sheets, z-order in the `SurfaceView` allows a developer to overlay a surface above or below the actual window on which typical views are rendered. Finally, the `SurfaceView` adds a property to reference the underlying `ISurfaceHolder` instance associated with this object.

The `ISurfaceHolderCallback` can be implemented on a `SurfaceView` to give a developer access to events and changes that occur to the surface. This interface is key to creating stable and functional `SurfaceView` objects. It exposes the following main events:

➤ `SurfaceCreated` is called right after the surface is created. This event is key because it indicates when the drawing process can occur. Attempting to draw to the surface before this event can have serious side effects, such as application locks or crashes.

➤ `SurfaceDestroyed` is called just before the `SurfaceView` is destroyed. Again, it is critical to avoid trying to draw anything to the surface when it does not exist. Consequently, this is where you will want to place any stop-processing logic.

➤ `SurfaceChanged` is called when changes have occurred to the surface structure, such as a difference in surface width or height. This allows a developer the opportunity to display changes, such as moving from a portrait display to a landscape.

With a new understanding of the `SurfaceView` object, you can now update the HTML5 logo so that it will run smoothly in the background. Within the same project as the previous example, add a new class called `HTML5Logo_SurfaceView.cs`. In this class, you need to inherit from the `SurfaceView` object and implement `ISurfaceHolderCallback`.

To set this new implementation to work properly, you need to slightly modify the same code examples that you used in the previous case. However, you do not have the luxury of simply inheriting from the `HTML5Logo` class. Listing 12-15 is the full implementation of the `SurfaceView` class. Portions that were covered in previous sections are marked with appropriate comments.

LISTING 12-15: Setting up the HTML5Logo SurfaceView

```
public class HTML5Logo_SurfaceView : SurfaceView, ISurfaceHolderCallback
{
        public Bitmap HTML5Bitmap { get; set; }
        public int Scale = 100;
        private int Velocity = 2;
        private Point CurrentPosition = new Point(1, 1);
```

```
public Boolean IsRunning = false;

private enum AxisDirection { Positive = 0, Negative = 1 };

private AxisDirection VerticalAxisDirection = AxisDirection.Positive;
private AxisDirection HorizontalDirection = AxisDirection.Positive;

public HTML5Logo_SurfaceView(Context context): base(context)
{
    this.Holder.AddCallback(this);
}

protected Bitmap CreateHTML5Bitmap()
{
    //Same as previous examples...
}

protected override void OnDraw(Canvas canvas)
{
    canvas.DrawColor(Color.Black);
    canvas.DrawBitmap(HTML5Bitmap, CurrentPosition.X, CurrentPosition.Y,
null);
}

protected void UpdatePosition(Canvas canvas)
{
    //Refactored from previous OnDraw() examples.
    //This will update the moving canvas's horizontal and vertical
    //directions.
}

private void RunLoop()
{
    Canvas c = null;

    while (IsRunning)
    {
        try
        {
            c = this.Holder.LockCanvas();

            UpdatePosition(c);
            this.OnDraw(c);
        }
        finally
        {
            if (c != null) this.Holder.UnlockCanvasAndPost(c);
        }
    }
}

public void SurfaceCreated(ISurfaceHolder holder)
{
    IsRunning = true;
```

continues

LISTING 12-15 *(continued)*

```
            ThreadPool.QueueUserWorkItem(o => RunLoop());
    }

    public void SurfaceDestroyed(ISurfaceHolder holder)
    {
        IsRunning = false;
    }

    public void SurfaceChanged(ISurfaceHolder holder,
        int format, int width, int height)
    {
    }

    private void DrawHTML5Text(Canvas canvas)
    {
        //Same as previous examples...
    }

    private void DrawHTML5InnerBackground(Canvas canvas)
    {
        //Same as previous examples...
    }

    private void DrawHTML5Background(Canvas canvas)
    {
        //Same as previous examples...
    }
}
```

Graphics_Canvas\Graphics_Canvas\HTML5Logo_SurfaceView.cs

Several parts of this listing should look familiar. In fact, all the code in the previous example was moved to this `SurfaceView` implementation and slightly modified. This includes the following:

➤ The logic to draw the HTML5 bitmap.

➤ The logic to keep a single instance of the HTML5 bitmap in memory between requests.

➤ The logic to update the position of the moving bitmap. This was refactored slightly into the `UpdatePosition()` method to clean up the `OnDraw()` method.

➤ The tracking variables to control velocity and scale.

In addition to these familiar methods, a few minor additions build on the same concepts as the previous example, but in a slightly different location:

➤ The constructor of this class adds a callback to the `ISurfaceHolder` object. This wires any `ISurfaceHolder` events to trigger within the instance of this class.

➤ The `SurfaceCreated` callback of the `ISurfaceHolder` class has been implemented. Within this class, you use the same `IsRunning` Boolean to indicate that the system can begin to run the drawing routines. As mentioned, this is important because you need to ensure that you do not try to draw to a null surface. After `IsRunning` is set to `true`, you use similar logic found in the previous example to queue a new background thread to start the looping draw updates.

➤ The `SurfaceDestroy` callback of the `ISurfaceHolder` is implemented. Just as with the create method, you flip the switch for the `IsRunning` variable to stop the drawing loop.

In addition, two key updates need special attention. The `RunLoop()` method represents the drawing routine used to create the animation effect of the `HTML5Logo` bitmap. Within this method, you create a new `Canvas` object. Then a `while` loop is initiated, checking the `IsRunning` Boolean to ensure that you are allowed to write to the `SurfaceView`.

Next, a `try/catch` block is added. The reason for this block is that, to draw to a `Canvas` object, the `SurfaceHolder` needs to be locked. When the `Holder.LockCanvas()` function is called, the surface is locked so that it can be updated. In addition, this function returns a `Canvas` object so that the bitmap can be updated and the canvas can be drawn on, as was done in previous examples. Last, the `finally` block is used to be sure that the `SurfaceHolder` will always be unlocked, even in the event of an error. This is important, because the view cannot render properly if the `SurfaceHolder` is locked.

Finally, the `OnDraw()` method looks similar to what we have come to expect. However, the initial draw command is a bit curious, because it seems odd to have to draw a black canvas before drawing the rendered bitmap. The reason for this is that the `Canvas` object is treated a little differently in a `SurfaceView`. Rather than being "blank" when you receive it, the `SurfaceHolder` returns the same `Canvas` object that was used in the previous draw commands. If you do not "blank" it out, you will draw your new `HTML5Logo` bitmap on a canvas that already has all the previous incarnations of it. This can result in an amusing error in which you have a long, snaking chain of HTML5 logos across your screen.

The code sample is ready to be tested. By either copying in the omitted results or downloading this sample project, finish updating your `SurfaceView` class so that it contains all the appropriate logic. Then update the Activity's `OnCreate` method to treat an instance of this class as the content view.

With all of this in place, run your example. You should be greeted by a bounding HTML5 logo that is running full throttle across the screen. The motion should be significantly smoother and should not impact the performance of the overall application interface.

Selecting the Best Approach

Within the previous examples, we walked through different use cases for animation techniques when interacting with the `Canvas` object. Specifically, we outlined two different approaches: overriding the `View` object or using the special `SurfaceView` class. Although these situations are somewhat contrived, they do exemplify the fact that selecting the best approach is often an iterative process and involves systematically testing the final result until you achieve the desired effect. In extreme cases, it can be quite clear which approach would be best; however, there are many cases in which one approach is as functional and performant as another.

When trying to decide whether to use an overridden, custom `Canvas` object or the `SurfaceView` object, you can consider a few key questions to assist in the selection process.

➤ **How complex is the graphic or animation effect?** Typical views and custom views are best for simple graphics or animation effects. If you are working on a very small one-time animation or if your effect is simple and linear, a custom view will make for a simple and elegant solution. As examples become more complex and resource-heavy, a `SurfaceView` is better suited to deal with heavy requirements.

➤ **How much is your application currently utilizing the UI thread?** A custom view approach needs to utilize the UI thread in order to redraw itself. If you are building some kind of background animation to an application that needs the UI thread for other purposes, this can make your application sluggish and unresponsive. Use a `SurfaceView` in situations where the UI thread is expected to be used for other purposes.

➤ **How essential is precision and timing for the animation?** As just stated, you need to call the `Invalidate()` function to *request* that the UI thread redraw the view for a custom view. This makes custom views poor choices for precision-dependent applications, such as action games. Use a `SurfaceView` in situations where you need the ability to precisely adjust and draw your graphics.

With these items in mind, you should have enough information to make a guess as to what the best approach would be for your animation needs. Despite this, making the right selection can sometimes be a trial-and-error process as you begin to add more features or more demands to your drawing process.

THE 2D GRAPHICS LIBRARY

In cases in which a developer does not want to work directly with the `Canvas` object, Android has a custom built-in 2D graphics library. This library does a great deal of heavy lifting and extends the capabilities of the underlying types. In fact, you have been working with this library already via the `Resources` class that leverages the 2D graphics library when using these items.

When working with the 2D graphics library on the Mono for Android platform, you will primarily deal with a special kind of resource known as a drawable. As you might guess, the `Drawable` class comprises a set of tools and functions for anything related to drawing. This can be custom art described programmatically or via XML files, physical image resources on the device, or a combination.

Drawables give a developer an amazing assortment of abilities. The framework has dozens of different implementations of these classes, each serving a specific need.

USING DRAWABLES

Drawables are used to describe anything that can be drawn in the Mono for Android platform. Although this functionality clearly overlaps with that of using graphic primitives and the canvas, these two groupings have some key differences:

➤ Drawables introduce a bit of overhead compared to working with the canvas directly. This has been stated several times; however, it is a key point. Do not be afraid to use drawables — just be aware of where and how you use them. By understanding the pros and cons of each option, you can make wise decisions about where and how to use them.

➤ Drawables can be expressed within the XML syntax of layouts. Using this, you can declare your `Drawable` object within layout files but still maintain them via code. This can greatly simplify the coding process and encapsulate drawables into reusable chunks.

Drawables play an important role in the framework. In addition to providing the mechanism to create universal style settings, drawables are often used as a generic way to pass graphical information between your code and the different framework toolsets.

Drawables as XML Resources

Although it is perfectly acceptable to define drawables via code, drawables are often utilized via XML expressions. Once a drawable has been defined via XML, it can be leveraged like any other drawable resource. This allows drawables to have a universal definition while still being accessible to any part of the system. When this feature is used correctly, it can make universal edits quite simple. In fact, many drawables are used to assist in global application definition, much the way CSS is used to make HTML styling universal across a website.

The process of defining an XML-based drawable is simple. You do so by adding an XML file under the Resources/Drawable directory and adding the appropriate syntax. After this file is added, the platform identifies it as a drawable resource, naming it according to the XML filename, minus the file extension. Once it recognizes the XML drawable as a resource, the drawable can be accessed using the typical methods that are used with standard drawable types, as shown in Listing 12-16.

LISTING 12-16: Declaring a drawable via XML and C#

```
<!-- Via XML Syntax in a Layout   -->
<Button android:id="@+id/SomeButton"
    android:layout_width="fill_parent"
    android:layout_height="wrap_content"
    android:background="@drawable/yourcustomdrawablename "
    android:text="Click Me!"/>

// Via code declaration:
View SomeView = new View(this);
SomeView.SetBackgroundDrawable(Resource.Drawable.YourCustomDrawableName);
```

Note that the resource reference in the XML syntax is lowercase. Android requires that all drawable resource references be lowercase. Mono for Android does quite a bit of work to support different cases of resource declarations, but not in the case of layout files. Using uppercase names within a drawable XML declaration will result in a complier error.

Using the drawable as an XML resource, you can easily create uniform layouts and backgrounds while maintaining the full flexibility of customized graphics.

> *For the following examples in this section, the XML declaration is the preferred means of expressing drawables. This does not imply that XML is the preferred way to work with drawables. Rather, the XML syntax is one of the unique features of drawables that makes it a handy toolset. In addition, the drawable implementation via code is rather straightforward, and using XML affords a change of pace.*

Simple and Compound Drawables

The framework has dozens of drawables. Since they are simple to extend and implement, modified implementations are prevalent throughout the framework as well as in several other third-party libraries. Consequently, any attempt to catalog or list every drawable type would be difficult and well beyond the scope of this chapter.

Despite their numbers, drawables tend to fall between two different delineations — simple drawables and compound drawables. Basically, *compound drawables* can merge several drawables within one unit, whereas *simple drawables* are singular units that provide a singular function. In addition to containing multiple units, compound drawables often offer transformative functionality that can be applied to their underlying units. When used in conjunction with one another, these two drawable types can be quite powerful and can provide a developer with scalable, crisp graphics that do not have the same kind of memory footprint as file-based resources.

Drawables in Action

Taking an approach similar to the one in the canvas section of this chapter, the following sections walk you through several use-case scenarios for XML-based drawables. Each use case expands a bit on the underlying lessons of the previous case in the hopes of building a complete story about how to interact with drawables in your application.

Case 1: Using Default Drawables

You have decided to create a simple application to assist with working with Android drawables. Within this application, you decide to display several rows of the Android robots, jokingly calling them your robot army. In addition to making sleek, stylistic robots, you want to add a bit of interaction with each individual robot.

To get started, create a new project called `GraphicsDrawables_RobotArmy`. Next, you need to choose a robot to use as a graphic for your robot army. For the sake of simplicity, this example uses a copy of the Android robot. Rename it "androidrobot," and add it as a drawable resource to the application's `Resources/Drawable` folder.

> With a quick search, you will find a number of variations on the Android robot. This example uses a converted version of the Android robot displayed on the Google Branding page: www.android.com/branding.html.
>
> Feel free to use whatever image you choose; however, ensure that it is in PNG format. In addition, the image should have a transparent background, because many of the examples that are covered will be hidden by an opaque background.
>
> A modified version of the Android robot image is included as part of the downloadable content for this project.

Once you have added the image for the robot to the application, you can begin the process of displaying a list of robots. Open the Main.axml file for this project. Rather than using the default LinearLayout, you will use a TableLayout to make listing the multitudes of robots much simpler.

Modify the Main.axml file, replacing the root layout with a TableLayout control. Next, add a TableRow node within the table layout, creating space for the first row of the upcoming robot army.

Finally, add four ImageButtons to the newly created TableRow, referencing the androidrobot drawable as the image source. When complete, the Main.axml file should look like Listing 12-17.

LISTING 12-17: Creating the table layout

```xml
<?xml version="1.0" encoding="utf-8"?>
<TableLayout xmlns:android="http://schemas.android.com/apk/res/android"
        android:orientation="vertical"
        android:layout_width="fill_parent"
        android:layout_height="fill_parent"
        android:stretchColumns="*"
        >
    <TableRow>
        <ImageButton android:src="@drawable/androidrobot" />
        <ImageButton android:src="@drawable/androidrobot" />
        <ImageButton android:src="@drawable/androidrobot" />
        <ImageButton android:src="@drawable/androidrobot" />
    </TableRow>
</TableLayout>
```

Graphics_Drawables\Graphics_Drawables\Resources\Layout\Main.axml

This layout is pretty typical of most table layouts. Within the table row, you create four robot instances. Rather than using a simple image control to display the robot graphics, you use the ImageButton. This helps you satisfy the need to add interactivity to each robot instance.

Finally, modify the activity's OnCreate() method so that it properly displays the contents of the Main.axml file. When complete, the resulting code resembles Listing 12-18.

LISTING 12-18: Setting up the activity's OnCreate() method

```
protected override void OnCreate(Bundle bundle)
{
        base.OnCreate(bundle);
        SetContentView(Resource.Layout.Main);
}
```

Graphics_Drawables\Graphics_Drawables\GraphicsDrawablesDemo.cs

With these steps complete, run the application and view the results. Using the default drawable tooling, you can quickly prototype version 1 of your robot army. Figure 12-6 shows how the result should appear.

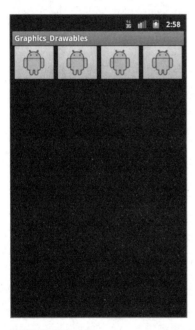

FIGURE 12-6

Despite the fact that the robots may be somewhat plain, you accomplished your two tasks with very little work!

Case 2: Adding Polish with the Shape Drawable

Although the application does have a row of robots that are interactive, they are still quite lackluster. In particular, the default look of the ImageButton is unappealing with its blocky corners and slate gray background. You decide that version 2 of your robots could stand an improvement in their overall style. You want to replace the blocky background with something sleek that has more tasteful colors.

Using the default properties of the `ImageButton`, you could begin to spruce up the final result of the `ImageButton` class by adding background colors, different spacing settings, and so on. However, this approach has two major drawbacks:

➤ Although the `ImageButton` does expose an impressive number of customization options, it cannot compare to the flexibility of using a custom drawable.

➤ Manually adjusting the attributes for each robot is manageable for the first four. However, as your robot army begins to grow to 8, 12, and 16 robots, this will result in quite a bit of repetitive code. Not only would the resulting layout be considerably larger, but it also would be a nightmare to update one setting on all the robots.

Rather than going with this approach, you can use a universal definition for each robot. This can be accomplished using a custom *shape drawable*.

Shape drawables are the one-stop-shopping source for drawing basic shapes on an Android device. They can be used to draw a wide variety of shapes, including ovals, rectangles, and arcs. Essentially, most of the shapes defined in the `Android.Graphics.Shapes` class can be drawn using a shape drawable.

In addition to creating general shapes, shape drawables contain tooling to assist in the application of other styles, such as borders, colors, and spacing of the final shape object.

As with any drawable, the shape drawable can be defined via code or XML. If you were to use a code-based shape drawable in this example, you would be forced to iteratively apply the drawable to each instance of a robot. You would succeed in defining the background in a single location for universal updates; however, this approach would still be rather tedious to apply. Rather than using this approach, you can declare the drawable via XML and allow the controls to specify where to use it.

As noted, drawables can be expressed via XML or within code. Consider the following questions when choosing an approach:

Under what circumstances do you plan to use the drawable? *When you work a lot with XML-based layouts and other XML-based drawables, the XML approach of using a drawable is handy. It has nice synergy with the other resources and is much less verbose than the code-based approach.*

What features do you require from the drawable? *Although the XML-based and code-based approaches offer some great tooling, the code-based approach is much more powerful because it offers a greater variety of options. In many cases, these additional options are not hard requirements for the usage scenario, but sometimes you can't get around having to use the code-based approach.*

On a final note, the drawable namespace is an excellent example of an area in which Android could vastly improve its documentation. In particular, some advanced usages of the XML-based approach require much patience and trial and error to achieve the desired results.

To get started, you create a new XML file within the `Resources/Drawable` directory, naming it `RobotBackground.xml`. Within this XML file, declare the shape drawable by using the `<shape>` node. Because the shape object is a generic container for many different shape types, the shape node exposes a property to define what kind of shape to render via the `android:shape` attribute. In this example, you use `rectangle` as the value. Other options are `oval`, `line`, and `ring`.

The shape XML object can contain several optional subnodes. These subnodes are additional drawables that can be associated with the shape or are ways to define how the shape is rendered. This example initially uses the following three subnodes of the shape object:

➤ The **corners node** lets you create rounded corners for the shape object. This subnode has several attributes that allow a developer to set the overall corner radius or specifically target individual corners. As you might imagine, this node is not appropriate for every shape type, but it adds a nice touch to objects with otherwise hard corners.

➤ The **solid node** lets you specify a color drawable to associate with the shape drawable. This node works with any shape type and is a simple way to establish a base color for the object.

➤ The **stroke node** lets you create an outline of the shape object. Additional properties include common items such as setting the stroke's width and color.

Using these elements, create a shape specification that would be appropriate to use as the background of each robot `ImageButton`. While working with these, bear in mind that any specifications made here are automatically shaped and scaled to the appropriate size of the object they are applied to. When you are finished, the final version of the file should resemble Listing 12-19.

LISTING 12-19: Creating the robot background drawable

```xml
<?xml version="1.0" encoding="utf-8" ?>

<shape xmlns:android="http://schemas.android.com/apk/res/android"
    android:shape="rectangle">
    <corners android:radius="5dp" />
    <solid android:color="#30577F"></solid>
    <stroke android:width="1dp" android:color="#FFFFFF" />
</shape>
```

Graphics_Drawables\Graphics_Drawables\Resources\Drawable\RobotBackground.xml

Within this code, the shape is defined as a rectangle with a blue background. The corners of the rectangle are set to be slightly rounded. Finally, the entire shape has a white border of minimal thickness.

Next, switch back to the `Main.axml` file. Rather than updating 'version 1' of the robot army, make a second row of robots to create a comparison point between version 1 and version 2 of the robot army.

Create a second `TableRow` by copying and pasting the information for the first `TableRow` in the layout. Within the second row, set the `android:background` property so that it uses the new `robotbackground` drawable as its background (do not forget to make sure it is lowercase). Finally, add a small amount of margin to each individual image to put a bit of space in the layout. Listing 12-20 shows how this new row should appear.

LISTING 12-20: Defining the robot background drawable in table view

```xml
<TableRow>
    <ImageButton android:src="@drawable/androidrobot" android:layout_margin="2dp"
        android:background="@drawable/robotbackground" />
    <ImageButton android:src="@drawable/androidrobot" android:layout_margin="2dp"
        android:background="@drawable/robotbackground" />
    <ImageButton android:src="@drawable/androidrobot" android:layout_margin="2dp"
        android:background="@drawable/robotbackground" />
    <ImageButton android:src="@drawable/androidrobot" android:layout_margin="2dp"
        android:background="@drawable/robotbackground" />
</TableRow>
```

Graphics_Drawables\Graphics_Drawables\Resources\Layout\Main.axml

Once this code is in place, the application should display eight robots within the robot army application, as shown in Figure 12-7. The first row represents the unmodified first version of the robot army. The second row is the newly added robot troops, using the custom drawable shape as the background.

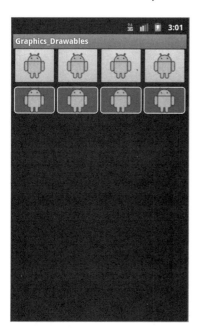

FIGURE 12-7

Case 3: Using the Gradient Drawable

Looking at the second version of the robot army, you can see that they are a vast improvement over version 1. However, you are not completely satisfied with the end result. You decide that if you were to add a nice gradient as the background to each robot, they would look trendier and more robot 2.0.

With *gradient drawables* you can create a large variety of gradients. In code-based scenarios, gradients are often used via the Shader class, which can be applied as a type of style on the Paint object. This approach is not used in this code sample, but when you work with code-based drawables, check out the Shader and ShaderFactory classes to find more information on displaying gradients.

For XML-based scenarios, gradients are expressed as a subnode of the shape XML drawable by using the <gradient> node. When you use the XML declaration of the gradient, you can define several different properties, as shown in Table 12-2.

TABLE 12-2: Gradient Drawable Attributes

ATTRIBUTE NAME	DESCRIPTION
angle	The angle attribute allows you to specify the overall angle at which the gradient is drawn. Acceptable values are in 45-degree increments. Note: Angle values for this might seem counterintuitive. Starting at 0 degrees, the gradient has the start color on its left and the end color on its right. As the value of the angle increases, the gradient rotates counterclockwise.
centerColor	This optional value can be used to create a three-point gradient. In addition to accepting hexadecimal values, this property can accept names of other color resources.
centerX and centerY	These float values indicate the center of the gradient. This value applies only to gradient types in which the concept of "center" is appropriate.
endColor	Specifies the color value at which the gradient will end. In addition to accepting hexadecimal values, this property can accept names of other color resources.
gradientRadius	When you use a radial gradient, this value indicates the gradient's radius value. This float value enables you to control the gradient's overall size and, consequently, how quickly the gradient transitions from start to end colors.
startColor	Specifies the color value at which the gradient starts. In addition to accepting hexadecimal values, this property can accept names of other color resources.
type	Indicates the type of gradient. Acceptable values are linear, radial, and sweep.

When working with gradients, you may encounter a scenario in which the rendered gradient no longer looks smooth but appears to have rings or lines stacked on one another (depending on the type). This effect is known as banding.

Typically, banding occurs when one color meets another within a gradient and the transition lacks the proper "noise" to make it appear to be blended. One way to combat banding on an Android device is to turn on dithering for the bitmap, drawable, or view on which you are applying the gradient.

Another possible reason for banding is that the pixel format of the rendering device or bitmap is too low. By increasing the PixelFormat of the device window or image to 32-bit (RGBA_8888), you increase the number of available colors to smooth the transition from the start to end colors.

Create a new XML file in the `Resource/Drawable` directory, and name it `RobotBackground_Gradient.xml`. Within this file, paste the contents of the previous drawable file, `RobotBackground.xml`. Within the new file, add a `<gradient>` node as a subnode to the shape declaration. When creating the gradient, specify its type as a linear gradient, and set its angle so that it that moves from the top to the bottom of the shape. Finally, add color values for the center, start, and end colors. Listing 12-21 displays what the gradient declaration could look like.

LISTING 12-21: Introducing the gradient drawable

```
<gradient
      android:type="linear"
      android:startColor="#FFFFFF"
      android:centerColor="#30577F"
      android:endColor="#30577F"
      android:angle="270"/>
```

Graphics_Drawables\Graphics_Drawables\Resources\Drawable\RobotBackground_Gradient.xml

Looking at this declaration, you can see that the added colors are intended to create a kind of "gleam" effect on the robot `ImageButtons`. The top of the button has a white glossy effect that dithers out somewhere around the middle of the button. By setting the angle to 270 degrees, you indicate that the linear gradient will flow from top to bottom.

Switching to the `Main.axml` file, you can go through the process of creating a version 3 of your robot army. As in the previous section, copy the contents of the previous `TableLayout` and paste them as a new, third row in the `TableLayout`.

For each `ImageButton` in the new `TableRow`, adjust the `android:background` attribute to use the `robotbackground_gradient` drawable rather than what they use in the previous example. When it is complete, the XML layout for the new third row should look like Listing 12-22.

LISTING 12-22: Defining the robot background gradient in table view

```
<TableRow>
    <ImageButton android:src="@drawable/androidrobot" android:layout_margin="2dp"
        android:background="@drawable/robotbackground_gradient" />
    <ImageButton android:src="@drawable/androidrobot" android:layout_margin="2dp"
        android:background="@drawable/robotbackground_gradient" />
    <ImageButton android:src="@drawable/androidrobot" android:layout_margin="2dp"
        android:background="@drawable/robotbackground_gradient" />
    <ImageButton android:src="@drawable/androidrobot" android:layout_margin="2dp"
        android:background="@drawable/robotbackground_gradient" />
</TableRow>
```

Graphics_Drawables\Graphics_Drawables\Resources\Layout\Main.axml

With this in place, run your application. When it loads, you have a comparative view of the first three iterations of the robot army. Assuming that all goes well, the device's final output should look like Figure 12-8.

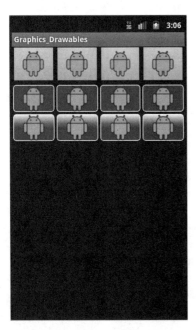

FIGURE 12-8

Case 4: Using the Compound Drawable

After looking over the third version of the robot army, you discover a problem. Previously, you created a gradient effect as the background for each ImageButton that represented a robot. Although this effect improved the previous look, the intent of this effect was to create something of a "gleam" on the top of the button to add depth and style to the robot display. Looking over the result, you can see that you succeeded in creating a stylistic but flat image. You decide that you need to take steps to add more depth to the next version of the robot.

In the previous sections, you created a robot army using the simple drawables of image and shape. Leveraging the framework, you added an image drawable of the robot multiple times, creating several rows of robots with increasingly complex background styling. Then, by using a shape XML resource, you adjusted the look of those multiple robots quickly and efficiently.

Although much can be accomplished with the use of a single drawable, this approach does have its limitations. What if you wanted more advanced integration between different drawables? What if you wanted to create overlay effects, thereby adding depth to the final image? What if you wanted a way to define attributes on a set of drawables while keeping their definitions separate from one another? When you reach this point, compound drawables can take your application to the next level.

As stated earlier in this chapter, compound drawables are a type of drawable that specializes in working with sets of other drawables. Although many have their own types of drawing actions, they excel at creating interaction points between one drawable and another. Consequently, they can act as a binding force between multiple drawable declarations, often merging them into a new and more interactive drawable.

To illustrate the use of compound drawables, we'll continue with the robot army example. In the last version, the gradient effect failed to please. Adding a simple gradient created a nice but flat-looking robot rather than adding depth. To fix this issue, you need to modify a couple of things:

➤ Rather than having a single background that is part gradient, you need two distinct backgrounds. One is the solid, simple background that you used in the second example. The other is an overlay that represents the gradient effect.

➤ To complete the effect, the overlying background needs to look as if it is not part of the other background. If you add a bit of transparency to the overlay, the underlying background will look as if it has curvature and depth.

Unfortunately, this kind of interaction is impossible with simple drawables. No matter how ingenious you are (short of importing an image resource), the resulting image will always be flat, or the entire layer will end up with some kind of transparency. However, this challenge is easily met via a compound drawable known as `LayerDrawable`, which can be used to manage a collection of underlying drawables. Using a list-based approach, items within a `LayerDrawable` are rendered one at a time, working from the first item to the last item in its collection. In an object-oriented understanding, you can think of a `LayerDrawable` as something akin to an array.

In addition, `LayerDrawable` has one aspect that sets it apart from many of the other list-like controls in Mono for Android. Unlike other listing controls such as `LinearLayout`, items within a `LayerDrawable` do not offset their draw position based on the ending position of the previous item. Rather, items in a `LayerDrawable` are drawn starting from the same origin point, unless instructed to do otherwise.

When working with the placement of drawables within the `LayerDrawable`, *you can often run into unexpected results if you do not intend the drawables to fully overlap one another. The reason for this is that drawables typically are scaled to fill the space allocated to them, often despite offset values that are given.*

Some drawables don't have a clear workaround to this issue. But workarounds are sometimes possible. For example, when you are working with basic drawables such as bitmaps, you can avoid the scaling issue by setting the gravity of the underlying bitmap to center. Although this case is documented within the Android developer docs, the overall documentation for this area is frustratingly light.

The XML declaration for a `LayerDrawable` is achieved using the `<layer-list>` node. Within this node, each "layer" of drawable is defined using a subelement tag of `<item>`.

The item node is a flexible container that can be used in two ways. First, the item exposes an attribute called `android:drawable`. You can use this attribute to specify the drawable that should be drawn, using the same drawable syntax that is used throughout Mono for Android, `@drawable\ drawable_name`. The second option is to define a custom drawable within the item node by adding any drawable declaration in XML.

Finally, an item node exposes several properties that allow you to define custom offsets for the top, bottom, left, and right of the item. This gives you some flexibility in regards to how each drawable is drawn onto the `Canvas` object.

Using the same `GraphicsDrawable_RobotArmy` project, you can begin to make the next version of your robot. Add a new XML file to the `Resources/Drawable` directory, naming it `RobotBackground_GradientOverlay.xml`.

Within this file, add the declaration for a `LayerDrawable` using the XML syntax of `<layer-list>`. Within this drawable, you will add two item subnodes to contain the following objects:

➤ **A reference to the `RobotBackground` drawable** gives you the basic, solid background for the robot `ImageButton`. Since you want a solid color for the initial background, this is the perfect resource to use. In addition, this is a good example of resource chaining. Even though this situation requires the merging of several drawables, you are not forced to hold the definition for a particular drawable in two different places.

➤ **A new shape object** forms the definition of the overlying gradient. Although this shape object will share the values for the corners and strokes of the original `RobotBackground` shape, this will have a special gradient to create the overlay effect. Next, to create a transparent effect, you add alpha blending information to the color hexadecimal string. In this case, you want a semitransparent white moving into a fully transparent white.

With these things in mind, add the two items to the `<layout-list>` node. When you're done, the result should look like Listing 12-23.

LISTING 12-23: Creating a layout list

```xml
<?xml version="1.0" encoding="utf-8" ?>
<layer-list xmlns:android="http://schemas.android.com/apk/res/android" >
    <item android:drawable="@drawable/robotbackground"></item>
    <item>
        <shape xmlns:android="http://schemas.android.com/apk/res/android"
            android:shape="rectangle">
            <corners android:radius="5dp" />
            <stroke android:width="1dp" android:color="#FFFFFF" />
            <gradient
                android:type="linear"
                android:startColor="#88FFFFFF"
                android:centerColor="#00FFFFFF"
                android:endColor="#00FFFFFF"
                android:angle="270"/>
        </shape>
    </item>
</layer-list>
```

Graphics_Drawables\Graphics_Drawables\Resources\Drawable\RobotBackground_GradientOverlay.xml

This listing is not too different from the previous examples, other than the fact that LayoutDrawable lets you define two simple drawables within one resource file. In regards to the new shape drawable, note the gradient's start, center, and end colors. As you can see, these colors specify the alpha transparency by adding two additional digits to the start of the hexadecimal string. Since a value of FF indicates opaque and 00 indicates transparent, this example uses a middle value of 88 as a start and becomes fully transparent somewhere near mid-image.

Now that the new drawable has been defined, go to the Main.axml file and copy the last row in the table layout. Paste in a new row, and adjust the background properties of each ImageButton so that they use the new drawable as their background. Listing 12-24 shows the updated row values.

LISTING 12-24: Defining the robot background gradient overlay in table view

```xml
<TableRow>
    <ImageButton android:src="@drawable/androidrobot" android:layout_margin="2dp"
        android:background="@drawable/robotbackground_gradientoverlay" />
    <ImageButton android:src="@drawable/androidrobot" android:layout_margin="2dp"
        android:background="@drawable/robotbackground_gradientoverlay" />
    <ImageButton android:src="@drawable/androidrobot" android:layout_margin="2dp"
        android:background="@drawable/robotbackground_gradientoverlay" />
    <ImageButton android:src="@drawable/androidrobot" android:layout_margin="2dp"
        android:background="@drawable/robotbackground_gradientoverlay" />
</TableRow>
```

Graphics_Drawables\Graphics_Drawables\Resources\Layout\Main.axml

After you add these items, run the application and check out the final result. You should see a new version of robot that looks stylistic, as if it has depth (see Figure 12-9).

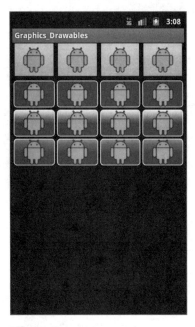

FIGURE 12-9

Case 5: Interacting with a Custom Drawable

Finally, the latest model of the robot army is visually perfect. When you look at the previous iterations, you can see that the robots' appearance has improved significantly. Now it is time to put on the finishing touches — giving the robots life so that they can interact with the device user.

As a way to help improve the utility of the robots, you want them to respond to being prodded by a finger. Specifically, you want them to give a visual cue that they have been pressed by updating the background color of the appropriate robot. Even though you could use a code-based approach by adding event handlers in C# to respond to the OnTouchEvent, you can do this in a much simpler and XML-based way by using the StateList drawable.

The StateList drawable, much like LayerDrawable, serves as a container for other drawables. Unlike LayerDrawable, StateList does not draw all the drawables contained within it at all times. Rather, it contains the logic to selectively draw the specific drawable items that satisfy certain predefined conditions.

 Whereas a LayerDrawable *acts like an array, a* StateList *acts much like a C# switch or series of* if *statements. When conditions are satisfied, the drawable associated with that switch is drawn. However, unlike a switch, several different cases can be true at the same time, resulting in multiple drawables being drawn.*

A `StateList` is defined using the `<selector>` tag. Just as with `LayerDrawable`, `StateList` uses the `<item>` subnode to define what drawables are part of the list. These items have several custom attributes specific to `StateList` that allow the developer to check for certain conditions. Table 12-3 shows the different possible conditions that may be checked against.

TABLE 12-3: State List Conditions

CONDITION	DESCRIPTION
state_pressed	Toggles if the item has been pressed
state_focused	Toggles if the item has focus by being highlighted via trackball or D-pad
state_selected	Toggles if the item is in a selected state, as with tabs or menus
state_checkable	Toggles if the item is checkable
state_checked	Toggles if the item has been checked
state_enabled	Toggles if the item can receive touch events
state_window_focused	Toggles if the item is in the foreground

Using these attributes, a developer has a great deal of flexibility in creating complex drawing behaviors. Each item can have any number of condition attributes. In addition, remember that you can specify behavior if the condition is true or if the condition is false. This gives you almost 100 different options that you can test for!

To give the newest model of the robot army a bit of life, you need to accomplish two things.

➤ First, you need to create a couple of extra resources that will represent a robot's "pressed" state.

➤ Next, you need to add the new `StateList` drawable to the code base, linking the appropriate drawables to the appropriate state conditions.

Within the `GraphicsDrawables_RobotArmy` project, navigate to the `Resources/Drawable` directory and make a copy of `RobotBackground.xml`, renaming it `RobotBackground2.xml`. Within the new file, alter the background color of the shape drawable to a color of your choice. You can do this by changing the `android:color` property of the `<solid>` node in the shape XML declaration. In this case, you use the color `#E01B4C` to give the robot image a red background.

Next, make a copy of `RobotBackground_GradientOverlay.xml`, naming it `RobotBackground_GradientOverlay2.xml`. You want to modify this file slightly so that the first shape in the list refers to the newly created background, `RobotBackground2`. If you wanted to avoid repeating code, you could refactor the gradient overlay background so that the second shape in each referred to the same drawable in a separate XML drawable file. However, for the sake of simplicity, leave the markup as is for this example.

With these things in place, you now have the appropriate resource chains set up so that you can clearly define the expected behavior. Thanks to the reusability of resource layouts, these modifications make for a clean, simple layout for the `StateList`.

Add a final drawable to the `Resources/Drawable` directory called `RobotBackground_StateAware`
`.xml`. Within this file, create two item nodes. The first item node should be active when there is no
pressed state, and the other should be active when pressed. Within each item, assign the correct
background drawable to its matching state representation. Listing 12-25 shows the proper declaration for the `StateList` drawable.

LISTING 12-25: Creating a state list

```
<?xml version="1.0" encoding="utf-8" ?>
<selector xmlns:android="http://schemas.android.com/apk/res/android" >
    <item android:drawable="@drawable/robotbackground_gradientoverlay"
        android:state_pressed="false"/>
    <item android:drawable="@drawable/robotbackground_gradientoverlay2"
        android:state_pressed="true"/>
</selector>
```

Graphics_Drawables\Graphics_Drawables\Resources\Drawable\RobotBackground_StateAware.xml

As shown in the listing, the first gradient overlay drawable is the default state of the robot
`ImageButton`. However, when pressed, the second gradient overlay drawable becomes active, high-
lighting the robot in red.

For the last step, update the `Main.axml` file to include a new series of robots. Copy the previous row,
and paste in the new row of robots, updating the background property of these robots to use the
`RobotBackground_StateAware` drawable. When you are done, the code should look like Listing
12-26, which depicts the final row's XML syntax.

LISTING 12-26: Defining the robot background state aware in table view

```
<TableRow>
    <ImageButton android:src="@drawable/androidrobot" android:layout_margin="2dp"
        android:background="@drawable/robotbackground_stateaware" />
    <ImageButton android:src="@drawable/androidrobot" android:layout_margin="2dp"
        android:background="@drawable/robotbackground_ stateaware" />
    <ImageButton android:src="@drawable/androidrobot" android:layout_margin="2dp"
        android:background="@drawable/robotbackground_ stateaware" />
    <ImageButton android:src="@drawable/androidrobot" android:layout_margin="2dp"
        android:background="@drawable/robotbackground_ stateaware" />
</TableRow>
```

Graphics_Drawables\Graphics_Drawables\Resources\Layout\Main.axml

Finally, launch the application and test the results. The last two rows in the application should
appear identical. However, when you press any individual robot in the last row, it alters its color to
the second drawable's settings. Figure 12-10 displays the expected result if the second robot in the
last row is pressed.

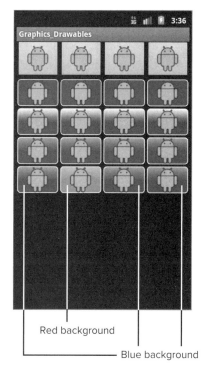

Red background

Blue background

FIGURE 12-10

SUMMARY

Graphics on the Android platform have the flexibility to accomplish tasks that range from simple, such as adding shaders and overlays, to complex, such as creating a fully animated 2D interaction. Despite this range of flexibility, Android's graphics story is quite unified. At the most basic level, working with graphics on Android essentially means working with views, resources, and primitives. All other, more advanced interactions build on this firm foundation, creating a full story.

One of the biggest strengths of Android graphics is their ability to generate CSS-like capabilities, using XML declarations as a way to generate separate, functional graphic units that can be easily applied and referenced throughout the entire application. This chapter has explored many different concepts:

➤ You have learned when to use the `Canvas` object versus when to use Android drawables.

➤ You have learned about performance considerations when utilizing different resources and various methods of keeping your memory footprint low.

➤ You have learned how to make custom animations on an Android device and also the basics of creating updating loops that are used in many game-development scenarios.

➤ You have learned how to handle different threading situations in Android and the appropriate time to use each different tool at your disposal.

➤ You have learned how to create custom drawables via XML syntax.

➤ You have learned how to reuse drawable declarations and create CSS-like styles to apply globally to your application.

➤ You have learned how to use compound drawable types to quickly handle state, image overlays, and other complex drawable interactions.

Finally, you have learned the foundations of how to begin using Android graphics in a real and intricate way. Even though graphics in general is a vast subject, using the information found in this chapter, you can begin building your graphics education to include many topics that were not covered here, such as 3D animation, animation drawables, and maintaining frame rates in game loops.

13

Working with Location Information

WHAT'S IN THIS CHAPTER?

➤ Understanding location-based services

➤ Choosing a location provider

➤ Finding a device's location

➤ Using geocoding to convert an address into a latitude and longitude

➤ Using reverse geocoding to convert a latitude and longitude into an address

➤ Configuring proximity alerts

➤ Using Google Maps

The display of location-specific information such as maps, addresses, and points of interest is a natural feature for mobile devices such as Android. Outside of some niche markets, location-specific information has never had great success on the desktop, primarily because a desktop PC is stuck in a single location. Mobile devices, on the other hand, are carried wherever the user goes. Therefore, as GPS technology has become smaller and cheaper, it has found its way into the cell phone market.

When smartphones appeared, their mapping and location applications were a couple of the key selling features — a perfect example of the possibilities presented by a multitouch user interface. Figure 13-1 shows the basic map application in an HTC EVO 4G.

Few other mobile devices had previously made navigating maps as elegant as the pinch-to-zoom, pinch-to-pan operation of maps on the Android screen.

FIGURE 13-1

This chapter shows you how to incorporate that same user experience for location and mapping into your own Mono for Android applications.

UNDERSTANDING LOCATION BASICS

Before you start looking at the mapping capabilities of Android and Mono for Android, here are some mapping terms that are used throughout this chapter:

➤ **Latitude:** The Y value of a location (90 to −90 degrees north to south).

➤ **Longitude:** The X value of a location (180 to −180 degrees east to west).

➤ **Heading:** Compass direction expressed in degrees (0 to 360).

➤ **GPS:** Global Positioning System. A collection of satellites using radio signals to enable Earth-based receivers to determine their location with a high degree of accuracy.

➤ **Geocoding:** Resolving a search string (such as an address, business, or landmark name) to a geographic location (latitude/longitude).

➤ **Reverse geocoding:** Finding the "human-readable" address for a specific latitude/longitude location.

Mono for Android provides easy access to these and other services to determine the user's location and heading and to map these services.

Determining Location

The location of a device is expressed in latitude and longitude and is typically determined by a GPS device. Consumer GPS devices were previously limited to bulky car navigation systems but are now small enough to fit inside a cell phone. These GPS services in a phone can fall into the following areas:

➤ Devices can calculate location information using cell tower triangulation. Using cell tower triangulation tends to provide a general area response; however, it is fairly low power.

➤ Some devices have dedicated GPS hardware within the device. The dedicated GPS hardware provides the most accuracy; however, it also uses the most power.

➤ There are services that will perform a lookup based on WiFi and known geographic location.

This means that a large proportion of Android OS devices have some sort of location services capability that you can program against.

Because Android uses different technologies to determine the device's position, the data's availability and accuracy can vary widely. The accuracy of this data depends on what technology is in the device. Devices with GPS capability can determine a very accurate latitude/longitude position under the right conditions (usually outdoors with a clear view of the sky). When no GPS is available and cell tower or wireless network information is used, the data is much less accurate. Each different data source offers a differing level of accuracy, from a few feet to a few miles.

Android location-enabled applications have options in performing location lookups. The applications will consider the accuracy of the data they receive to ensure they don't present misleading information. Thankfully, Android provides a `Criteria` class. This class allows the system to best determine the location provider to use based on the needs of the application.

Location-Based Data Interruptions

Sometimes Android is unable to provide data for several reasons:

➤ A GPS reading cannot be taken because the user is inside or otherwise out of range of GPS signals.

➤ Other location providers cannot be accessed, such as cell towers or WiFi network information.

➤ The user has prevented the device from supplying data to your application. To prevent applications from accessing a user's location without his or her knowledge, the application asks the user's permission upon installation before sending the data to your application. This location preference is stored within the `AndroidManifest.xml` file.

➤ The user has disabled location services. For privacy or battery-saving reasons, location services can be turned off in Settings. You should always check whether location services are available and for any error condition (including the user's denying access) before using location data in your code. It is possible to determine if location services are available. If they have been turned off and your application attempts to access location data, a message is displayed to prompt the user to turn Location Manager back on.

Using Location-Based Services

Location-based services (LBS) is a general term that encompasses all the technologies associated with the device's location. Android provides two main LBS components:

➤ **Location Manager** provides options when working with LBS. Typically, developers program to the Location Manager, and it communicates with the various providers installed on the device. With the Location Manager, a developer can do the following:

➤ Determine the device's current location.

➤ Track the device's movement.

➤ Interact with the various Location Providers on the device.

➤ Interact with proximity alerts. This includes detecting when the device moves into and out of a defined proximity.

➤ **Location Providers** represent the different location-finding technologies.

Configuring Location-Based Applications on the Emulator

Obtaining the location of a device depends on the device providing the necessary support. Unfortunately, the Android emulator does not have this hardware. Luckily, the emulator provides the capabilities to test location-based applications without device hardware. The emulator lets a developer work with emulated Location Providers and allows the developer to test applications without a physical device.

DDMS is the Dalvik Debug Monitoring Service. It provides debugging services and is provided by the Android SDK. Some of the services that DDMS provides are device screen capture, logging information, thread and heap information, location spoofing, and other debugging services. In this chapter, we are interested in the location data spoofing capabilities of DDMS. The location spoofing is available on the Emulator Control tab.

Figure 13-2 shows the Manual tab in the DDMS, which allows the developer to use specific latitude/longitude pairs. This is location data spoofing.

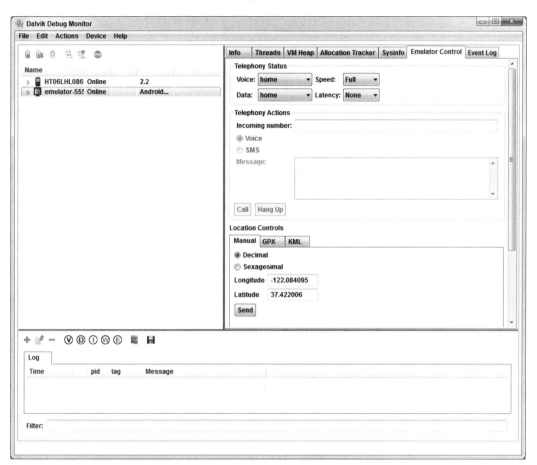

FIGURE 13-2

There are other ways to configure the DDMS. Figure 13-3 shows the configuration using the Keyhole Markup Language (KML) tab. As soon as the points are loaded, selecting a point allows the emulator to simulate being at that location. In addition, it is possible to simulate being at a series of locations sequentially.

FIGURE 13-3

KML is a file format that is used to describe geographic data. This data can be used inside many of Google's applications. In this case, KML data is used within the Android emulator. KML is an XML-defined format.

To see the KML setup file that is a part of this chapter's download, look in the kml/test.kml *file. The chapter download is available at* www.wrox.com.

SELECTING A LOCATION PROVIDER

As noted earlier in the chapter, Android devices can use multiple technologies to determine the device's current location. These technologies vary according to the device. Each technology has capabilities that function differently in terms of power consumption, accuracy, device heading, altitude, and other items.

To get an instance of a specific provider, calling `LocationManager`'s `.GetProvider` method and passing the provider's name returns an instance:

```
String providerName = LocationManager.GpsProvider;
LocationProvider gpsProvider;
String serviceString = Context.LocationService;
lm = (LocationManager)GetSystemService(serviceString);
gpsProvider = (lm.GetProvider(providerName));
```

This can be useful for obtaining the features and abilities of a given provider.

Determining Which Providers Are Available

The `LocationManager` class provides the `LocationManager.GpsProvider` and `LocationManager` `.NetworkProvider` static string constants for common Location Providers. Android devices may have any provider. To obtain a list of all enabled providers on the device, make the following call:

```
IList<string> providers = lm.GetProviders(true);
```

Finding Location Providers with Criteria

The providers are typically different on different Android devices. Therefore, it's unlikely that a developer will want to hard-code with only one specific provider. It's more common to use a set of criteria that are passed to Android and then have Android determine the best provider to use.

The `Criteria` class is used to request a provider that most accurately meets the application's requirements. The criteria can be set according to the following:

➤ **Accuracy of the location**

➤ **Desired power requirements**

➤ **Altitude:** Does the provider provide altitude information?

➤ **Bearing/heading:** Does the provider provide bearing/heading information?

➤ **Speed:** Does the provider provide speed information?

➤ **Cost:** Is there a financial cost?

Code Listing 13-1 creates a `Criteria` class, sets its values, and uses it to get location updates.

LISTING 13-1: Finding location providers based on criteria

```
cr = new Criteria();
cr.Accuracy = Accuracy.Coarse;
cr.PowerRequirement = Power.Low;
cr.AltitudeRequired = false;
cr.BearingRequired = false;
cr.SpeedRequired = false;
cr.CostAllowed = true;
String serviceString = Context.LocationService;
lm = (LocationManager)GetSystemService(serviceString);
bestProvider = lm.GetBestProvider(cr, false);
lm.RequestLocationUpdates(bestProvider, 5000, 500f, this);
```

You can find this code in the LocationListener project.

In this case, the activity must implement `Android.Locations.ILocationListener`. Listing 13-2 shows the methods that the activity implements:

LISTING 13-2: Implementing Android locations

```
public void OnLocationChanged(Location location)
{
    this.RunOnUiThread(() => tvLat.Text = location.Latitude.ToString());
    this.RunOnUiThread(() => {
        tvLon.Text = location.Longitude.ToString();
        GetAddress(location.Latitude, location.Longitude);
    });
}

public void OnProviderDisabled(string provider)
{
}

public void OnProviderEnabled(string provider)
{
}

public void OnStatusChanged(string provider, Availability status, Bundle extras)
{
}
```

You can find this code in the LocationListener project.

To get location information, the application needs access to the location permissions. This can be set by selecting the entries in the project's Required Permissions interface, as shown in Figure 13-4. The figure shows the project properties for setting `AssemblyManifest.xml`.

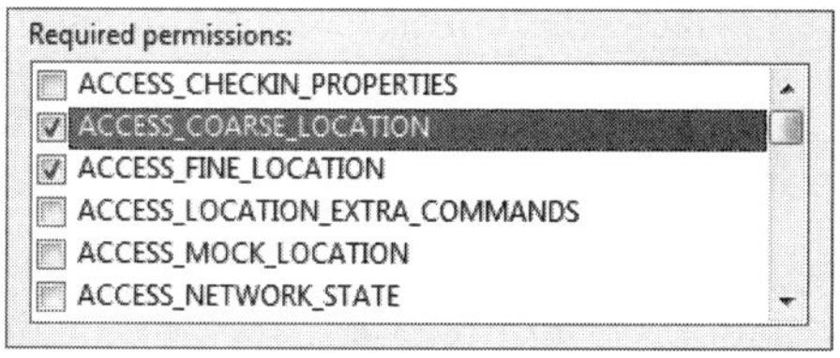

FIGURE 13-4

Additionally, the permission issue can be set directly in the `AndroidManifest.xml` file:

```
<uses-permission android:name="android.permission.ACCESS_FINE_LOCATION" />
<uses-permission android:name="android.permission.ACCESS_COARSE_LOCATION" />
```

> *The* `ACCESS_FINE_LOCATION` *permission uses more battery than the* `ACCESS_COARSE_LOCATION` *permission.*

If there is a need to stop listening for a location, the call to `.RemoveUpdates()` stops the location updates:

```
lm.RemoveUpdates(this);
```

GEOCODING

This section describes the two types of geocoding:

➤ **Forward geocoding** is the process of obtaining a latitude and longitude from an address.

➤ **Reverse geocoding** is the process of obtaining an address from a latitude and longitude.

Forward Geocoding

Forward geocoding, also just called geocoding, allows a street address to be translated into a pair of latitude/longitude map coordinates. This information can be used with map-based activities, services, and other location-based applications and activities.

> *Geocoding lookups are done over the Internet. Because of this, the application must get permission. This is done by adding the Internet permission in the* `AssemblyManifest.xml` *file in the project. The setting is as follows:*
>
> ```
> <uses-permission android:name="android.permission.INTERNET"/>
> ```

Listing 13-3 shows some sample code to perform forward geocoding. The user must provide an address. In this case, the user puts data into an EditView. The Geocoder class performs the lookup and returns a list of Address objects from the call to GetFromLocationName. GetFromLocationName returns a list with a maximum number of address objects. The address object list that is returned contains as much information as can be returned. This information might include latitude and longitude as well as the other pieces of information that might be in the Address object.

LISTING 13-3: Forward geocoding

```
//There is a bug in the emulator that results in an error.
//This code works properly on a device.
var add = Convert.ToString(et.Text);
Geocoder geocoder = new Geocoder(this, Java.Util.Locale.Default);
IList<Android.Locations.Address> result = geocoder.GetFromLocationName(add, 10);
if (result != null)
{
    tvLat.Text = "Latitude: " + result[0].Latitude.ToString();
    tvLon.Text = "Longitude: " + result[0].Longitude.ToString();
}
```

You can find this code in the GeoCode project.

If the data that GetFromLocationName method returns is null, no data could be found based on the address that was input.

Forward geocoding is performed synchronously and runs over the data connection. Because it runs synchronously, the calling thread is blocked. With slow data connections, this can cause an issue, and the user may see the Force Close dialog box. Instead of confusing the user with this message, consider performing the address lookup in some type of background thread or service.

Figure 13-5 shows the output of a geocode lookup for an address.

Reverse Geocoding

Reverse geocoding is the process of getting physical location information based on latitude and longitude coordinates. To perform this lookup, a program passes a latitude and longitude to the geocoder's .GetFromLocation method. This method returns a list of addresses that match the location. The list of addresses increases from most specific to least specific. Listing 13-4 exemplifies this process:

FIGURE 13-5

LISTING 13-4: Reverse geocoding

```
IList<Address> al;
Geocoder geoc = new Geocoder(this, Java.Util.Locale.Default);
al = geoc.GetFromLocation(Lat, Lon, 10);
Addresstv.Text = String.Empty;

if (al != null)
{
    for(int i = 0; i < al.Count; i++)
    {
        Addresstv.Text += String.Format("Location #{0}" +
                System.Environment.NewLine, i + 1);
        if (!String.IsNullOrEmpty(al[i].GetAddressLine(0)) )
                Addresstv.Text += al[i].GetAddressLine(0) +
                System.Environment.NewLine;
            if (!String.IsNullOrEmpty(al[i].GetAddressLine(1)))
                Addresstv.Text += al[i].GetAddressLine(1) +
                System.Environment.NewLine;
            if (!String.IsNullOrEmpty(al[i].Locality))
                Addresstv.Text += al[i].Locality + System.Environment.NewLine;
            if (!String.IsNullOrEmpty(al[i].PostalCode))
```

continues

LISTING 13-4 *(continued)*

```
                Addresstv.Text += al[i].PostalCode +
                System.Environment.NewLine;
        }
    }
    else
    {
        Addresstv.Text = "No addresses found.";
    }
```

LocationListener\LocationListener\Activity1.cs

The list of addresses that is returned is populated with as much data as is known about the location. Multiple addresses are returned, each with various degrees of specificity. For example, one address may have a street, city, state, and zip code. The next may have only the city, state, and zip code. The next may have only the city. This could go on until only the country is returned, as shown in Figure 13-6.

FIGURE 13-6

CONSTRUCTING PROXIMITY ALERTS

Applications often need to know when a user or device moves into a specified area or passes a certain proximity threshold. So when a user moves into or out of the general area of a certain location, an alert should be fired to let the system/application know.

To set up an alert for proximity, you need the following:

➤ Latitude and longitude of a center point

➤ Radius from that point

➤ Time period for the alert

When the device moves across the boundary defined by the radius and within the time frame specified, the alert is fired.

Listing 13-5 sets up a proximity with a radius and permanent time frame.

LISTING 13-5: Configuring proximity alerts

```
private static String MYPROXIMITY = "com.monodroid.alert";
protected override void OnCreate(Bundle bundle)
{
    base.OnCreate(bundle);
    SetContentView(Resource.Layout.Main);
    Button button = FindViewById<Button>(Resource.Id.MyButton);
    button.Click += delegate { SetProximityAlert(); };
}

private void SetProximityAlert() {

    String locService = Context.LocationService;
    LocationManager locationManager;
    locationManager = (LocationManager)GetSystemService(locService);
    double lat = 35.89988475;
    double lng = -84.12312175;
    float radius = 100f; // meters
    long expiration = -1; // do not expire

    Intent intent = new Intent(this, typeof(RecieveProximityMessages));
    PendingIntent proximityIntent = PendingIntent.GetBroadcast(this, -1,
        intent, 0);
    locationManager.AddProximityAlert(lat, lng, radius, expiration,
    proximityIntent);
    IntentFilter filter = new IntentFilter(MYPROXIMITY);
    RegisterReceiver(new ReceiveProximityMessages(), filter);
}
```

ProximityAlerts\ProximityAlerts\Activity1.cs.

When the proximity is triggered by a location change, a message is sent to a class that inherits from `BroadcastReceiver`. This call then processes the message. In this case, a `Toast` is sent to the UI. Many other things could be done; Listing 13-6 is just one example:

LISTING 13-6: Proximity alerts BroadcastReceiver

```
[BroadcastReceiver(Name = "com.monodroid.alert")]
public class ReceiveProximityMessages : BroadcastReceiver
{
public override void OnReceive(Context context, Intent intent)
{
```

continues

LISTING 13-6 *(continued)*

```
    String locService = Context.LocationService;
    LocationManager locationManager;
    locationManager = (LocationManager)context.GetSystemService(locService);
    String key = LocationManager.KeyProximityEntering;
    Boolean entering = intent.GetBooleanExtra(key, false);
    ShowToast(context, entering);
}
void ShowToast(Context context, bool entering)
{
    var text = "Entering: " + entering.ToString();
    Toast.MakeText(context, text, ToastLength.Short).Show();
}
}
```

ProximityAlerts\ProximityAlerts\Receiver1.cs.

USING GOOGLE MAPS

To include Google Maps in your application, you need to download both Google APIs for Android and create a virtual device that targets the Android OS with the Google APIs.

First, navigate to your Android SDK location, go to Tools, and run the Android file. This is the Android SDK and AVD Manager you have used in the past. Select Available Packages and select the Google APIs by Google Inc. for the relevant API level you want to target. An example is shown in Figure 13-7.

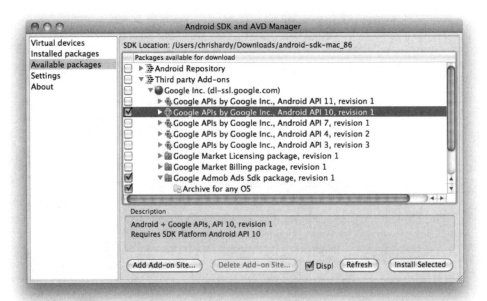

FIGURE 13-7

Once all that is installed, create a virtual device using the Google API as the target, as shown in Figure 13-8. Once this is set up, you will need to have a Google Maps API key to use the maps in this application. You can download this from the Android developer website at `http://code`
`.google.com/android/maps-api-signup.html`.

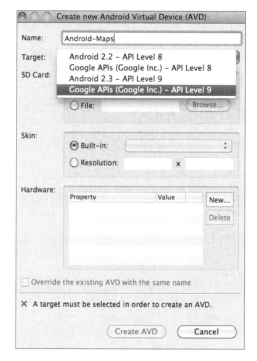

FIGURE 13-8

Without an API key, the Map view will not download the tiles used to display the map.

To obtain a key, you need to specify the MD5 fingerprint of the certificate used to sign your application. Generally, you will sign your application using two certificates — a default debug certificate and a production certificate. The following sections explain how to obtain the MD5 fingerprint of each signing certificate used for your application.

Getting Your Development/Debugging MD5 Fingerprint

With Mono for Android, each application will be signed with a default debug certificate unique to that application. To view map tiles while debugging you will need to obtain a Maps API key registered via the MD5 fingerprint of the debug certificate.

Typically the debug keystore is stored in the following location:

➤ **Windows Vista/7:** `C:\Users\[USERNAME]\AppData\Local\Xamarin\Mono for Android\`
   `debug.keystore`

➤ **OSX:** `/Users/[USERNAME]/.local/share/Xamarin/Mono for Android/debug.keystore`

This location is created when you first deploy any Mono for Android application, so make sure that you do this first before trying to create a MD5 fingerprint.

To find the MD5 fingerprint of your debug certificate, use the `keytool` command from your Java installation, as shown here:

```
keytool -list -alias androiddebugkey -keystore debug.keystore -storepass android
-keypass android
```

Getting Your Production/Release MD5 Fingerprint

Before you sign your application for release, you will need to obtain a Maps API key using the MD5 fingerprint for your release certificate.

You will need to create the certificate for yourself when creating a release build by using the following command (modify as needed). This will ask you to provide information about the certificate and to give passwords for the keystore and alias.

```
keytool -genkey -v -keystore my-release-key.keystore -alias my-android-alias
-keyalg RSA -keysize 2048 -validity 10000
```

Find the MD5 fingerprint using the `keytool` command and specifying the `-list` parameter and the keystore and alias you will use to sign your release application.

```
keytool -list -alias my-android-alias -keystore my-android-keystore
```

You will be prompted for your keystore and alias passwords before the MD5 fingerprint is returned. More information about signing your application for the Android Market can be found in Chapter 16.

Creating the Maps-Based Activity

The Android maps library is included in Mono for Android as an assembly file that you can add called `Mono.Android.GoogleMaps`. Since Maps require the use of the Internet and a `uses-library` tag, these technicalities are handled for you in the `GoogleMaps` assembly with the following assembly attributes:

```
[assembly: UsesPermission (Name = "android.permission.INTERNET")]
[assembly: UsesLibrary (Name = "com.google.android.maps")]
```

The maps package as described here is not part of the standard Android open source project. It is provided within the Android SDK by Google and is available on most Android devices. However, be aware that because it is a nonstandard package, an Android device may not feature this particular library.

Now you will want to create an activity that uses a map. When a map is used in an activity, the activity must use the MapActivity as a subclass. This class will take care of starting and stopping the location services for your map and the life cycle of the activity. You can have only one map activity per process running as running multiple map processes can cause unwanted issues. When you subclass an activity with a MapActivity, you will need implement the IsRouteDisplayed method. This is shown in Listing 13-7.

LISTING 13-7: **Empty map activity**

```
using Android.App;
using Android.GoogleMaps;
using Android.OS;

namespace MapExample
{
    [Activity (Label = "MapExample", MainLauncher = true)]
    public class Activity1 : MapActivity
    {

        MapView mapView;

        protected override void OnCreate (Bundle bundle)
        {
            base.OnCreate (bundle);

            // Set our view from the "main" layout resource
            SetContentView (Resource.Layout.Main);

            mapView = FindViewById<MapView>(Resource.Id.mapView);

        }

        #region implemented abstract members of Android.GoogleMaps.MapActivity
        protected override bool IsRouteDisplayed {
            get {
                return false;
            }
        }
        #endregion
    }
}
```

MapExample\MapExample\Activity1.java

Creating a Map in a Layout File

If you run the preceding code, you will notice that no map is displayed. This is because, although we have told the activity it will include a map, the actual map has not been added yet. You can update the Main.axml layout file to include the MapView that you want to display. This is shown in Listing 13-8.

LISTING 13-8: Main.axml layout file

```xml
<?xml version="1.0" encoding="utf-8"?>
<LinearLayout xmlns:android="http://schemas.android.com/apk/res/android"
    android:orientation="vertical"
    android:layout_width="fill_parent"
    android:layout_height="fill_parent"
    >

    <com.google.android.maps.MapView
        android:id="@+id/mapView"
        android:layout_width="fill_parent"
        android:layout_height="fill_parent"
        android:enabled="true"
        android:clickable="true"
        android:apiKey="YourAPIKeyHere"
    />

</LinearLayout>
```

MapsExample\MapsExample\Resources\layout\Main.axml

As you can see from the final line in the `com.google.android.maps.MapView` tag, there's an attribute for an *apiKey*. This is where you need to enter the API key that was created earlier. Hit run and you will see something that looks like Figure 13-9.

FIGURE 13-9

Using the MapView Controller with an Overlay

The `MapView` has a `Controller` property that enables you to set the pan and zoom of the map programmatically. To do this, you have a few methods that you can utilize, such as `SetZoom`, which takes an integer between 1 (being the widest, most zoomed out) and 21 (being the closest, most zoomed in). This can be used by calling the following method:

```
mapView.Controller.SetZoom(5);
```

As well as controlling the zoom, you may want to focus on a particular area on a map; this can be done in two different ways.

➤ You can use the `SetCenter` method, which takes a `GeoPoint` parameter on the location you want to center the map.

➤ Alternatively, you can use the `AnimateTo` method, which again takes a `GeoPoint` parameter, but this will smoothly fly from the current location to the `GeoPoint` set rather than jumping straight to the location.

To display an item on a map, you will want to use an overlay that will go over the top of the current map to display useful information in your application. The Google Maps API provides a `MyLocationOverlay` for you to use, which places the current location of the user onto the overlay. To use this overlay, you would create a new instance of the `MyLocationOverlay` class. You can see this in Listing 13-9.

LISTING 13-9: MapOverlayExample layout file

```
using System;

using Android.App;
using Android.Content;
using Android.Runtime;
using Android.Views;
using Android.Widget;
using Android.OS;
using Android.GoogleMaps;

namespace MapOverlayExample
{
    [Activity (Label = "MapOverlayExample", MainLauncher = true)]
    public class Activity1 : MapActivity
    {
        MapView mapView;
        MyLocationOverlay myLocationOverlay;

        protected override void OnCreate (Bundle bundle)
        {
            base.OnCreate (bundle);

            // Set our view from the "main" layout resource
            SetContentView (Resource.Layout.Main);

            mapView = FindViewById<MapView>(Resource.Id.mapView);
            mapView.Controller.SetZoom(19);

            myLocationOverlay = new MyLocationOverlay (this, mapView);
            myLocationOverlay.RunOnFirstFix (() => {
                mapView.Controller.AnimateTo (myLocationOverlay.MyLocation);
```

continues

LISTING 13-9 *(continued)*

```
            });
            mapView.Overlays.Add (myLocationOverlay);
        }

        protected override void OnResume ()
        {
            base.OnResume ();

            myLocationOverlay.EnableMyLocation();
        }

        protected override void OnStop ()
        {
            base.OnStop ();

            myLocationOverlay.DisableMyLocation();
        }

        #region implemented abstract members of Android.GoogleMaps.MapActivity
        protected override bool IsRouteDisplayed {
            get {
                return false;
            }
        }
        #endregion
    }
}
```

MapOverlayExample\MapOverlayExample\Activity1.cs

 Since MyLocationOverlay *uses location data, do not forget to add in permissions for either* ACCESS_FINE_LOCATION *or* ACCESS_COARSE_LOCATION.

You can see that after we create the new myLocationOverlay object, we set up the method RunOnFirstFix; this will fire the event when the first location of the user is fixed. From here you will want to use the AnimateTo method to move the map to display the location of the current user. Since you will have a location for the current user from the overlay, you can use the MyLocation property from the overlay and pass this into the AnimateTo method.

Once the new overlay is created and set up, you can add this to the MapView overlays by using the Add method on the Overlays property. The OnResume and OnStop methods are used to start and stop searching for a location when the app is open and closed, respectively. Hit run and you should see something like Figure 13-10.

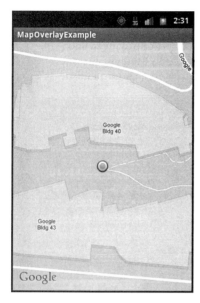

FIGURE 13-10

SUMMARY

This chapter looked at location-based services in Android. Location-based services are a natural fit for Android. Android devices are by definition mobile. Getting the current location allows an application to present the user with location-specific information. Along with the current location of the device, other forms of location-based services allow for presenting helpful information to the user, such as the approximate street address to speed up data entry. The chapter also looked into using the Google Maps API to provide maps to be utilized in applications and how this can be used to display a user's location. The topics covered in this chapter include:

➤ Using `ILocationListener` to get the device's location.

➤ Performing geocoding to convert an address into a latitude and longitude.

➤ Performing reverse geocoding to convert a latitude and longitude into an address.

➤ Using proximity alerts for when a user passes through a boundary.

➤ Using a map within an activity.

➤ Displaying a user location on a map using overlays.

14

Internationalization and Localization

Internationalization and localization are two different aspects of providing multilingual and multicultural support for software applications. Although the exact definitions of these two terms may vary, the two concepts can be broadly defined as follows:

➤   **Internationalization** refers to the process of globally enabling an application to handle multicultural settings without specifically designing to any particular locale.

➤   **Localization** refers to the effort of designing an application to cater to the needs of a specific locale by specifically targeting the desired locale via application code and settings adjustments.

Using internationalization, you enable your application to handle a number of different language and cultural scenarios. In many ways, you can think of internationalization as enabling multiple-language support on more of a global application level. In the context of Mono for Android, you can largely achieve this by leveraging the tools within the .NET Framework. Internationalization endeavors may include the following:

➤   Making list storing sensitive to language

➤   Adhering to local specific formatting on different data units such as date and time

➤ Adjusting for differences in symbology for items such as currency and general numbers

➤ Representing measurements such as temperature, weight, and distance in appropriate units

➤ Appropriately accepting input and displaying addresses, telephone numbers, and government identification numbers

➤ Properly accepting multiple text encoding formats as inputs

Using localization, you can fine-tune your application to target an individual culture. In conjunction with tooling in the .NET Framework and therefore Mono for Android, the Android architecture is designed to ease the difficulty of this process. Localization endeavors may include the following:

➤ Identifying text areas and displaying them in the target language

➤ Customizing your layout and image-based text displays to match the target locale

➤ Adjusting tooltips and application flow to match the locale

➤ Adjusting the entire user interface to cater to a specific locale

When speaking broadly of both internationalization and localization, people often use the term globalization. Since these two concepts often overlap, it is often more concise to use this term. In fact, the .NET Framework does just this via its namespace, `System.Globalization`, which is used to create multilingual applications.

Figure 14-1 shows the home menu of an Android phone under different localization settings. Using this chapter, you can achieve similar results in your applications and increase the level of exposure that your application has on the growing Android Market!

FIGURE 14-1

The terms internationalization and localization are often shortened to i18n and L10n, respectively. The numbers refer to the number of characters between the first and last letter of each word.

SELECTING A LOCALIZATION STRATEGY

Before you begin to localize your application, you should consider several factors. In a perfect world, we would have the time and resources to localize for every culture and locale. Unfortunately, this is not the case. In many cases, we have to make precise and informed decisions when choosing what to target for localization. Localization can give your application more exposure. However, the key to a successful localization is maintaining the balance between supporting as many users as possible and keeping your initial development time and overall development overhead low.

To keep that balance, you may want to ask yourself several questions before you begin investing in localization:

➤ **What is the locale of your target audience(s)?** From the outset of your application development process, you should have a general idea of who your target customers are. Are they specific to a particular locale? Do specific features of your ideal customer make you want to target a locale?

➤ **What exposure do you expect for your application?** Beyond the metrics found in the Android Market, you should consider the avenues you will use to advertise your app. In addition, consider the locales that your advertising partners support so that you can match those as well to maximize your advertising initiatives.

➤ **Does your application limit itself to particular locales?** Some application types do not cater to every locale. Often there are cultural, economic, or political reasons why an app would be more successful in some areas than in others. Be wary of your app's subject matter, cost, and specificity to a culture as you consider what locales to support.

➤ **How will your application's behavior vary from locale to locale?** Page layout, text directions, and even interface behavior expectations can vary from culture to culture. If you intend to fully support a different locale, take time to understand these differences, and adjust your application accordingly.

➤ **What resources can you utilize that are locale-neutral?** If you are working on an app that has many different locales that you want to support, strive for locale-neutral resources. Simple ideas, such as avoiding images with static text, can save you a great deal of time and effort in the long run when you are supporting multiple locales.

➤ **What resources do you have at your disposal to provide localization services?** When working to provide full localization services for your application, it is easy to forget some of the finer points, such as the fact that you do not fluently speak the language for which you want to localize. Aligning with resources who fluently speak both your language and your target language will ensure not only that you support the target locale but also that you sound professional in doing so.

➤ **When someone tries to access your app from an unsupported locale, what does your application do?** It is impossible to accommodate every possibility. Rather than trying for the impossible, accept that there are points where your app will fail, and ensure that it will fail gracefully.

Finally, you would be remiss not to consider the Android operating system's current level of exposure. Although Android is rapidly gaining exposure across the globe, currently it does not have the same diversity as its competitors on other mobile platforms. Understanding who the key users of the Android operating system are will go a long way in helping you make your localization decisions. Here are a couple of good resources for mobile phone usage statics and locales:

➤ **AdMob Mobile Metrics:** `http://metrics.admob.com`

➤ **Nielsen data:** `http://blog.nielsen.com/nielsenwire`

UPDATING LANGUAGE AND REGIONAL SETTINGS

To test localization, you need to be familiar with the process of updating the language and regional settings on your devices. The steps to update these settings differ, depending on whether you are using an emulated device or testing on an actual hardware device.

You can change your local and regional settings on your physical Android device by accessing the System Settings ➪ Language & Keyboard screen. Under this screen you can set your language and region via the Select Language menu option. On this screen, the language name is displayed on the left, and the selected region, if any, is displayed in parentheses to the right of the language. You will notice that the user-friendly names, not the codes themselves, are displayed on this screen.

There are many other settings on the physical device that can apply to language and regional settings. In addition, different features and additions may have more or less support in this area, including dictionaries and custom keyboards.

When you are working with the emulator, the process of updating your language and regional settings is much simpler. On your emulator home screen, you can find an application named Custom Locale. Under this application, you will find a long list of different language and regional settings to choose from, listed by their regional codes. By doing a long press on any of these items, you update your device's settings. Figure 14-2 shows the process of updating your emulator.

Be sure to make a note of where this application is located on your menu, or it might be hard to find your way back.

By changing these settings, you affect how the Android OS and .NET display content and the formatting for some types. Thankfully, both use the same language and region naming conventions to delineate between these selections. Here are the two codes you need to change these settings:

➤ **Language code:** The two-letter ISO 639-1 code is the preferred method to identify languages. Common examples are en for English, ja for Japanese, es for Spanish, fr for French, and de for German.

➤ **Region code:** The two-character ISO 3166-1 code that identifies a region or locale that speaks a specific language. Examples are UK for the United Kingdom and US for the United States.

Combined, these two values create a locale. Although two countries may speak the same language, they may have different approaches to the spelling of common words or the formatting of data types, such as telephone numbers or addresses. This is why identifying the locale is important.

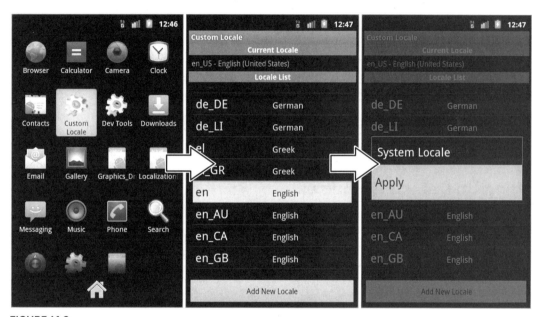

FIGURE 14-2

In addition to identifying locales by languages and regions, some areas have custom or special tags used to identify them. You can define custom locale tags within the emulator locale settings.

 Locale identifiers vary between .NET and the Android platform. In .NET, a locale is defined as <language>-<REGION>, as in en-US. In the Android OS, the formatting for a locale is often <language>-r<REGION>, as in en-rUS. This gets slightly more confusing when considering Java, which prefers an underscore as the delimiter between language and region. Additionally, most areas follow the convention of leaving the language code in lowercase and using uppercase for the region.

To learn more about the use of locale tags and other ISO standards, or to view a comprehensive list of codes, visit the International Organization for Standardization at www.iso.org.

UNDERSTANDING THE MECHANICS OF ANDROID LOCALIZATION

On the Android platform, the process of setting up for localization is simple, thanks to the adoption of a type of design by convention for localization purposes. This design allows you to quickly create locale-specific resource settings. In conjunction with the process of establishing default resources in your application, the localization process is fully extensible and also provides quite a bit of fail-safety.

CONVENTION VERSUS CONFIGURATION

If you're familiar with ASP.NET MVC, you should understand the concept of design by convention. It focuses on decreasing an application's complexity by establishing and maintaining known conventions or accepted standards rather than using complex configuration techniques. In ASP.NET MVC, this is accomplished using the provided folder structures and the framework when dealing with Models, Views, and Controllers. The Android operating system uses a similar approach for resource handling.

Setting Up Default Resources

The first step of supporting localization is to set up default resources for your application. Resources can be strings, graphics, layout patterns, sounds, or just about any other static files or data that your application requires. A resource is considered a default resource when it is located in a nonspecific default directory for that resource type. You can also consider these resources *locale-neutral* because, hopefully, they do not contain any locale-specific information.

 Keep in mind that if it is a resource, you can localize it. This is true of not only text but also images, views, and other resource types.

Having a default resource is critical, because the Android operating system uses default resources when it can find no other alternatives. If a resource is not found in a given scenario, the Android operating system throws an application exception. Considering the rate at which alternative Android devices are being created, this is the only way to provide a measure of fail-safety or, at the very least, an elegant failure.

Currently the Android operating system has several default folders to contain resources. None of these folders are required to exist in order for your application to run properly; they should only be added on an as-needed basis. Table 14-1 describes the most frequently used default folders for localization. By placing resources in these default folders, you can ensure that the Android operating system always has a source for that resource in situations where an unsupported locale is requested.

TABLE 14-1: Android Default Folders

FOLDER NAME	GENERAL USAGE
drawable/	Contains image files or XML files that are used for graphics that can be drawn on the screen.
layout/	Contains configuration files that specify different kinds of user interface layouts.
menu/	Contains configuration files that contain the definitions for the Options and Context menus and submenus.
values/	Contains XML files that specify basic values, such as string values, color settings, and general styles.
xml/	Contains miscellaneous XML files that can be read at runtime. Typically used in more user-defined contexts

 You can find more information about folder conventions by visiting `http://developer.android.com`*.*

Adding Localization Support

After the default resource folders are placed, you can begin adding support for additional locales. To have a resource that targets a specific device setting, you create another directory that contains the same name as the default directory and set specific text. The additional text used to target a specific setting is known as a configuration qualifier name. For localization purposes, Android uses a `<DirectoryName>-<Language>-r<region>` pattern for its naming convention.

In Figure 14-3, the layout directory has several different configurations: a default drawable folder, a drawable folder specifically targeting those whose language is set to English (en), and a drawable folder for those who not only speak French but also live in the region of France.

FIGURE 14-3

In this case, if the application requested `icon.png`, the Android runtime would select the specific folder that matched the device's current configuration. Assuming that your Android device was set to en-US, you would be served `icon.png` under the en directory. If your locale were set to fr-rCA, you would be served `icon.png` under the default `drawable` directory, because the locale would not match your device settings.

Resource Selection in Detail

When an Android application is run, the Android operating system attempts to select and load the resources that best match the Android device's settings and current configuration. This approach not only simplifies the process of supporting localization but also creates additional flexibility in the development process, because the developer can use a system of specificity when supporting localization.

Android uses the following process to determine the correct resource:

1. You request a resource from within the application.

2. Android finds every possible directory match for that resource and eliminates anything that conflicts with the device configuration.

3. If several possible matches are found, Android starts with the most specific directory and looks for the resource. Then it iterates through all available directories until the first match is found for the resource.

4. If no matches are found, Android falls back to the default resource.

5. If no default resources are found, Android throws an exception.

Although the folder-naming convention does simplify the process of adding support for other locales, several other configuration qualifier names target different application settings. Those settings may include different screen densities, screen orientation, and application modes. For every deviation from the default resource that you need to specifically target, you need to create an additional directory as well as an accompanying resource. As you might imagine, managing the number of deviations as well as fully understanding the resource selection process is critical.

Although this topic is beyond the scope of this section, Android documentation does define qualifier precedence. Since some qualifiers are ranked higher in consideration than others, in some situations more specific names could be outranked by names with higher qualifiers. See http://developer.android.com *for more information.*

One major drawback of using the directory names as a convention for identifying the correct resources is that it greatly limits your ability to organize resources in any other way. In addition, currently the Android operating system does not support subdirectories in these resources' subfolders.

SUPPORTING MULTIPLE LANGUAGES

Typically, when developers write applications without considering localization, they often hard-code string values within either the UI or the application code. With some applications, this can be a bad practice, because it can lead to some very painful refactoring if you have to localize a code base that is already complete. Furthermore, developers tend to bypass the localization process because it is perceived as additional work or seems to be harder to maintain. In this section, you will see that not only is the process of localizing strings simple, but it also can actually make your development process smoother.

Utilizing the Strings.xml File

To support easy translation of text values, you can use the strings configuration file located under `/Resources/Values/Strings.xml`. The `strings.xml` file lets you specify key-value pairs of strings. By using this file, you can separate the text to display from the actual application code. This approach lets you swap in different desired text or languages without having to modify the view or application code. The following code snippet is an example of the default `strings.xml` file in a new Mono for Android application:

```xml
<?xml version="1.0" encoding="utf-8"?>
<resources>
    <string name="hello">Hello World, Click Me!</string>
    <string name="app_name">Test</string>
</resources>
```

The `name` attribute acts as the key value to the string, and the text between the string tags is the actual text values. As your application is compiled, the key value of the string resources is added as a property of the special `Resources` class. This allows you to declaratively access your text values and also gives you compile-time checking for existing keys.

Although the `Strings.xml` file is a simple concept, you should keep in mind a few rules when adding values:

➤ When using a single or double quotation mark as the value for a given string, you must escape the character properly. You can accomplish this by using the backslash (\ ) as an escape character or by wrapping the entire text value in enclosing quotes that are not the same as the type of quote character you are trying to escape. Here are two examples of using this escape method:

```xml
<string name="Example1">Android\'s awesome!</string>
<string name="Example2">"Android's awesome!"</string>
```

➤ The `Strings.xml` file supports the use of some formatting tags, as shown in Table 14-2.

TABLE 14-2: Valid Formatting Tags within the String Value

STYLE	EXAMPLE
Bold text	`<b>This is bold text!</b>`
Italic text	`<i>This is italic text!</i>`
Underline text	`<u>This would be underlined!</u>`

➤ HTML-style comments, such as `<!-- This is a comment -->`, are permitted within the `Strings.xml` file as well.

Translating Text

In the first example of this chapter, we will walk through the process of creating a simple translation scenario. Starting with a default Mono for Android project in Visual Studio, open the `Strings.xml` file located under the `Resources/Values` directory. Modify this file so that it looks like this:

```xml
<?xml version="1.0" encoding="utf-8"?>
<resources>
    <string name="Hello">Hello, Mono for Android!</string>
```

```
            <string name="Goodbye">Goodbye, Mono for Android!</string>
      </resources>
```

Next, modify `Main.axml` by adding two button controls. These buttons will provide the mechanism by which to display our localized strings. For the time being, give one button the text value of `"Say Hello"` and the other button the text value of `"Say Goodbye"`. Upon completion, your code should look something like this:

```xml
<?xml version="1.0" encoding="utf-8"?>
<LinearLayout xmlns:android="http://schemas.android.com/apk/res/android"
      android:orientation="vertical"
      android:layout_width="fill_parent"
      android:layout_height="fill_parent">
<Button
      android:id="@+id/HelloButton"
      android:layout_width="fill_parent"
      android:layout_height="wrap_content"
      android:text="Say Hello"/>
    <Button
      android:id="@+id/GoodbyeButton"
      android:layout_width="fill_parent"
      android:layout_height="wrap_content"
      android:text="Say Goodbye"/>
</LinearLayout>
```

All snippets for this example can be found in `Localization01`.

Now that the controls are in place, you can write the application code to utilize the new string resources you have defined. In the `Activity1.cs` file, replace the `OnCreate` function with the following code:

```csharp
protected override void OnCreate(Bundle bundle)
{
      base.OnCreate(bundle);

      // Set our view from the "Main" layout resource
      SetContentView(Resource.Layout.Main);

      // Get our buttons from the layout resource,
      // and attach an event to it
      Button HelloButton = FindViewById<Button>(Resource.Id.HelloButton);
      HelloButton.Click += delegate {
          Toast.MakeText(this, Resource.String.Hello, ToastLength.Long).Show(); };

      Button GoodbyeButton = FindViewById<Button>(Resource.Id.GoodbyeButton);
      GoodbyeButton.Click += delegate {
          Toast.MakeText(this, Resource.String.Goodbye,
          ToastLength.Long).Show(); };
}
```

When you add event handlers to each button's `Click` event, the appropriate string values can be displayed in a small toast window. Notice that you can access your string's value by specifying the appropriate key using the special `Resource` class.

When everything is in place, run the example. You should see the default locale for your application, along with the two buttons you created. When you click the buttons, you see the screens shown in Figure 14-4.

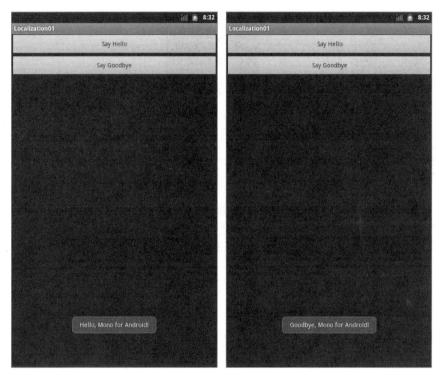

FIGURE 14-4

Now that the baseline is set up, you can begin adding localization support. Create another directory within the `Resources` directory, called `Values-es`. Within this directory, create a file called `Strings.xml`, and add the following content to that file. Now your application will support translations for devices whose language settings are set to `es`, the language code for Spanish:

```xml
<?xml version="1.0" encoding="utf-8"?>
<resources>
    <!--  The keyboard shortcut for the "¡" character is Alt+0161. -->
    <string name="Hello">¡Hola, Mono for Android!</string>
    <!--  The keyboard shortcut for the "ó" character is Alt+0243. -->
    <string name="Goodbye">¡Adiós, Mono for Android!</string>
</resources>
```

Now you can load your new application into your device. Before you open the application, change your device settings to use Spanish as your primary language via the appropriate methods discussed earlier. Then open your application and see its new, translated values (see Figure 14-5).

FIGURE 14-5

 Remember, when adding resources that are to be accessed via the Resource *class, as we did in this example, be sure to change their build action to* AndroidResource *so that they will be properly added to the build. You can do this by right-clicking the target resource, selecting Properties, and changing the build action from the configuration screen. Failing to do this will result in compilation errors or, in this case, utilization of the default resource rather than the one just added.*

At this point, you have added translation support for your application. By using the previously mentioned naming convention, you can begin adding support for other languages and locales. As with other resources, requests for a string value begin at the most specific directory and work to the most generic. If you have a key that is not located in a specific directory, but is located in your default, the Android OS loads the default key's value. This means that, although you have targeted a different locale via the more-specific Strings.xml file, you do not have to give a translation for every key in every file.

Translating Control Text

Now that we have established the process of assigning the Strings.xml file's values in the application code for simple toast messages, let's look at the process of adding localization support for different controls. As you might imagine, the process is very similar to what we used in the preceding examples.

You can add localized text to a control in two ways:

➤ Bind the resource text to an appropriate property on the control via the application code. This was shown in the example in the previous section.

➤ Use the control's XML layout to define the matching string key for the given property.

Starting from the `Localization01` example, we can begin adding support for localization in controls. In the preceding example, we introduced two button controls that would display a localized text message when clicked. However, the text on the buttons themselves was hard-coded, which requires our localized users to know what those buttons mean in English before they can get to their translated text. Let's fix this mistake.

For this example, add the following lines to the `Strings.xml` file. These items will be text source for our button text that is displayed when the application loads:

```
<string name="HelloButtonText">Hello</string>
<string name="GoodbyeButtonText">Goodbye</string>
```

If desired, we could set the control's text property in the application code. If we were to do so, it would look something like this:

```
Button HelloButton = FindViewById<Button>(Resource.id.HelloButton);
HelloButton.Text = Resource.@string.HelloButtonText;
```

The problem with this approach is that it is quite a bit of code to achieve a basic result. Furthermore, as you begin adding more controls to your page, your line count increases considerably, as does your maintenance cost.

The alternative approach is to use the control's XML configuration to specify the string key mapping to the given control's property. This binding is accomplished using the following syntax:

```
@[package_name:]<resource_type>/<resource_name>
```

In our case, the package name is unnecessary, because the resource is located in the same package as the one we are currently working in. Since we are referencing a text value in `Strings.xml`, the resource type is `String`. Finally, the resource name is the string key within the `Strings.xml` file we are looking for.

To localize the button text, modify the button's XML markup in the `Resources/Layout/Main .axml` file. Within the XML configuration, replace the hard-coded string value in the control's text property with the appropriate string key using the `@string/key` syntax. After you have done so, your code should look something like this:

```
<Button android:id="@+id/HelloButton"
    android:layout_width="fill_parent"
    android:layout_height="wrap_content"
    android:text="@string/HelloButtonText" />
<Button android:id="@+id/GoodbyeButton"
    android:layout_width="fill_parent"
    android:layout_height="wrap_content"
    android:text="@string/GoodbyeButtonText"/>
```

All snippets for this example can be found in `Localization02`.

If you were to run your code at this point, you would be greeted with a screen that looked very similar to the previous example, despite whatever localization settings you may have. By adding the following snippet to your `Resources/Values-es/Strings.xml` file, you add Spanish localization support for your button text:

```
<string name="HelloButtonText">Hola</string>
<string name="GoodbyeButtonText">Adiós</string>
```

When you have completed this step, you can change your phone's locale settings between en and es. Figure 14-6 shows the newly translated page.

Although the example in this section is specific to buttons, the process of binding resources to any control or any control property works in a similar fashion. By using the XML binding syntax or by simply binding via application code, you can localize almost every control in your application.

FIGURE 14-6

 As you are adding controls to your application, it is a good practice to proactively add localized strings for every text value. This not only ensures that you have full localization support, but also makes text resources and control configuration very easy to maintain.

LOCALIZING OTHER RESOURCES

As with strings, the process of adding localization support for other resources involves the same steps of creating the additional locale-specific resource, adding it to the appropriately named directory, and referencing the resource using the `Resource` special class or via the proper XML syntax. Because an Android resource can be anything from application strings to images to even views themselves, an Android developer has great flexibility in defining what resources load for what locales.

Keeping that in mind, pick up where you left off in the preceding example (or grab the `Localization02` download) so that you can begin the process of adding other localized resources. In the sample application, you will add two common images and their translated text captions to the screen. Before you start adding XML markup, however, you need to define the string keys and values you will use in the example.

ADDED TO /RESOURCES/VALUES/STRINGS.XML

```
<string name="RestaurantText">Restaurant</string>
<string name="FlagText">Flag</string>
```

ADDED TO /RESOURCES/VALUES-ES/STRINGS.XML

```
<string name="RestaurantText">El Restaurante</string>
<string name="FlagText">Bandera</string>
```

Now, it's time to add the controls to the application. Basically, you will add two images along with some descriptive text. For the sake of easy layout, these controls are contained in a table structure. Add the following code to `Resources/Layout/Main.axml`:

```
<TableLayout xmlns:android="http://schemas.android.com/apk/res/android"
     android:layout_width="fill_parent"
     android:layout_height="fill_parent">
<TableRow>
     <ImageView
          android:layout_height="wrap_content"
          android:layout_width="wrap_content"
          android:layout_margin="5dip"
          android:src="@drawable/flag" />
     <TextView android:id="@+id/tvFlag"
          android:layout_height="fill_parent"
          android:layout_width="wrap_content"
          android:text="@string/FlagText"
          android:gravity="center_vertical|center_horizontal"
          android:padding="3dip" />
</TableRow>
<TableRow>
     <ImageView
          android:layout_height="wrap_content"
          android:layout_width="wrap_content"
          android:layout_margin="5dip"
          android:src="@drawable/restaurant" />
     <TextView android:id="@+id/tvRestaurant"
          android:layout_height="fill_parent"
          android:layout_width="wrap_content"
          android:text="@string/RestaurantText"
          android:gravity="center_vertical|center_horizontal"
          android:padding="3dip" />
</TableRow>
</TableLayout>
```

All snippets for this example can be found in `Localization03`.

As you can see, the XML configuration contains two image controls that are looking for two images called `flag` and `restaurant`. Since your application will not run properly without those resources, add two appropriate images to the `Resources/Drawable` directory with those same names.

Once everything is in place, run your application in the emulator. You should see the screen shown in Figure 14-7.

For the sake of this example, assume that our target audience is not only Spanish speakers but also those who live in Spain. The locale setting for Spanish-speaking Spain is `es_ES`. Add a directory under the `Resources` directory called `Drawable-es-rES`. Finally, add an image of the Spanish flag to that directory, making sure that the image name and type mirror that of the flag image in the default directory.

The sample images `flag` *and* `restaurant` *and a copy of a Spanish flag image all can be found in the* `Localization03` *download for this chapter.*

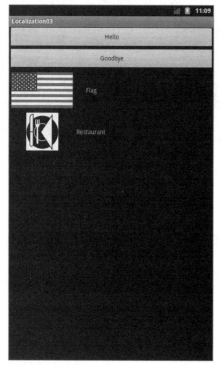

FIGURE 14-7

Now the application is ready to be tested. Run the application and change your locale to `es-ES`. After you do so, you should see the screen shown on the left of Figure 14-8. Notice that the text is in Spanish and that the screen displays the Spanish flag. Now, if you selected `es` as your choice language and left your locale at its default location (assuming that your default region is US), you would end up with an application that targets Spanish-speaking Americans. The image on the right shows what this configuration would look like. Notice that the American flag (our default resource) loaded because the flag in the `Drawable-es-rES` directory had a configuration that contradicted the default region of the device.

 As you are adding the flag images, be sure to set their content type to Android Resource.

This application displayed how you can achieve different and possibly unexpected results when unplanned locale settings are chosen. Also, keep in mind that even though we focused on image localization, *any* resource can be localized by using the Android folder-naming convention.

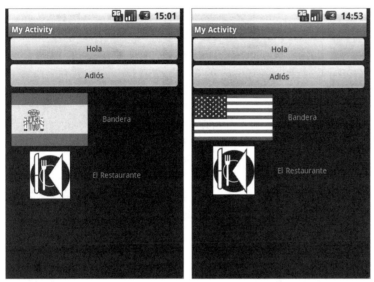

FIGURE 14-8

Localizing the Menu Icon and Application Name

In the Android OS, the menu icon and the application name are what you see when your application is on the home screen. The process of localizing that view is very simple.

For starters, localizing the icon follows the same pattern as localizing any other image. First, add a different image called Icon.png to a more specific locale directory that targets that locale. Next, the icon can be localized using the same @string/key syntax used in any controls in conjunction with the Activity attribute.

The application name can be localized within the Activity attribute as well. Modify the Activity attribute on your main activity class so that it mirrors the following code:

```
[Activity(Label = "@string/app_name", MainLauncher = true, Icon="@drawable/icon")]
```

The Icon value will set the appropriate value in the Android manifest, using the same localization rules as those used for any other drawable. Also, assuming that you have a corresponding key of app_name in the appropriate Strings.xml file, your application name is now localized in the same manner.

LOCALIZATION SERVICES

It is always a good idea to have a person who is fluent in your target language as well as familiar with any specific regional dialects that you choose to support. Although many developers tend to be multilingual in a programming sense, it is often difficult to find the resources to provide translations for your application text. With that in mind, here are two good sources for translations:

➤ **Localization services:** Several sites online are dedicated to providing professional and detailed translation services for application developers as well as numerous other professions. As with many services, their prices and quality of service vary greatly.

➤ **Local colleges:** If your localization needs are minimal, colleges are an excellent place to request assistance for localization services. For free or for a small cost, college professors and classes often are happy to take on a small translation project.

Direct translation services such as Google Translate or even word-to-word translations via dictionaries are never a good idea. These services have their place, but they frequently make mistakes in connotation and proper sentence structure.

ADVANCED USAGE OF STRINGS.XML

Because we have extensively covered the basic usage of the `Strings.xml` file, you can incorporate a few additional features to make the process of localization much easier. This section summarizes these special usages.

String Array

Within `Strings.xml`, you can specify an array of strings that can be used for binding to list-type controls. For the most part, this practice should be reserved for displaying data that is completely static. Here's the syntax for defining an array of strings:

```
<string-array name="NameArray">
    <item>Nathan</item>
    <item>Crystal</item>
    <item>Kitara</item>
</string-array>
```

In your application code, you can access this array via the special `Resources` class by using `Resource.Array.NameArray` and binding it to the appropriate property on a listing control.

Plurals

In many applications, developers find themselves in situations where they need a way to programmatically handle the usage of plurals in their response text. One example is in search results where you specify how many results were found. Although it is acceptable to use "(s)" to indicate a potential plural noun, the plurals feature of `Strings.xml` can allow you to handle these situations with greater finesse.

By using the plurals section in the `Strings.xml` file, you can specify different messages to a single string key based on whether there are one or many results. The syntax for using this feature is as follows:

```
<plurals name="BookSearchResults">
        <item quantity="one">Your search found only one book.</item>
        <item quantity="other">Your search found many books!  Hooray!</item>
</plurals>
```

In this case, the `quantity` attribute of the item node has only two valid values. As you might guess, `one` refers to when you have only a single item in the plural, and `other` refers to having many results. To use this feature in code, you simply have to access the special `Resource` class in conjunction with the application instance of the `Resources` class. Here's an example of its usage:

```
List<Book> BooksQuery = GetAllBooksInDatabase();
string ResultsMessage = Resources.GetQuantityString
   (Resource.plurals.BookSearchResults, BooksQuery.Count);
```

String Replacements

Working with dynamic strings is always a challenge, especially in localization scenarios. In many cases, programmers find themselves having to juggle several banks of intersecting strings to provide full dynamic support. In situations like this, it is best to leverage the framework's string-replacement functions to do as much work as possible for you.

Imagine that you need to create a simple, localized number-counting application that returns a localized string in conjunction with a text version of a specific number. In this case, you need to support only the integers 1, 2, and 3.

In a Mono for Android application (or picking up from `Localization03`), add the following values to the appropriate `Strings.xml` file. These values represent the string values of the dynamic number text you want to display.

ADDED TO /RESOURCES/VALUES/STRINGS.XML

```
<string-array name="NumberArray">
        <item>one</item>
        <item>two</item>
        <item>three</item>
</string-array>
```

ADDED TO /RESOURCES/VALUES-ES/STRINGS.XML

```
<string-array name="NumberArray">
        <item>una</item>
        <item>dos</item>
        <item>tres</item>
</string-array>
```

With these strings in place, you can create a response string in `Strings.xml` that is preset to leverage .NET's string-replacement tools. In C#, you can accomplish string replacement via the

`String.Format()` static string. By using the proper index syntax, such as `{0}`, you can identify locations in a template string that are to be dynamically replaced. In showing the logic for localizing the counting response string, the following example adds localized text that will be used for the counting button itself.

ADDED TO /RESOURCES/VALUES/STRINGS.XML

```
<string name="CountButtonText">Count to three...</string>
<plurals name="CountingResponse">
    <item quantity="one">You have counted {0} time.</item>
    <item quantity="other">You have counted {0} times!</item>
</plurals>
```

ADDED TO /RESOURCES/VALUES-ES/STRINGS.XML

```
<string name="CountButtonText">Cuente hasta tres...</string>
<plurals name="CountingResponse">
    <item quantity="one">Usted ha contado {0} vez.</item>
    <item quantity="other">Se han contado {0} veces!</item>
</plurals>
```

As you can see, we have not only added support for a dynamic string, but we have also leveraged plurals to localize the conversion from singular to multiple items. Using logic much like the previous plurals example, we can easily support multiple localization scenarios with a little configuration.

Next, we need to update the `Resources/Layout/Main.axml` by adding a button that will initiate the counting process. Within the file, create a button with an ID of `@+id/btnNumberCounter` and then set its text value to the appropriate string resource. When complete, the button text should look something like the following snippet:

```
<Button android:id="@+id/btnNumberCounter"
    android:layout_width="fill_parent"
    android:layout_height="wrap_content"
    android:text="@string/CountButtonText"/>
```

Finally, add the appropriate logic to the button's CLICK event that will display a `Toast` message, indicating the number of clicks that have transpired. The code to do this is as follows:

```
protected override void OnCreate(Bundle bundle)
{
    base.OnCreate(bundle);

    // Set our view from the "Main" layout resource
    SetContentView(Resource.Layout.Main);

    // Get our buttons from the layout resource,
    // and attach an event to it
    Button HelloButton = FindViewById<Button>(Resource.Id.HelloButton);
    HelloButton.Click += delegate {
        Toast.MakeText(this, Resource.String.Hello, ToastLength.Long).Show(); };

    Button GoodbyeButton = FindViewById<Button>(Resource.Id.GoodbyeButton);
    GoodbyeButton.Click += delegate {
        Toast.MakeText(this, Resource.String.Goodbye, ToastLength.Long).Show(); };

    Button NumberCounter = FindViewById<Button>(Resource.Id.btnNumberCounter);
```

```
        NumberCounter.Click += delegate { DisplayNumberCounterToastMessage(); };
}

public int NumberOfPresses = 0;

public void DisplayNumberCounterToastMessage()
{
    String[] NumberArray = Resources.GetStringArray(Resource.Array.NumberArray);
    NumberOfPresses =
        NumberOfPresses == NumberArray.Length ? 1 : NumberOfPresses + 1;
    string Message = string.Format(Resources.GetQuantityString(Resource
        .Plurals.CountingResponse, NumberOfPresses), NumberArray.GetValue
            (NumberOfPresses - 1));

    Toast.MakeText(this, Message, ToastLength.Short).Show();
}
```

A working example of this code can be found in `Localization04`.

After this is added, the application displays the template message with the dynamic string value whose index is equal to the `NumberOfPresses` variable. In addition, this same variable is used to indicate whether or not to pluralize the template message. In this simple example, the application resets the press counter to 1 when the `NumberOfPresses` variable is equal to the array's length.

Run the example and try it out in both languages. You should be greeted by the following screens (Figure 14-9)!

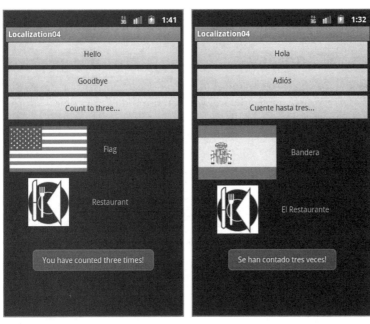

FIGURE 14-9

WORKING WITH FORMAT CONVERSIONS

Another step in the process of supporting other locales is to respect the user's preference for displayed dates, times, and numbers. This can be critical in things such as date formats, where a format can look similar in different locales but can have very different meanings.

Since Mono for Android uses the .NET Framework as its underlying technology, supporting these custom formats is similar to the process of supporting them in any other .NET project. The big bonus for you as a developer is that .NET knows the locale setting set in your Mono for Android application. Consequently, a large chunk of your work is already handled in the framework.

Formatting Dates

Providing locale-aware dates in .NET is as simple as using the `DateTime` object. Consider the following code:

```
DateTime LocalizedDate = DateTime.Now.ToShortDateString();
```

Because you used the `DateTime` object to identify your date, the system automatically determines the best way to display the date according to the locale settings of the Android device. Consequently, the code to get a short date string is identical to the one you would use to access it in a non-localized code base.

> *One key thing to beware of is to make sure that you do not specify custom date format strings in your code. Using the following code, your application will no longer utilize your application's localized settings, because you have specifically instructed the .NET runtime how to format your date:*
>
> ```
> DateTime LocalizedDate = DateTime.Now.ToString("dd-mm-yyyy");
> ```

Formatting Numbers and Currency

Formatting numbers and currency in .NET is very similar to the process of formatting dates. Since .NET can reflect the local settings of your Android device, you can use the `string` object's format function to handle your formatting issues automatically. In the following code snippet, the given number is formatted according to the region settings of the Android device:

```
double BigNumber = 1234567890.11;
string FormattedNumber = String.Format("{0:N}", BigNumber);

// This same formatting can be achieved in an object's ToString() method.
string FormattedNumber = BigNumber.ToString("N")
```

Depending on your locale settings, you will see varying results. Table 14-3 shows what the results would look like in a few different locale settings.

TABLE 14-3: Number Formatting Results

LOCALE	RESULT
en-US	1,234,567,890.11
fr-FR	1 234 567 890,11
es-ES	1.234.567.890,11

In the code example, we told the framework the kind of number formatting we wanted by using a basic number formatting specifier. In this case, we used the N specifier, which means that we wanted our number to be a general number with separators. In addition to this specifier, several others in .NET can be used to define different types of number formats. Table 14-4 shows many of the common specifiers used for localization purposes.

TABLE 14-4: String Number Specifiers

SPECIFIER	TYPE
C	Currency
D	Decimal
N	Number with commas
E	Scientific number
F	Fixed-point number
G	General number

SUMMARY

The Android OS has become one of the large players in the mobile marketplace. People around the world are being exposed to the Android Market as the official centralized location for reviewing, purchasing, and downloading Android applications. Therefore, it is critical for an Android developer to support as many potential customers as possible via localization.

Additionally, the process of localizing your application gives you separation of concerns, makes updates easier to manage, and is as simple a process as any other approach. By proactively localizing your application, you will prepare yourself for an easier development experience while enabling yourself to target a broader audience.

15

Sharing Code between Mono for Android, MonoTouch, and Windows Phone 7

WHAT'S IN THIS CHAPTER?

➤ Understanding the mobile platforms

➤ Using class libraries on different platforms

➤ One class library to rule them all

➤ Building an application that shares code

This chapter guides you through the popular mobile platforms and shows you how you can leverage your .NET and C# skills to develop for each platform. You also will discover how you can share code between these platforms and the possibilities of using one assembly across all three platforms.

To finish the chapter, you will create a sample application that will work across these platforms, learning about interesting differences as you go along.

OVERVIEW OF THE THREE PLATFORMS

You can potentially develop for many mobile platforms. The three platforms I am referring to are iOS, Android, and Windows Phone 7. Why these three? You can develop on these platforms using C# and the .NET framework: MonoTouch for iOS, .NET on Windows Phone, and Mono for Android on Android devices. Let's delve into these platforms.

Mono for Android

The Mono for Android default project structure should be relatively familiar to you now, since you likely have been working with Mono for Android through the book. Figure 15-1 shows the default project structure. You can see that you have `mscorlib`, `System`, `System.Core`, `System.Xml`, and `System.Xml.Linq` assemblies all included by default. As well as these assemblies, you have a `Mono.Android` assembly, which contains all the bindings to the Android APIs.

By default, Mono for Android project structures also include an Assets folder and a Resources folder. The Assets folder is the place where you may store files, such as audio files, to be used in your application. The Resources folder contains three other folders (Drawable, Layout, and Values) and a `Resource.designer.cs` file. You should be familiar with these different files and folders after working through this book.

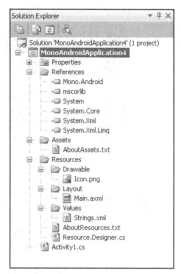

FIGURE 15-1

With this default project structure, you also get an `Activity1.cs` file, which sets up a main launching activity for your application. This means that you can simply press Run on your project, and it will build and run straight through to the Android emulator without any other configuration.

MonoTouch

In 2009, MonoTouch was released, which was a set of tools allowing .NET developers to develop for the iPhone and iPod Touch. This wasn't a way to port over Silverlight applications to run on these devices. Instead, it was a way to develop against the iPhone SDK in a familiar way by using the .NET framework and the C# language. To be able to develop on these devices, you need a machine running Mac OS X. This steps up the barrier of entry somewhat compared to having integration directly into a more familiar environment with Visual Studio.

The bindings for MonoTouch work by directly calling into the iOS SDK for iOS-specific APIs (such as UI controls). MonoTouch also spins up the Mono framework and runs all .NET code through this from C# code compiled into ARM code. This means that .NET developers can use the familiar APIs and syntax from the .NET framework and C# programming language while being able to take full advantage of the iOS infrastructure.

Figure 15-2 shows the default project structure of a MonoTouch application. As you can see, the default `System`, `System.Core`, and `System.Xml` assemblies are included in our application. Comparing this to Figure 15-1, which is the Mono for Android default project structure, you see these are common across both platforms. They differ in that MonoTouch includes a `MonoTouch.dll` reference, and Mono for Android includes a `Mono.Android.dll` reference.

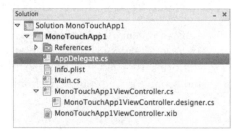

FIGURE 15-2

These two assemblies differ on both projects because `MonoTouch.dll` targets the iOS APIs and `Mono.Android.dll` targets the Android APIs.

Figure 15-2 also shows a `Main.cs` file, `AppDelegate.cs` file with `MonoTouchApp1ViewController.cs`, and `MonoTouchApp1ViewController.designer.cs` and `MonoTouchApp1ViewController.xib` files. Because MonoTouch applications are invoked through the `UIApplication` call, the `Main` file manages this, then goes into the `AppDelegate.cs` file to manage any custom displaying of views. Mono for Android has the concept of Activities. Handling an application's loading is deferred to an Activity, so by default your `Activity1.cs` file manages this application's launch (as long as it is declared with the `MainLauncher` attribute as true in the `Activity` attribute).

MonoTouch uses a `UIWindow` as the first view of the application, and then multiple views are loaded onto the window and pushed and popped as the application is built. This is why the `UIWindow window` property is initialized. This is very different in Android, as you have learned throughout this book. Hence the extra Resources folder, which handles how a view is laid out and displayed.

Just like Mono for Android, MonoTouch integrates with the iOS tools that a developer using Objective-C would use. This allows the developer to use the real iPhone/iPad simulator to get the same experience. This of course means that MonoTouch can easily integrate when a new platform comes out (such as the iPad device) and can continue to use the native tools. With MonoTouch, working in Visual Studio is possible, but only to write and compile code. You can't run your MonoTouch application through Visual Studio; this requires a Mac machine and the iOS SDK to work with it.

Sometimes while doing iOS development, you might need to solve a problem that you can't quite work out with the provided iOS APIs. You would ask the question on Stack Overflow, and an Objective-C developer would answer your MonoTouch question. Because the two are so closely tied together, it is easy to translate an Objective-C answer into a MonoTouch one.

The core libraries on the .NET side are the same as the ones that Mono for Android provides. This means that if you have any business logic code in a MonoTouch application, it should be easy to move over the code and reuse it on Mono for Android applications. This approach comes with some caveats, though, as explored further throughout this chapter.

Windows Phone 7

Windows Phone 7 is the development platform that allows developers to develop in C# and the .NET framework. Since the platform is tightly integrated with Silverlight, Visual Studio, and Expression Blend, a developer can easily reuse his or her existing skills in a familiar environment, especially if he or she has developed using the Silverlight toolset before.

The Windows Phone 7 default project, shown in Figure 15-3, contains many references to assemblies, including `mscorlib`, `System`, `System.Core`, and `System.Xml`; these are the same as the Mono for Android references. As well, you will see `Microsoft.Phone` and `Microsoft.Phone.Interop`. These two assemblies are the phone-specific APIs that you can use when programming against the Windows Phone 7 platform. Another assembly that is included in the application that isn't included by default with Mono for Android is `System.Windows`. Since Windows Phone 7 makes heavy use of Silverlight APIs, these are mostly covered in this assembly. They include things such as Sliders,

Grids, Buttons, and other non-UI-specific classes such as `Observable Collections` and `Dispatcher` to handle multithreading (similar to the `RunOnUIThread` method in Mono for Android).

The Windows Phone 7 project also contains three default images that are used for the `ApplicationIcon`, the Tile icon for the application (when it is pinned on the home screen), and the splash screen for displaying when the application loads. The other two files are `.xaml` files. `App.xaml` is the file that is first hit when the application loads and is where the setup of the first page is initialized. By default, this is set to load the `MainPage.xaml` file, which is autocreated and set up with the application name and page name. By default, the application name isn't set to a string that can be changed in a `String.xml` file, as with Mono for Android. It is instead just hard-coded.

When you install the Windows Phone developer tools, the program installs a Windows Phone Simulator. It has limited functionality compared to a real device and is similar to the iPhone simulator. Because it is a simulator, the performance can be much better or much worse than when the application is run on a device.

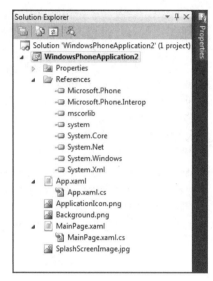

FIGURE 15-3

Because the .NET framework is part of the Windows Phone OS, applications can be very small — minimal to the point that an application can be around 15KB. In contrast, a compressed MonoTouch application is about 4MB. With today's 3G speeds and easy access to WiFi, 4MB isn't much of a problem.

USING CLASS LIBRARIES TO SEPARATE THE CODE

Class libraries exist so that you can create reusable code to use across multiple projects. Most of the time, these libraries are used across the same type of project (such as a web application project). Since we're talking about sharing with multiple devices, unfortunately this also means that class libraries exist for each of the different platforms, so a different class library is needed for MonoTouch, Mono for Android, and Windows Phone 7.

It's time to take a deeper look at each of the class libraries and what they have to offer each platform.

Using Preprocessor Directives

Preprocessor directives allow you to selectively compile sections of code according to predefined constants in the build configuration for that project. This generally gives you code that looks like the following:

```
#if DEBUG
    var email = "debug@example.com";
#elif
    var email = "live@example.com";
#endif
```

Since you are sometimes going to need to include platform-specific code, this can come in useful when targeting code that works on one platform and not another. Constants (known as conditional compilation symbols) are defined in PropertyGroups in your `csproj` file under the DefineConstants tag; the following sections will tell you what constants you should use for these for each platform and how to use them.

Mono for Android

In Mono for Android class libraries, the `csproj` file uses the following project type GUIDs:

```
<ProjectTypeGuids>{EFBA0AD7-5A72-4C68-AF49-83D382785DCF};
                  {FAE04EC0-301F-11D3-BF4B-00C04F79EFBC}</ProjectTypeGuids>
```

`EFBA0AD7-5A72-4C68-AF49-83D382785DCF` is the important GUID to remember because it signifies a Mono for Android class library project. `FAE04EC0-301F-11D3-BF4B-00C04F79EFBC` indicates that this is a Windows C# project.

Also import the following line:

```
<Import Project="$(MSBuildExtensionsPath)\Novell\Novell.MonoDroid.CSharp.targets"
  />
```

to ensure that Visual Studio knows how to build the project.

Although there is no default preprocessor directive that you should use for a Mono for Android project, it would be safe to assume that `MONOANDROID` would be fine. You can add this to all your PropertyGroups like so:

```
<DefineConstants>DEBUG;TRACE;MONOANDROID</DefineConstants>
```

or you can use the GUI to set the conditional compilation symbols for you, which ends up producing the same `csproj` settings as editing the `csproj` directly. This is shown in Figure 15-4.

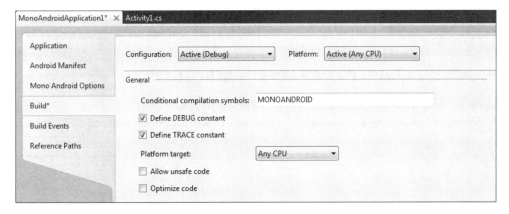

FIGURE 15-4

Windows Phone 7

Similar to the Mono for Android class library, the Windows Phone 7 class library has its own project type GUID too:

```
<ProjectTypeGuids>{C089C8C0-30E0-4E22-80C0-CE093F111A43};
  {fae04ec0-301f-11d3-bf4b-00c04f79efbc}</ProjectTypeGuids>
```

and it also uses the same Windows C# project GUID.

The class library also has a few Silverlight/Windows Phone 7–specific items, but you don't need to worry about them when trying to use your class libraries across different platforms.

Similar to the Mono for Android project, the Windows Phone 7 class library imports two targets:

```
<Import Project="$(MSBuildExtensionsPath)\Microsoft\
Silverlight for Phone\$(TargetFrameworkVersion)\
Microsoft.Silverlight.$(TargetFrameworkProfile).Overrides.targets" />

<Import Project="$(MSBuildExtensionsPath)\Microsoft\Silverlight for Phone\
$(TargetFrameworkVersion)\Microsoft.Silverlight.CSharp.targets" />
```

The class library uses SILVERLIGHT and WINDOWS_PHONE as the default conditional compilation symbols.

MonoTouch

Like the previous two class libraries, MonoTouch comes with its own GUID. Aside from that, the Mono for Android and MonoTouch class libraries are the same.

```
<ProjectTypeGuids>{6BC8ED88-2882-458C-8E55-DFD12B67127B};
{FAE04EC0-301F-11D3-BF4B-00C04F79EFBC}</ProjectTypeGuids>
```

MonoTouch class libraries include the following line:

```
<Import Project="$(MSBuildBinPath)\Microsoft.CSharp.targets" />
```

to allow for these to be built with MSBuild.

Like the Mono for Android class library, the MonoTouch library doesn't use a default conditional compilation symbol, but it has been commonplace to use MONOTOUCH as a conditional compilation symbol for MonoTouch projects.

Now that you know the subtle differences between the three class library projects, you are ready to take a deeper look at the code libraries they provide.

ASSEMBLIES AVAILABLE ON EACH PLATFORM

Table 15-1 lists the default assembly references that are available to each of the different class libraries. Most of these are available across platforms, and others are just available for MonoTouch and Mono for Android. For example, System.Core and System.Xml are supported on all three platforms. So is every method available on each profile? Sadly, this is not the case.

TABLE 15-1: Assembly Availability on Mobile Platforms

ASSEMBLY	MONOTOUCH	MONO FOR ANDROID	WINDOWS PHONE 7
mscorlib	Yes	Yes	Yes
System	Yes	Yes	Yes
System.Core	Yes	Yes	Yes

ASSEMBLY	MONOTOUCH	MONO FOR ANDROID	WINDOWS PHONE 7
System.Data	Yes	Yes	No
System.Json	Yes	Yes	No
System.Runtime. Serialization	Yes	Yes	Yes
System.ServiceModel	Yes	Yes	Yes
System.ServiceModel.Web	Yes	Yes	Yes
System.Transactions	Yes	Yes	No
System.Web.Services	Yes	Yes	No
System.Xml	Yes	Yes	Yes
System.Xml.Linq	Yes	Yes	Yes
System.Device	No	No	Yes
System.Observable	No	No	Yes
System.Windows	No	No	Yes

Although some assemblies are not included in the profile for a specific platform, such as `System .Json`, you can still use this assembly by directly referencing it from the Silverlight assemblies. The final section of this chapter has an example.

There is a disconnect between platforms because certain things are either restricted or simply unavailable on the targeted platform. If you plan to write code to target multiple platforms, you need to be aware of this. For example, let's focus on the `File` class in the `System.IO` namespace, which is part of the `mscorlib` assembly.

A common method you may use when doing file access with .NET is the `ReadAllText` method. This method takes a string path to a file and an optional encoding type. Since MonoTouch and Mono for Android use the same common code across these two platforms, we can assume that this method will exist on both platforms.

When you go to reuse this code on Windows Phone 7, you will quickly realize that this method doesn't exist on this platform. You might worry about how you need to reimplement code that exists on the .NET platform — not an easy task. Luckily the Mono project team has done this for you — hence, the Mono framework allowing this functionality. What you can do is go to the repository for the Mono code on GitHub at `https://github.com/mono/mono/blob/master/mcs/ class/corlib/System.IO/File.cs` and navigate to the code to do this.

Listing 15-1 displays the source code for the missing `ReadAllText` method.

LISTING 15-1: The System.IO.File class displaying code for ReadAllText

```
//
// System.IO.File.cs
//
// Authors:
//   Miguel de Icaza   (miguel@ximian.com)
//   Jim Richardson    (develop@wtfo-guru.com)
//   Dan Lewis         (dihlewis@yahoo.co.uk)
//   Ville Palo        (vi64pa@kolumbus.fi)
//
// Copyright 2002 Ximian, Inc. http://www.ximian.com
// Copyright (C) 2001 Moonlight Enterprises, All Rights Reserved
// Copyright (C) 2004, 2006, 2010 Novell, Inc (http://www.novell.com)
//
// Permission is hereby granted, free of charge, to any person obtaining
// a copy of this software and associated documentation files (the
// "Software"), to deal in the Software without restriction, including
// without limitation the rights to use, copy, modify, merge, publish,
// distribute, sublicense, and/or sell copies of the Software, and to
// permit persons to whom the Software is furnished to do so, subject to
// the following conditions:
//
// The above copyright notice and this permission notice shall be
// included in all copies or substantial portions of the Software.
//
// THE SOFTWARE IS PROVIDED "AS IS", WITHOUT WARRANTY OF ANY KIND,
// EXPRESS OR IMPLIED, INCLUDING BUT NOT LIMITED TO THE WARRANTIES OF
// MERCHANTABILITY, FITNESS FOR A PARTICULAR PURPOSE AND
// NONINFRINGEMENT. IN NO EVENT SHALL THE AUTHORS OR COPYRIGHT HOLDERS BE
// LIABLE FOR ANY CLAIM, DAMAGES OR OTHER LIABILITY, WHETHER IN AN ACTION
// OF CONTRACT, TORT OR OTHERWISE, ARISING FROM, OUT OF OR IN CONNECTION
// WITH THE SOFTWARE OR THE USE OR OTHER DEALINGS IN THE SOFTWARE.
//

public static string ReadAllText (string path)
{
    using (StreamReader sr = new StreamReader (path)) {
        return sr.ReadToEnd ();
    }
}

public static string ReadAllText (string path, Encoding encoding)
{
    using (StreamReader sr = new StreamReader (path, encoding)) {
        return sr.ReadToEnd ();
    }
}
```

File.cs

This is nothing more than a convenience method around a `StreamReader`. However, it makes a big
difference when simple methods are not easily reusable across platforms. You will also notice that
`WriteAllText` is missing from the `System.IO.File` class. Again, you grab the code you need and use it
with your Windows Phone 7 projects as well as your MonoTouch and Mono for Android projects.

ONE CLASS LIBRARY TO RULE THEM ALL

Shouldn't this be easier? Shouldn't you just be able to compile one assembly and have it run everywhere? You can — sort of.

The Portable Library Tools aim to allow the reuse of code from one assembly but provides a base set of APIs that will work across multiple platforms, whether those are .NET, Silverlight, Xbox 360, or Silverlight for Windows Phone 7 projects. It does this by providing a limited subset of the .NET framework that is almost guaranteed to exist on each of the platforms just mentioned and that is most likely to exist on other platforms such as MonoTouch and Mono for Android.

 You can find the portable library tools at `http://bit.ly/portablelibrarytools`

To see a good example of this, you can take a look at a sample application that converts an alphanumeric telephone number into a regular telephone number. For example, the number 1-888-0CHRISNTR would translate into 1-888-024747687.

To integrate this library, first you create a new portable library class project. You create a static class with a single public method that returns the converted number as a string. For clarity reasons, Listing 15-2 displays the class that you will want to use in the portable library.

Available for
download on
Wrox.com

LISTING 15-2 The telephone converter class

```
using System.Text;

namespace TelephoneConverter
{
    public static class TelephoneStringConverter
    {
        public static string ConvertEntryToNumber(string rawTelephoneString)
        {
            var newNumber = new StringBuilder();
            var trimmedAndReplacedTelephone =
rawTelephoneString.Trim().ToUpperInvariant().Replace("-", "");
            foreach (var c in trimmedAndReplacedTelephone)
            {
                var result = ExtractNumberFromLetter(c);
                if (result == null)
                    newNumber.Append(c);
                else
                    newNumber.Append(result);
            }
            return newNumber.ToString();
        }

        static int? ExtractNumberFromLetter(char c)
        {
            if (c >= 'A' && c <= 'C')
```

continues

LISTING 15-2 *(continued)*

```
        {
            return 2;
        }
        else if (c >= 'D' && c <= 'F')
        {
            return 3;
        }
        else if (c >= 'G' && c <= 'I')
        {
            return 4;
        }
        else if (c >= 'J' && c <= 'L')
        {
            return 5;
        }
        else if (c >= 'M' && c <= 'O')
        {
            return 6;
        }
        else if (c >= 'P' && c <= 'S')
        {
            return 7;
        }
        else if (c >= 'T' && c <= 'V')
        {
            return 8;
        }
        else if (c >= 'W' && c <= 'Z')
        {
            return 9;
        }
        return null;
    }
  }
}
```

TelephoneConverter\TelephoneConverter\TelephoneStringConverter.cs

The implementation of the logic is not the important part of the class. The important point is to notice that the implementation only relies on the `StringBuilder` class in `System.Text` (and `mscorlib`). When you now build the project, you see `TelephoneConverter.dll` in the `bin` folder. This assembly can now be moved to the platform-specific application and referenced as an assembly.

Now you need to build the UI-specific logic for each platform. For this you can just use a text box and a clickable button and then display the result in an alert.

Mono for Android

With Mono for Android, you use a `Button` and an `EditBox` to interact with the portable library project. You can then use an `AlertDialog` and associated builder to display the result to the user.

Most of the UI work is declared in the layout. Listing 15-3 displays the code that invokes the shared code.

LISTING 15-3: Convert code implemented in a Mono for Android application

```
Button button = FindViewById<Button>(Resource.Id.MyButton);
EditText textBox1 = FindViewById<EditText>(Resource.Id.TextBox1);

button.Click += delegate
{
    if (!String.IsNullOrEmpty(textBox1.Text.ToString()))
    {
        var result =
            TelephoneConverter.TelephoneStringConverter.
            ConvertEntryToNumber(textBox1.Text.ToString());
            new AlertDialog.Builder(this).
                SetMessage(result).
                SetNeutralButton("Ok", delegate {}).Show();
    }
    else
    {
        new AlertDialog.Builder(this).
            SetMessage("No number entered").
            SetNeutralButton("Ok", delegate { });
    }
};
```

TelephoneConverter\MonoDroidTelephone\Activity1.cs

Most of the UI work can be found in the `Main.axml` file, so make sure you download the sample project to see this example running in full. Figure 15-5 shows the result on the emulator.

FIGURE 15-5

> *You can download relevant code from this chapter at this book's website at* www.wrox.com. *The Telephone Converter Mono for Android code project can be found at TelephoneConverter\MonoDroidTelephone\MonoDroidTelephone.sln in this chapter's code download.*

MonoTouch

You will find that the MonoTouch sample doesn't differ much from the Mono for Android version. Just like the Mono for Android version, you need to add in the portable library project assembly and reference it. After referencing the assembly you only have to use one line to call your portable library project's static class, and then you use the native alert method on the platform to display the converted number. With the MonoTouch solution, again you can set up the UI mostly in Interface Builder (which is part of Xcode). Download the sample project to see the code running for the MonoTouch example. (You need a Mac to run this example and the evaluation version of MonoTouch.)

Listing 15-4 shows the code needed to handle the `TouchUpInside` method (the equivalent `Click` method on a button in MonoTouch) and display the MonoTouch native alert message with the converted number.

LISTING 15-4: Convert code implemented in a MonoTouch application

Available for
download on
Wrox.com

```
button.TouchUpInside += (sender, e) => {
      if (!String.IsNullOrEmpty(textBox1.Text.ToString()))
      {
         var result = TelephoneConverter.TelephoneStringConverter.
                    ConvertEntryToNumber(textBox1.Text.ToString());
         var alert = new UIAlertView("Call", result, null, "Ok!", null);
         alert.Show();
      }
      else
      {
         var alert = new UIAlertView("Oops", "No Number entered", null, "Ok!",
                    null);
         alert.Show();
      }
   };
```

TelephoneConverter\MonoTouchTelephone\MonoTouchTelephoneViewController.cs

Figure 15-6 shows the application running and successfully converting the telephone number.

> *You can download the relevant code from this chapter at this book's website at* www.wrox.com. *The Telephone Converter MonoTouch code project can be found at TelephoneConverter\MonoTouchTelephone\MonoTouchTelephone .sln in this chapter's code download.*

FIGURE 15-6

Windows Phone 7

In Windows Phone 7, again you just copy over the portable library assembly and get the project to reference it. Most of the display is generated in the designer service, so you only need to hook up the button click event in code. The button click event is shown in Listing 15-5.

LISTING 15-5: Windows Phone 7 implementation

```
private void button1_Click(object sender, RoutedEventArgs e)
{
    if(!String.IsNullOrEmpty(textBox1.Text))
    {
        var result = TelephoneConverter.TelephoneStringConverter.
                    ConvertEntryToNumber(textBox1.Text);
        MessageBox.Show(result);
    }
    else
    {
        MessageBox.Show("No number entered");
    }
}
```

TelephoneConverter\WP7Telephone\MainPage.xaml.cs

When you enter text into the textbox and press the button, the phone number is converted, as shown in the Windows Phone 7 emulator in Figure 15-7.

FIGURE 15-7

 You can download the relevant code from this chapter at this book's website at www.wrox.com. *The Telephone Converter Windows Phone 7 code project can be found at TelephoneConverter\WP7Telephone\ WP7Telephone.sln in this chapter's code download.*

 You should never use a `MessageBox` in a real Windows Phone 7 application, because it is a blocking method and will cause your application to close.

Looking deeper into the Portable Library Tools, you will find that the tools don't support `XmlDocument`, `System.Linq.Xml`, and many more commonly used .NET classes. This is done to enable a core base that will cover the widest spread of platforms, although this makes it harder to reuse code that uses unsupported code.

The Portable Library Tools really do make your code portable. But the library's current limited nature makes it hard to use the library to solve more complex code reuse, so knowing how to share source files across these platforms is useful. The Portable Library Tools are definitely something to keep an eye on as the project's iterations keep coming.

PUTTING IT ALL TOGETHER: CREATING A CROSS-PLATFORM APPLICATION

At the moment, creating reusable code across Mono for Android, MonoTouch, and Windows Phone 7 with the Portable Library Tools probably won't work for a lot of tasks, because the portable library contains only the underlying core .NET assemblies with limited functionality. So to create a cross-mobile platform application, this section gets into what you need to do.

To show an example of an application that shares code and also works on the three platforms mentioned near the beginning of this chapter, I have developed a relatively straightforward Twitter application. When the user enters a username, the application returns a list of tweets for that user.

To start the application, you will just create a new Windows Phone 7 application. From there you can create a Windows Phone 7 class library and then share the code across the different class libraries and rewrite the UI to work on Mono for Android and MonoTouch.

In the Windows Phone 7 class library, you create a generic `Tweet.cs` class that contains your Twitter data. You also create a `TwitterReceiver.cs` class, which is a static method to go off to the Twitter API. Then you parse the JSON results and pass them back to whatever called the method. Listing 15-6 shows the code that will be reused in each of the applications. It's worth noting that this code uses the Silverlight `System.Json` assembly reference to parse the JSON result.

LISTING 15-6: The GetTweetsForUser implementation

```
public static void GetTweetsForUser
                    (string userName, Action<List<Tweet>> actionResult)
{
   var client = new WebClient();
   client.DownloadStringCompleted += (s, e) =>
   {
      var listOfTweets = new List<Tweet>();
      if (e.Error != null)
      {
         actionResult(listOfTweets);
      }
      else
      {
         var jsonResults = JsonValue.Parse(e.Result);
         if (jsonResults != null)
         {
            foreach (JsonValue item in jsonResults["results"])
            {
               var text = HttpUtility.HtmlDecode(item["text"]);
               var user = HttpUtility.HtmlDecode(item["from_user"]);
               var profileImage =
                   HttpUtility.HtmlDecode(item["profile_image_url"]);
               listOfTweets.Add(new Tweet() {
                       FromUser = user,
```

continues

LISTING 15-6 *(continued)*

```
                              ProfileImageUrl = profileImage, Text = text
                    }
               );
           }
        }
        actionResult(listOfTweets);
     }
   };
   client.DownloadStringAsync(new
              Uri(String.Format("http://search.twitter.com/
                         search.json?q=from:{0}", userName)));
}
```

TwitterUser\WindowsPhoneTwitter\TwitterHelper\TwitterReceiver.cs

To build the UI for the Twitter application on Windows Phone 7, you can use simple XAML code to add a bindable UI and then use the code-behind to gather data for it to display. You can use a `ListBox` to do this with a data template, which uses a stack panel to lay out content. The XAML looks like Listing 15-7.

LISTING 15-7: XAML for laying out the UI on Windows Phone 7

```xml
<Button Content="Search" Height="72" HorizontalAlignment="Left" Margin="296,0,0,0"
  Name="searchButton"
VerticalAlignment="Top" Width="160" Click="SearchButtonClick" />

<TextBox Height="72" HorizontalAlignment="Left" Name="userNameBox" Text="chrisntr"
VerticalAlignment="Top" Width="290" />

<ListBox Name="listBox1" Margin="0,78,0,0" ItemsSource="{Binding}"
DataContext="{Binding}">
   <ListBox.ItemTemplate>
      <DataTemplate>
         <StackPanel Orientation="Horizontal" Height="Auto">
            <Image Source="{Binding ProfileImageUrl}" Height="73" Width="73"
VerticalAlignment="Top" Margin="0,10,8,0"/>
            <StackPanel Width="370">
               <TextBlock Text="{Binding FromUser}" Foreground="#FFC8AB14"
FontSize="28" />
               <TextBlock Text="{Binding Text}" TextWrapping="Wrap"
FontSize="24" />
            </StackPanel>
         </StackPanel>
      </DataTemplate>
   </ListBox.ItemTemplate>
</ListBox>
```

TwitterUser\WindowsPhoneTwitter\WindowsPhoneTwitter\MainPage.xaml

You can see that you're using the binding syntax to model against `ItemsSource`. In the code-behind you call your class library and set the `ItemsSource` directly; there's nothing much else to it. Since you're looking for a click (or button press) when you want to load the new tweets, you hook onto the Click event, as shown in Listing 15-8.

LISTING 15-8: The SearchButtonClick event

```
private void SearchButtonClick(object sender, RoutedEventArgs e)
{
    if(!String.IsNullOrEmpty(userNameBox.Text))
    {
        TwitterReceiver.GetTweetsForUser(userNameBox.Text, tweets =>
    Dispatcher.BeginInvoke(() => listBox1.ItemsSource = tweets));
    }
}
```

TwitterUser\WindowsPhoneTwitter\WindowsPhoneTwitter\MainPage.xaml.cs

Since you're going to be running the download method on a background thread, you need to use the Dispatcher.BeginInvoke method to allow you to manipulate anything on the UI thread.

When you run the application, it should look something like Figure 15-8.

When you click Search, you should see something like Figure 15-9.

FIGURE 15-8

FIGURE 15-9

Again, you can download this example as part of the book's code download on ww.wrox.com. You can find it in this chapter's folder under the folder name "TwitterUser," which also includes the two projects that work with Mono for Android and MonoTouch.

To get a Mono for Android version running, you want to create a Mono for Android project. Because the Mono for Android project and the Windows Phone 7 projects are incompatible, you will want to create solution folders to split up the two kinds of projects. You can do this by right-clicking the solution, selecting Add, and then selecting New Solution Folder. Rename the existing solution folder something relevant (I recommend "Windows Phone 7"), and then move over the two Windows Phone 7 projects.

FIGURE 15-10

Create another solution folder for Mono for Android, and add a new Mono for Android project as well as a new Mono for Android class library. This should leave you with something that looks like Figure 15-10.

Since you want the Mono for Android project to use the same code you used in the Windows Phone 7 project, in your Mono for Android class library, add a reference to `System.Json`, as you would have done with the Windows Phone 7 project. You then need to add "Existing file..." for each source file used in the Windows Phone 7 class library. When you add the source files as existing files, you need to make sure you add them via "Add As Link." Figure 15-11 displays how this looks in Visual Studio 2010. This means that instead of creating the file inside that folder, it just creates a link directly back to the existing file.

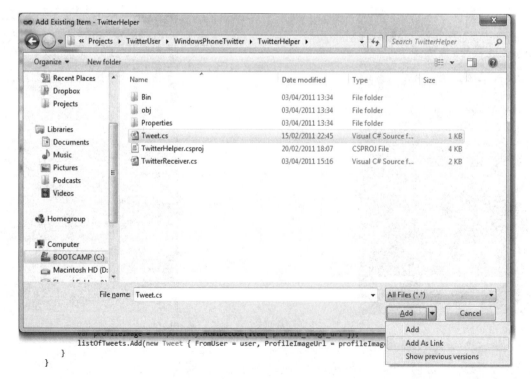

FIGURE 15-11

The first thing you should notice when building the new Mono for Android project is that it doesn't compile. This is because `HttpUtility.HtmlDecode` is included in the `System.Windows` assembly for

Windows Phone 7. Recall that Mono for Android does not have a reference to `System.Windows`. To resolve this issue, you can instead reference `System.Web.Services`, the location of `System.Web.HttpUtility` on Mono for Android. Since you don't want the Windows Phone 7 project to try and resolve the `System.Web` namespace, you want to wrap it with the preprocessor directive to successfully get the application compiling. The snippet below shows how the `using` statements look for the `TwitterReceiver.cs` file. (Note that you can add in MONOTOUCH and MONOANDROID, since the location for the `HttpUtility` is the same on both platforms.)

```
using System;
using System.Collections.Generic;
using System.Json;
using System.Net;
#if MONOANDROID || MONOTOUCH
using System.Web;
#endif
```

To set up the UI, you need to modify the `Main.axml` file to include your `EditText` box and a search `Button` with a `ListView` for displaying tweets. You should have something that looks like Listing 15-9.

LISTING 15-9: Mono for Android AXML for UI layout

```xml
<?xml version="1.0" encoding="utf-8"?>
<LinearLayout xmlns:android="http://schemas.android.com/apk/res/android"
    android:orientation="vertical"
    android:layout_width="fill_parent"
    android:layout_height="fill_parent"
    >

<EditText android:id="@+id/UserNameBox"
    android:layout_width="fill_parent"
    android:layout_height="wrap_content"
    android:text="chrisntr"
    />

<Button
    android:id="@+id/SearchButton"
    android:layout_width="fill_parent"
    android:layout_height="wrap_content"
    android:text="Search"
    />

<ListView
        android:id="@+id/ListView"
        android:layout_width="fill_parent"
        android:layout_height="fill_parent"
    />
</LinearLayout>
```

TwitterUser\MonoDroidTwitter\MonoDroidTwitter\Resources\Layout\Main.axml

The other part of the UI you need to set up is the individual view for a row in the `ListView`. You need to create a new `.axml` file that lays out a singular row and then binds against each value. This row will contain two text fields and an `ImageView` to bind to, as shown in Listing 15-10.

LISTING 15-10: View for a single item in a ListView

```xml
<?xml version="1.0" encoding="utf-8"?>
<LinearLayout xmlns:android="http://schemas.android.com/apk/res/android"
    android:id="@+id/widget28"
    android:layout_width="fill_parent"
    android:layout_height="80px"
>

<ImageView
    android:id="@+id/imageItem"
    android:layout_width="wrap_content"
    android:layout_height="wrap_content"
    android:layout_gravity="center_vertical"
/>

    <LinearLayout
        android:id="@+id/linearText"
        android:layout_width="wrap_content"
        android:layout_height="fill_parent"
        android:orientation="vertical"
        android:layout_marginLeft="10px"
        android:layout_marginTop="10px"
    >

        <TextView
            android:id="@+id/textTop"
            android:layout_width="wrap_content"
        android:layout_height="wrap_content"
        android:text="TextView"
        />
        <TextView
        android:id="@+id/textBottom"
        android:layout_width="wrap_content"
        android:layout_height="wrap_content"
        android:text="TextView"
        />
        </LinearLayout>
</LinearLayout>
```

TwitterUser\MonoDroidTwitter\MonoDroidTwitter\Resources\Layout\CustomListItem.axml

Since you don't have any easy binding like you do in Windows Phone 7, you need to create a custom adapter to display and bind this data. You want to create a custom array adapter to take the list and display it accordingly. The array adapter is shown here:

```csharp
public class TweetArrayAdapter : ArrayAdapter<Tweet>
{
    private readonly Activity _context;
    private readonly List<Tweet> _tweets;
    private readonly int _resource;

    public TweetArrayAdapter(Activity context, int resource, List<Tweet> tweets) :
```

```
base(context, resource, tweets)
  {
    _resource = resource;
    _context = context;
  }

public override View GetView(int position, View convertView, ViewGroup parent)
  {
    var item = GetItem(position);

    LinearLayout view;

    if (convertView == null)
       view = (LinearLayout)
              _context.LayoutInflater.Inflate(_resource, parent, false);
    else
       view = (LinearLayout) convertView;

    //Find references to each subview in the list item's view
    var imageItem = view.FindViewById(Resource.Id.ImageItem) as ImageView;
    var textTop = view.FindViewById(Resource.Id.TextTop) as TextView;
    var textBottom = view.FindViewById(Resource.Id.TextBottom) as TextView;

    // Get image...
    var path = System.Environment.GetFolderPath
                    (System.Environment.SpecialFolder.Personal);

    if (!Directory.Exists(String.Format("{0}/twitter-images", path)))
       Directory.CreateDirectory(String.Format("{0}/twitter-images", path));

    string file =
          String.Format("{0}/twitter-images/{1}.jpg", path, item.FromUser);

    if (System.IO.File.Exists(file))
       imageItem.SetImageURI(Android.Net.Uri.Parse(file));
    else
    {
       var wc = new WebClient();
       wc.DownloadFile(item.ProfileImageUrl, file);
       imageItem.SetImageURI(Android.Net.Uri.Parse(file));
    }

    textTop.SetText(item.FromUser, TextView.BufferType.Normal);
    textBottom.SetText(item.Text, TextView.BufferType.Normal);

    //Finally return the view
    return view;
  }
}
```

TwitterUser\MonoDroidTwitter\MonoDroidTwitter\Activity1.cs

From the line Get image... you may notice something a little odd. To allow the application to display an image from the Web, first you need to download the image to the device, and then you can display it in an `ImageView`. This means that the application can check to see if the image exists first before trying to re-download the image every time it is displayed in the `ListView`.

Now that you have the adapter set up and the UI in place, you need to hook these two together to display some real results. Since you want the web request to get the tweets on a background thread, you want to use the `ThreadPool.QueueUserWorkItem` to enable this. The code to request the tweets is similar to the Windows Phone 7 code. Listing 15-11 shows how this adapter is set up.

LISTING 15-11: Setting up the ListView adapter

```
protected override void OnCreate(Bundle bundle)
{
    base.OnCreate(bundle);

    SetContentView(Resource.Layout.Main);

    var button = FindViewById<Button>(Resource.Id.SearchButton);
    var userNameBox = FindViewById<EditText>(Resource.Id.UserNameBox);
    var listView = FindViewById<ListView>(Resource.Id.ListView);

    tweet = new List<Tweet>();
    istView.Adapter = new TweetArrayAdapter
                        (this, Resource.Layout.CustomListItem, tweet);

    button.Click += delegate
    {
        ThreadPool.QueueUserWorkItem( o =>
            TwitterReceiver.GetTweetsForUser(userNameBox.Text.ToString(), tweets => {
                this.RunOnUiThread(() => {
                        listView.Adapter = new TweetArrayAdapter
                            (this, Resource.Layout.CustomListItem, tweets);
                });
            })
        );
    };
}
```

TwitterUser\MonoDroidTwitter\MonoDroidTwitter\Activity1.cs

When you put this all together and run the code, you should see the screen shown in Figure 15-12. When you click Search, you should see a list of tweets, as shown in Figure 15-13.

You may notice that when you run the project, the Windows Phone 7 simulator starts at the same time. You can modify the configuration and optionally stop certain types of projects from deploying. It might be worth creating different profiles to use on the different platforms in the solution so that you can easily switch between projects.

FIGURE 15-12

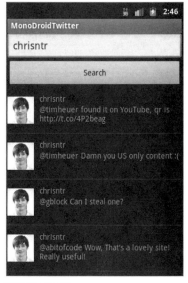

FIGURE 15-13

To get the same code running in MonoTouch, you need to fire up MonoDevelop on a Mac. As with the Mono for Android example, you want to add in both a MonoTouch Window-based project (which is just a default MonoTouch project) and a MonoTouch Library project. Since MonoDevelop cannot have the same project name twice, even with different solution folders, the sample calls the Twitter helper MonoTouch Library project MTTwitterHelper. For the layout, you can use Interface Builder, an Apple tool that allows you to click and drag controls onto an iPhone layout. In here you just add the layout that you are looking for (using a table view to list your data, a button, and a text box). Figure 15-14 shows what the layout looks like.

In a similar way that you used the `ArrayAdapter` in the Mono for Android Twitter User application, to bind data to your table view in MonoTouch, you want to create a custom table source to handle displaying this data. Instead of having a `GetView` like you had in Mono for Android adapters, you have a `GetCell` method. This is where you are going to handle the binding of the data from your list of tweets and display them appropriately. Listing 15-12 shows the implementation of the `TableViewSource` class.

LISTING 15-12: Setting up the TableViewSource class

```
public class TweetTableViewSource : UITableViewSource
{
    public AppDelegate _delegate { get; set; }

    public TweetTableViewSource(AppDelegate delegte)
    {
        _delegate = delegte;
    }

    public override int RowsInSection (UITableView tableview, int section)
    {
```

continues

LISTING 15-12 *(continued)*

```
            return _delegate._tweet.Count();
        }
    public override UITableViewCell GetCell
                            (UITableView tableView, NSIndexPath indexPath)
    {
        var cell = tableView.DequeueReusableCell("myCell");
        if(cell == null)
        {
            cell = new UITableViewCell(UITableViewCellStyle.Subtitle, "myCell");
        }

        cell.DetailTextLabel.Text = _delegate._tweet[indexPath.Row].FromUser;
        cell.TextLabel.Text = _delegate._tweet[indexPath.Row].Text;

        var path = Environment.GetFolderPath (Environment.SpecialFolder.Personal);

        if (!Directory.Exists (string.Format ("{0}/twitter-images", path)))
            Directory.CreateDirectory (string.Format ("{0}/twitter-images", path));

        string file = string.Format ("{0}/twitter-images/{1}", path,
                                _delegate._tweet[indexPath.Row].FromUser);

        if (File.Exists (file))
        {
            var img = UIImage.FromFile
                            (string.Format ("../Documents/twitter-images/{0}",
                                    _delegate._tweet[indexPath.Row].FromUser));

            if(img != null)
                cell.ImageView.Image = img;
            else
                cell.ImageView.Image = null;
        }
        else
        {
            var wc = new WebClient ();
            wc.DownloadFile (_delegate._tweet[indexPath.Row].ProfileImageUrl, file);
            this.InvokeOnMainThread (delegate {
                var img = UIImage.FromFile
                                (string.Format ("../Documents/twitter-images/{0}",
                                        _delegate._tweet[indexPath.Row].FromUser));
                if(img != null)
                    cell.ImageView.Image = img;
                _delegate.ReloadData();
            });
        }

        return cell;
    }
}
```

TwitterUser\MonoTouchTwitter\MonoTouchTwitter\Main.cs

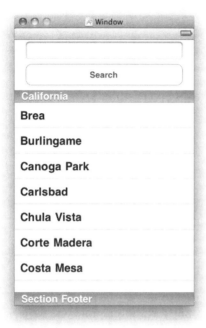

FIGURE 15-14

Now you have created the `TableViewSource` class, you need to implement the button's `TouchUpInside` method to call your shared code, return back the list of tweets, and reload the table view's data with the new information. In MonoTouch, you use an `InvokeOnMainThread` delegate, unlike in Mono for Android where you would use a `RunOnUiThread` method. Either way, this runs code on the UI thread in both cases. Listing 15-13 shows the button and table view getting set up with the `TableViewSource` that was created in Listing 15-12.

LISTING 15-13: Connecting up the TableViewSource with a button

```
public override bool FinishedLaunching (UIApplication app, NSDictionary options)
{
    // When keyboard return is pressed, hide keyboard
    userNameBox.ShouldReturn = (tf) => {
        tf.ResignFirstResponder ();
        return true;
    };

    _tweet = new List<Tweet>();

    button.TouchUpInside += (s,e) =>
    {
        var username = userNameBox.Text.ToString();
        ThreadPool.QueueUserWorkItem( o =>
            TwitterReceiver.GetTweetsForUser(username, tweets =>
```

continues

LISTING 15-13 *(continued)*

```
        {
            InvokeOnMainThread(() =>
            {
                _tweet = tweets;
                tableView.ReloadData();
            });
        })
    );
};

    tableView.Source = new TweetTableViewSource(this);

    window.MakeKeyAndVisible ();

    return true;
}
```

TwitterUser\MonoTouchTwitter\MonoTouchTwitter\Main.cs

Now that you have hooked together the button, the shared code, and the table view, you should notice that the code for MonoTouch is quite similar to the Mono for Android solution, despite the fact that they target two different platforms. Now running the application should get you something that looks a little bit like what is shown in Figure 15-15.

FIGURE 15-15

To learn more about MonoTouch development, check out the Wrox book Professional iPhone Programming with MonoTouch and .NET/C# *(ISBN 978-0-470-63782-1).*

Using this technique to lay out your projects lets you share code that works on all three platforms but still allows you to use the preprocessor directives mentioned earlier to write platform-specific code. This allows you to abstract complexities with, for example, a file system or accessing contacts and not have the application worry about how to do so. This is something that the portable library project will never allow you to do.

SUMMARY

In this chapter, you have learned about the main different mobile platforms and how you can write C# and .NET code across each one. Writing for each platform allows for the reuse of a familiar language and a common framework. However, there is still a disconnect between what parts of the .NET framework are available on these platforms and devices and what you can and cannot use on each.

When the Portable Library Tools come into fruition and are out in the wild with version 1.0, library creators will hopefully start to move over to writing their libraries to work with the portable library. This would allow many people to use their libraries and allow the creators to write their code only once.

16

Preparing and Publishing Your Application to the Market

WHAT'S IN THIS CHAPTER?

➤ Preparing your application: best testing practices and tools

➤ Creating the final build

➤ Signing your application

➤ Deploying to the Android Market

After spending grueling hours writing, designing, developing, and testing your application, you're finally ready to put your application on the market. Whether you are releasing a free or for-pay application, you know that the first impression your application makes on a potential user means everything toward your success. The goal of this chapter is not only to help you successfully publish your application but also to help you ensure that your application succeeds.

Although you have already put a significant amount of work into your application, you still have quite a few additional steps to take when approaching application publication. Regardless, it is essential that you take your time and not cut any corners, because a few moments of impatience can result in dismal sales or downloads. With that in mind, this chapter is broken into two sections that focus on two different aspects of application publication:

➤ **"Preparing Your Application"** focuses on the steps required to get your application ready for uploading to the application market. In addition to including the typical checklists, this section suggests tools and processes you can use to perform the final tests for your application.

➤ **"Publishing Your Application to the Android Market"** covers how the current Android Market works. In addition, this section walks through the process of uploading an application and describes common gotchas in the publication process.

This chapter also gives essential tips to remember while working through the publication process. However, do not limit your endeavors to the ideas listed in this chapter. Instead, use this chapter as a foundation to build a custom publication and maintenance strategy that makes the most of your application and its market.

PREPARING YOUR APPLICATION

As developers, we tend to get excited as our application nears completion. In fact, we get so enthusiastic about our application that we sometimes skip critical steps whose omission could prove detrimental to the success of our application in the Android Market. The purpose of this section is to help keep this enthusiasm in check by giving you a few tips, tricks, and items to consider before you begin the publishing process. In addition, this section spends some time covering the steps involved in dealing with licensing issues, preparing for the final deployment, and avoiding common gotchas.

Testing Your Application

Testing is the most important step in this chapter. It is critical and essential that you fully test your application before publication. Even though you have probably spent much time testing your application, several steps are still important before you release your application into the wild.

Why do we stress testing so much? Beyond the obvious reasons, releasing applications into the application market is very different from releasing applications in other areas. The phone application market is a unique animal, both in how its users react and in what kind of hardware your application will face. Extensive testing is important for the following reasons:

➤ **Users are much less forgiving of phone applications than they are of other applications, such as desktop apps.** In a world in which thousands of applications compete for your users' time, your application needs to shine much brighter than anything around it. Simple mistakes such as random stop errors and missing menu items can instantly ruin an otherwise good relationship with a user. Nothing is worse than seeing Figure 16-1 on an application launch.

➤ **Applications have reviews — and the users give them great weight.** The worst thing that can happen to an application is for it to be launched, only to have a bad initial rating. Users put great stock in application reviews and often simply listen to others' opinions rather than trying an application for themselves. It can be difficult to recover from a bad initial review, so it is best to avoid getting them.

➤ **Android runs on a large variety of platforms.** From tablets to TV boxes to Kindles to a large variety of phones, Android is rapidly spreading to many different hardware platforms. Even though your application may not need to target every one of those hardware devices, it is important not only to test all your target audience's devices but also to fail with grace with unsupported modes.

We probably have driven the need for testing into the ground, but it is an important step and not one to take lightly. Luckily, remembering a few key testing areas can help you focus on getting the job done, and a large number of tools and utilities can help you in your testing endeavors.

FIGURE 16-1

Hitting the Key Testing Areas

While you are going through the testing process before publication, your focus should be a bit broader than just debugging for errors in your application. Although general application stability is important, you should consider several other key aspects of your application:

➤ **UI thread performance is the number-one culprit for causing user dissatisfaction.** While testing your application, rigorously check to make sure that you are doing as little on the UI thread as possible. For new Android developers, this is a common mistake. The UI thread is often overworked because just about every process in an application runs on the UI thread unless specifically handled by the developer. It is always a good idea to review your final product, making sure that you use the UI thread at the appropriate places and use background threads for the rest. The pitfalls of overusing the UI thread are covered in more depth in Chapter 12.

➤ **Screen orientation changes can do strange things to your layout and design.** Therefore, it is a great idea to test every view of your application in both Landscape and Portrait modes. It is surprising how many developers can miss these items. Furthermore, if you are doing any screen animations or anything that requires a calculation of the screen size, remember to detect orientation changes and update any calculations accordingly.

➤ **Different device settings on an Android device can cause unintended results in your application.** In fact, in some cases device settings can render your application unusable. Know how your application will behave under a variety of settings. In particular, be sure to try different values for the following settings:

➤ **Localization:** How does your application behave with different language and region settings? Are you supporting your expected user base in this way? Do you have a default option for every resource?

➤ **The input method (keyboard):** Does your system behave correctly when supporting different keyboard types? What if the keyboard is unavailable? Does the keyboard disappear after text is edited? Does the keyboard complement your application rather than blocking entry fields? Should you include any specialty keys or keyboard options as part of the input methods?

➤ **Different screen sizes and densities:** This is not a device setting so much as an aspect of a device; however, it is a good idea to treat it as a setting and test different values on devices. Do the application's resources reflect the right density level? Does your layout flow work correctly for different screen sizes?

➤ **Device citizenship is another area where developers often miss important testing opportunities.** The difficult thing with device citizenship is that it is such a broad category because it refers to integration that your device has with the Android OS or other applications running on the device. Thankfully, you can follow a couple basic rules that you probably heard while growing up:

➤ **Waste not, want not.** Memory is the key resource for a mobile device because it is a scarce resource that many different applications are vying for. In typical application programming, you can become a little lazy, because the ever-faster hardware of the typical PC gives you a great buffer for writing suboptimal code. Currently, the mobile world is a different story. Therefore, focus on using as little memory as possible, for as short a period of time as possible.

Also, if memory is the key resource, the device's battery reserves are a close second. Be aware of how much of an impact your application has on overall battery life. Be sure to use system resources such as GPS efficiently. Finally, if you are writing any kind of service, take time to use a battery profiling application to understand the full impact of your service on overall power consumption over time. Inordinate battery consumption is another pet peeve of many users and will quickly result in your application's being removed from their devices.

➤ **Clean up after yourself.** When running a process, take the time to fully handle situations in which the application no longer has focus. There is no reason to maintain an animation if the application is no longer in the foreground. By using the correct events in the life cycle, you can ensure that the app runs a little smoother.

In addition, be wary when using system devices such as the camera. When not using them, release them as soon as possible to free the resource for other applications. This is a key trait of good citizenship with other applications, because you can have some effect on the performance of other applications in the system by consuming system resources unwisely.

Another important part of cleaning up is to handle any unsaved user data just before an application closes or crashes. Whether your application has been sitting in the background long enough to be collected, or your application encounters an unexpected error, do your best to save pertinent data as the application is closing. Not only does this save the user trouble, it is rather impressive when executed correctly.

➤ **Finally, check your application's dependencies on other services and resources.** More importantly, check to see how your application behaves when those services and resources are not there. Here are some things to check out:

   ➤ How does your application perform when it does not have network connections?

   ➤ What if it is missing Bluetooth or GPS?

   ➤ How does it act when it cannot access the device's camera?

   ➤ How does your device handle situations where no SD card exists?

Elegantly dealing with these failures is one of the quickest ways to make a great impression on your application's user. Conversely, failing to do so can quickly result in negative feedback.

Tools for the Testing Trade

When working on a Mono for Android application, you are in a rare position. Not only can you leverage tools found on the Android/Java side of things, but you also can leverage many of the tools found in the Visual Studio/.NET stack. This gives you quite a bit of power to test your application in a variety of ways.

You have numerous toolsets at your disposal. In an effort to introduce as many tools as possible, the following sections give a high-level overview of many of the available tools and how to leverage them in your project.

Unit Testing

It is rare today to go very far into programming without hearing about unit testing. Developers may hold different views on various unit-testing procedures, such as the pros and cons of test-driven development (TDD) or integration testing. Regardless, unit tests are excellent tools to assist in the development process. Even though it may seem late in the game, it is never too late to add a few tests.

Unit testing on the Mono for Android platform still is not completely seamless. Currently no tools for Visual Studio can assist with any kind of UI testing. Despite this, do not forget that most of Android was built with the MVC pattern in mind. This means that you should not have difficulty isolating a large portion of your logic into separate layers or DLLs, affording great testability options.

With that in mind, almost any unit-testing framework that works with Visual Studio (or despite Visual Studio) can apply to a Mono for Android class library. In addition, many of the class types used as parameters are interfaces. Even though you may never succeed in getting 100 percent coverage, unit testing is a viable option when working on Mono for Android. In particular, unit testing comes in handy as you begin to respond to user feedback, begin updating your logic, or even in special cases such as stress testing or preventing bug regression.

DDMS

The Dalvik Debug Monitor Server (DDMS) is a specialized debugging tool created by Google that installs with the Android SDK. Of all the tools mentioned in this section, the DDMS is probably one of the most versatile and useful for tracking down just about any information about your running application.

The exciting thing about this tool is that it operates by connecting directly to a running emulator. This means that it works seamlessly with both Android and Mono for Android projects. Also, it gives information not only on the emulator, but also on any Android device connected to the computer and running in Debug mode, whether that is a physical phone or tablet. Thus, this tool is an excellent choice when you are doing the final checks on your application.

In a way, the DDMS acts much like the Windows Task Manager or the activity monitor on Linux, in that it can give you information on memory allocation, performance statistics, and other OS-related information. Of course, this tool does much more:

➤ **The DDMS provides tooling to track heap usage for any given process.** This is a great place to get a snapshot of your memory heap usage. Figure 16-2 gives the heap statistics used for the `SurfaceView` application created in Chapter 12.

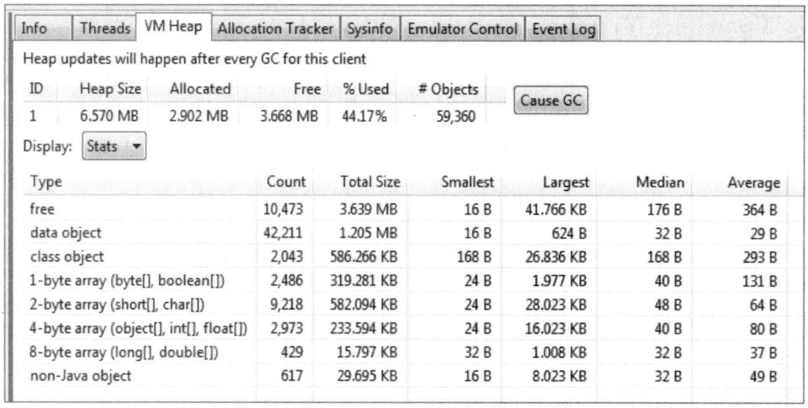

Info	Threads	VM Heap	Allocation Tracker	Sysinfo	Emulator Control	Event Log

Heap updates will happen after every GC for this client

ID	Heap Size	Allocated	Free	% Used	# Objects	
1	6.570 MB	2.902 MB	3.668 MB	44.17%	59,360	Cause GC

Display: Stats ▼

Type	Count	Total Size	Smallest	Largest	Median	Average
free	10,473	3.639 MB	16 B	41.766 KB	176 B	364 B
data object	42,211	1.205 MB	16 B	624 B	32 B	29 B
class object	2,043	586.266 KB	168 B	26.836 KB	168 B	293 B
1-byte array (byte[], boolean[])	2,486	319.281 KB	24 B	1.977 KB	40 B	131 B
2-byte array (short[], char[])	9,218	582.094 KB	24 B	28.023 KB	48 B	64 B
4-byte array (object[], int[], float[])	2,973	233.594 KB	24 B	16.023 KB	40 B	80 B
8-byte array (long[], double[])	429	15.797 KB	32 B	1.008 KB	32 B	37 B
non-Java object	617	29.695 KB	16 B	8.023 KB	32 B	49 B

FIGURE 16-2

➤ **The DDMS has a feature that lets you track the allocation of objects to memory.** You can delve into your running application and gauge how your classes and threads allocate memory to different objects. The only downside of this feature is that, because Mono for Android "translates" your application for you, it can be a bit more difficult to track down which object is what in Visual Studio. Of course, this can be overcome with a small amount of deductive reasoning, making this one of the best locations to track down memory consumption issues.

Figure 16-3 gives an example of object usage in different threads of the `HTML5Logo_Bouncing` application used in Chapter 12.

➤ **The DDMS has LogCat embedded as a window pane.** Although this functionality is provided within Visual Studio via the Android Device Logging screen, this is a nice feature in the DDMS. Unlike the Visual Studio tools, the embedded LogCat screen lets you toggle message verbosity, quickly filter messages by type (warning, debug, error), or simply export selected portions to a `.csv` file. Figure 16-4 shows the LogCat view.

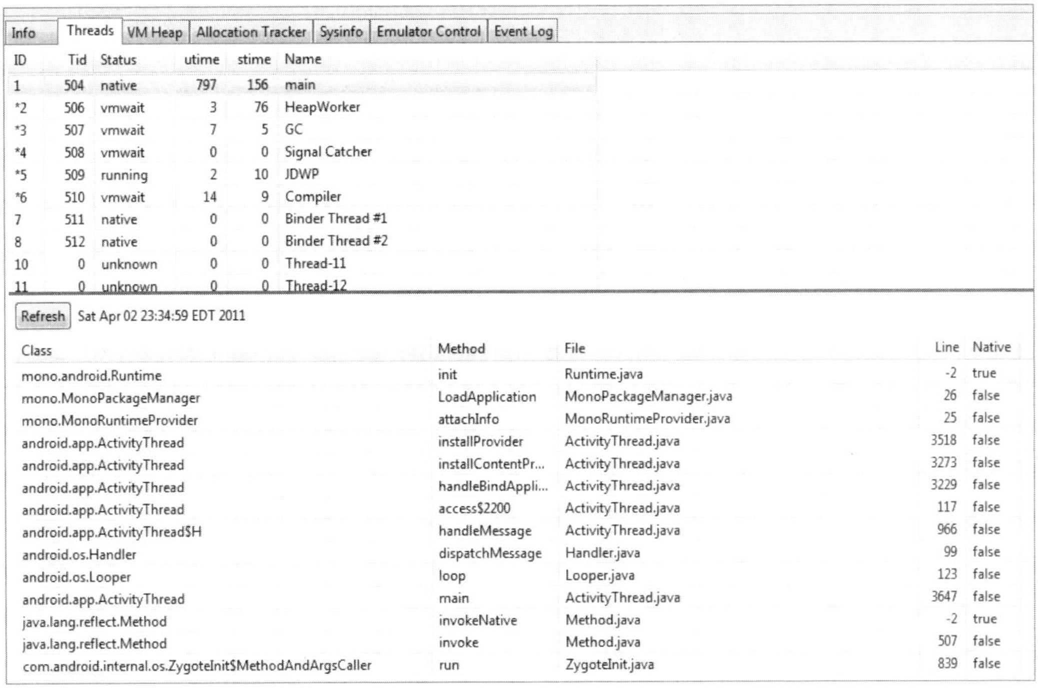

Info	Threads	VM Heap	Allocation Tracker	Sysinfo	Emulator Control	Event Log

ID	Tid	Status	utime	stime	Name
1	504	native	797	156	main
*2	506	vmwait	3	76	HeapWorker
*3	507	vmwait	7	5	GC
*4	508	vmwait	0	0	Signal Catcher
*5	509	running	2	10	JDWP
*6	510	vmwait	14	9	Compiler
7	511	native	0	0	Binder Thread #1
8	512	native	0	0	Binder Thread #2
10	0	unknown	0	0	Thread-11
11	0	unknown	0	0	Thread-12

Refresh   Sat Apr 02 23:34:59 EDT 2011

Class	Method	File	Line	Native
mono.android.Runtime	init	Runtime.java	-2	true
mono.MonoPackageManager	LoadApplication	MonoPackageManager.java	26	false
mono.MonoRuntimeProvider	attachInfo	MonoRuntimeProvider.java	25	false
android.app.ActivityThread	installProvider	ActivityThread.java	3518	false
android.app.ActivityThread	installContentPr...	ActivityThread.java	3273	false
android.app.ActivityThread	handleBindAppli...	ActivityThread.java	3229	false
android.app.ActivityThread	access$2200	ActivityThread.java	117	false
android.app.ActivityThread$H	handleMessage	ActivityThread.java	966	false
android.os.Handler	dispatchMessage	Handler.java	99	false
android.os.Looper	loop	Looper.java	123	false
android.app.ActivityThread	main	ActivityThread.java	3647	false
java.lang.reflect.Method	invokeNative	Method.java	-2	true
java.lang.reflect.Method	invoke	Method.java	507	false
com.android.internal.os.ZygoteInit$MethodAndArgsCaller	run	ZygoteInit.java	839	false

FIGURE 16-3

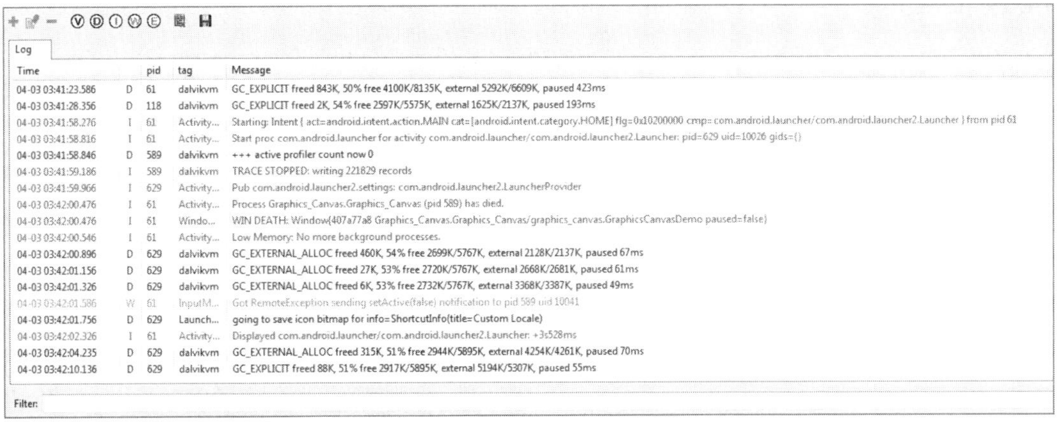

Time	pid	tag	Message
04-03 03:41:23.586	D 61	dalvikvm	GC_EXPLICIT freed 843K, 50% free 4100K/8135K, external 5292K/6609K, paused 423ms
04-03 03:41:28.356	D 118	dalvikvm	GC_EXPLICIT freed 2K, 54% free 2597K/5575K, external 1625K/2137K, paused 193ms
04-03 03:41:58.276	I 61	Activity...	Starting: Intent { act=android.intent.action.MAIN cat=[android.intent.category.HOME] flg=0x10200000 cmp=com.android.launcher/com.android.launcher2.Launcher } from pid 61
04-03 03:41:58.816	I 61	Activity...	Start proc com.android.launcher for activity com.android.launcher/com.android.launcher2.Launcher: pid=629 uid=10026 gids=()
04-03 03:41:58.846	D 589	dalvikvm	+++ active profiler count now 0
04-03 03:41:59.186	I 589	dalvikvm	TRACE STOPPED: writing 221829 records
04-03 03:41:59.966	I 629	Activity...	Pub com.android.launcher2.settings: com.android.launcher2.LauncherProvider
04-03 03:42:00.476	I 61	Activity...	Process Graphics_Canvas.Graphics_Canvas (pid 589) has died.
04-03 03:42:00.476	I 61	Windo...	WIN DEATH: Window{407a77a8 Graphics_Canvas.Graphics_Canvas/graphics_canvas.GraphicsCanvasDemo paused=false}
04-03 03:42:00.546	I 61	Activity...	Low Memory: No more background processes.
04-03 03:42:00.896	D 629	dalvikvm	GC_EXTERNAL_ALLOC freed 460K, 54% free 2699K/5767K, external 2128K/2137K, paused 67ms
04-03 03:42:01.156	D 629	dalvikvm	GC_EXTERNAL_ALLOC freed 27K, 53% free 2720K/5767K, external 2668K/2681K, paused 61ms
04-03 03:42:01.326	D 629	dalvikvm	GC_EXTERNAL_ALLOC freed 6K, 53% free 2732K/5767K, external 3368K/3387K, paused 49ms
04-03 03:42:01.586	W 61	InputM...	Got RemoteException sending setActive(false) notification to pid 589 uid 10041
04-03 03:42:01.756	D 629	Launch...	going to save icon bitmap for info= ShortcutInfo(title= Custom Locale)
04-03 03:42:02.326	I 61	Activity...	Displayed com.android.launcher/com.android.launcher2.Launcher: +3s528ms
04-03 03:42:04.235	D 629	dalvikvm	GC_EXTERNAL_ALLOC freed 315K, 51% free 2944K/5895K, external 4254K/4261K, paused 70ms
04-03 03:42:10.136	D 629	dalvikvm	GC_EXPLICIT freed 88K, 51% free 2917K/5895K, external 5194K/5307K, paused 55ms

Filter:

FIGURE 16-4

Beyond these key features, the DDMS offers lots of great utilities: spoofing locations, calls, and text messages; adjusting device states such as network connectivity, latency, and speed; and various smaller tasks such as taking screenshots, doing method profiling, and providing graphical layouts of performance statistics. Figure 16-5 shows an emulator's running memory usage.

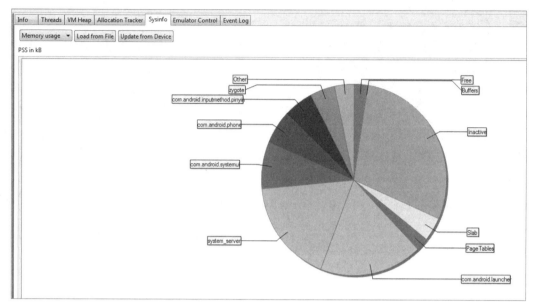

FIGURE 16-5

When you consider the massive potential of the DDMS, this tool is worth your time to investigate. It can prove essential when you are trying to put that final polish on your application's performance.

The Emulator

Although you are probably familiar with the emulator tool by now, it has quite a few other options you can use to test a variety of phone conditions. In addition to testing a diversity of system settings, such as localization, the emulator has a series of command-line switches that launch it into different states. These options vary from giving you different screen densities to simulating different phone load scenarios. Table 16-1 is a short list of some of the available phone configuration switches.

TABLE 16-1: Common Emulator Command-Line Switches

OPTION NAME	DESCRIPTION
-dpi/-scale	Scales the emulator screen size by the desired scaling factor.
-netspeed	Allows the developer to specify a target network speed setting to emulate low- versus high-speed connections.
-netdelay	Specifies network latency on the device.
-cpu-delay	Can simulate a CPU under stress by applying an abstract delay factor on emulator requests.

These are just a few of the typical command-line switches available for emulators. You can view a more exhaustive list at `http://developer.android.com/guide/developing/tools/emulator.html`.

In addition to the command-line switches, emulators have a variety of configuration settings that can be leveraged for testing, such as adding/removing SD card access. When you are testing with emulators, it often helps to generate a suite of different emulator images to represent different states. Although this is a bit of a pain to maintain, it's a great way to ensure that your application behaves consistently under certain conditions.

Finally, the testing abilities of the DDMS and the emulator overlap in some situations. Typically, the DDMS is the faster tool for approaching a single process and testing one aspect of it. The emulator provides a way to test many scenarios in a whole environment and has the added feature of saving testing scenarios.

 It's important to remember that the emulator and DDMS do not replace the need to test your application on the physical devices. Use these options for initial testing and for scenarios in which you cannot physically access a phone type or re-create the phone condition.

Traceviews

Another excellent tool provided by the Android SDK is Traceview, which allows you to graphically view tracing and execution data from your Android device. It accomplishes this by building an application timeline based on the timestamps of recorded debugging messages for each running thread. When working with the timeline windows, you can slice portions of time to zoom into and inspect deeply. These slices go down to portions of a millisecond, which gives you great visibility into how every step of your application runs. Figure 16-6 shows the timeline view of the Traceview tool.

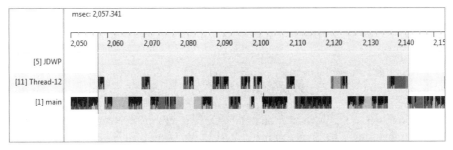

FIGURE 16-6

This figure shows examples of the timelines on several running threads. This application uses switching to background threads (Thread-12) to do heavy processing before pushing those updates onto the main thread. Notice how you can easily see the staggering execution between each thread, as well as the overall time spent in each "hop."

In addition to providing timeline information, you can use Traceview to profile the expense and time lapse for any given process. This is easily accomplished by selecting a spot in the timeline and clicking the area. Traceview then fills the profile window with a summary of all the time spent with the selected method. In addition, you can move up and down the profile window, getting a feel for how long each individual method or group of methods takes to execute. Figure 16-7 shows a drawing function's profile view.

Name	Incl %	Inclusive	Excl %	Exclusive	Calls+Recur...	Time/Call
8 android/view/ViewGroup.dispatchDraw (Landroid/graphics/C	27.3%	5431.616	1.7%	330.681	334+668	5.421
9 android/view/ViewGroup.drawChild (Landroid/graphics/Canv	26.6%	5293.755	4.3%	852.424	334+1002	3.962
Parents						
8 android/view/ViewGroup.dispatchDraw (Landroid/grap	100.0%	5293.755			334/1336	
Children						
self	5.1%	271.509				
8 android/view/ViewGroup.dispatchDraw (Landroid/grap	89.1%	4715.213			334/1002	
37 android/graphics/Canvas.quickReject (FFFFLandroid/	1.7%	89.082			334/1336	
53 android/graphics/Canvas.save ()I	1.0%	52.565			334/1002	
54 android/graphics/Canvas.clipRect (IIII)Z	0.8%	43.841			334/1002	
60 android/view/View.getDrawingCache (Z)Landroid/gra	0.6%	29.942			334/1002	
51 android/graphics/Canvas.restoreToCount (I)V	0.5%	28.726			334/1336	
64 android/view/View.getAnimation ()Landroid/view/an	0.4%	21.406			334/1336	
67 android/view/View.computeScroll ()V	0.4%	21.255			334/1002	
50 android/graphics/Canvas.translate (FF)V	0.4%	20.216			334/1670	
(context switch)	0.0%	0.000			28/3708	
Parents while recursive						
Children while recursive						
10 android/os/Handler.handleCallback (Landroid/os/Message;)'	15.4%	3072.384	1.1%	218.359	2397+0	1.282
11 mono/java/lang/IRunnableAdapter.run ()V	14.4%	2854.025	1.1%	222.825	2397+0	1.191

FIGURE 16-7

You can see the total time spent within the selected method call. You also can view all the underlying child methods within the selected method, giving you an excellent view of where your longer-running requests are occurring. Finally, the Calls+RecurrCalls/Total column shows how many calls were made to this particular method. By combining this value with the overall time spent on a method, you can quickly realize the best places to improve your application's performance.

Traceview can be initiated on an application in two different ways. The first and simplest way is to start tracing via the DDMS tool. When you open the DDMS, select a given running application on a listed device. Then start method profiling by clicking the corresponding button in the main window of the DDMS. This initiates tracing on your application. Once tracing is enabled, it captures the process calls in that application. When you are ready to stop tracking, simply click the same button that initiated tracing. The Traceview window appears with the collected data because the DDMS tool launches Traceview automatically.

You also can initiate a tracing session through code. This is a great way to focus on one particular function call and remove the noise of other operations. To do this, simply use the `Debug` class to initiate a tracing method, as shown in Listing 16-1.

LISTING 16-1: Writing trace information to the SD card via code

```
private void RunLoop(View TargetView)
{
    Debug.StartMethodTracing("DemoTracing");
    while (IsRunning)
    {
        Thread.Sleep(10);
        RunOnUiThread(() => TargetView.Invalidate());
    }
    Debug.StopMethodTracing();
}
```

When you use the Debug class to capture tracing messages, you need to ensure that your emulator or Android device has an SD card and that your application has WRITE_EXTERNAL_STORAGE permission. With these in place, the file is written to the root directory of the SD card with the name you specified and the .trace file extension.

Stress Testing via the Application Exerciser Monkey

The Exerciser Monkey, or simply the Monkey, is an application that runs on an emulator in tandem with the application you are developing. Using its many configuration options, the Monkey can be used to stress-test the application to generate a series of clicks, presses, and events on the Android device. Each of these events occurs in a semirandom pattern.

The strength of the Monkey is that it can be executed using basic commands from within the adb executable. In addition to specifying the number of events to generate, you can configure the Monkey in three other areas:

➤ **Constraints:** Within the command-line arguments, you can constrain the Monkey to generate events only on target packages. Furthermore, random events can also be locked down to only certain categories of activities.

➤ **Debugging:** You can specify how the Monkey responds to numerous events, exceptions, or time-outs. Typically, the Monkey stops functioning when it encounters an issue such as a time-out or application error. Using the command-line arguments, you can fine-tune what kinds of situations the Monkey can ignore.

➤ **Events:** This area represents the kinds of events the Monkey generates, such as touch events, motion events, trackball events, navigation events, application switches, and a few others. Using command-line arguments, you can lock down the frequency of these random events to target different types of stress scenarios.

Needless to say, the Monkey is an excellent way to stress-test an application to ensure that you have adequately handled many different touch scenarios and events. Not only is it a handy tool, but it is also easy to use. With the emulator running, open a command window and navigate to the default install directory of your Android SDK. Find the adb executable, located under the platform-tools directory. Once you are there, begin a basic stress test by using the following command:

```
adb shell monkey -v 100
```

Using this command, the Monkey exercises 100 random events on every package installed on the Android device. As you might imagine, this can be quite a lengthy process. However, you can single out a package by using the Monkey's -p argument.

The Monkey is an excellent tool for stress testing. It's worth the time to learn more about it. For more information and a full list of all the possible switches, refer to the Android documentation at http://developer.android.com/guide/developing/tools/monkey.html.

UI Testing via the Monkeyrunner

In addition to running stress tests on your application, you may find that you want to specify a series of clicks and events in a preset pattern. Although the Monkey tool can generate a series of pseudo-random events, it cannot perform any scripted tasks. For situations such as these, you can use another tool called Monkeyrunner.

Monkeyrunner is an interface to an API that can interact with running Android emulators. Via this API, the Monkeyrunner can accomplish many different tasks, such as deploying applications, causing various UI/touch events, taking screenshots, and so on. Using this tool, you can create a full suite of UI testing functions that can be performed repeatedly in a unit-testing-style methodology.

One of the biggest challenges that a C# developer would have with using Monkeyrunner is that instructions for it are written using Python. Consequently, this option is not for the novice developer, but it's well worth your time to understand and use it within your builds. For more information about Monkeyrunner, visit the Android documentation at http://developer.android .com/guide/developing/tools/monkeyrunner_concepts.html.

Although each of the tools described in this section can and should be used during the main development process, they also provide a nice way to inspect your application's overall health and performance in prepublication scenarios. In addition, they can be used to quickly ferret out many difficult application issues, such as memory leaks, threading errors, and heavy methods.

Involving Peers and Users in the Testing Process

Once you have established that your application can pass your self-imposed rigorous tests, it is generally a good idea to share some of the testing burden with your peers or any willing device user. This can greatly increase your application's stability by ferreting out any unexpected errors. It's also a great way to collect some initial user feedback and make any last-minute modifications.

When selecting beta users for your application, it is important to consider a few different factors. Although it is great to have a close friend or relative review your application, you run the risk of receiving overly positive feedback or not actually testing against your target audience. The following list offers a few quick tips for choosing the right beta testers:

➤ **Consider including both power users and casual users.** Power users typically are willing to go through more steps for greater functionality but can often be much less forgiving of common mistakes. Conversely, casual users often appreciate direct, intuitive interfaces and sometimes are less annoyed by an occasional glitch in the process flow.

➤ **Consider the types of devices that your beta users will use.** It is critical that you test your application on as many different hardware devices as possible. By leveraging your beta user base, you can satisfy your testing requirement without a significant financial investment in hardware.

➤ **Choose people who give balanced feedback.** People who are ridiculously critical or who are likely to give only positive feedback add very little value.

➤ **Offer some initial tips on how to give feedback.** Most people are not experts at giving feedback. "This is great" or "This is awful" is not valuable feedback. Encourage them to detail what makes them feel this way and how they think your application could be better.

➤ **Provide clean, easy-to-use feedback channels.** Forcing your beta users to fill out long forms or log in through several screens will result in less feedback. Be respectful of their time and efforts.

➤ **Within feedback iterations, it is acceptable to ask for focused attention on a particular aspect of the application.** However, avoid overloading the user with too many focus questions; they can detract from the feedback value when overdone.

Establishing a testing group is a great way to help your application become a stable and usable product. In addition, a good testing group can serve as a sanity check, especially after you publish your application and begin receiving user feedback.

PUBLISHING YOUR APPLICATION TO THE ANDROID MARKET

Let's assume that your application is ready to go. You have optimized it to the point that it runs at peak performance. You have tested for and eliminated all known bugs. Finally, you have gone through multiple iterations of feedback testers, and you believe you have an awesome application ready to go. The last hurdle to cross is publishing your application to the Android Market.

With your application fully developed and tested, it is time to make the final modifications to your Mono for Android application to prepare it to be uploaded to the Android Market. Although a couple of these steps are specific to either Mono for Android or Visual Studio, the steps in this process are almost identical to those of any typical Android application.

Versioning Your Application

The first step of preparing your application for publication is to assign it a proper application name, package name, version number, and version name. These values are important to your application, because they are what the Android OS uses to identify your application, track any dependencies, and ascertain whether a more recent version is available on the Android Market. More specifically, versioning is a critical step in the publication process for several reasons:

➤ Versioning is useful if you intend to upgrade or maintain your application after it has been published to the Android Market. It acts as a simple, visible cue to assign update notes and tell the users what features are in what version.

➤ Android uses your application's version number to automatically inform the user that an update of your application is available. Of course, this happens only when a user checks for updates in the Android Market. Any other update notifications or version restrictions must be handled by the developer in-application.

➤ Versions are used to assist in tracking dependencies and compatibility between applications. In particular, if your application is part of a suite of applications, the application's version number can be leveraged to ensure that everything is using the correct build.

In Android, the version of an application can be expressed via two values. The first value is Version Name. Consider this string value to be the typical version information listing, using the *MajorVersion.MinorVersion.PointVersion* pattern. The Android OS does not use this value for anything other than informational purposes. This serves as a visual clue to your application users and other services that would track updates of your application.

The other value that Android requires for versioning is the Version Code. The Android OS uses this integer-only number to determine if one version of your application is newer than another. Assuming that your initial release of the application is version 1, Android considers any application with a version code greater than 1 to be an update. Since this is considered an "internal" value, this version is invisible to the users.

In a way, the versioning system in Android is a compromise to allow developers to define their own versioning standards and styles while maintaining a simple, quick way to ascertain upgrade and downgrade information programmatically.

Adding versioning information to your application is a basic task. In typical Android development, you can specify an application's version number by manually editing the Android Manifest file, which acts much like the `web.config` file in ASP.NET programming. In Mono for Android, the developers have simplified this process by adding Android Manifest menu options in the application's Properties window.

In your application, go to the Properties window and select the Android Manifest tab. Within this screen, you see the appropriate fields to edit your version number, as well as several other values, as shown in Figure 16-8.

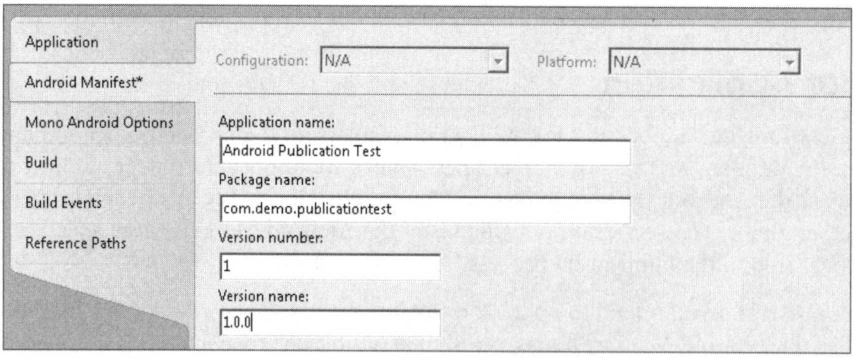

FIGURE 16-8

The cautious reader may have noticed that Figure 16-8 shows the name "Version Name" rather than "Version Code" as a field in the Visual Studio properties. This is not a mistake. Although the Android Manifest expects an element of Version Code, the Visual Studio tooling has renamed this to the more globally used term, Version Name.

Creating the Final Build

The next step of preparing your application is to create a final build within Visual Studio. As with most applications within Visual Studio, there are at least two separate types of build configurations: Debug and Release. Up to this point, you have most likely been operating under the Debug mode configuration.

The Debug mode configuration is important because it is a configuration setting that favors the process of building and debugging an application for testing at the expense of optimization or build size. In addition to the typical debug advantages found in any Visual Studio application, a few aspects pertain to only Mono for Android:

> ➤ **Debug builds use the Mono for Android shared runtime rather than existing as a singular package on the development device.** This means that when an application is first deployed to a debugging device, two applications are installed: the application you are working with, and the Mono for Android runtime. The runtime includes all of Mono for Android's libraries. Therefore, it can be a rather large installation on the first publication. But it is much smaller and faster for subsequent application pushes, because the Mono for Android runtime has to be deployed only the first time.

> ➤ **Applications deployed under the Debug configuration are automatically signed by the Mono for Android runtime.** The Android system requires that all applications be digitally signed with a private key that belongs to the application developer. In the case of debugging applications, a debugging key is generated and associated with your application.

The Release configuration is used when the application is ready for deployment. Within the context of Visual Studio, this configuration is optimized for best performance and size. In addition, Mono for Android no longer autosigns your builds with the developer key. Finally, the runtime chooses what packages are required from the Mono for Android framework, bundles those with your application, and creates a single release in the form of an .apk file.

With that in mind, you can begin the process of creating the final build. First, change the configuration mode in Visual Studio to Release rather than Debug. Typically, this can be accomplished by changing the value of the appropriate drop-down list within Visual Studio's standard toolbar. Figure 16-9 displays this process.

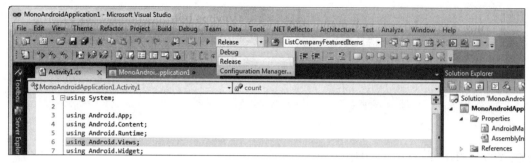

FIGURE 16-9

Alternatively, you can alter your configuration settings by right-clicking the solution in the Solution Explorer window, selecting Properties, and viewing the Configuration section of the property pages.

When you switch from Debug to Release on a Mono for Android project, the Mono Android Options for the application should be updated simultaneously to no longer use the Shared Runtime. To double-check this process (or to remove this default setting), go to the application's Properties ⇨ Mono Android Options and ensure that the Use Shared Runtime option is clear, as shown in Figure 16-10.

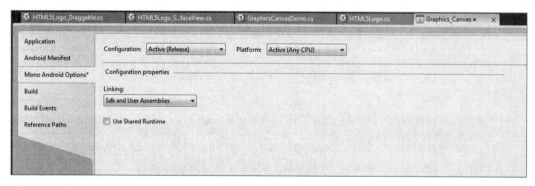

FIGURE 16-10

Your application is now ready to build. The final step in the build process is to test your application one more time in the Release configuration.

Although you have already fully tested your application, moving to Release mode makes a massive change to your underlying application. Therefore, quickly deploy your application one more time, and ensure that it behaves as intended.

Signing Your Application

With a final build in place, you can begin the process of signing your application. The purpose of doing so is twofold:

➤ First, it ensures the application's security during deployment. This is important, because a signed application includes the means to verify the publisher's identity and verify that the downloaded application matches the actual application via a checksum.

➤ The second purpose is that Google uses the signing mechanism to uniquely identify the application's developer (or development team) and to determine if they have the permission to update an application on the Android Market.

To sign an application, you need to generate a certificate. This certificate acts as something of an ID or license for your application. In many cases, a certificate authority is required to create the certificate. Certificate authorities can be a good thing; however, they also can be rather pricey. Consequently, they can become an extra, needless expense for the already tightly budgeted Android developer. Thankfully, in Android, Google allows developers to generate their own self-signed certificates. This not only saves you money but also gives you full authority to manage your applications' ID(s) as you see fit.

Creating a Private Key

Self-signing an application starts with generating a private key. The private key is the credentials by which you can manipulate a signed application. Therefore, it is paramount that you keep your private key safe and secure. Because a private key is used to generate a certificate, the terms are often used synonymously.

Here are a few things to keep in mind about private keys and certificates:

➤ The private key is a mechanism by which an application's certificate is generated. This makes a private key something like an authentication credential or password. However, unlike a password, you cannot "reset" a private key. If a key is lost, you must create a new one, which in turn forces you to make a new certificate.

➤ The certificate and, therefore, your private key are something of an agreement between you and your customer's Android device. When issuing updates, the device must receive a matching certificate from the updating software. If you have had to regenerate the certificate (due to loss of your key or some other reason), the application is unable to update and installs as a new instance instead.

➤ Your certificate and key represent you as a developer or development group. Your credibility as a developer is tied to this key, which means that, if it is stolen and used maliciously, it is done under your credentials.

➤ Certificates and private keys can be used across multiple applications. This also is the only means by which two applications can run within the same system process. This adds a large amount of modular potential to your application, because you can package and group multiple pieces of applications under a single certificate.

➤ Your private key should have a validity period of 25 years or more. Currently, the Android Market expects an application's key to be valid through 2033.

Generating a private key for a Mono for Android application is rather simple. Within the Java SDK that was installed with the Android SDK is a tool appropriately named `keytool`. Using this command-line tool, you can quickly create a keystore for your application. A keystore is basically a database for private keys. Table 16-2 lists the different switches that can be used when generating a keystore.

TABLE 16-2: Keytool Command-Line Options

COMMAND	DESCRIPTION
-genkey	Commands the tool to generate a new public and private key.
-v	Enables verbose output from `keytool`.
-alias	Specifies an eight-character maximum alias for the generated key.
-keyalg	Allows the developer to choose the encryption algorithm to use for the private key. Currently, RSA and DSA are supported.
-dname	The distinguished name that describes who created this key. In most cases, this is your name or that of the development company you are working for. If this value is specified, it is used in the issuer and subject fields of the self-signed certificate.
-keypass	Allows you to specify the key's password. However, if this is not supplied, `keytool` prompts you to enter a password. Typically, waiting for the prompt is the more secure method.
-validity	The number of days that this key is valid. The recommended length is 25 years or approximately 10,000 days.
-keystore	The name of the keystore that will be used to contain the key.
-storepass	The keystore's password. Again, if this password is not added, `keytool` prompts you to provide it.

Using `keytool`, you can generate the private keys for your application. Open a command window, navigate to the installation directory of the JDK on your system, and find the directory for `keytool.exe`. The default path on a Windows 7 64-bit machine is

```
C:\Program Files (x86)\Java\jdk<version>\bin\
```

Once there, use `keytool.exe` and the command-line arguments listed in Table 16-2 to generate your private key. The following is a sample command for generating a private key:

```
keytool -genkey -v -keystore <keystore-name>.keystore -alias <key-name>
-keyalg RSA -keysize 2048 -validity 10000
```

As you walk through this command, you are greeted with a series of questions that require identifying information about the owner of this key. After you have answered all the questions, you should have your own private key and keystore, as shown in Figure 16-11.

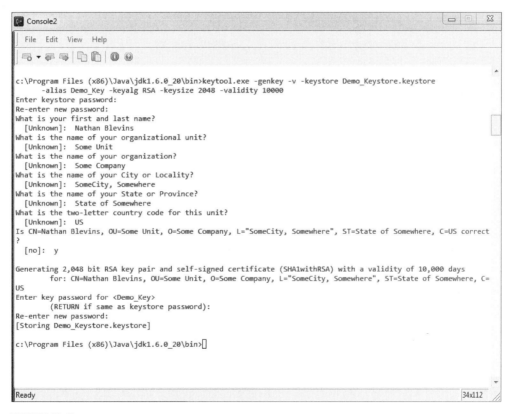

FIGURE 16-11

 When you run these tools from the command line in Windows 7, make sure that they are running with administrator privileges. Otherwise, this tool will be unable to create the appropriate keystore files.

Creating a Self-Signed Certificate

After your private key has been created, you are ready to sign your application. As in the previous section, you can use the tooling included in the JDK to sign the application package. To complete the signing process, you need to have three things prepared:

➤ **The target application as an unsigned package.** When you created your final build, Mono for Android created a release version of your application within the `Bin\Release` directory. If you look in the directory, you will find two versions of your application. One has `-Signed` appended to its name. That version is meant for local deployment and testing, because it is still signed with the autogenerated debug key. Use the unsigned version of your application. Figure 16-12 shows these different files.

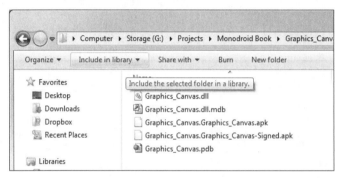

FIGURE 16-12

➤ **Access to the private key and keystore that were just created.** These will be used to create the self-signed certificate. By default, generated keystores are saved in the same directory as the `keytool` executable.

➤ **The `jarsigner` tool found in the JDK.** As with `keytool`, you use `jarsigner` to combine the unsigned `.apk` and the private key to create a signed package for upload. In Windows 7 64-bit, `jarsigner` is found under `C:\Program Files (x86)\Java\jdk<version>\bin\`.

To use the `jarsigner` tool, you simply call it using the command line and provide the appropriate arguments. The following is an example of using the `jarsigner` command-line tool:

```
jarsigner -verbose -keystore <my-keystore-name>.keystore <package .apk> <key-name>
```

After this is run, the system prompts you for the passwords to the keystore and the target key. You can verify that your application signing was successful by using the `-verify` switch of the `jarsigner` tool:

```
jarsigner -verify <package.apk>
```

Congratulations. You have now applied your own self-signed certificate to the application.

Aligning the Final Package

After you perform the preceding steps, you have a fully signed package. However, one more step is needed before the process is complete. Within the Android SDK is a tool called `zipalign`. Provided by Google, it is a simple tool used to ensure that your application runs as smoothly as possible.

Although technically you can deploy your application without taking this step, it is not a good idea to bypass it unless you have good reason.

The purpose of this tool is to align uncompressed bytes within the package so that it can be read and handled more efficiently. For the most part, the process by which `zipalign` does this is not essential to understand — beyond the fact that the net result is that your application consumes slightly less device RAM when running.

`zipalign` can be found under the default installation path of your Android SDK, in the `tools` directory. When running it, you basically need to provide the current project name and a name for the output project. Here's an example of what the `zipalign` tool command looks like:

```
zipalign -v 4 <current unaligned project>.apk<output project name>.apk
```

> Looking at the command for the `zipalign` tool, you will notice a 4 after the verbose switch. When using `zipalign`, *always include that 4 and never any other number. This command indicates the byte boundary by which the* `zipalign` *tool optimizes the code.*
>
> *For any Android application, the memory address size is 16 bits, or 4 bytes. If you align appropriate items in code to a 4-byte boundary, Android can access them directly using the* `mmap()` *function. This decreases the amount of overall RAM required to run your application.*
>
> *You can read more about* `zipalign`, `mmap`, *and memory addresses at the following links:*
>
> ➤ **zipalign:** `http://developer.android.com/guide/developing/tools/zipalign.html`
>
> ➤ **mmap:** `http://en.wikipedia.org/wiki/Mmap`
>
> ➤ **Memory addresses:** `http://en.wikipedia.org/wiki/Memory_address`

With this final step, your application is now signed, optimized, and ready for publication to the Android Market!

Uploading to the Android Market

Publishing an application to the Android Market typically is a pretty quick process. To publish, you and your application need to meet a few requirements:

➤ You must be registered as an Android developer. This costs $25 and takes just a few minutes. To sign up, visit `http://market.android.com/publish`.

➤ You need an application in its final build, signed, and aligned. Specifically, you need to ensure that your application's license does not expire before 2033.

➤ You must have properly versioned your application.

➤ Your application must specify both a label and an icon within its definition.

Assuming that those things are covered, you can now publish your application! Visit the publication site at `http://market.android.com` and log in using the developer credentials you specified when you signed up for your developer account.

After you log in, you can select to upload your application by choosing the Upload Application button on the lower-right side of the page, as shown in Figure 16-13.

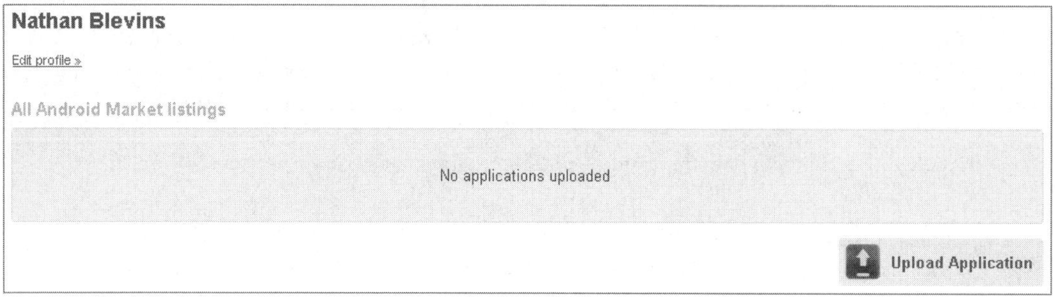

Nathan Blevins

Edit profile »

All Android Market listings

No applications uploaded

Upload Application

FIGURE 16-13

On the next screen, add the appropriate information about your application. First, you are asked to upload a draft version of your application. The term "draft" is a little confusing. Basically, this is a staging upload until you complete all the application information and select the Publish button at the bottom of the page.

After uploading your `.apk` file, fill in the rest of the form as completely and honestly as possible (see Figure 16-14). This information mainly pertains to what the users will see when your application is listed on the Android Market. Take the time to include adequate screenshots, descriptions, and other information, because they will be the first things a potential user sees about your application.

After you have filled in the necessary information, select the Publish button. Congratulations! You have now published an application to the Android Market!

SUMMARY

Deploying your application is a huge milestone for any developer. It is a target for which developers strive from the time they write their first line of code. While working toward this goal, it is important not to become overeager, because many different steps within the publication process still need your full consideration.

Testing is by far the most important step in the publication process. Lack of testing can keep your application from succeeding in the Android Market, thereby wasting your development efforts. Luckily, many tools can assist you, ranging from performance monitoring to UI testing to application testing. Finally, using a bank of beta testers is an excellent way to gauge your product's overall usability while ferreting out those last few bugs that you may have overlooked.

FIGURE 16-14

After your application passes your rigorous testing process, it can be quickly deployed to the Android Market efficiently and securely.

17

Android Tablets

WHAT'S IN THIS CHAPTER?

➤   Designing a tablet user interface (UI)

➤   Working with the action bar to use the extra screen space effectively

➤   Working with fragments to divide the screen and use the extra real estate effectively

Android 3.0 (Honeycomb) has been available since early 2011. Unfortunately, the initial Android tablets based on Android 3.x were not well accepted in the market. Thankfully, Android tablet shipments have ticked up with the release of Android 4.0 (Ice Cream Sandwich (ICS)). Android 4.0 brings together features from the phone and tablet in much the same way that the Apple iPad and iPhone operating systems were separate until iOS 4.2.

EXAMINING THE ANDROID TABLET MARKETPLACE

The tablet marketplace has seen explosive growth. Tablets have been available for many years in the Microsoft Windows ecosystem. I can remember Pen Windows from the early 1990s. In the early 2000s, Microsoft tried to reenergize tablet devices. Unfortunately, these efforts met with limited success, outside of a few niche areas, and never achieved large consumer demand. This was primarily due to the clunkiness of the hardware, with its large size and weight, as well as the stylus, which was easy to lose.

In 2010, Apple released the iPad. This device — with its tie-in to iTunes, various book resellers, size, and weight — was definitely accepted in the marketplace. Consumers could not purchase enough of them. There were large lines at Apple stores. Deliveries took weeks when ordered online.

The iPad has many great features, including:

➤ **Size:** The iPad is smaller than a laptop but bigger than a phone, making it appropriate for casual usage.

➤ **Weight:** The iPad is easy to carry around on the go or to meetings without having to put it and its supporting peripherals into a bag.

➤ **Preexisting apps:** The iPad offers a large number of preexisting apps due to the fact that its operating system is based on the Apple iPhone operating system.

➤ **Touch:** Although a stylus can be used with the iPad, fingers are the default input mechanism. I know that the four stylus devices I lost over the years with various tablets makes touch-based tablets very appealing.

It's into this marketplace that Android's developers started looking at how to bring Android into the world of tablets. In early 2011, the first Android tablet shipped, the Motorola Xoom. The Xoom shipped with Android 3.0 (Honeycomb). Honeycomb is the code name for the Android operating system that is optimized for tablet usage. Android 3.0 is a tablet-only version of Android 4.0 and is not available from device manufacturers in a phone version.

Android 3.0 has undergone several iterations and is currently giving way to the next major update to Android, called *Ice Cream Sandwich* (ICS) — also referred to as *Android version 4.0*. Android 4.0 is the version of Android designed to run on phones and tablets and provides a common API across these devices. If history is any indication, it will be a while before Android 4.0 becomes available on existing devices, and many existing devices won't be upgraded to Android 4.0. However, that won't stop us from taking a look at some of the important features in Android 4.0, as well as creating applications for Android tablets running Android 3.0 and Android 4.0.

One word of warning as you build applications that target Android tablets: A number of tablets are 7 to 10 inches in their form factor. These tablets look like tablets; however, they run Android 2.x as their operating system. Although these devices fit the physical form factor for a tablet, their operating system isn't Android 3.0 or Android 4.0. Therefore, your Android 3.0/4.0 applications won't run on these devices. Be aware of this during the application development process.

DESIGNING A TABLET UI

Before diving into code, it is important to think about what tablet applications need to be successful. If you think about an Android 2.x or phone application, the UI is a set of activities and users navigate through each individual activity, as necessary, to get work done. Only one activity is available to users at a time. Users perform the work in activity A, go to activity B, select the back button to go to activity A, may end up in activity C, and so on, until their work is complete (see Figure 17-1).

This can be a little bit jarring for users if they need to remember something from one activity screen to another. When thinking about your tablet UI, consider how you can group together information so that the user can be successful. For example, suppose that you have Twitter clients that support multiple user IDs at the same time. In the part of your application that allows users to tweet, it might be helpful to show them which Twitter ID this tweet will go to. And if the users are replying to other users, it might be helpful for the users to see the content that they are replying to, as well as who they are logged in as. For example, the UI flow could be something like that shown in Figure 17-2.

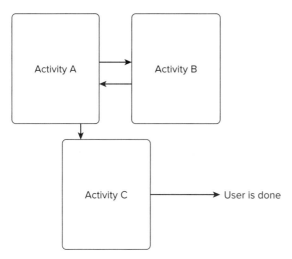

FIGURE 17-1

Twitterid: @wbm

@migueldeicaza: We have just completed support for Android Jelly Bean. Download and build something wonderful!

Tweet

@migueldeicaza this is GREAT! You have made the community VERY HAPPY!

Virtual Keyboard

FIGURE 17-2

In this example, the reply is to @migueldeicaza's statement. You can see who you are logged in as, so you know which account this will be posted to, and you know what exactly you are replying to. This will give the user more context as they work on a response.

USING THE ACTION BAR

Along with the various parts of the screen, you need to think about how users navigate within an application. Android 2.x phone applications use a menu system that allows users to act and navigate within an application. On the other hand, Android 3.0 and Android 4.0 tablet applications offer much more screen real estate with which to work. And desktop applications in Mac OS X and Windows have a menu system that aligns across the top of a screen. This is shown running on Windows in Figure 17-3.

FIGURE 17-3

So, how do you implement this navigation in Android 3.0 and Android 4.0? Thankfully, there is a facility for this, called the *action bar*. The action bar is a widget for activities that replaces the Android title bar that appears at the top of a screen. By default, the application logo appears on the left side of the screen, followed by the title of the activity. Finally, available items are displayed within the options menu within the action bar. These items are referred to as *action items*. The action items provide immediate access to important user actions. Menu items that do not appear as action items are placed in an overflow menu, which is shown as a drop-down list in the action bar. Additional features in the action bar include the ability to provide tabs for navigating between fragments, to provide support for navigation with a drop-down list, and to provide action views.

The action bar is included by default in all activities that target SDK level 11. Specifically, the action bar is included with all Android activities that use the "holographic" theme. This theme is included in any application that targets Android 3.0.

Note that an Android application is set to target a given version of the SDK when its `android:minSdkVersion` or `android:targetSdkVersion` attribute is set to 11 or greater in the `AndroidManifest.xml` file. This can be updated via the project properties in Visual Studio, as shown in Figure 17-4.

FIGURE 17-4

Removing the Action Bar

You can remove the action bar in several ways:

➤ Use the `Theme.Holo.NoActionBar` Android Activity.

➤ If the application has a custom Android Activity theme, set the `android:windowActionBar` property to `false`.

➤ Call the `.Hide()` method of an action bar. The `.Hide()` method is a companion to the `.Show()` method. You can use the `.Show()` method to show the action bar after it has been hidden. If the action bar is hidden, the Android operating system will update the activity so that the content fills all of the screen real estate.

If you remove the action bar using a theme, the action bar will not be available at all. The call to get the `.ActionBar` property will return a null.

Adding Items to the Action Bar

By default, an action item is a menu item. As you learned in Chapter 4, you can create a menu by overriding the default action in `OnCreateOptionsMenu`. When users press a menu key, the `OnMenuItemSelected` method is called and the program will determine which menu item was selected. Listing 17-1 shows how to set up menu items in the action bar.

LISTING 17-1: Loading the action bar

```
[Activity(Label = "HCExample", MainLauncher = true, Icon = "@drawable/icon")]
public class Activity1 : Activity
{
    ActionBar ab;

    protected override void OnCreate(Bundle bundle)
    {
        base.OnCreate(bundle);

        // Set our view from the "main" layout resource
        SetContentView(Resource.Layout.Main);

        // Get our button from the layout resource,
        // and attach an event to it
        Button button = FindViewById<Button>(Resource.Id.MyButton);
        ab = this.ActionBar;

        button.Click += delegate {
```

continues

LISTING 17-1 *(continued)*

```
            if (ab.IsShowing)
            {
                ab.Hide();
            }
            else
            {
                ab.Show();
            }
        };
    }

    public override bool OnCreateOptionsMenu(IMenu menu)
    {
        //return base.OnCreateOptionsMenu(menu);
        MenuInflater inflater = new Android.Views.MenuInflater(this);
        inflater.Inflate(Resource.Layout.menu, menu);
        return true;
    }

    public override bool OnOptionsItemSelected(IMenuItem item)
    {
        return base.OnOptionsItemSelected(item);
    }

    public override bool OnMenuItemSelected(int featureId, IMenuItem item)
    {
        var item1 = FindViewById(Resource.Id.item01);
        var item2 = FindViewById(Resource.Id.item02);

        if (item1.Id == item.ItemId)
        {
            Android.Util.Log.Info("ActionBar",
                String.Format("Item 1 selected. Item: {0}.", item1.Id));
        }
        if (item2.Id == item.ItemId)
        {
            Android.Util.Log.Info("ActionBar",
                String.Format("Item 2 selected. Item: {0}.", item2.Id));
        }
        return base.OnMenuItemSelected(featureId, item);
    }
}
```

HCExample/HCExample/Activity1.cs

Listing 17-2 shows the defined XML menu code to create a menu system directly in the action bar. In this case, the menu system shows an example of using icons, submenu items, as well as the show-AsAction attribute. The icons and submenu items were discussed in the chapter on User Interface controls (Chapter 4).

The showAsAction attribute has the following options:

➤ ifRoom: If there is room for an item, it will be placed in the action bar.

➤ withText: The text specified by the android:title attribute will be included with the item.

➤ never: The item will never be placed in the action bar.

➤ always: The item will always be placed in the action bar. Use this value with care. If you set too many items with the always value, you can get overlapping items and confusion in the action bar.

➤ collapseActionView: Introduced in API level 14, this item will be marked as collapsible.

LISTING 17-2: Action bar menu definition

```
<menu xmlns:android="http://schemas.android.com/apk/res/android"
  android:name="Embedded Resource - Context Menu">
  <item
  android:id="@+id/item01"
  android:icon="@drawable/jellyfishsmall"
  android:title="Menu item 1"
  android:showAsAction="ifRoom|withText">
    <menu>
      <item
      android:id="@+id/item06"
      android:title="Submenu item 1">
      </item>
      <item
      android:id="@+id/item07"
      android:title="Submenu item 2">
      </item>
      <item
      android:id="@+id/item08"
      android:title="Submenu item 3">
      </item>
      <item
      android:id="@+id/item09"
      android:title="Submenu item 4">
      </item>
      <item
      android:id="@+id/item10"
      android:title="Submenu item 5">
      </item>
    </menu>
  </item>
  <item
  android:id="@+id/item02"
  android:checkable="true"
  android:title="Menu item 2"
  android:showAsAction="ifRoom|withText">
  </item>
```

continues

LISTING 17-2 *(continued)*

```
<item
android:id="@+id/item03"
android:numericShortcut="3"
android:alphabeticShortcut="3"
android:title="Menu item 3"
android:showAsAction="ifRoom|withText">
</item>
<item
android:id="@+id/item04"
android:title="Submenu items"
android:showAsAction="ifRoom|withText">
  <menu>
    <item
    android:id="@+id/item05"
    android:title="Submenu item 1">
    </item>
  </menu>
</item>
</menu>
```

HCExample\HCExample\Resources\Layout\menu.xml

As you can see, the action bar can have multiple top-level menu items, and each menu item can have its own options.

Figures 17-5 and 17-6 show the action bar with menu items in it. Figure 17-5 shows what users see when the application initially loads. Figure 17-6 shows what users see when they touch "Menu item 1" and how the submenu items are expanded.

FIGURE 17-5

FIGURE 17-6

Using the Application Icon

You've probably noticed that the application's icon appears on the left side of the action bar. This is by default. One of the things that the application icon can do is respond to a user click. This is similar to selecting action items in the menu. Typically, you will want your application to return to the opening/home activity when the user taps the application icon in the top left-hand portion of the screen when the app is running. When the user performs the tap, the system will call the activity's `OnMenuItemSelected` method.

To handle tapping the App Icon, add the code in Listing 17-3 to the `OnMenuItemSelected` method. The following are key parts of this code to note:

➤ When the App Icon is tapped, the `Android.Resource.Id.Home` value is passed for the id of selected control.

➤ This code sample shows that a test is performed to verify that the application is not currently displaying the start activity. If that is the case, there may/may not be a reason to go back. This is can be left to the discretion of the application.

➤ If the application is currently buried down in the hierarchy of the application, the appropriate flag will be set to clear the activities above the current one in the stack and to take the user back to the original activity.

LISTING 17-3: Navigating to the top level activity

```
if (Android.Resource.Id.Home == item.ItemId)
{
    var topClass = (new Activity1()).Class;
    if (this.Class != topClass)
    {
        Intent intent = new Intent(this, topClass);
        intent.AddFlags(ActivityFlags.ClearTop);
        StartActivity(intent);
    }
}
```

HCExample\HCExample\Activity1.cs

Note that the `ActivityFlags.ClearTop` will clear all the activities above the current one in the stack. This will remove any activities in the stack between the current one and the original class.

Navigating "Up" the Stack

Another valid use of the App Icon is to navigate "up" the stack from the user's current activity. This is helpful when an application is within a fairly rigid workflow of activities. The activities appear in a specific order, like a wizard layout. In this type of workflow, using the App Icon to navigate to the previous activity is perfectly valid. There are two steps necessary to get this to work:

1. Call the action bar's `.SetDisplayHomeAsUpEnabled(true)`. This will add the arrow to the App Icon.

2. Update the `OnMenuItemSelected` method to return to the previous activity. This can be done by updating the code in Listing 17-4 with the correct activity.

LISTING 17-4: Pseudo code for navigating up the stack

```
// ActivityName is just an example name and would map to any activity
// within your application.
var actClass = (new ActivityName()).Class;
Intent i = new Intent(this, actClass );
//  Add the appropiate flags as necessary
//Intent.AddFlags(ActivityFlags.BroughtToFront);
StartActivity(i);
```

Another option is to call the `.Finish()` method on the current Activity.

Adding and Using Action Items

An action view is a widget that appears in the action bar. It is a substitute for an action item. By adding the following XML to the menu definition, a `SearchView` is added to the action bar.

```
<item android:id="@+id/menu_search"
    android:title="Search"
    android:showAsAction="ifRoom|withText"
    android:actionViewClass="android.widget.SearchView" />
```

Figure 17-7 shows this search option.

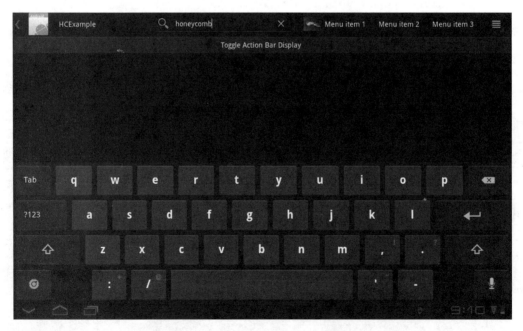

FIGURE 17-7

Creating a Tabbed Interface

Besides creating a menu system in the action bar, it is possible to create a tabbed interface based on the action bar. This can be created without using the TabWidget. The Android operating system will adapt the action bar tabs based on screen size. The action bar's tabs are placed on the normal action when there is enough screen real estate. When there is not enough screen real estate, tabs will be displayed on a separate bar, called the *stacked action bar.*

The steps for the process are as follows:

1. Associate a `ViewGroup` with a tab.

2. Implement the `ActionBar.ITabListener` interface. This interface means that code will implement `OnTabSelected`, `OnTabUnselected`, and `OnTabReselected`. These methods are called as a user navigates through the tabs.

3. For each tab added, define a `TabListener`. In this specific example, this is handled by the `Activity` class.

4. Add each tab to an action bar by calling `.AddTab`.

Listing 17-5 shows some sample code to set up a simple tabbed interface in Android 3.0 on a tablet.

Available for download on Wrox.com

LISTING 17-5: Tabbed interface code

```
[Activity(Label = "HCExampleTabbedInterface", MainLauncher = true, Icon =
    "@drawable/icon")]
public class Activity1 : Activity, ActionBar.ITabListener
{
    protected override void OnCreate(Bundle bundle)
    {
        base.OnCreate(bundle);

        var bar = ActionBar;

        for (int i = 0; i < 3; i++)
        {
            bar.AddTab(bar.NewTab().SetText(String.Format("Tab {0}", i))
                .SetTabListener(this));
        }
        bar.DisplayOptions = ActionBarDisplayOptions.ShowCustom |
            ActionBarDisplayOptions.UseLogo;
        bar.NavigationMode = ActionBarNavigationMode.Tabs;
        bar.SetDisplayShowHomeEnabled(true);
    }

    public void OnTabReselected(ActionBar.Tab tab, FragmentTransaction ft)
    {
        Android.Util.Log.Info("tab", String.Format("Tab ReSelected: {0}", tab
            .Text));
    }
```

continues

LISTING 17-5 *(continued)*

```
public void OnTabSelected(ActionBar.Tab tab, FragmentTransaction ft)
{
    Android.Util.Log.Info("tab", String.Format("Tab Selected: {0}",
        tab.Text));
}

public void OnTabUnselected(ActionBar.Tab tab, FragmentTransaction ft)
{
    Android.Util.Log.Info("tab", String.Format("Tab UnSelected: {0}",
        tab.Text));
}
}
```

HCExampleTabbedInterface\HCExampleTabbedInterface\Activity1.cs

Figure 17-8 shows the output of the code on an Android 3.0 tablet.

FIGURE 17-8

PARTIAL SCREEN CONTROL USING FRAGMENTS

Consider an Android application running on a smartphone. With it, you think of having control of the entire screen. The entire screen is controlled via an activity. This is done because an activity is "about the right size" to control the application. However, a tablet application typically has much more space associated with it. An Android tablet device typically has approximately 7 to 10 inches of space to display content. Because of this additional space, you can provide the users with so much more in an application.

The release of Android 3.0 (SDK 11) introduced fragments to provide the ability to support screen sections and to reuse UI components across an application. A fragment is a portion of a UI of an activity. You can combine multiple fragments in a single activity to create a UI, and you can use fragments across multiple activities. Think of a fragment as a mini- or sub-activity. Fragments have their own life cycles and receive their own events; therefore, a developer is responsible for setting them up.

You can provide a user with so much more information that makes sense to provide within the same screen. For example, you can provide a user with a search screen that displays a list of search results in a simple format. When the user selects a single search item, he or she gets more detailed information regarding the selected item. In this scenario, you could have the following:

➤ **A SearchView in the action bar:** A SearchView provides the user with a UI that displays the search text field and the button to start the search.

➤ **A List/Master fragment:** When the user clicks the button, a search is done against a data source, such as Twitter, and then the data is displayed in the List fragment.

➤ **A Detail fragment:** When the user selects an item in the List fragment, the detail of the item selected is displayed.

Figure 17-9 shows an example layout conceptually.

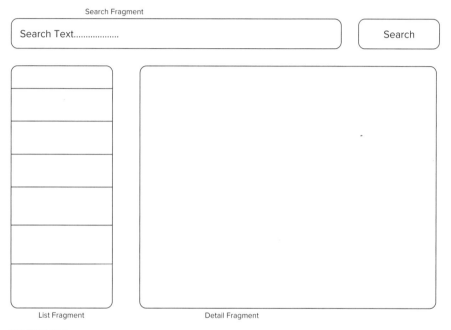

FIGURE 17-9

Creating Fragments

The process to create a fragment is not that much different from creating an Android activity:

1. Inherit classes from a fragment. The following classes can be inherited from a fragment:

➤ `Fragment`: The fragment class is the base class for fragments. Inheriting from the class gives the developer access to all the standard methods of a fragment.

➤ `DialogFragment`: The dialog fragment class allows for the display of a floating dialog. This class is an alternative for using the dialog helper methods.

➤ `ListFragment`: The list fragment class displays a list of items that are managed by an adapter. This is conceptually similar to a list activity.

➤ `PreferenceFragment`: The preference fragment class displays a list/hierarchy of preference objects as a list. This is similar to a preference activity.

2. Implement the necessary life cycle events:

➤ OnCreate(): Similar to an activity's OnCreate method, this method is called when a fragment is created. This method is useful for initializing the UI components and other essential items of a fragment.

➤ OnCreateView(): This method is called when a fragment is instructed by the operating system that it is time to draw a UI. The method must return a view. This view is the root of a fragment's layout. A null can be returned if a fragment does not have a UI.

➤ OnPause(): The operating system calls the OnPause method when the user is leaving a fragment. This doesn't mean that the fragment is necessarily destroyed; the user can return. This method is a good place to store the user's current session information.

Now that you understand the basics of fragments, let's implement an example. In this example, we'll have two fragments named Frag1 and Frag2. These fragments are used to show how to set up a tablet application and then to show some communication between the two fragments. Frag1 will have a button on it. When that button is clicked, a TextView in Frag2 is updated with the current time. The first step is to create the layout shown in Listing 17-6:

LISTING 17-6: Activity layout

```xml
<?xml version="1.0" encoding="utf-8"?>
<LinearLayout xmlns:android="http://schemas.android.com/apk/res/android"
    android:orientation="horizontal"
    android:layout_width="fill_parent"
    android:layout_height="fill_parent"
    >
  <fragment android:name="com.wallym.example.hcfrag.Frag1"
        android:id="@+id/list"
        android:layout_weight="1"
        android:layout_width="100dp"
        android:layout_height="match_parent" />
  <fragment android:name="com.wallym.example.hcfrag.Frag2"
        android:id="@+id/viewer"
        android:layout_weight="2"
        android:layout_width="100dp"
        android:layout_height="match_parent" />
</LinearLayout>
```

HCFragmentExample\HCFragmentExample\Resources\Layout\Main.axml.

This layout has a linear layout of fragments. You can think of the fragments within the activity's layout as containers for the fragment's respective layouts.

The next step is to create the layouts for the various fragments. Listing 17-7 shows the fragment on the left-hand side of the screen.

LISTING 17-7: Fragment 1 layout

```xml
<?xml version="1.0" encoding="utf-8"?>
<LinearLayout xmlns:android="http://schemas.android.com/apk/res/android"
    android:orientation="vertical"
    android:layout_width="fill_parent"
    android:layout_height="fill_parent"
    >
  <TextView
    android:id="@+id/tv1"
    android:layout_width="wrap_content"
    android:layout_height="wrap_content"
    android:text="TextView 1"
    ></TextView>
  <Button android:id="@+id/btn"
    android:layout_width="wrap_content"
    android:layout_height="wrap_content"
    android:text="Update"/>
</LinearLayout>
```

HCFragmentExample\HCFragmentExample\Resources\Layout\frag1layout.axml.

Listing 17-8 shows a simple layout on the right-hand side of the screen.

LISTING 17-8: Fragment 2 layout

```xml
<?xml version="1.0" encoding="utf-8"?>
<LinearLayout xmlns:android="http://schemas.android.com/apk/res/android"
    android:orientation="vertical"
    android:layout_width="fill_parent"
    android:layout_height="fill_parent">
  <TextView
    android:id="@+id/tv2"
    android:layout_width="wrap_content"
    android:layout_height="wrap_content"
    android:text="TextView 2"
    ></TextView>
</LinearLayout>
```

HCFragmentExample\HCFragmentExample\Resources\Layout\frag2layout.axml.

These two fragments will be placed by the Android operating system within the activity's containers for each respective fragment within the activity's layout.

Now that you have seen the layouts for the activity and the fragments, look at the code behind the scenes (see Listing 17-9). The code for the activity, which looks very simple, loads the activity's layout and is shown next.

LISTING 17-9: The activity's class file

```
[Activity(Label = "HCFragmentExample", MainLauncher = true,
        Icon = "@drawable/icon")]
public class Activity1 : Activity
{
    int count = 1;

    protected override void OnCreate(Bundle bundle)
    {
        base.OnCreate(bundle);
        SetContentView(Resource.Layout.Main);
    }
}
```

HCFragmentExample\HCFragmentExample\Activity1.cs.

Now that you have seen the activity, look at the fragment on the left side, which is referred to as
Frag1 (see Listing 17-10). This code will manually inflate the layout. After creating the layout in
OnCreateView, you can create a reference to controls. With the reference to a control, you can
create the events on a control. In this situation, when the user pushes the button, a reference to
the second fragment needs to be tested for. This is performed by calling the FragmentManager's
FindFragmentById method and passing in the container's view ID. Finally, in the button's click
event, you can set a property on the fragment.

LISTING 17-10: Fragment 1 source code

```
public class Frag1 : Fragment
{
    public override void OnCreate(Bundle bundle)
    {
        base.OnCreate(bundle);

        // Create your application here
    }
    Button btn;
    Frag2 f2;
    public override View OnCreateView(LayoutInflater inflater,
        ViewGroup container, Bundle savedInstanceState)
    {
        base.OnCreateView(inflater, container, savedInstanceState);
        var vw = inflater.Inflate(Resource.Layout.frag1layout,
          container, true);
        btn = vw.FindViewById<Button>(Resource.Id.btn);
        btn.Click += new EventHandler(btn_Click);
        return vw;
    }

    void btn_Click(object sender, EventArgs e)
    {
        var dt = DateTime.Now.ToShortTimeString();
```

```
            if (f2 == null)
            {
                f2 = FragmentManager.FindFragmentById<Frag2>(Resource.Id.viewer);
            }
            f2.Update = dt;
        }

        public override void OnPause()
        {
            base.OnPause();
        }
    }
```

HCFragmentExample\HCFragmentExample\Frag1.cs.

Frag2 is a fragment with an Update property (Listing 17-11). When the Update property is set, a TextView in the fragment is updated.

LISTING 17-11: Fragment 2 source code

```
public class Frag2 : Fragment
{
    public string Update
    {
        set { tv2.Text = value; }
    }
    TextView tv2;

    public override void OnCreate(Bundle bundle)
    {
        base.OnCreate(bundle);

        // Create your application here
    }

    public override View OnCreateView(LayoutInflater inflater,
        ViewGroup container, Bundle savedInstanceState)
    {
        base.OnCreateView(inflater, container, savedInstanceState);
        var vw = inflater.Inflate(Resource.Layout.frag2layout, container,
            true);
        tv2 = vw.FindViewById<TextView>(Resource.Id.tv2);
        return vw;
    }

    public override void OnPause()
    {
        base.OnPause();
    }
}
```

HCFragmentExample\HCFragmentExample\Frag2.cs.

Figure 17-10 shows the output when a user clicks the Update button and the `TextView` in the second fragment is updated with the current time.

FIGURE 17-10

More Fragments

Having covered the basics of fragments, I now want you to see a somewhat more complicated and realistic example. This example uses a `SearchView` to get Twitter timelines — specifically, the public timeline of @wbm. In the action bar at the top of the page, there is a `SearchView` control. The user will input a Twitter user ID. After this, a search is done via a call to the Twitter Search API, and the results are displayed in the left side of the tablet's screen in a `ListView`. When the user touches an item in the `ListView`, additional information is displayed on the right side of the screen. This additional information includes the Twitter avatar of the user and the date of the tweet.

The first thing to do is to create the fairly simple layout for the activity, as shown in Listing 17-12. In this code, the screen is divided into two parts, each containing a fragment. The fragment on the left will take up one third of the screen, and the fragment on the right will take up two thirds of the screen. This weighting is defined within the `android:layout_width` attribute. The fragments defined in our layout will be containers for the fragments, as well as cue the fragments to load.

LISTING 17-12: Activity layout source code

```xml
<?xml version="1.0" encoding="utf-8"?>
<LinearLayout xmlns:android="http://schemas.android.com/apk/res/android"
    android:orientation="horizontal"
    android:layout_width="fill_parent"
    android:layout_height="fill_parent"
    >
  <fragment android:name="com.wallym.example.hcfrag.Frag1"
        android:id="@+id/list"
        android:layout_weight="1"
        android:layout_width="100dp"
        android:layout_height="match_parent" />
  <fragment android:name="com.wallym.example.hcfrag.Frag2"
        android:id="@+id/viewer"
        android:layout_weight="2"
        android:layout_width="100dp"
        android:layout_height="match_parent" />
</LinearLayout>
```

HCFragmentSearch\HCFragmentExample\Resources\Layout\Main.axml.

The next step is to create the layouts for the fragments. Listing 17-13 shows the Fragment 1 source code. It merely has a `ListView`.

LISTING 17-13: Fragment 1 source code

```
<?xml version="1.0" encoding="utf-8"?>
<LinearLayout xmlns:android="http://schemas.android.com/apk/res/android"
    android:orientation="vertical"
    android:layout_width="fill_parent"
    android:layout_height="fill_parent"
    >
  <ListView
    android:id="@id/android:list"
    android:layout_width="match_parent"
    android:layout_height="match_parent"
    android:background="#00FF00"
    android:layout_weight="1"
    android:drawSelectorOnTop="false"  />
</LinearLayout>
```

HCFragmentSearch\HCFragmentExample\Resources\Layout\frag1layout.axml.

The next step is to create the layout for Fragment 2. In this layout, there is an ImageView and several TextViews. This is shown in Listing 17-14.

LISTING 17-14: Fragment 2 source code

```
<?xml version="1.0" encoding="utf-8"?>
<LinearLayout xmlns:android="http://schemas.android.com/apk/res/android"
    android:orientation="vertical"
    android:layout_width="fill_parent"
    android:layout_height="fill_parent">
  <ImageView
    android:id="@+id/twitterImage"
    android:layout_width="wrap_content"
    android:layout_height="wrap_content" />
  <TextView
    android:id="@+id/TwitterId"
    android:layout_width="wrap_content"
    android:layout_height="wrap_content"
    android:text=""
    ></TextView>
  <TextView
    android:id="@+id/status"
    android:layout_width="wrap_content"
    android:layout_height="wrap_content"
    android:text=""
    ></TextView>
  <TextView
    android:id="@+id/dateofstatus"
    android:layout_width="wrap_content"
    android:layout_height="wrap_content"
    android:text=""
    ></TextView>
</LinearLayout>
```

HCFragmentSearch\HCFragmentExample\Resources\Layout\frag2layout.axml.

The layout for the action bar is listed next (Listing 17-15). In this situation, it is a single item — the `SearchView`.

LISTING 17-15: Action bar source code

```
<menu xmlns:android="http://schemas.android.com/apk/res/android"
android:name="Embedded Resource - Context Menu">
    <item android:id="@+id/menu_search"
        android:title="Search"
        android:showAsAction="ifRoom|withText"
        android:icon="@drawable/searchmag"
        android:actionViewClass="android.widget.SearchView" />
</menu>
```

HCFragmentSearch\HCFragmentExample\Resources\Layout\search.axml.

Listing 17-16 shows the activity source code. The layout for the activity is loaded via `SetContentView`. In the `OnCreateOptionsMenu`, the layout for the action bar is loaded. Once the layout is loaded, a reference to the `SearchView` is created and the event for it is wired up.

LISTING 17-16: Activity source code

```
[Activity(Label = "HCFragmentExample", MainLauncher = true,
            Icon = "@drawable/icon")]
public class Activity1 : Activity
{
    SearchView sv;
    Frag1 f1;
    protected override void OnCreate(Bundle bundle)
    {
        base.OnCreate(bundle);

        // Set our view from the "main" layout resource
        SetContentView(Resource.Layout.Main);

        // Get our button from the layout resource,
        // and attach an event to it
    }
    public override bool OnCreateOptionsMenu(IMenu menu)
    {
        //return base.OnCreateOptionsMenu(menu);
        MenuInflater inflater = new Android.Views.MenuInflater(this);
        inflater.Inflate(Resource.Layout.search, menu);
        sv = (SearchView)menu.FindItem(Resource.Id.menu_search).ActionView;
        sv.Click += new EventHandler(sv_Click);
        return true;
    }

    void sv_Click(object sender, EventArgs e)
    {
        if (f1 == null)
```

```
            {
                f1 = FragmentManager.FindFragmentById<Frag1>(Resource.Id.list);
            }
            f1.UserId = sv.Query;
        }
    }
```

HCFragmentSearch\HCFragmentExample\Activity1.cs

Finally, you can see that when the .Click event fires in the SearchView, the sv_Click method is called. When the method is called, a reference is created to the loaded ListView fragment. Once the reference exists, the .UserId property of Frag1 is assigned.

Once a value is passed to the .UserId property of Frag1, an asynchronous request is made against the Twitter API. When a result comes back, a List<Tweet> is created. The status is then bound to the ListView. See Listing 17-17.

LISTING 17-17: Fragment 1 source code

```
public class Frag1 : ListFragment
{
    Frag2 f2;
    string _uid = String.Empty;
    List<Tweet> twt;
    public string UserId
    {
        get { return _uid; }
        set
        {
            _uid = value;
            string Url =
                "http://api.twitter.com/1/statuses/user_timeline.xml?screen_name="
            + _uid;
            try
            {
                // Create the web request
                HttpWebRequest request = WebRequest.Create(Url) as HttpWebRequest;

                request.Method = "GET";
                request.ContentType = "application/xml";
                request.BeginGetResponse(new
                    AsyncCallback(ProcessRestXmlLINQHttpResponse), request);
            }
            catch (WebException we)
            {
                Android.Util.Log.Error("http request", "Exception: " + we.Message);
            }
            catch (System.Exception sysExc)
            {
                Android.Util.Log.Error("http request", "Exception: " +
                    sysExc.Message);
```

continues

LISTING 17-17 *(continued)*

```
            }

        }
    }

    public override void OnCreate(Bundle bundle)
    {
        base.OnCreate(bundle);

    }
    public override View OnCreateView(LayoutInflater inflater,
      ViewGroup container, Bundle savedInstanceState)
    {
        base.OnCreateView(inflater, container, savedInstanceState);
        var vw = inflater.Inflate(Resource.Layout.frag1layout, container, true);
        return vw;
    }
    public override void OnPause()
    {
        base.OnPause();
    }

    void ProcessRestXmlLINQHttpResponse(IAsyncResult iar)
    {
        try
        {
            HttpWebRequest request = (HttpWebRequest)iar.AsyncState;
            HttpWebResponse response;
            response = (HttpWebResponse)request.EndGetResponse(iar);
            System.IO.StreamReader strm = new System.IO.StreamReader(
                response.GetResponseStream());
            System.Xml.Linq.XDocument xd = XDocument.Load(strm);
            twt = (from x in xd.Root.Descendants("status")
                      where x != null
                      select new Tweet
                      {
                          StatusId = x.Element("id").Value,
                          UserName = x.Element("user").Element("screen_name")
                              .Value,
                          ProfileImage =
                              x.Element("user").Element("profile_image_url")
                              .Value,
                          Status = x.Element("text").Value,
                          StatusDate = x.Element("created_at").Value
                      }).ToList<Tweet>();
            var st = new List<String>();
            foreach (Tweet t in twt)
            {
                st.Add(t.Status);
            }

            var s = new ArrayAdapter<String>(Activity,
              Android.Resource.Layout.SimpleListItem1, st.ToArray());
            Activity.RunOnUiThread(() =>
```

```
                {
                    this.ListAdapter = s;
                }
            );
            Android.Util.Log.Debug("http response", "finished");
        }
        catch (System.Exception sysExc)
        {
            Android.Util.Log.Error("http response", "Exception Message: " +
                sysExc.Message);
            Android.Util.Log.Error("http response", "Exception Stack Trace: " +
                sysExc.StackTrace);
            var iExc = sysExc.InnerException;
            while(iExc != null )
            {
                Android.Util.Log.Error("http response", "Exception Message: " +
                    iExc.Message);
                Android.Util.Log.Error("http response", "Exception Stack Trace: " +
                    iExc.StackTrace);
                iExc = iExc.InnerException;
            }
        }
    }

    public override void OnListItemClick(ListView l, View v, int position, long id)
    {
        base.OnListItemClick(l, v, position, id);
        if (f2 == null)
        {
            f2 = FragmentManager.FindFragmentById<Frag2>(Resource.Id.viewer);
        }
        var thisTweet = twt[position];
        f2.TId = thisTweet.UserName;
        f2.TDate = thisTweet.StatusDate;
        f2.TStatus = thisTweet.Status;
        f2.TwitterImage = thisTweet.ProfileImage;
    }
}
```

HCFragmentSearch\HCFragmentExample\Frag1.cs

Once an item in the ListView is a selected, several properties are updated in the Frag2. These properties will update the views in Fragment 2. In the downloading of the image, the ThreadPool is used
to download the file. This provides a better user experience because the download operation is performed off the main thread of the application. See Listing 17-18.

LISTING 17-18: Fragment 2 source code

```
public class Frag2 : Fragment
{
    public string TId
    {
        set { twitterId.Text = value; }
```

continues

LISTING 17-18 *(continued)*

```
        }
    public string TStatus
    {
        set { twitterStatus.Text = value; }
    }
    public string TDate
    {
        set { twitterDate.Text = value; }
    }
    public string TwitterImage
    {
        set
        {
            var imgUrl = value;
                string documents = System.Environment.GetFolderPath
                (System.Environment.SpecialFolder.Personal);
            string fileName = System.Guid.NewGuid().ToString();
            string file = System.IO.Path.Combine(documents, fileName);
            //this is a synchronous download, so its bad.
            var ptt = new PassToThread() { FileName = file,
                imageV = twitterImg, UrlToDownload = imgUrl };
            System.Threading.ThreadPool.QueueUserWorkItem(new
                System.Threading.WaitCallback(downloadImage), ptt);
        }
    }
    TextView twitterId;
    TextView twitterStatus;
    TextView twitterDate;
    ImageView twitterImg;
    public override void OnCreate(Bundle bundle)
    {
        base.OnCreate(bundle);
    }

    public override View OnCreateView(LayoutInflater inflater,
        ViewGroup container, Bundle savedInstanceState)
    {
        base.OnCreateView(inflater, container, savedInstanceState);
        var vw = inflater.Inflate(Resource.Layout.frag2layout, container,
            true);
        twitterId = vw.FindViewById<TextView>(Resource.Id.TwitterId);
        twitterStatus = vw.FindViewById<TextView>(Resource.Id.status);
        twitterDate = vw.FindViewById<TextView>(Resource.Id.dateofstatus);
        twitterImg = vw.FindViewById<ImageView>(Resource.Id.twitterImage);
        return vw;
    }

    public override void OnPause()
```

```
    {
        base.OnPause();
    }

    private void downloadImage(Object o)
    {
        try
        {
            var ptt = (PassToThread)o;
            var wc = new System.Net.WebClient();
            wc.DownloadFile(ptt.UrlToDownload, ptt.FileName);
            Activity.RunOnUiThread(() =>
                ptt.imageV.SetImageURI(Android.Net.Uri.Parse(ptt.FileName)));
        }
        catch (System.Net.WebException wec)
        {
            Android.Util.Log.Error("twitter timelines", wec.Message);
        }
    }

    private class PassToThread
    {
        public string UrlToDownload { get; set; }
        public string FileName { get; set; }
        public ImageView imageV { get; set; }
    }
}
```

HCFragmentSearch\HCFragmentExample\Frag2.cs

Note that RunOnUiThread is used in this code. In and of itself this is not surprising. The key thing to notice is that RunOnUiThread is from the .Activity property of the fragment. The .Activity property provides access to many of the properties that developers are used to when moving from Android 2.x phone design to the Android 3.x and later tablet design.

Figure 17-11 shows the output of the application.

FIGURE 17-11

SUMMARY

This chapter took a short look at Android tablets in Android 3.0 and Android 4.0, including:

➤ Using the action bar with menu items

➤ Creating a search interface with the action bar

➤ The basics of fragments and how to divide the screen real estate to use it effectively

➤ Communicating between fragments in a Twitter search application

Tips for Developers and the Future of Mono and Android

WHAT'S IN THIS APPENDIX?

➤   Reviewing best practices, hints, tips, and gotchas

➤   Introducing Android 3.0: Honeycomb and 4.0: Ice Cream Sandwich

➤   Discussing fragments support

➤   The future of Mono for Android

Every platform has its quirks, and Android is no different. Just because you can write in C# for Android does not mean you are exempt from these oddities and abnormalities. This book has noted and explained some of these Androidisms. This appendix describes some of the best practices, tips, and gotchas that may not fit anywhere else. You will also become acquainted with Android 3.0: Honeycomb and 4.0: Ice Cream Sandwich. You will explore new features that your apps can take advantage of, while learning how to maintain compatibility with older Android versions.

Finally, the future of Mono Android will be discussed. You will get the inside scoop on where the platform is headed, and what to expect down the road.

BEST PRACTICES, HINTS, TIPS, AND GOTCHAS

As a Mono for Android developer, there are a few hints, tips, and gotchas that you should be aware of. The following points of information will hopefully increase your proficiency by keeping you from making common mistakes and help you learn some time-saving tricks:

➤ **Remove old versions from your device:** It's best practice to remove all installed Mono for Android applications as well as any shared runtime or anything otherwise Mono-related from your device or emulator when a new version of Mono for Android is released. Though the team tries to make upgrades seamless, this simple practice can save a lot of headaches!

➤ **Get familiar with ADB:** Mono for Android runs on the Android toolset. Become familiar with the various ADB command-line tools:

  ➤ **adb device** shows a list of currently attached devices, including all emulator sessions that are currently running.

  ➤ **adb kill-server** will stop the currently running ADB server on the PC.

  ➤ **adb start-server** will start ADB again.

➤ **Try out DDMS:** This is a tool which is not well known. It is a graphical utility which will list processes running on all connected devices and emulator sessions, as well as a decorated view of adb logcat output, with the ability to create filters. It will allow you to track memory allocation, heap usage, and running threads. Finally, you can use it to control the emulator, simulating SMS messages, phone calls, and location.

➤ **User software can cause problems:** Software such as HTC Sync may cause issues for developers. Try uninstalling such software from your vendor if you run into problems.

➤ **Emulators need larger than default partitions:** By default the Android emulators you create will start with a 64MB partition size. This is simply too small to install the Mono for Android shared runtime and your applications on for debugging. You should either create and start your emulators through the Mono for Android tools, or specify `-partition-size 512` or larger through the command line when starting your emulators.

➤ **Virtual keyboard:** In some emulator versions, you must set keyboard support to false in the emulator properties to allow the virtual keyboard in Android to display and be used.

➤ **Use dots in your project name:** Android requires that package names include at least one dot (.). If you create a project with a name that does not contain a dot, Mono for Android automatically creates a name that has one. In many cases this works just fine, but if you ever need to refer to your package name later, confusion may arise. The best practice is to always use a dot in your project name to avoid any such confusion.

➤ **Use .axml files for your user interface instead of .xml files:** Mono for Android recognizes `.axml` as a special file type for defining Android XML layout files. The content is no different from that in `.xml` files, but using this `.axml` extension tells Mono that it should treat the file a specific way. The result is that you will get some IntelliSense support in Visual Studio (see Figure A-1), and you will have better error message information when you encounter a problem.

➤ **Use DroidDraw for user interface creation and editing:** You can edit layout files by hand, but using a free tool such as DroidDraw reduces the likelihood of errors in the markup syntax.

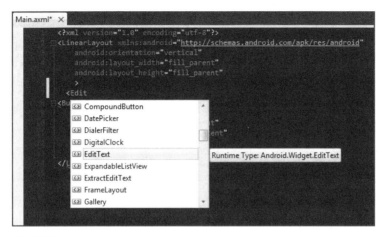

FIGURE A-1

 You can find more information about DroidDraw at `http://www.droiddraw`
`.org/.`

➤ **Turn up the MSBuild output verbosity level:** If you get an error that makes no sense, try
going into Visual Studio Options, in the Projects and Solutions section, under Build and Run,
and set the MSBuild project build output verbosity to a higher level (see Figure A-2). This
should cause more meaningful errors to be output to help you debug the problem.

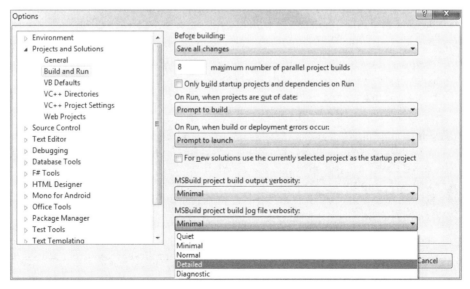

FIGURE A-2

➤ **View ADB logcat output in Visual Studio:** Mono for Android includes a window that can be found in Other Windows in Visual Studio called Android Device Logging (see Figure A-3). This can be used to display the logcat output from ADB right within your IDE. Of course, you can display logcat output by running the command `adb logcat` in your command prompt (assuming you have included the `platform-tools` folder from your Android SDK installation in your windows `PATH` variable).

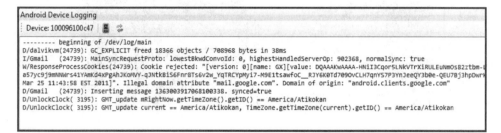

FIGURE A-3

➤ **Debugging on a physical device requires WiFi:** The Mono for Android debugger requires WiFi to be enabled on your physical device. It also requires the device to be on the same network as the machine you want to debug from. The debugger connects via TCP/IP, so it won't work without this!

➤ **Samsung Galaxy S devices require Android 2.2 or newer:** A bug in the kernel of Android 2.1 for all Samsung Galaxy S devices causes Mono for Android not to work. You must have 2.2 or higher to run Mono on these devices.

➤ **Beware of async code that updates the UI:** Anytime you want to run code that will update the UI, you should run it inside `RunOnUIThread()` to ensure that the code will be run on the same thread as the UI. If you don't do this, unexpected behavior will occur.

➤ **Large assets cannot be compressed:** For some reason, Android will not compress assets that have file sizes greater than 1MB. The workaround is to tell Android not to compress file extensions for files that will be larger than this. Unfortunately, files can be excluded only on a per-extension basis, not on a single-file basis.

➤ **Strings and CharSequences:** In Android, most text display properties are not exposed as simple string types (even in Java). This is because Android supports the notion of formatted text (such as a `SpannableString`). In Mono, all cases of this behavior include overloads or properties, both for a simple string type and for an `ICharSequence` type. In the case of a `TextView`, there is a `Text` property (string) and a `TextFormatted` property (`ICharSequence`).

➤ **Default debugging device:** In the Visual Studio Options, in the Mono for Android section, you can select a default device to use when debugging so that you don't always have to select your device from the list (see Figure A-4).

➤ **Preserve user data between deployments:** In the Visual Studio Options, in the Mono for Android section, there is a checkbox option to data/cache between application deployments. Use this to ensure your preferences and local files don't get deleted between builds while debugging.

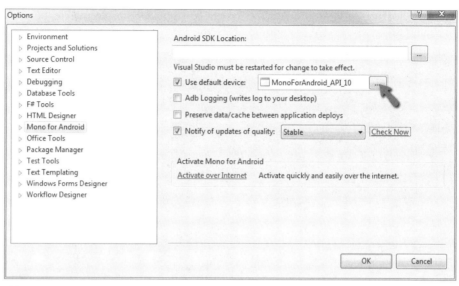

FIGURE A-4

➤ **Clean and rebuild:** In many cases, doing a Clean and Full Rebuild of your solution can solve problems you can't explain. When in doubt, it is recommended you try this.

➤ **Improve emulator performance:** Try starting your emulator image manually, specifying the parameters `-no-boot-anim -scale .75 -partition-size 512`. Removing the boot animation and changing the scale may increase the speed of the emulator. The partition size of 512 is needed by Mono for Android.

ANDROID HONEYCOMB (3.0) AND ICE CREAM SANDWICH (4.0)

The iPad inspired and defined the tablet market. The first real response to the iPad — the Motorola Xoom — arrived on the scene with Honeycomb (Android 3.0), a version of Android that never made it to phones, as it was designed specifically with tablets in mind. This release brought many optimizations for Android on the tablet form factor, and helped shape the release of Ice Cream Sandwich (Android 4.0), which brought Android back to a common code base to target both phone and tablet form factors simultaneously. As an Android developer, you should be aware of a number of new things in these new Android versions, some of which relate specifically to tablets:

➤ **Optimized home screen:** The home screen for tablets (Figure A-5) now has a much larger grid space for placing widgets and displaying a great deal more information than there would be room for on a smaller phone display.

➤ **Action Bar:** The top of the screen always shows an Action Bar. The content of this bar can be controlled by the application directly, so the actions on the bar can be changed depending on the current application, as well as the context within the application.

➤ **System Bar:** Android 3.0 takes the concept of soft keys a step further by incorporating the Home and Back buttons into the System Bar as touch screen controls, instead of requiring them to be hardware buttons on the device. Also, the new Recent Apps button is essentially a multitasking button. It displays a scrollable list of recently opened applications, with a snapshot of their latest display. The System Bar is always visible and rotates with the device, so it's always located at the bottom of the display.

FIGURE A-5

➤ **Relocated menu and search:** New applications designed for Android 3.0 and Android 4.0 can take advantage of the Action Bar to relocate menu options to the top-right corner (see Figure A-6). This gives developers greater flexibility as to which menu options are always visible. With previous versions of Android, users had to just know to press a single menu button. For legacy support, applications that still require the menu button cause a menu button to be displayed on the System Bar.

➤ **Notifications:** Gone is the old pull-down notification bar. In its place are new growl- or toast-like notifications. Notifications are displayed in the bottom-right corner for a few seconds (see Figure A-7); they disappear if they are not tapped. Tapping the clock in the bottom-right corner of the System Bar causes the notifications that have not been cleared to be shown again in case you missed them.

➤ **Two-pane UI:** The Gmail app has been updated to use a two-pane interface (see Figure A-8), much like the Mail app for the iPad. This UI can be used in other applications with the new fragments API.

➤ **Encryption:** Google has recognized the need for encryption, which is important to many business users. Android 3.0 has an option to encrypt the entire device with a PIN. This process takes some time, but because it's a must-have for some business users, the option is now available.

FIGURE A-6

FIGURE A-7

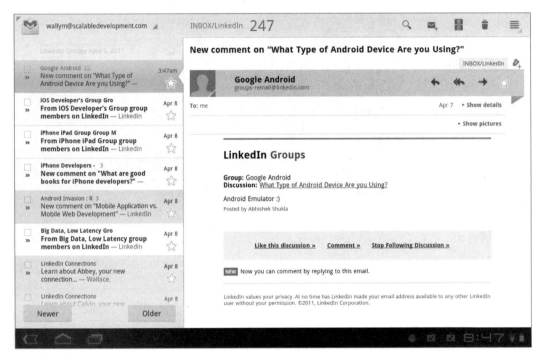

FIGURE A-8

FRAGMENTS FOR ALL!

Android 3.0 Honeycomb achieves some of its new features with a new library containing support for fragments. Fragments let you create user interfaces with multiple displays coexisting in a single activity.

Take, for example, the Gmail application: on an Android phone device, Gmail shows a list of e-mails that takes up the entire screen. When the user taps an e-mail, another activity is opened with the details of the email, removing the list of e-mails from the user's view. Since there is more screen real estate on a tablet, it makes sense to show both the list of e-mails and the selected e-mail's detail on the screen at the same time, using the fragments library.

Fragments allow you as a developer to display what are typically two or more activities on the screen at the same time. Figure A-9 illustrates the traditional way of using multiple activities on the left, and the new use of fragments to display multiple activities at once, on the right.

Since fragments are such an important new UI element, Google has decided to incorporate the functionality into a static library that is compatible all the way back to Android 1.6. This is especially important for tablet devices still running Android 2.2 or 2.3.

Traditional use of activities

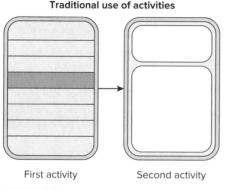

First activity   Second activity

New use of fragments

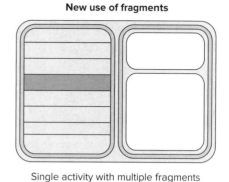

Single activity with multiple fragments

FIGURE A-9

As of the 4.0 Release, Mono for Android supports fragments only for Android 3.0 and higher. It does not yet support the fragments compatibility library. It is expected that bindings for this library will be included in a later release, as the Mono for Android team is currently developing a utility to help bind .jar *Android libraries to .NET. In the meantime, it is possible for you to write your own bindings using Managed and Android Callable Wrappers, which allow you to call Android or Java code directly. You can learn more about this on the Mono for Android Support site created by Xamarin (*http://support.xamarin.com/*).*

ANDROID VERSION AND DEVICE FRAGMENTATION

In just two short years, Android has gone from version 1.5 to version 3.0, with many changes to how the platform operates on devices and the capabilities offered. From a developer's perspective, Google has done a good job of maintaining backwards compatibility with their APIs. Unfortunately, it was inevitable that some Android versions contained new features unavailable in older versions (such as Cloud 2 Device Messaging). This makes deciding when to use new features in your application more difficult as a developer. You don't want to exclude users on an older Android version; however, you also want to give users with newer versions the best experience possible!

The versioning problem is exacerbated by the open nature of Android and the fact that many different manufacturers and carriers use Android on their devices. Since Google does not manufacture their own devices, they do not have control over when (if ever) a manufacturer or carrier should choose to offer updates to their users' devices. This means some users simply can't ever get the latest version of Android on their device even though Google has released it. Other users may have to wait for their device manufacturer to release an update to them, trailing months behind Google's release of the latest Android version.

Google makes available the percentage of active Android devices on each version of their operating system. You can find this information at http://developer. android.com/resources/dashboard/platform-versions.html.

The other problem developers face is device fragmentation. Again, since Google does not control which hardware Android runs on, many different manufacturers create many different combinations of hardware. Different processor speeds, memory sizes, storage capacities, and screen resolutions mean a potentially infinite combination of devices to target.

If you follow best practices for developing user interfaces on Android, in most cases, your applications should be able to scale to accommodate any screen resolution. You should also always aim to make your application as efficient as possible. This will help ensure your application runs smoothly regardless of how powerful a device is.

Google is aware of these fragmentation issues and they are trying to address them in a few ways:

1. **Moving applications out of the core operating system:** Google has moved Gmail, Maps, and some other applications into the Market instead of releasing updates to Android just to address these applications. This means they can focus on updates to the core operating system only, and hopefully release updates a bit less frequently.

2. **Releasing new APIs as libraries:** The fragments library is compatible all the way back to Android 1.6, meaning developers can use these new features, regardless of Android version.

3. **Early access program:** Google is planning to tighten control over Android by enforcing non-fragmentation policies as a requirement for manufacturers to gain early access to future versions of Android.

Despite Google's attempts to limit fragmentation, it is a reality that you as an Android developer must continue to deal with. Test your applications on a variety of devices and configurations if possible, code with best practices in mind, and the issue of fragmentation won't be as scary as it sounds!

WHAT'S NEXT FOR MONO FOR ANDROID?

Mono for Android 1.0 was a major milestone, with compatibility for MonoDevelop on OSX and Visual Studio 2010 on Windows. The release came with full emulator and on-device debugging support, as well as bindings to most of the Java Android APIs (bindings are what allow us to call Java Android API methods from .NET code). Version 1.2 brought some much needed stability improvements and further bindings. Version 4.0 is the most significant release to date, and it includes many improvements over previous releases:

➤   Android 3.0 and Android 4.0 API support

➤   Google Map API bindings

➤   Reduced startup performance — roughly 50 percent improvement can be seen in startup times and deployment sizes

➤ Garbage collection fixes and faster deployment for debugging

➤ Java 7 support

The first release of Mono for Android was just the beginning, and there are already several new features planned for future releases. Below are some of the things you can expect in upcoming Mono for Android versions:

➤ **More Android bindings:** While most of the crucial bindings are already included in Mono for Android, there are still some that are missing. Expect more complete coverage of the Java Android APIs in the future.

➤ **More .NET-oriented APIs:** Java APIs don't always translate well into optimal .NET APIs. Expect to see more event patterns, native .NET type usage, and other .NET patterns for the Java Android APIs. This has improved dramatically in version 4.0, with better support for .NET style events and compatibility with Java style constants for easier porting of Java code, but the team continues to work on exposing the Android APIs in a more .NET friendly way.

➤ **Binding generation utility:** The Mono for Android developers are working on a utility that will allow developers to generate .NET bindings to any Java library (.jar). This means you will be able to use any third-party Android or Java library directly in Mono for Android!

➤ **Fragments library:** Currently there are bindings to the fragments library in Mono for Android only if you use version 4.0 and target the Android Honeycomb (3.0) API level. Hopefully, future versions of Mono for Android will support the fragments compatibility library as well.

➤ **Bug fixes:** There is constantly work being done to address bugs that crop up. Expect more stable releases with fewer bugs in the future.

➤ **GUI designer:** At the time of writing, Xamarin has begun working on a graphical designer for Android XML layouts. This should be available in the next version of Mono for Android.

 You can submit bugs that you find at http://bugzilla.xamarin.com/. *This is the best way to get your issues addressed quickly!*

➤ **Performance improvements:** The main focus for the initial release of Mono for Android has been getting things working. As more bugs are fixed, focus will naturally shift to improving the performance of Mono for Android applications, including faster application execution and start-up time, lower memory usage, and smaller application packages.

Using Xamarin.Mobile for Cross-Platform Mobile Functionality

One of the new initiatives that Xamarin is working on is called Xamarin.Mobile. With Mono for Android, MonoTouch, and Windows Phone 7, it's already possible to share some common C# code between all three mobile platforms. However, platform-specific code still needs to be written for APIs such as User Interfaces, Contacts, and Calendar. This is where Xamarin.Mobile steps in.

Its aim is to create a common library for such APIs, so that you can code once for things such as Location Services and have it work on all three platforms.

At the time of writing, Xamarin.Mobile only supports Geolocation, but there are already plans to incorporate several other features into the library:

➤ Contacts

➤ Geolocation

➤ Compass and accelerometer

➤ Video and audio

➤ Notifications

Xamarin.Mobile should continue to make developing cross-platform mobile applications in C# a breeze. Even if you're only targeting Android, this library should simplify using the functionality it contains in your Android applications.

Android has taken the mobile world by storm, and now accounts for a significant share in the mobile space. It has become a very functional and powerful product. Thanks to Mono for Android, it is possible for you to create awesome native mobile applications for Android. With the roadmap ahead, the future looks great for Mono for Android developers, and it only gets better from here!

INDEX

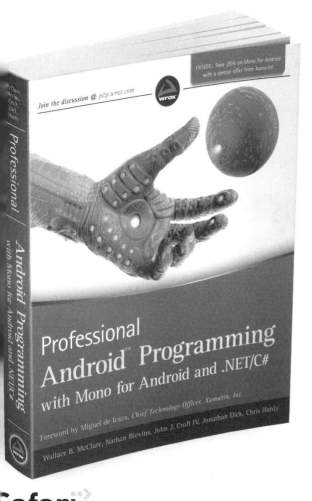